Nabokov's Dark Cinema

Vladimir Nabokov, Montreux, 1964.
(Photo by Henry Grossman)

"A good deal of Kinbote's commentary [in *Pale Fire*] was written here in the Montreux Palace garden, one of the most enchanting and inspiring gardens I know, now disfigured by a tennis court and a parking lot. I'm especially fond of its weeping cedar, the arboreal counterpart of a very shaggy dog with hair hanging over its eyes," says Nabokov.

NABOKOV'S DARK CINEMA

ALFRED APPEL, JR.

NEW YORK OXFORD UNIVERSITY PRESS 1974

Copyright © 1974 by Oxford University Press

Library of Congress Catalogue Card Number: 74-79617

Printed in the United States of America

To Nina, Karen, and Richard

Acknowledgments

I would like to thank the following for permission to quote:

Doubleday & Company, Inc., for passages from "The Assistant Producer," copyright 1943 by The Atlantic Monthly Company; from "Lance," copyright 1952 by Vladimir Nabokov; from " 'That in Aleppo Once . . .'," copyright 1943 by The Atlantic Monthly Company; from "Time and Ebb," copyright 1944 by The Atlantic Monthly Company, all included in *Nabokov's Dozen* by Vladimir Nabokov, copyright © 1958 by Vladimir Nabokov; and from *Pnin* by Vladimir Nabokov, copyright © 1953, 1955, 1957 by Vladimir Nabokov.

McGraw-Hill Book Company, for passages from *Ada* by Vladimir Nabokov, copyright © 1969 by McGraw-Hill International, Inc.; from *Bend Sinister* by Vladimir Nabokov, copyright © 1947 by Vladimir Nabokov; from *Glory* by Vladimir Nabokov, copyright © 1971 by McGraw-Hill International, Inc.; from *King, Queen, Knave* by Vladimir Nabokov, copyright © 1968 by Vladimir Nabokov; from *Lolita: A Screenplay* by Vladimir Nabokov, copyright © 1961 by Metro-Goldwyn-Mayer, Inc., Foreword copyright © 1974 by McGraw-Hill International, Inc., reprinted by permission of McGraw-Hill International, Inc.; from *Mary* by Vlamidir Nabokov, copyright © 1970 McGraw-Hill International, Inc.; from *Poems and Problems* by Vladimir Nabokov, copyright © 1970 by McGraw-Hill International, Inc.; from *Strong Opin-ions* by Vladimir Nabokov, copyright © 1973 by McGraw-Hill International, Inc.; from *Transparent Things* by Vladimir Nabokov, copyright © 1972 McGraw-Hill International, Inc.

Vladimir Nabokov, for passages from *Camera Obscura* by Vladimir Nabokov, copyright 1936 by Vladimir Nabokov; from *Nikolai Gogol* by Vladimir Nabokov, copyright 1944 by New Directions; from *Speak, Memory* by Vladimir Nabokov, copyright 1947, 1948, 1949, 1950, 1951 by Vladimir Nabokov, © 1960, 1966 by Vladimir Nabokov.

New Directions, for passages from *Laughter in the Dark* by Vladimir Nabokov, copyright 1938 by Vladimir Nabokov, reprinted by permission of New Directions Publishing Corporation; from *The Real Life of Sebastian Knight* by Vladimir Nabokov, copyright 1941, © 1959 by New Directions Publishing Corporation, reprinted by permission of New Directions Publishing Corporation; from *The Day of the Locust* by Nathanael West, copyright 1939 by the Estate of Nathanael West, © 1966 by Laura Perelman, reprinted by permission of New Directions Publishing Corporation; from *Miss Lonely-hearts* by Nathanael West, copyright 1933 by Nathanael West, © 1960 by Laura Perelman, reprinted by permission of New Directions Publishing Corporation.

G. P. Putnam's Sons, for passages from *The Defense* by Vladimir Nabokov, © 1964 by Vladimir Nabokov; from *De-spair* by Vladimir Nabokov, © 1965, 1966 by Vladimir Nabokov; from *The Gift* by Vladimir Nabokov, copyright © 1963 by G. P. Putnam's Sons; from *Invitation to a Beheading* by

Vladimir Nabokov, © 1959 by Vladimir Nabokov; from *Lolita* by Vladimir Nabokov, © 1955 by Vladimir Nabokov; from *Pale Fire* by Vladimir Nabokov, copyright © 1962 by G. P. Putnam's Sons.

Picture credits (unless noted in captions): Richard W. Bann, 104, 164 (left); Richard W. Bann and Leonard Maltin, 98, 106; Kevin Brownlow, 90, 122 (top), 275, 276; Chicago Tribune–New York News Syndicate, 77 (top), Copyright © 1974 Chicago Tribune–New York News Syndicate; Cinemabilia, 289; Collie-Smith photograph, 186, courtesy of Mary C. Lyons; Culver Pictures, 285 (left); The Homer Dickens Still Archive, New York, 300; courtesy of Robert Frank, 15, 206, 217, 219; courtesy of Lee Friedlander, 254; Impact Films, 277 (left, bottom; right); Doug Lemza and Films, Inc., 7 (left), 40, 51, 141 (top), 148 (top), 178 (top), 243 (top), 295 (left); Movie Star News, 291; Movie Story Shop, 162 (left, top); Collection, The Museum of Modern Art, 23, 70 (Gift of the photographer), 204, 217, 266 (Gift of Peter H. Deitsch); The Museum of Modern Art/Film Stills Archive, cover illustration, 2, 5, 8, 11 (left), 35 (right), 38, 42, 96 (left; right), 97, 101 (right), 105, 114 (top; bottom), 122 (bottom), 143, 145, 149, 156, 162 (left, bottom), 165 (right), 173 (right, top and bottom), 179, 198, 200 (top), 202, 214, 215, 220 (left), 221, 226 (bottom), 230, 253 (bottom), 272, 281 (right, top), 284 (bottom), 286 (top; bottom), 287 (top; bottom), 290, 297, 303; courtesy of Véra Nabokov, 28, 160, 169, 247, 248, 269, 298, copyright © 1974 by Véra Nabokov, all rights reserved; National Film Archive (London), 39 (top; bottom), 49, 54, 99, 100 (top; bottom), 102 (right), 103 (left; right), 110 (left; right), 124, 125, 137, 138, 140, 142 (top; bottom), 146, 147, 159, 162 (right, bottom), 163 (left; right, top), 164 (right), 165 (left, bottom), 166 (left, top; right, bottom), 172, 173 (left), 177, 178 (bottom), 192, 194, 197, 200 (bottom), 205, 208, 209, 211, 212, 213, 220 (right), 224, 225, 226 (top), 227 (top; bottom), 228 (top; bottom), 240, 242, 243 (bottom), 249, 251, 252, 253 (top), 273, 277 (left, top), 281 (left, top), 282 (top; bottom), 283 (top; bottom), 284 (top), 299, 301; National Periodical Publications, Inc., 158, copyright © 1946, McClure Syndicate; Transworld Feature Syndicate, Inc., frontispiece; Wisconsin Center for Theatre Research, 45, 111.

I am grateful to the John Simon Guggenheim Memorial Foundation for the 1972-73 Fellowship that enabled me to write this book. The Research Committee of Northwestern University defrayed the costs of my illustrations and I wish to acknowledge their kindness. Patience as well as kindness can be credited to Véra and Vladimir Nabokov, gracious hosts who endured my questions. Vivian Darkbloom's contributions cannot be overlooked or underestimated; his influence is most discernible in my seventh chapter. Mary Corliss of The Museum of Modern Art, New York, was most helpful in regard to movie stills, and the museum's Department of Photography, John Szarkowski and Diana Edkins in particular, also offered valuable assistance. I am especially grateful for the advice and suggestions provided by my friends Elizabeth Dipple, Frank McConnell, and Barbara Heldt Monter, and by Stephanie Golden and James Raimes of the Oxford University Press. Among other things, the dedication page acknowledges the assistance of two *Batman* scholars.

Evanston, Ill.   A.A.
June 1974

Contents

Nabokov's Dark Cinema

Susan Hayward and Gregory Peck
in *David and Bathsheba*.

1
Frederick's of Hollywood

"Why can't you be more like Gregory Peck," said J. S., casting a disappointed look in my direction as we left the Playhouse Theatre after a showing of *David and Bathsheba,* summer of '52, and re-entered the real world. I straightened up and stretched skyward as far as my suddenly puny five feet ten would allow—full growth, alas, for an eighteen-year-old dispossessed by popular culture. She glided along in her Capezio flats with sullen grace, a tight-sweatered silhouette against the harsh neon lights of drugstores and all-nite snack shops, and I lamented the season: if only it had been autumn; at least I could have turned up the collar of my old leather jacket with a redeeming Brandoesque panache and assumed a manly *On the Waterfront* slouch. Scholarship and criticism are sometimes said to be disinterested enterprises, detached and deliber-

ate, cool and calm in method. A middle-aged child of the nineteen-forties and fifties confronting the subject of movies knows better.

Most people now accept the film as An Art Form Worthy of Serious Study, but this opinion shouldn't be taken for granted. Only in the last decade has the commercial American cinema become critically respectable, and a case *can* be made against this not always artful form. The worst minds of my generation (*pace* Allen Ginsberg) were softened by the cinema, and several of the best ones had to struggle to survive the popular cinema's pernicious effects on our social and political and sexual attitudes, the darkest, most private recesses of our psyches. Walker Percy's novel *The Moviegoer* (1962) is a failure because it doesn't go far enough in suggesting the ways in which movies form and succor their viewers. When Jean-Paul Belmondo stands before the icon-like poster of Bogart in *Breathless* (1959), touches his own curled lip, and intones "Bogey!" director Jean-Luc Godard gives us a deathless image of the degree to which life *does* imitate art, in the most willful and fatal sense of that cliché. Godard himself appears in the film to denounce his hero to the police, a self-consciously symbolic act that articulates the director's ambivalent feelings toward his own creation as well as the manner in which American gangster films may have in turn created *him*, unhappily enough.

Breathless and the childlike gunplay of *Band of Outsiders* (1964) suggest that little Jean-Luc, the son of a Swiss doctor, would have been at home with my playmates growing up in the movie houses of middle-class Long Island. Our choices in touchstones of masculinity were determined by ethnic and religious criteria, though short boys of every persuasion were buoyed by Alan Ladd's example and the box he reputedly had to stand on in order to kiss droopy-lidded actresses. Wasps could imitate the laconic strength of Gary Cooper or Henry Fonda, Italo-Americans mimed Richard Conte, Irish Catholics had as their imagos the pugnacity of early Spencer Tracy and Jimmy Cagney, but Jewish boys had a problem. Yes, Little Caesar was really Emanuel Goldenberg, but by the mid nineteen-forties Robinson had also become a "dramatic actor"—which is to say a weakling

in *The Woman in the Window* (1944) and *Scarlet Street* (1945), defeated in both films by Joan Bennett, who preferred Dan Duryea, a sleazy Irish charmer. The problem was solved by the young scholar who discovered that John Garfield, who had his way with platinum Lana Turner in *The Postman Always Rings Twice* (1946), was né Julius Garfinkle; his war efforts on land (*Pride of the Marines*, 1945), sea (*Destination Tokyo*, 1944), and air (*Air Force*, 1943) assumed a new luster. The same boy, an early fan of Kirk Douglas—a heel rather than a hero in his first films, but absolved by his birth as Issur Danielovitch—returned from summer camp steeled by the fact that one of his bunkmates was first cousin to Louis Lepke of Murder, Inc., infamy, recently claimed by Sing Sing's electric chair. If toughness was genetic *and* transferable, my friend's lot had clearly improved; Albert Einstein was not a sufficient cultural hero. Could one win fist fights and impress girls by earning a grade of one hundred in geometry?

Rhetorical questions vex and persist: how many psyches have been withered and twisted by the conjunction of manhood and violence celebrated in American popular culture? We laughed at the cowardly antics of Charlie Chan's colored chauffeur as played by Mantan Moreland ("Feets, do your stuff!"), but at a Harlem theatre c. 1962 I was amazed when the all-Negro audience cheered Tarzan's one-man triumph over the tribe of craven natives that had re-

Narcissistic eroticism of the forties, Julius Garfinkle in Wonderland: Lana Turner and John Garfield in *The Postman Always Rings Twice.*

belled against a band of white uranium seekers. My friends and I outdistanced our laughter (of course), and surely it's no accident that a famous poster of Huey Newton, c. 1965, shows the Minister of Defense seated on a mock-African throne, flanked by Black Panthers carrying jungle spears and shields—a parody of a *Tarzan* "visual," a witty protest and defense against the deracinating images of popular culture, a campy version of Frantz Fanon's teachings. The Panthers would shortly activate their fantasies.

Too young to serve our country in World War II, we fought the war through the movies, staging and enacting our own *Wake Island* (1942), *Guadalcanal Diary* (1943), *Back to Bataan* (1945), et al. in the dense woods, roughs, and sand traps of the Soundview Golf Course, closed for the duration and fated to disappear beneath one hundred postwar "ranch homes." Paving the way for progress, the developer's bulldozers would level the hills and destroy all but a few trees; scattered half a mile apart, their branches shorn by the falling limbs of other trees, they stood amidst the settling dust, dazed survivors of a saturation bombing. In our earnest Soundview productions the tallest boy was Sergeant John Wayne, the fattest was Corporal William Bendix, and the entire hospital area was played by an asthmatic boy who, carried away by his new Superman costume, had tried to fly from the roof of his garage and broken both arms; when the casts were removed he became permanent combat medic and insisted upon being called "Doctor." The smallest and weakest boys were Japs, a not entirely hateful fate since the role allowed for histrionic theatrics. One short fellow dislocated his shoulder tumbling to his death down the ninth fairway, the steepest incline, while another died several hundred times during the course of 1942 before his family moved away. A hopelessly stunted boy, hoarse from shouting *"Banzai!"* waited three years to rise in the cast: to playing a Chinese guerrilla on the eve of V-J Day in our adaptation of *Dragon Seed* (1944). Sitting in Kregle's Ice Cream Parlor after seeing a submarine opus (*Destination Tokyo*?) my friends and I discuss the whereabouts and possible exploits of our relatives in the service. We notice the poster above the booth, "A Slip of the Lip May Sink a Ship," and proceed in a whisper, for Mr. Kregle has a German accent. "WAR DAY!" declared the summary Playhouse Theatre marquee, advertising a 1944 Saturday matinee that paired *The Fighting Sullivans* with *The Fighting Seabees*. The excitement during the show is so great that several boys lose control, creating another version of the yellow peril, and the furious "matron," a fat masculine woman in a soiled white uniform, rolls up and down the center aisle like an amphibious tank—cursing, clapping us on the head, cutting at least one ear—my sole war wound, as it turned out.

At *The Purple Heart* (1944) a few weeks later, we endured the trial and torture of the surviving pilots from General Doolittle's airstrike against Tokyo. "You will die, Yankee dogs!" exclaims the bucktoothed yellow rat judge. "Our planes will darken your skies!" replies the doomed airman (Dana Andrews), getting in the last word in the best sense of the phrase, and we cheer through the mists and monsoons of our no longer furtive tears. Out in the sunshine again, the Air Corps Song from the soundtrack ringing in our heads, we forsake a soda to loiter by the U.S. Army recruitment office, staffed by a beribboned sergeant resembling Randolph Scott. Wearing our wool-lined aviators' headgear despite the June heat, perspiration coursing down our faces in place of tears, we stroll through Woolworth's and admire the new Dick Tracy Crime Stopper kits and the servicemen from the nearby USO who are flirting with the fast high-school girls who work at Woolworth's, where the big cooling blades of the overhead fans revolve so slowly, so insinuatingly, humming the Army Navy Air Force mat-

Right: Storming the ninth green on the Soundview Golf Course: left to right, Lee Bowman, Thomas Mitchell ("Wait for me, fellas [puff puff]"), Robert Taylor, and Lloyd Nolan in *Bataan* (1943). Far right, top: Securing the ninth green, as dramatized in *The Fighting Seabees*. Far right, bottom: Victory! Richard Jaeckel and William Bendix in *Guadalcanal Diary*, completing the Soundview montage.

ing song. If only we could enlist, experience action like the USO heroes or the Boy Commandos of comic book fame, be part of a children's crusade or a legion of midgets; American Japs, we know, have *their* army division—we've seen a picture-story in *Look*—and our bitterness and frustration know no equal. Our war games were particularly vicious that day.

Ten years later I finally had my military opportunity, anti-climactically, an experience considerably less wondrous than the Soundview campaigns and in certain ways eerie indeed. On the bayonet course in Infantry Basic Training we were supposed to shout "Kill!" as we ran along the line thrusting our steeled rifles into freely suspended straw-filled dummies. The final target was a huge stationary sandbag. Running through the course shouting "Kill!" I remembered Soundview and started to exaggerate my performance, yelling with manic glee, a soul-saving parody quite independent of any film I had ever seen. At the stationary sandbag I became a crazed Method actor, thrust the lethal blade in again and again—"Kill! Kill! *Kill!*"—and then delivered two blows with the rifle's butt, strokes that were not in the scenario. The canvas bag exploded, sand poured out from the wound, and in a few moments only a large limp rag remained, a tattered flag above my sandbox. Horrified, I had a sudden vision of a term in a *From Here to Eternity*-like stockade. The bayonet instructor, a big-bellied six-foot-four sergeant from Georgia, fresh from com-

Airmen Dana Andrews (second from left), Farley Granger, and Sam Levene face Richard Loo in *The Purple Heart*.

bat in Korea, his helmet tilted over his eyes, put a massive arm around my shoulder and said, looking down at me, "Nice goin', young killer." At every turn in our training the various combat instructors would say, "Don't place the naked bayonet in your belt like John Wayne, you'll cut your friggin' leg"; "Don't hold a machine gun by the barrel like John Wayne—that's Hollywood, troopers; you'll burn your hands to a crisp"; "Don't pull the [grenade] pin with your teeth like John Wayne, meatheads, you'll have nothin' left." At the end of our "graduation" ceremony an infantry captain asked if we had any last questions; his answer might save a life or two. "Yes," said a draftee from Newark, "could you tell me what the United States Army has against John Wayne?" Speechless in the face of tumultuous laughter, recoiling like Dracula before wolfbane, the captain dismissed Company K of the 342nd Infantry, an impossible assemblage of college misfits and urban wise-guys.

It would seem, actually, that the U.S. Army is profoundly indebted to Sgt. John Wayne and Hollywood. Everyone knows how the American Legion ethos and Cold War rationale sustained the Indochina war. Would it be too fanciful or facile to suggest that the xenophobic patriotism and racism of American war movies played their part, too? Following the lead of a movie-star-like American president whose own exploits literally became a war movie, more than one survivor of the Soundview Golf Course remained a war hawk to the end. "I felt sorry. I don't know why I felt sorry. John Wayne never felt sorry," a Vietnam veteran told Robert Jay Lifton (quoted in his *Home From the War*, 1973). "He's driven out, away, east . . . in a dented green Lagonda by his batman, a Corporal Wayne," writes Thomas Pynchon early in *Gravity's Rainbow* (1973); and the chauffeur's name —a tiny particle in a vast Pop cosmos or cinematic montage of death—is appropriate to the inferno of buzz-bombed London, 1944, as staged by another Long Island movie-goer of the nineteen-forties who has at least managed to reduce John Wayne in rank.

The iconography of popular culture—to risk a grand phrase—creates and controls and cripples us in more ways than we recognize or would like to know. Unlike the movies' influence on war games of whatever scale, the interaction between the cinema and one's sexual attitudes and expectations is as complicated as a DNA molecule. The signal event of my war-torn 1944 was a movie titled *Phantom Lady*. It starred Ella Raines as a prim, well-scrubbed secretary whose page-boy hairdo folded softly on her fashionably wide shoulders. She loves her boss from afar in the manner then prescribed for nice Midwestern girls transplanted to the Big City. When her boss is arrested and falsely charged with murder, virginal Ella enters and explores the rainwashed nightscapes of the urban demimonde to discover the real killer. In order to seduce crucial information from a wild-eyed jazz drummer (Elisha Cook, *The Maltest Falcon*'s gunsel), Ella assumes a new name and transforms herself into a "hep-kitten" (a nineteen-forties groupie): wetly painted lips, a mole on her chin, upswept hairdo, pounds of costume jewelry, platform shoes, a suddenly excellent figure tightly encased in a black satin dress slit along the side Dragon Lady-style—the kind of frock luridly advertised by Frederick's of Hollywood in the back pages of movie magazines we had covertly perused at the neighborhood newsstand. Elisha Cook was enchanted by Ella Raines, and so was I—the transformed Ella, that is, the short-lived Ella Number Two who bungled the seduction by dropping her purse, thereby exposing her identification card. For several weeks I forgot the war completely and almost missed the D-Day invasion of Normandy, which we restaged on the narrow, condom-infested beaches of Long Island Sound. At night, trying to fall asleep on my stomach, I thought of Ella Number Two, and would experience a strange discomfiture. Although the swashbuckling screen freedoms enjoyed by a Jon Hall or a Cornel Wilde had their dream equivalents too (eighty-three ways to sneak into a harem), Elisha Cook's lost chance was far more stimulating. Miniature versions of Ella One, the neighborhood girls became ghostly transparent things. N. S., a year or two older than the other girls, had already disappeared from view, having decided to dedicate her life to the maintenance of a massive Don Ameche scrapbook.

The glamor of Ella the Second seemed representative. A constellation of actors and actresses would soon enthrall both girls and boys, and a close student of such phenomena could easily locate the Hollywood sources of our hair styles and various mannerisms, a sexual role-playing twice distanced from life inasmuch as it was modeled on stylized celluloid behavior. If one couldn't be as tall as Gregory Peck, one could at least spread the rumor that G. R., another sullen vamp, stuffed her bra with bobby sox because, like all middle-class girls, she was loath to risk her reputation at the self-improvement counter of Woolworth's, staffed by a well-endowed lower-class fast girl who would tell all.

A recent TV presentation of *Phantom Lady* provided two large surprises: the movie is quite good (a *film noir*, we'd call it now), and the "sexy" Ella Raines turns out to be a grotesque—German refugee director Robert Siodmak's sly parody of vacuous nineteen-forties movie glamor. The first Ella is clearly the preferable girl, and Number Two is cleverly played for laughs: she stumbles slightly in her wedgies, her "seductive" voice is too sharp, too shrill, and she chews her gum to the drumbeat with a comic, vulgar gusto. Her transformed figure is obviously the product of at least two plastic or padded insertions. Worst anti-

Ella Raines and Elisha Cook, Jr. (with drumstick), in *Phantom Lady*.

Comic strip eroticism of the forties: a gift to the author (1943) that now serves to remind us how Hollywood ideals of style and glamor once constituted a monolithic presence. The posy females in Alex Raymond's *Flash Gordon* were modeled on anonymous starlets but the Dragon Lady (right) in Milton Caniff's *Terry and the Pirates* resembled Hedy Lamarr and Luise Rainer. Burma—the strip's wise-cracking "blonde bombshell"—recalled Jean Harlow, Ginger Rogers, Carole Lombard, and other independent "thirties girls." The Dragon Lady provided Vietnam's Madame Nhu with a sobriquet c. 1962, another reminder of how Pop, our lingua franca, functions as folklore or mythology.

climax of all, my prefabricated dream Ella is terrified by the prospect of a genuine sexual encounter with the drummer, rather in the manner of my own response to a similar opportunity a year or so later when, age twelve, wearing my tweed topcoat and little gray fedora—an outfit reserved for biannual Special Occasions—I took the train into New York City to visit my grandmother. As I was striding along Forty-second Street past the stores that then offered old stamps and coins, a man sidled up beside me and, mistaking me for a young buck or a dapper dwarf, said, "Hey, buddy, want a piece of ass?" My pale stricken face and widened eyes—like Bambi's in the forest fire—sent him scurrying around the corner. Grandma took me to a movie, a far safer terrain. She greatly enjoyed that afternoon's fare—Rita Hayworth in *Gilda* (1946)—but my pleasure quotient had been compromised and reduced by shame. A more troubled sleeplessness ensued, producing nightmares in which I appeared in my seventh-grade social studies class clad only in precariously fastened pajama bottoms and one slipper, unable to recite the presidents of the United States for a hideously grinning teacher played alternately by an Ella Raines and a Rita Hayworth whose faces had been made up by Bob Kane, the artist who gave us the Joker in *Batman*. Suspended above my bed as in a comic strip balloon, terrible laughter sounded through my head.

That composite, shifting dream figure was an unredeeming substitute for our real-life teacher, a very pretty but strict and sarcastic spinster who, one day after class, confided to my friend and me that in high school she had dated actor Ronald Reagan, and that her fiancé, a sailor, had more recently perished in the Battle of the Coral Sea on the same battleship as the five Sullivan brothers, whose story had been told in *The Fighting Sullivans* and, she continued, had just been marked by a handsome purple commemorative postage stamp. Sure, we knew it; a terrific picture, and I'd bought an entire sheet of those stamps. Had we seen Ronnie in *This Is the Army*, she asked, her eyes brimming with tears.

The artifice of cinema is real enough, animating the regressive pastoral of nostalgia or directing our sentient lives. Recalling in tranquility the affair with Ella that unreeled in the roomy projection booth of my young skull, I would propose, belatedly, a simple if utopian experiment: given the opportunity to see *Phantom Lady* on a subsequent annual basis, when would I have recognized the truth about Ella? How many years later? The experiment is of more than local interest, given the movie-inspired mummery and cranial cinema indulged in by adolescents of all ages, sexual charades that sustain rather than narrow the distance separating two people.

Twenty years after that initial viewing of *Phantom*

Lady I visited Hollywood for the first time. After unpacking my suitcase I left the hotel, turned left, and started walking along Hollywood Boulevard in search of local color. I was brought to a stop by a store façade: FREDERICK'S OF HOLLYWOOD. It really existed, two large windows filled with feminine merchandise forming a kind of Darwinian order of disguise, head to foot and then inward: wigs of all shapes, sizes, and colors; fake eyelashes of moth-like dimensions; slinky clinging gowns like the one worn by Ella in *Phantom Lady;* fur-trimmed nighties and negligees, uncensored variants of kept-woman fashions in films of the forties such as *Scarlet Street;* high-heeled shoes with gravity-defiant five-inch spikes, a threat to rug or person, and furry bedroom platform slippers recalling Meret Oppenheim's famous fur-lined cup and saucer set. An imaginative range of undergarments is featured: laff-riot brassieres with clutching black fingers printed over their cups and bras with open spaces for nipples; bottomless underpants and a pair that has "Pay as you enter" embroidered on its nether region. A multitude of exotically colored little see-thru items is suspended by threads, floating freely through this aquarium of larger deep-sea oddities. Illusion is paramount behind the glass of Frederick's of Hollywood: padded stockings to fill out the legs of skinny or bow-legged creatures; mountainous false breasts, of course, but padded hips and buttocks too, with straps and strings as complicated as those of any orthopedic devices. These are but a few of Frederick's components, an array of erotic parts and props sufficient to the sundry needs of sado-masochists, transvestites, fetishists, onanists, and voyeurs, all part of a vast army of sad and ordinary disappointed dreamers. I started to enter the shop, when the door flew open and a woman rushed out, forcing me to step aside quickly, matador-style. Well under five feet, but a shade too tall to be called a dwarf, sixty years of age under her heavy makeup, heart-shaped sunglasses, and platinum blond wig (slightly askew), she was wearing a miniature version of Ella Raines's black dress. Not only was she burdened by several large packages, her precarious balance was threatened further by skyscraper heels and the spastic shudders that shook a body swollen fore and aft by Frederick's padding. Later, at lunch at the Paramount Studio commissary, I started at the sight of actor Cornel Wilde seated at a nearby table, the same Cornel Wilde (or was it Jon Hall?) who had swooped onto Maria Montez's balcony and carried her into my dreams during the nineteen-forties. To my knowledge, he hadn't made a film in years. His patent-leather black hair free of gray, his wrinkle-proof face as handsome as ever, its suntan radiant against a cream-colored sportcoat, he was a Hollywood Wax Museum image of himself. Two sets of identical twin girls, cousins wearing matching pink coats, descended upon him. "May we please have your autograph, Mr. Curtis?" Wilde's shrill laughter filled the room. "Yeah, I *know*, you're gonna make me a *star!*" snarled a plump middle-aged woman to two Mexican youths on Sunset Boulevard that night. Her nose was red, she had a giant box of Kleenex under one arm, and her not unattractive face looked familiar to me. One of the young men cursed her in Spanish while the other slowly removed a non-filter cigarette from behind his ear and placed it between his curled lips, from which it may still be dangling, unlit. An accident had created a traffic jam, and cars were bumper to bumper on Sunset Boulevard—old Buicks, Chevys, Olds 98s, sparkling with their simonized Saturday night facelifts, their horns howling in rage at the evening's lost opportunities. A week later, lecturing on Nathanael West's *The Day of the Locust*, I was able to offer the class what we in the business call a "new insight": among other things, Nathanael West was a good reporter, and photographers such as Weegee (*"Who?* Spell it, please") and Robert Frank didn't have to search too far for their subject matter.

Popular culture has produced an unfair share of psychological mutants, a theme that has engaged many writers. In Sean O'Faolain's "The Woman Who Married Clark Gable" (1948), a common man's moustache makes a Samson-like conjugal difference. Grim as it is, O'Faolain's tale renders a truth as representative as it is pathological. American family scrapbooks

An army of dreamers: at a Hollywood premiere, photograph by Weegee (Arthur Fellig), c. 1950.

are filled with old snapshots of loved ones resembling George Brent and Sylvia Sidney, if not Gable and Garbo, and one can imagine, twenty-five years hence, the historically informed children of today's college students looking up from *their* family albums, and saying, "Gee, Dad [or Mom], you looked like Mick Jagger." I was leaving a movie theater recently with my wife and two children after seeing John Wayne in *True Grit;* we passed a brightly lit "head" shop, its window crowded with counter-culture implementa. A boy and girl, eighteen years old or so, pale and thin, were slumped in the doorway, alternately nodding and giggling, and I remembered the phantom lady of Frederick's and *David and Bathsheba,* a summery performance, and turned up my collar against the wind.

Modern fiction has frequently attacked the pervasive, debilitating aura of popular culture. Since critical or scholarly detachment is highly esteemed, the personal past must give way to the professional present, and an annotated reading list. Nabokov's *Lolita* (1955), a vision of the 1947-52 period, succeeds better than any other postwar American novel in its rendering of the ways in which songs, ads, magazines, and movies create and control their consumers. The destructive Pop mythopoesis of the nineteen-thirties

Detroit, a photograph by Robert Frank, c. 1957. The Joan Crawford film is *A Woman's Face.*

has been definitively fixed by several writers: West, particularly in *The Day of the Locust* (1939; *The Cheated* was its working title); James Thurber in "The Remarkable Case of Mr. Bruhl" (1935; the mild little man's identity is engulfed by that of "Shoescar," a Capone-like gangster) and "The Secret Life of Walter Mitty" (1939); Horace McCoy in *They Shoot Horses, Don't They?* (1935; the dance marathon is literally a crippling fad); James M. Cain in *Mildred Pierce* (1941; young Veda Pierce models her cold, cruel "phony toniness" on Constance Bennett's screen persona); Irvin Faust in his Thurberesque tale "Into the Green Night" (1964; adolescent movie-goer Armand LaRue becomes the immortal movie star Lucky LaRue); and, more gently, by Robert Hemenway in *The Girl Who Sang with the Beatles and Other Stories* (1970) and by Manuel Puig, the Argentinian novelist. The girls of *Heartbreak Tango: A Serial* (1969) dream of Robert Taylor and Tyrone Power, duty-free export products, and Puig quietly makes a political point about America's influences on its poor neighbors. *Heartbreak Tango* and his *Betrayed by Rita Hayworth* (1968) demonstrate that life in a provincial Argentinian town in the nineteen-thirties and forties was in many ways similar to a Pop-conditioned childhood and adolescence in Dublin, Des Moines, or underdeveloped Long Island.

Where *Phantom Lady* was the Pop apogee of 1944,

Hail the Conquering Hero, with Ella Raines, marked the year's nadir, my worst war experience. I was drawn to the theater by the promising title and Ella's presence, but the film turned out to be a satire (a word not then in my vocabulary) of our myths and dreams of heroism, a send-up too of several other national pieties we shared with the larger audience. Woodrow LaFayette Pershing Truesmith (Eddie Bracken), the hapless son of a Marine hero, has left town because his hay fever has barred him from the service. He is befriended by six Marines on leave, who transform him into an honorably discharged hero of Guadalcanal, an updated version of the Buster Keaton daydreamer. Although many of the film's ironies (another word we wouldn't have used) surely escaped us, the high comedy of Woody's "triumphal" return devastated us. Nor was solace to be found in the fact that Ella finally loves him for what he is, a sweet and innocent incompetent. We weren't ready to see ourselves in Woody, and in 1944 no one went to the movies to laugh at himself. We were able to forget *Hail* quickly, however, and resume our games, for its broad manner was an isolated, aberrant phenomenon. American *films noirs* of the period—*Phantom Lady*, *Woman in the Window*, *Scarlet Street*—also took their measure of certain pieties and assumptions, but unlike *Hail the Conquering Hero* they did it quietly, working subversively from within the safe confines of established and expected conventions. The fat and freckled Boy Scout who discovers the murder victim in *Woman in the Window* is obviously a figure of fun—and we laughed at him—but he only appears briefly, in a newsreel, a film-within-the-film that separates him from the action and contains the satire, which was too short-lived to upset the Scouts seated in the audience. Comedy had to be respectful. Swashbuckler Errol Flynn could laugh at his own stunts yet manage to remain in character, the neighborhood show-off having the time of his life; his mirth was not directed at the film itself.

Since wartime producers were not about to undercut their audiences, Hollywood genre films of the forties rarely mocked their own conventions. The Bing Crosby–Bob Hope *Road* movies were a notable exception, which is probably why we avoided this popular series. Miraculously pre-conditioned by the literary criticism of F. R. Leavis, we demanded responsible "realism." When Groucho Marx spoke to the audience from the screen we could accept that intrusion because his greasepaint moustache made it clear that the clown's world was special, totally unreal, a circus transferred to the cinema. The same held for Bugs Bunny's one-way conversations with the viewer: an animated cartoon was by definition artifice, a brief and frivolous prelude to the afternoon's serious business that only sharpened our anticipations. But when Hope or Crosby employed direct address, winked at the camera, or questioned their presence in this "terrible picture" ("What are we doing here, Bing?"), thereby breaking the spell of illusion and audience identification with their adventures or pursuit of Lamour, we could only recoil; we had been recognized in the darkness, our voyeuristic privacy had been violated and compromised. Self-conscious art (such as it was) and psychic distancing had no place in our sense of movie-going, our primal aesthetic experience. "Stupid," we'd say, taxing our vocabularies and paraphrasing Leavis's verdict on *Tristram Shandy*.

Self-consciousness prevails today, of course, in all the arts, and the "anti-" film—the send-up of the Western, thriller, horror, or war movie—has in itself become a cycle or genre whose popular antecedents can be located in certain comic books and strips of the 1943-53 period. *The Spirit* satirized movies, while *Plastic Man* took care of superheroes; *Mad* magazine, Nichols and May, radio's Bob and Ray, and *Your Show of Shows* on TV extended their range of burlesque through the nineteen-fifties. To Lenny Bruce, the world *was* Show Biz, a meretricious amusement palace in which everyone had their con, their number, their *schtick*. Lesser artists, buoyed by the prestige of the printed page but lacking Bruce's controlled rage or moral equilibrium, are now busily tapping his deep vein of anarchic Pop comedy (Philip Roth's *Our Gang,* 1971, or Pynchon's interminable *Gravity's Rainbow—Plastic Man* writ large). If movies are unable to create our myths as they once did, it is partly because of this kind of comedy, and Pop culture's new-found ability to make fun of itself; even radio and TV commercials are self-referential in the manner of the most advanced fiction (Barthelme's *Snow White* through Gardner's *Grendel,* the reading list in the college courses of current and future advertising copywriters). A recent ad on Chicago radio, promoting a local bank, spoofed the old *Green Hornet* program. When the Hornet asks Kato to make a deposit, he refuses. "What you think I am, your faithful valet?" he snarls, rejecting his subservient "racist" role and self-consciously adapting the introductory tag that was used by the original announcer but never by Kato, who would not have heard it, since he existed in the realistic dimension of the story. A contemporary child may watch an actor on a TV thriller at 7:00 P.M. and an hour later see him return as the "guest star" of a variety show sketch which mocks his role as a handsome and virile and fearless private eye. "Quick, Dad, come here," yelled my ten-year-old son recently. "They're doing a parody of *Mannix.*" My son and his friends do not play any Soundview games.

Parody is a cleansing exercise, a healthy presence in any culture, and the reappraisal of the American cinema that has occurred in the last decade has doubtless profited from this new self-consciousness as well as from more literal kinds of distance: the geographic remove enjoyed by French film critics of the fifties and sixties (André Bazin and his colleagues on *Cahiers du Cinema*), which recalls the Gallic redemption of jazz in the thirties; and the inevitable passage of time, which has enabled American *cinéastes* to isolate the films of the past as they would any artifact or text. Moreover, cultural critics have been partially disarmed by the fact that movies are no longer our principal distraction and narcotic. To suggest that Hortense Powdermaker's *Hollywood, the Dream Factory* (1950) is now dated is not to be sanguine about the effects of today's screen violence or pornography; it's a matter of seeing the difference between past and present fields of force. If such a book were now possible or necessary, it would first address itself to television or, more likely, the rock or counter-culture, since the distractive environment of the TV set, a piece of furniture, is so distant from the dreamy, enveloping gigantism of the movie screen. As pernicious as it was, a film such as *Easy Rider* (1969) reinforced rather than created the attitudes of but one segment of its youthful audience, something quite different from the awesome sway of old Hollywood.

Since younger readers do not remember or perhaps cannot imagine a time when Pop music went uncelebrated and motion pictures were not respected, let alone revered, it is worth noting that the literary culture has traditionally scorned and resisted the popular arts, even when it has quietly absorbed and built upon them. Apollinaire's poem *Zone* (1913) is an early and important exception. "Weary of this oldtime world," the French prophet of American Pop Art recommends the poetry of commercial prospectuses, catalogues, and posters, the prose of newspapers and detective stories, the miscellany of a thousand modern items—an injunction that reflected or influenced the performances of his friends among the typographically inclined Cubists. Unlike the élitist Braque, who continued to mount the names of classical composers, Juan Gris included in his still life *Violin* (1914) a fragment of sheet music from "Auprès de ma blonde," a pun that savors three Parisian commodities (*blonde* is also French slang for "beer"). Picasso's *Ma Jolie* paintings of 1911-14 saluted a love by way of a banal song; and composers as various as Stravinsky, Ravel, Ives, and Kurt Weill had all made use of popular music by the advent of *Finnegans Wake* (1939), but Joyce, a musical wordman, viewed it as the indigestible offal of a technological culture:

We now romp through a period of pure lyricism of shamebred music (technologically, let me say, the appetising entry of this subject on a fool chest of vialds is plumply pudding the carp before doevre hors) evidenced by such words in distress as *I cream for thee, Sweet Margareen*, and the more hopeful *O Margareena! O Margareena! Still in the bowl is left a lump of gold!*[1]

The opposite of Gris's song and beer conundrum, Joyce's horse/hors/whore pun is summary, suggesting the difference between the music-hall melodies of *Ulysses* (1922), a community sing, and the manufactured, counterfeit emotions of a subsequent decade's product—margarine instead of butter. The verbal *leitmotifs* of *Ulysses* had already been compared to cinematic montage, but the cinema itself receives low grades in the *Wake*, where young females are seen "at the movies swallowing sobs and blowing bixed mixcuits over 'childe' chaplain's 'latest' or on the verge of the gutter with some bobbedhair brieffrocked babyma's toddler."[2] *Ulysses*'s simple nursemaid Gerty MacDowell had lost herself in the sentimental pulp fiction of 1904, but her avatars choose the movies, an accurate observation on Joyce's part. Bloom's self-abuse, provoked by Gerty's exhibitionism, is linked with her lameness and "Mutoscope pictures,"[3] and this allusion to the turn-of-the-century peepshow machine telescopes Bloom's crippled psychic condition as well as the voyeuristic nature of the film-going experience. Joyce, however, is not about to condemn such needs categorically. No friend to Onan, as the chapter makes clear, Joyce does not suggest, as West or Nabokov would, that Mutoscope and pulp fiction have formed their consumers; water seeks its own level, as Bloom would say. Joyce is less generous toward cheap journalism, as the singularly violent "Cyclops" chapter proves, but his ripostes and parodies are never strident. "K.M.R.I.A.," proclaims a newspaper headline in "Aeolus" (= "kiss my royal Irish arse"), prefiguring contemporary journalism's penchant for what Daniel Boorstin would one day call non-events.

Joyce's cultural sympathies were widely inclusive, tolerant and humane, and he himself enjoyed the cinema immensely. His negative images (no pun is intended) are the gleanings of an anthropologist rather than the product of a consistent and concerted "highbrow" attack on contemporary vulgarities; out of context, however, they appear to be quite in keeping with his literary generation's less complicated and closed opinions about mass culture in general—opinions which extend all the way back to Plato's *Gorgias*, where Socrates, the premier critic of kitsch, makes the basic Platonic distinction between the enlightening, rational arts and the pleasureful, rhetorical, and hence counterfeit non-arts (or "knacks"). "The 'movies' have killed the drama," wrote literary critic James Huneker in 1916. "No doubt, when we all own a motor-car, the 'movies,' too, will go out of business."[4]

The silent cinema did have its literary advocates. *The Little Review*, which would serialize *Ulysses*, saluted Chaplin's *The Tramp* in 1915, the same year that the poet Vachel Lindsay published *The Art of the Moving Pictures;* but three decades would pass before a *littérateur* would again expend his energies on a book about movies (Parker Tyler). Dreiser, among others, also wrote enthusiastically about film during the nineteen-twenties, particularly on Mack Sennett, whose spirit did not animate Dreiser's other endeavors. By the thirties, however, a negative attitude prevailed, for the advent of talkies and Ford-like assembly-line production had completely overrun the literary community's romantic sense of art (one man, one work—almost possible in the earlier American cinema). Except for an acknowledged trove of silent classics (mainly Soviet), and perhaps the Marx Brothers (didn't T. S. Eliot admire Groucho?), most intellectuals on both sides of the Atlantic now regarded movies with a hostility, or at best an indifference, based on aesthetic and sociopolitical principles. Rudolf Arnheim's *Film* (1933), first published in Germany (expanded and reprinted as *Film as Art*, 1957), argued that the arrival of sound and color represented a decline in artistic form, while the sociological and anthropological poles of opinion were defined by such books as Leo Rosten's *Hollywood: The Movie Colony, The Movie Makers* (1941) and Powdermaker's *Hollywood, the Dream Factory*. The talkies demanded more dialogue, of course, and Hollywood turned toward the East as never before.

With the exception of Hemingway, who sold his novels rather than himself to Hollywood, all the major and a good many minor American writers worked in

California as screenwriters during the thirties. Filthy lucre and artistic exhaustion were not the only forces that sent them westward. By failing to buy novels or attend plays, the American public could sentence a writer to a season or more in hell, as life "out there" was deemed; the writer, in turn, could revile the entire enterprise, audience included. The writers, most of them leftist, set the tone of the anti-Hollywood bias, their bitterness compounded by the fact that in Hollywood's social and creative hierarchies, screenwriters were near the bottom. An ugly, rarely acknowledged aspect of the bias was articulated by Spencer Tracy when he said, "Out here the Kellys are working for the Cohens."[5] "You're doing pretty well for a 'Heeb,'" said Hemingway to M-G-M producer Bernard Hyman when his employee, scenarist F. Scott Fitzgerald, proudly brought his famous friend into Hyman's office in the Thalberg Building at Metro.[6] "Must you talk to me? This is a Gentile's house, you know," says screenwriter Clare Quilty to gun-toting refugee Humbert Humbert in *Lolita*.[7] Membership in the Communist Party and donations to Loyalist Spain aside, anecdotes told at the expense of illiterate immigrant producers were the principal immediate solace for the slumming "successful" novelist or playwright who was down on his luck or as greedy as any mogul (see S. N. Behrman's charming memoir, *People in a Diary*, 1972). The Hollywood novel (there

are more than a hundred) was supposed to even all sorts of scores; like the anti-academic "satires" of later decades, however, it usually shot down easy targets and collapsed in self-pity. And cynical, guilt-ridden old Hollywood hands, writing their memoirs at poolside, downgraded their own real achievements, however few, and told everyone what they wanted to hear about life in a Babylonian brothel (see Ben Hecht's *A Child of the Century*, 1955). "Hollywood" became a synonym for "tawdry," "delusive," or "meretricious" (see *The American Heritage Dictionary*), and these biases were confirmed by the findings of documentary photographers from Walker Evans and Weegee to Robert Frank and Diane Arbus, who cover a range of more than thirty years. Arbus's shots of (and at) a nocturnal, eerily quiescent Disneyland and the façade of a movie-lot mansion silhouetted against the sky—her sole "landscape" ventures, bereft of freakish people—provide contemporary addenda to Nathanael West and Edward Weston, who anticipates Arbus in his 1940 photographs of the M-G-M lot, with its *trompe-l'œil* sets and naked, disjointed wardrobe mannequins crowded and stacked on crude wooden shelves like the corded living dead in a Dachau dormitory. Antonioni sets the stills of such photographers in motion in *Zabriskie Point*, but his vision of an apocalyptic Southern California is hardly fresh news in 1970—and his Death Valley setups merely duplicate the landscape photography of Ansel Adams (1954) and Weston (1938), whose desolate images of Zabriskie Point seem to document the rule of entropy. "Strictly From Hunger"; "The Love Nest"; "Crazy Sunday"; *The Last Tycoon; The Slide Area;* "The World in the Evening"; "The City Was in Total Darkness"; *The Day of the Locust*—the titles of the best Hollywood stories and novels are self-explanatory.[8] Like *Zabriskie Point*, they constitute a compendium of received opinions, a doomsday ambience.

Another aspect of the *de rigueur* prejudice against Hollywood and its alleged sop-for-the-masses product was expressed by Edmund Wilson in *The Boys in the Back Room* (1940-41), where he claimed that screenwriter-novelist James M. Cain had corrupted his genuine gifts by writing novels tailored for the screen (eight did indeed find their way there); in his five-page "Postscript," Wilson laid at Hollywood's feet the early deaths and unfulfilled destinies of Scott Fitzgerald and Nathanael West, his recently deceased friends. If one of those "boys," Raymond Chandler, an extraordinary novelist, could not be accepted by critics who dismissed him because of his genre, then at least he could establish his credentials and self-respect by scorning Hollywood and his own script-writing assignments, a stance which made him as much of an artist, prostitute, and martyr as anyone else.[9] Murray Kempton orchestrates the martyrdom theme in *Part of Our Time: Some Monuments and Ruins of the Thirties* (1955), adding to Wilson's honor roll the name of Daniel Fuchs, who, having published an estimable trilogy of novels in the mid thirties, disappeared from literary view in Hollywood. It would be easy enough to update Kempton by ridiculing Fuchs's Recognized Achievements—an Oscar for *Love Me or Leave Me* ("Best Motion Picture Story" of 1955)—but his credits as scenarist also included *Criss Cross* (1949), a fine *film noir* whose verbal wit recalls screenwriter William Faulkner's contributions to *The Big Sleep* (1946) and *To Have and Have Not* (1944).[10] But gangster films and thrillers had no content, it was said (wrongly), and were thus worthless; the properties of *film noir* had yet to be identified.

That a talented person should write for or about the movies seemed either tragic or absurd. Curious editorial procedures formulate such views: a posthumous, award-winning collection of William Troy's essays (1967) omits the first-rate film criticism he wrote in the thirties, which included a remarkable 1933 review of Fritz Lang's *M* that accurately predicted the way the cinema would displace the naturalistic drama. To Alfred Kazin (*Starting Out in the Thirties*, 1965), Otis Ferguson's film reviewing (1934-41) was simply

Houses and Billboards in Atlanta, a photograph by Walker Evans, 1936. The ironic counterpointing became a convention.

the realization of a willful anti-literary stance; the massive, posthumous *Film Criticism of Otis Ferguson* (1971) suggests otherwise, and that there are less taxing ways to become an *épateur* (grow a long beard, punch a professor). After a brilliant start as a film critic in the early thirties, Dwight Macdonald turned to politics; only with the exhaustion of those hopes did he return to the fold in the late fifties. James Agee and Robert Warshow, the best American film critics of the forties and fifties, were hectored by their friends to do truly serious work, and the defensive publishers of *Agee on Film* (1958) chose to preface that posthumous volume with W. H. Auden's condescending praise of Agee, originally a 1944 letter to the editors of *The Nation:* "I do not care for movies very much and I rarely see them," he wrote, but Agee's excellent criticism "transcends its . . . unimportant subject." That hostile ambience, as it prevailed at Columbia University in the late forties, has been nicely described by critic Andrew Sarris, who survived.[11] John Hollander's excellent poem "Movie-Going" (1960), a celebration and an elegy ("I remember: the RKO COLONIAL; the cheap / ARDEN and ALDEN both"),[12] dismayed our mutual friend, Hollander's colleague at *Partisan Review,* who said, "John's lost his mind!" When Lionel Trilling reviewed Ingmar Bergman's *Four Screenplays* (1960), he admitted that he had never *seen* one of the films, but would comment on them as literature.[13] The Bergmania (as *Time* might then have said) of the popular reviewers had not aroused Trilling's curiosity, and the considered critical praise in *Film Quarterly* was hardly relevant, since, its university press imprimatur notwithstanding, that journal would never have reached his desk. "That reminds me of a movie I saw the other night," digressed Professor F. W. Dupee, lecturing on Henry James c. 1960 to a class of solemn Columbia graduate students, who gasped aloud as one at such a blatant breach of Seriousness. Dupee recoiled, half in mock-horror, as helpless and speechless as John Wayne's enemy, the infantry captain at K Company's graduation ceremony.

Film is now in the curriculum, but these attitudes persist, despite the almost heroic efforts in several quarters to rescue and redeem the American cinema. "At first sight, it seems a terrible waste to ask a writer as gifted as Miss Kael to criticize films," stated reviewer Anatole Broyard in 1973, echoing Auden's "praise" of Agee; at second sight he is grateful for her ability to recognize nonsense.[14] Jay Martin, a youngish academic critic writing in 1970 about Nathanael West's crucial Hollywood years, complements his seniors by offering a shopworn Marxist overview of the Dream Factory: "As a consequence of these [commercial] interests, the movies of the thirties portrayed a world in which economics, politics, race, and religion were absent, a world strangely polarized between historical Western adventure and bedroom farce, attempting to convince its patrons that this was the normal lot of mankind."[15] Martin, a professor of American Studies, seems unaware of the decade's muckraking protest films, such as *I Am a Fugitive from a Chain Gang* (1932), *Wild Boys of the Road* (1933), *The Power and the Glory* (1933), *Our Daily Bread* (1934), *Fury* (1936), and *The Great McGinty* (1940), all culminating in *Citizen Kane* (1941); or of John Ford's excellent historical films (*Young Mr. Lincoln,* 1939), adaptations of social and political novels (*The Informer,* 1935, *The Grapes of Wrath,* 1940), and classic improvement upon Eugene O'Neill (*The Long Voyage Home,* 1940); or of the socioeconomic commentaries explicit in the era's best gangster films; or of social satires as various as *Dinner at Eight* (1933), *Modern Times* (1936), and *Nothing Sacred* (1937). Nor does he admit the truly subversive comedies of the Marx Brothers or W. C. Fields, whose grotesqueries are not altogether unlike West's, and whose scabrous version of the American family functions—along with Faulkner's *The Hamlet* (1940)—as an antidote to Norman Rockwell's sentimental image. The campiest entertainment of the thirties is also lost on Martin—unfortunately, since it too has its "Westian" interludes. In the "Lullaby of Broadway" number in Busby Berkeley's *Gold Diggers of 1935,* a Manhattan working girl (Wini Shaw) who lives in a drab walk-up apartment is swept away by her dream, a fantastic and frenzied nightclub whirl (with Dick Powell) that ends with her scream as she falls to her death from glamorous heights, the victim of the kind of escapism eviscerated by Nathanael West and usually indulged by Berkeley.

The relationship between high art and popular art is troublesome indeed, complicated in recent years by the literary critics who have Gone Over to the Other Side, such as Leslie Fiedler, Susan Sontag, and younger exegetes who, often under the spell of French structuralism, are exercising their cleverness, if not intelligence, in behalf of grade-Z movies, pornography, comic books, and *Doc Savage* reprints. *King Kong* threatens to become the *Moby-Dick* of another industry. Over-zealous, uncritical "readings" of Pop, the obverse of the sociological ruminations of the fifties, have inspired a retrograde mandarin backlash, reinforcing old lines, which is also lamentable.[16] Literary historians who ignore popular culture are ahistorical; as critics, busily patrolling the interstices between high and low forms, they cannot perceive or describe the exact achievements of the many "serious" writers since Joyce who have variously absorbed and utilized popular materials (West, Graham Greene), nor recognize the excellence of "popular" writers who worked within and transcended the limitations of sub-literary genres (Dashiell Hammett, Raymond Chandler, and the numerous science-fiction authors whose dystopias have fueled William Burroughs's *Naked Lunch*, 1959, and *Nova Express*, 1964). Those hard-boiled writers, we are told, imitated Hemingway; "The Killers" (1927), however, was influenced by the *Black Mask* pulp writers. Although Hemingway would never have publicized such slumming expeditions, Jorge Luis Borges's essays of 1935-36 on G. K. Chesterton's Father Brown make it clear that the Argentinian's epistemological tales could not exist without the example of the popular detective genre. Similarly instructive is Borges's tribute to the H. G. Wells romances that are frequently dismissed as potboilers; *The War of the Worlds* (1898) helped beget Borges's anti-utopian "Tlön, Uqbar, Orbis Tertius" (1939/47), whose invaders arrive more quietly. When Anthony Burgess in *The Wanting Seed* (1962) generously names characters Heinlein and Asimov after the well-known sci-fi writers, he is acknowledging a source of inspiration and underscoring a fact that critics would avoid or resist: "art" is not always served by arbitrary distinctions. Writers certainly don't observe them.

Constance Rourke's *American Humor* (1931) ends with the hope that American writers may soon achieve an instinctive alliance between native materials and old world themes or traditions. Nathanael West was realizing her wish as she wrote (*Miss Lonelyhearts*

was begun in 1931), and contemporary American novelists have more than obliged her; the democratic aesthetic of recent American poetry, an extension of Apollinaire or Whitman, is typified by Edward Field's adulation of popular iconography in *Variety Photoplays* (1967), whose zone ranges from *The Bride of Frankenstein* to Joan Crawford. Who, besides Saul Bellow, *isn't* using popular materials (e.g., sports) or Pop culture these days? Vladimir Nabokov, another admirer of Chesterton and Wells, would add his name to the list. He says that he "loathes popular pulp," "vulgar movies" in particular, as he told an interviewer who has written a book on the not always artful films of Samuel Fuller.[17] A taxonomic survey of Nabokov's work both supports and contradicts his claim. Certain pervasive attitudes, effects, and techniques in his fiction could not have been achieved without a knowledge of cinema, and this book will argue that popular forms have exerted a positive influence on a body of work whose themes are not exclusive to high art. The same could be said of several other writers, and they will not be neglected here, but Nabokov's strong opinions and "highbrow" credentials make him an especially suitable subject, the ideal lens through which to study a large and open-ended "interdisciplinary" field. Movie stills, which abound in this book, are rarely an exact replica of the scene we think we remember. They are the result of restaged or re-

The ideal lens: Basil Rathbone as Sherlock Holmes (c. 1942), a more assiduous observer than several of Nabokov's narrators and readers, whose search for clues and a solution casts them, frustratingly enough, as detectives. As a boy, Nabokov was an avid reader of Conan Doyle; that enthusiasm has waned, but nevertheless left its mark. Hermann, the narrator of Nabokov's

arranged scenes, or, at best, the original set-up shot from a slightly different angle. Memento mori of happy occasions, they equal the ways in which artists and nostalgists color or transmute the past. Many of the names, titles, and players introduced in this chapter will weave in and out of the following pages, duplicating the surround of popular culture; Vladimir Nabokov will actually meet John Wayne. The associative method has its obvious pitfalls, but my intentions are modest enough. "And if my private universe scans right, / So does the verse of galaxies divine / Which I suspect is an iambic line," writes John Shade in *Pale Fire* (1962).[18]

Despair (1936), addresses Conan Doyle directly: "What an opportunity, what a subject you missed! For you could have written one last tale concluding the whole Sherlock Holmes epic; one last episode beautifully setting off the rest; the murderer in that tale should have turned out to be not the one-legged bookkeeper, not the Chinaman Ching and not the woman in crimson, but the very chronicler of the crime stories, Dr. Watson himself—Watson, who, so to speak, knew what was Whatson. A staggering surprise for the reader"—and a description of Nabokov's own narrative strategies, the surprises in store for the readers of *Despair* and the many other works which parody and/or transmute the plots and techniques of the "tale of ratiocination." Has Hermann, a "Rascalnikov" in every way, read Agatha Christie's *The Murder of Roger Ackroyd* (1926), whose narrator (a Watson-like doctor) turns out to be the killer? No matter; Nabokov's surprises, unlike Christie's mere trick, posit the mysteries of character, of identity and self-knowledge.

Cover design of the *émigré* first edition of *Camera Obscura,*
by "V. Sirin," Nabokov's *émigré* pen name.

2
Negative Images

"The twilight before the Lumières," laments *Ada's* (1969) Van Veen in regard to the dark, muddy tonalities of an old photograph ("a sumerograph," he calls it, invoking Sumer, the ancient region of Babylonia, and *sumerki*, a Russian word for "twilight").[1] Although Nabokov admires certain classic films and loves the screen comedies of Keaton, Chaplin, Lloyd, Clair, Laurel and Hardy, and the Marx Brothers, Van's metaphor is paradoxical. In Nabokov's fiction the descendents of those pioneering French cinematographers, the Lumières, would seem to have produced a commercial product that obfuscates rather than illuminates its human subjects. *Laughter in the Dark* (1938) was originally titled *Camera Obscura* (1932), and the root meaning of *obscura* survives and persists in Nabokov's vision of a popular cinema that is dark indeed.

Because Nabokov is, with Borges and Raymond Queneau, the most learned and mandarin of living writers, his numerous allusions to movies might also seem paradoxical. They are, in fact, consistent with an aesthetic shared by Nabokov and several other great writers. Though he is a fantast and artificer who believes in the fictiveness of fiction, the texture of his prose nevertheless incorporates an extraordinary amount of material drawn from *his* quotidian: tags from Italian opera and Russian popular songs; allusions if not *tableaux vivants* copied from Flemish Old Masters and old French comic strips; literary references from Catullus to Updike; gleanings, and intrusions from Nabokov's recondite researches and pastimes, his passion for chess and lepidoptery. The latter vocation—for Nabokov is a professional—helps to define his particular sensibility. No more isolated in Montreux than was Joyce in Trieste, where his Aunt Josephine kept him supplied with Dublin information, Nabokov the biologist regularly exercises a cool curiosity about all facets of life, and his walk to the well-stocked neighborhood news kiosk in Montreux is a daily ritual. *L'Erald Tribune* (as it's called in *Transparent Things*), *Le Monde, Time, Newsweek, The New Yorker, The Saturday Review, Playboy, Esquire, Encounter, The Listener, The Spectator, The New Statesman, Punch*, the London Sunday newspapers, the *TLS, The National Review,* and *The New York Review of Books* provide a balanced diet and satisfy a literary anatomist's penchant for sub-literary but culturally significant details, glittering additions to whatever mosaic the writer has in progress (or mind).

As in his 1,086-page *Eugene Onegin* Commentary (1964), novelist Nabokov assembles the quirky, compendious materials one associates with the bedside library, the great literary anatomies such as Burton's *Anatomy of Melancholy* (1651) or those *sui generis* masterpieces such as *Gargantua and Pantagruel* (1564), *Moby-Dick* (1851), and *Ulysses* (1922), in which the writer makes fictive use of all kinds of learning and unpromising bits and pieces of trash and trivia, effecting verbal collages which give pleasure and vividly communicate a sense of what it was like to be alive at a given moment in space and time. Delightful *objets trouvés* displace omniscience as a means of rendering a character's psychology. Obsessed by the warp and woof of coincidence, John Shade incorporates a very old newspaper headline in his poem *Pale Fire:* "A Curio: *Red Sox Beat Yanks 5-4/On Chapman's Homer*, thumbtacked to the door" (ll. 97-98). Unearthed by Nabokov in the stacks of the Cornell Library, the headline refers to Ben Chapman, a Red Sox outfielder (1937-38, to be exact). Charles Kinbote, his blinders in place, glosses it as "A reference to the title of Keats' famous sonnet (often quoted in America) which, owing to a printer's absentmindedness, has been drolly transposed, from some other article." His ignorance of baseball and Keats' journalistic prestige is touching as well as amusing because it adumbrates the exile's total isolation, the madman's inability to "read" reality, let alone a poem. More typical of the anatomist's methods as a cultural observer is the note to line 91 of *Pale Fire*, which quotes rather than parodies two ads from 1937 and 1949 issues of *Life*, since their absurdity cannot be outdone. That note is titled "trivia," in an allusive tribute to the great age of literary anatomy—Sterne, Swift, Johnson —by way of John Gay's *Trivia, or the Art of Walking the Streets of London* (1716).

Transparent Things (1972), with its Swiss locale and international local color, succinctly demonstrates how Nabokov makes aesthetic capital of a browse in a souvenir shop for tourists, a walk to the kiosk, and a quick perusal of unpurchased journals. Early in the novel, Nabokov notes a sign on a snapshot booth and laments how "The masculine ending and the absence of an acute accent flawed the unintentional pun."

3 Photos Poses

is incorporated in the text;[2] *osé* is French for "bold," "risqué." Both the booth and that sign, crying out for corrective graffiti, exist—across the street from Nabokov's news kiosk. "Dennis the Menace doesn't look like his father. Could he be illegitimate?" wonders

Nabokov, back at the hotel, looking up from the comics page of *The Herald Tribune*. "Shall I inquire in a letter to the editor?" asks *Onegin*'s scholiast. "I wish you wouldn't," says Véra Nabokov. "They never printed your letter complaining about the plot inconsistencies in *Rex Morgan*."[3] Sweet Reason prevails, but Dennis (or his cuckolded father) may yet surface in a Nabokov work. He is not, as some friendly critics have suggested, totally hostile to the "actual world," and its fictions—large and small—clearly fascinate him. Except for his positive view of screen comedy, Nabokov's references to cinema are the product of an anatomist's tour of the contemporary world, rather than a *cinéaste*'s total recall, a film buff's enthusiasm. The result is a kind of cultural criticism.

The *émigré* narrator of "Spring in Fialta" (1938), Nabokov's own favorite among his many stories, is a representative for a European film company and, his gentility notwithstanding, a representative figure. He is acquainted with a Nabokov-like "Franco-Hungarian writer," and subsequently "even turned out to be of some use to him: my firm acquired the film rights of one of his more intelligible stories, and then he had a good time pestering me with telegrams." As with Nabokov's own experience in the thirties with two film options on *Camera Obscura*, nothing comes of that project. Depressed by the prospect of an unexpected reunion with the writer, the narrator admits

The anatomy of literary anatomy. Note 91 of Kinbote's commentary, a gloss on "trivia," is based on the ads pictured here: "Among these was a scrapbook in which over a period of years (1937-1949) Aunt Maud had been pasting clippings of an involuntarily ludicrous or grotesque nature. John Shade allowed me one day to memorandum the first and the last of the series; they happened to intercommunicate most pleasingly, I thought. Both stemmed from the same family magazine *Life*, so justly famed for its pudibundity in regard to the mysteries of the male sex; hence one can well imagine how startled or titillated those families were. The first comes from the issue of May 10, 1937, p. 67, and advertises the Talon Trouser Fastener (a rather grasping and painful name,

by the way). It shows a young gent radiating virility among several ecstatic lady-friends, and the inscription reads: *You'll be amazed that the fly on your trousers could be so dramatically improved.* The second comes from the issue of March 28, 1949, p. 126, and advertises Hanes Fig Leaf Brief. It shows a modern Eve worshipfully peeping from behind a potted tree of knowledge at a leering young Adam in rather ordinary but clean underwear, with the front of his advertised brief conspicuously and compactly shaded, and the inscription reads: *Nothing beats a fig leaf.*

"I think there must exist a special subversive group of pseudo-cupids—plump hairless little devils whom Satan commissions to make disgusting mischief in sacrosanct places."

that "one thing, however, considerably cheered me up: the flop of his recent play."[4] (Nabokov's play, *Sobytie* [*The Event*], had a brief Parisian run in 1938.) His is the entrepreneur's hostility toward the artist, and Nabokov more than returns it in kind; it pervades his work, especially in his conception of cinematic *poshlost'*, to use one of the two words he has fixed in our language—if *Time* is grist for your lexicon (*vide* June 10, 1974, p. 93).

Like Lolita, but no nymphet, Margot in *Laughter in the Dark* "was mad on the movies."[5] She daydreams of stardom while serving as an usherette at the Argus, named after the hundred-eyed monster of Greek mythology, who was set to watch Io, a maiden loved by Zeus. "Good name for a cinema," thinks Albinus (p. 22), whom Margot will destroy after he has been figuratively and then literally blinded. Argus is slain by Hermes, who transforms lovely Io into a cow—quite appropriate to Hermes-Nabokov's attitude toward the popular cinema, his reductive mockery of Margot. An ironic and surprisingly antic image of sightlessness, the Argus is Nabokov's movie emblem and stamp of disapproval, his answer to M-G-M's imposing Leo the Lion, 20th Century–Fox's crisscrossing beams of light, Columbia's torch-bearing American goddess.

Employing a Flaubertian shorthand of characterization, Nabokov continually uses movies, as well as novels, paintings, and magazines, to define the minds and souls of his creations, the total nature of their existence. "The glasses he had got were very becoming. He looked like the actor Hess in *The Hindu Student,* a movie," thinks Martha of Franz, her provincial, unglamorous lover in *King, Queen, Knave* (1928).[6] Throughout the novel a "Cinépalace" is being erected which will premiere the film version of the stage play *King, Queen, Knave,* in an infinite regress that comments on the trashiness of Franz's and Martha's murder plot, quite apart from the novelistic artistry which contains them. "Plagiarizing villainy," Martha avidly posits several scenarios. "From [the door's] threshold [Franz] would fire half a dozen times in quick succession, as they do in American movies" (p. 179), or they might kill her husband in the woods, after which Franz would shoot Martha through the hand—"Yes, that's necessary, darling, it is always done, it must look as if we had been attacked by robbers" (p. 180). "Martha . . . would tell [her cuckolded husband] in breathless detail the entire foolish film as the preface and price of a submissive caress" (p. 92). Whatever the price of sexuality, all warmth seems to have been neutralized by the aura of the silver screen or the novel's austere and white-walled Art Deco environment. "Yes, Franz and Martha certainly like the flicks, but I'm quite indifferent to them," says Nabokov, patiently enduring his guest's disquisition, his willingness to share taxonomic discoveries.

The death of Argus, as documented by an ancient Greek painter.

"From its threshold he would fire . . . as they do in American movies": the shadow of an actor in *The Drag Net* (1928), directed by Josef von Sternberg, as was the 1927 hit *Underworld*, famous early gangster films contemporary with *King, Queen, Knave*. "When in doubt, have a man come through a door with a gun in his hand," said Raymond Chandler, shooting down the standardized pulp detective fiction of the twenties and early thirties. Those Sternberg films begot J. L. Borges's first story, "Streetcorner Man" (1933), *his* "Killers"—a gangster tale whose colloquial, laconic prose and slyly "naive" narrator have affected such contemporary Latin American writers as Puig, Cabrera Infante, and García Márquez.

One doesn't need a microscope to see that almost every Nabokov novel takes its measure of the "cine-monkey," and that a far from indifferent attitude is sharply fixed. Hermann, the fatuous chocolate manufacturer of *Despair* (1936), asks Felix, "what is the opinion you have formed of me?" "Maybe you're an actor," answers the tramp whom Hermann has murderously and mistakenly cast as his "Double."[7] "You've guessed. . . . Yes, I'm an actor," says Hermann. "A film actor, to be accurate," and Felix, no fool in at least one matter, "seem[s] . . . disappointed" (p. 88). At the end of the novel, Hermann, the cornered "arch-criminal," watches the gendarmes closing in, but his shouts out the window—added by Nabokov to the 1966 translation—are directions addressed to the film company he imagines to be assembled below: "*Attention!* I want a clean getaway. That's all. Thank you," and he steps into the medium deemed appropriate to a self-styled "mystery story" as misconceived and muddled as his has been. In search of a definitive composite picture of *his* identity, the *émigré* narrator of *The Eye* (1930) indulges "the fantasy that directs life"[8] and performs a trick even more difficult than Hermann's self-perpetuating murder: suicide followed by a free-wheeling ghostly return that would allow him a calm outside view of himself and easy access to at least all the spoken and written versions of his self. "I walked homeward and on the way had a wonderful idea. I imagined a sleek movie villain reading a document he has found on someone else's desk. True, my plan was very sketchy," and it is as doomed to inevitable failure as any movie villain's quest (p. 67).

Satirical thrusts at a character's movie preferences do not necessarily undermine our sympathetic responses. In *The Defense* (1930), Grandmaster Luzhin's wife, a most ordinary woman, "made his acquaintance . . . the way they do in old novels or in motion pictures: she drops a handkerchief and he picks it up—with the sole difference that they interchanged roles."[9] After his nervous collapse, she takes Luzhin to the very first film he has ever seen, an awful production, and Nabokov carefully and wittily paraphrases its trite plot, which includes a chess game (pp. 191-92). By having him cry at the film, Nabokov telescopes Luzhin's provincial, regressive, vulnerable innocence and isolation—the toll of his genius and circumscribing obsession—and underscores once more his mate's commonplace turn of mind. " 'Very, very good—that picture,' " Luzhin says the next day. "He thought a bit more and added: 'But they don't know how to play [chess]. 'What do you mean, they don't know?' said his wife with surprise. 'They were first-class actors' " (p. 192).

Glory (1932) is more sparing of Martin Edelweiss, perhaps because the young *émigré*, a daring and attractive fellow, has been vested with many of Nabokov's experiences at Cambridge. *Glory*'s lachrymose

Uncle Henry "even cried at the movies,"[10] but Nabokov affectionately indulges all the "immemorial and tender banalities" which deeply stir Martin. His hapless infatuation with flirtatious, dark-eyed Sonia ignites a series of banal nocturnal fantasies familiar to any man who was ever young, and its culmination—if not climax—fully demonstrates that Martin is as naively romantic as he is keenly sensitive:

But while the bond of [dancing] bodies is still unbroken, the outlines of a potential love affair begin to form, and the rough draft already comprises everything: the sudden silence between two people in some dimly lit room; the man carefully placing with trembling fingers on the edge of an ashtray the just-lit but impedient cigarette; the woman's eyes slowly closing as in a filmed scene; and the rapt darkness, and in it a point of light, a glossy limousine traveling fast through the rainy night, and suddenly, a white terrace and the dazzling ripple of the sea, and Martin softly saying to the girl he has carried off, "Your name —what's your name?" Leafy shadows play on her luminous dress. She gets up, she goes away. The rapacious croupier rakes in Martin's last chips, and he has nothing left but to thrust his hands into the empty pockets of his dinner jacket and descend slowly into the casino garden and, then, sign on as a longshoreman—and there she is again, aboard someone else's yacht, sparkling, laughing, flinging coins into the water.

"Funny thing," said Darwin [his more sophisticated friend] one night, as he and Martin came out of a small Cambridge cinema, "it's all unquestionably poor, vulgar, and rather implausible, and yet there is something excit-ing about all that flying foam, the *femme fatale* on the yacht, the ruined and ragged he-man swallowing his tears."

"It's nice to travel," said Martin. "I'd like to travel a lot" (pp. 82-83).

Martin does travel, third-class, to Germany and France, where he retraces Nabokov's postgraduate itinerary of 1923. "A ragged he-man" in the best sense, Martin gloriously transcends his fears and fearful circumstances by mountain-climbing, one of the "exploits" referred to by the novel's original title, *Podvig*.

Nabokov is less indulgent of well-traveled Pnin, who, unlike his creator, fails to respond properly to the most delightful and ageless cinema artistry. At the fortnightly college presentation of "rather highbrow music and unusual film offerings,"

three ancient movie shorts bored our friend: that cane, the bowler, that white face, those black, arched eyebrows, those twitchy nostrils meant nothing to him. Whether the incomparable comedian danced in the sun with chapleted nymphs near a waiting cactus, or was a prehistoric man (the supple cane now a supple club), or was glared at by burly Mack Swain at a hectic night club, old-fashioned, humorless Pnin remained indifferent.[11]

Pnin's travails make him an *émigré* version of the Little Tramp, but he is far too earnest—and pedantic —to accept the mirror proffered by cinema. "Even . . . Max Linder used to be more comical," he snorts, identifying Chaplin's French precursor and possible early influence (p. 81).

As befits their form, short stories make the most of fleeting movie references. Suffering is the only certain coin in the illusory material world of "The Leonardo" (1933), a story about a gentle old counterfeiter whose insubstantial existence and subsequent murder are projected by "the specters" on a movie screen, another counterfeited surface. In "Spring in Fialta," staged in the misty season, cinema is but one of several shams equated with the untrustworthy performances of memory. The *émigré* actor Lik (= Russian for "face," especially the representation of a saint, and for "appearance"), the title character in one of Nabokov's finest stories (1938), had "won some fame, thanks to a film in which he did an excellent job in the bit part of a stutterer."[12] Lik's is no mere *tour de force*. The cruel, unfortunate role and Lik's thespian mimicry are equivalent to the precariousness of his very being: poverty, hypersensitivity, a state of loneliness as incurable as his medically diagnosed heart ailment.

Nabokov's cinematic means are often succinct indeed: one of the "burly comrades" of Margot's brother in *Laughter in the Dark* "had eyes like the film actor Veidt" (p. 27), an image of intensity and villainy that draws on several nightmarish German films, and Paul Pahlovich's second wife in *The Real Life of Sebastian Knight* (1941) says that his first marriage to the mys-

Chaplin and "chapleted nymphs" in *Sunnyside*. Pnin also views *His Prehistoric Past* (1914, with Mack Swain) and *The Immigrant* (1917), where, to strike a pedantic note in the manner of Pnin, Charlie is in fact glared at by Swain's successor as "heavy," Eric Campbell.

"He had eyes like the film actor Veidt," who specialized in macabre roles. Conrad Veidt's horrific, heavily mascaraed eyes were featured in numerous German films, most famously in *The Cabinet of Dr. Caligari,* in which he played Cesare the somnambulist (1919). They appear at left in *Waxworks* (1924), Veidt as Ivan the Terrible.

Veidt in the American film *The Man Who Laughs* (1928)—because his mouth has been sculpted into a permanent grin. Here he celebrates the fact that the blind girl cannot see him. Adapted from Victor Hugo's story, the film inspired the Joker in the *Batman* comic book, as its creator has admitted, thereby serving history. Veidt traveled to America again, and his cinematic travails will be documented.

terious Nina (alias Madame Lecerf) "was merely a
bad dream after seeing a bad cinema film."[13] "I
shouldn't be surprised if she turned out to be an international spy. Mata Hari! That's her type. Oh, absolutely," says her former husband (p. 145), possibly
drawing upon a memory of Greta Garbo's slinky title
performance in *Mata Hari* (1932). Nina was "shallow
and glamorous," says the narrator, "for all I knew she
might be in jail or in Los Angeles" (p. 163). She
"went to movies, bicycle races and boxing matches,"
says Humbert Humbert of his first wife, Valeria, "his
big-breasted and practically brainless *baba*" (p. 28).
His contempt for her is projected in appropriate cinematic terms; when he learns of Valeria's infidelity,
Humbert alludes to "the backhand slap with which I
ought to have hit her across the cheekbone according
to the rules of the movies" (pp. 31-32). His next wife,
the slimmer Charlotte Haze, is described as a diluted
Marlene Dietrich (p. 39), and when she announces
her plans for a trip to Europe, Humbert says, "I can
well imagine the thrill that you, a healthy American
gal, must experience at crossing the Atlantic on the
same ocean liner with Lady Bumble—or Sam Bumble,
the Frozen Meat King, or a Hollywood harlot"
(p. 92).

However cruel Humbert's characterizations may
be, Nabokov is equally unsparing of his own person.
No longer the sylphish 140-pounder of Berlin *émigré*
days nor the lean Wellesley lecturer of 1941-48, Nabo-

"Mata Hari! That's her type": Garbo in *Mata Hari.*

kov savors his memory of the New York premiere of Stanley Kubrick's film version of *Lolita*: "Date: June 13, 1962. Setting: Loew's State, Broadway at Forty-fifth Street. Scene: Crowds awaiting the limousines that drew up one by one, and there I, too, ride, as eager and innocent as the fans who peer into my car hoping to glimpse James Mason but finding only the placid profile of a stand-in for Hitchcock."[14] And in *Transparent Things*, the person of "R.," a famous and aging "Nabokovian" novelist, unpleasant in several ways, is reduced to a celluloid transparency by the authenticity of Hugh Person's infatuation with Armande, a girl he has recently met. "All sham and waxworks," Hugh's interview with R. *becomes* a movie and, dressed like an old Hollywoodian mobster, R. is subjected to a summary cinematic comparison consistent with "the illusory quality" of the entire "stiffly written scene" staged in a "bogus bar" for "the benefit of an invisible audience":

Baron R. had coarse features, a sallow complexion, a lumpy nose with enlarged pores, shaggy bellicose eyebrows, an unerring stare, and a bulldog mouth full of bad teeth. The streak of nasty inventiveness so conspicuous in his writings also appeared in the prepared parts of his speech, as when he said, as he did now, that far from "looking fit" he felt more and more a creeping resemblance to the cinema star Reubenson who once played old gangsters in Florida-staged films; but no such actor existed (p. 30).

The actor, of course, is Edward G. Robinson, the film is *Key Largo* (1948), and only in a figurative sense do they not exist.

Particularly appalling to Nabokov is the content of the fiction-film, as it is sometimes called, to distinguish it from the documentary form—fictions whose plots and players are equally cartoon-like. "An actress with a little black heart for lips and with eyelashes like the spokes of an umbrella was impersonating a rich heiress impersonating a poor office girl," writes Nabokov of a film which Franz views in *King, Queen, Knave* (p. 93). Jilted in *Laughter in the Dark* by Axel Rex, her initial lover, distressed Margot "went to a dance hall as abandoned damsels do in films." There she is accosted by "two Japanese gentlemen," stock erotic threats to Aryan girls in many German films of the twenties (p. 38); earlier, in Cecil B. De-Mille's *The Cheat* (1915), the "evil" sexuality of the villain (Sessue Hayakawa) was based on his Burmese nationality, a "Yellow Peril" most blatant in *The Mask of Fu Manchu* (1932, the year of *Camera Obscura's* publication). "She was so pretty," Nabokov says of Garbo, "but except for *Ninotchka* [1939], the films themselves were always so awful, the stories so absurd." He could not remember which Garbo films they had seen in the twenties and early thirties, though his wife recalled *Flesh and the Devil* (1927), a perfect example of trashy content almost transcended by various kinds of technical perfection.

After Margot has casually told Albinus that she has mailed a letter to his home (surely to be intercepted by his wife), she picks up a book "and turned her back to him. On the right-hand page was a photographic study of Greta Garbo. Albinus found himself thinking: 'How strange. A disaster occurs and still a man notices a picture'" (p. 79). That distractive allure and those extraordinary technical means make the fiction-film easily susceptible to *poshlost'*.

Poshlost', says Nabokov, discussing Gogol and defining one of his favorite Russian words, "is not only the obviously trashy but also the falsely important, the falsely beautiful, the falsely clever, the falsely attractive,"[15] a blending of pretentiousness, vulgarity, and cliché, insidious and cruel when it unintentionally mocks or parodies human needs and desires. Coldly cataloguing American *poshlost'*, vintage 1943, observed in *Life* magazine, Nabokov noted how "kind people send our lonely soldiers silk hosed dummy legs modeled on those of Hollywood lovelies and stuffed with candies and safety razor blades" (p. 67). Considerably less innocent are the variegated Soviet propaganda films, preeminent *poshlost'*, which Nabokov scorns in several books. In *The Gift* (1937-38), Fyodor and his mother visit a Berlin cinema, c. 1925, "where a Russian film was being shown which conveyed with particular brio the globules of sweat rolling down the glistening faces of the factory workers—while the factory owner smoked a cigar all the

"But those caricatures are all the same": factory owners in *Strike*.

time."[16] Asked for the source of that image, Nabokov replied, "One of the big boys—Pudovkin's . . . what *was* the title? *Sister? Brother? MOTHER!* [1926]. From Gorky's novel." It's probably distilled from Eisenstein's *Strike* (1924). "Perhaps. But those caricatures are all the same," he continued, "and *Krokodil* [the Soviet "satirical" magazine] picked them up." Manipulating life *and* literature in the most fundamental of ways, the totalitarian state in *Bend Sinister* (1947) tries to enlist the cooperation of philosopher Adam Krug by kidnapping his young son, David. Transported to the State's infamous experimental station, where David is imprisoned, Krug is shown an ineptly projected "scientific" film intended as further "persuasion." An inscription appears upside down, a nurse giggles, and finally

A trembling legend appeared on the screen: Test 656. This melted into a subtle subtitle: "A Night Lawn Party." Armed nurses were shown unlocking doors. Blinking, the inmates trooped out. "Frau Doktor von Wytwyl, Leader of the Experiment (No Whistling, Please!)" said the next inscription. In spite of the dreadful predicament he was in, even Dr. Hammecke could not restrain an appreciative ha-ha. The woman Wytwyl, a statuesque blonde, holding a whip in one hand and a chronometer in the other, swept haughtily across the screen. "Watch Those Curves": a curving line on a blackboard was shown and a pointer in a rubber-gloved hand pointed out the climactic points and other points of interest in the yarovization of the ego.[17]

The curvaceous teaching aid was probably modeled on an imaginative infantry instructor's variant of World War II's most famous pin-up pose, published in *Look*, a bottomless wellspring of *poshlost'*. It pictured Betty Grable in that swimsuit, coyly looking back over her shoulder, squared grid coordinates superimposed on her curves, the smiling sergeant indicating with his donnish pointer "How to Read a Map."

Following another filmed sequence, "The Little Person Appears" on the screen: a still healthy David, dispatched down "floodlit marble steps" by a nurse. "David had his warmest overcoat on, but his legs were bare and he wore his bedroom slippers. The whole thing lasted a moment: he turned his face up to the nurse, his eyelashes beat, his hair caught a gleam of lambent light. . . . His face became larger, dimmer, and vanished. . . . The nurse remained on the steps, a faint not untender smile playing on her dark lips. 'What a Treat,' said the legend, 'For a Little Person to be Out Walking in the Middle of the Night' . . ." (p. 223). A cinematic specter, Nabokov's Rudy Bloom,[18] David has vanished in more ways than one; the State has already murdered him, by mistake. "Your child will be given the most scrumptious burial a white man's child could dream up," one of the Elders tells Krug (p. 226). Torture is inflicted upon Pnin by the "impressive Soviet documentary film" which is exhibited as part of that highbrow evening program:

"Handsome, unkempt girls marched in an immemorial Spring Festival with banners bearing snatches of old Russian ballads such as '*Ruki proch ot Korei*' ["Hands off Korea"]. . . . In a mountain pasture somewhere in legendary Ossetia, a herdsman reported by portable radio to the local Republic's Ministry of Agriculture on the birth of a lamb. . . . Eight thousand citizens at Moscow's Electrical Equipment Plant unanimously nominated Stalin candidate from the Stalin Election District of Moscow" (p. 81). Pnin, a lone *émigré* seated amidst American faculty fellow travelers, is moved to tears. Post–World War II neo-realism briefly flickers in *Pnin* as international *poshlost'*. One of "the obvious sources of Victor's fantasies" is "an Italian film made in Berlin for American consumption, with a wild-eyed youngster in rumpled shorts, pursued through slums and ruins and a brothel or two by a multiple agent" (p. 86)—*The Bicycle Thief* (1949) in reverse gear, "social comment" as a new context and one more excuse for cheap thrills, or what Van Veen in *Ada* calls "the *fokus-pokus* of a social theme" (p. 426).

Classless and universal, *poshlost'* is as rampant in intellectual and arty discourse as in advertising copy. Aiming a double-edged barb, Humbert tells the Beardsley School that he will return as soon as he has completed his "Hollywood engagement," hinting he is to be "chief consultant in the production of a film dealing with 'existentialism,' still a hot thing at the time" (1949; his "engagement" punningly embraces *engagé*, the existentialist requisite [p. 210]). When Victor Vitry, "a brilliant French director," bases a "completely unauthorized picture" on Van Veen's first book, *Letters from Terra* (p. 579), written fifty years before (1891), its enormous popularity is in part due to the way in which "the lovely leading lady, . . . Gedda Vitry, after titillating the spectators with her skimpy skirts and sexy rags in the existential sequences, came out of her capsule on Antiterra stark naked . . ." (p. 582). At age fourteen, Ada abandons botany in favor of movie-acting. She studies with "Stan Slavsky (no relation, and not a stage name), [who] gave her private lessons of drama, despair, hope. Her debut was a quiet little disaster" (p. 426). Stan's "theories" burlesque "the Method" psychologizings of Lee Strasberg's Actor's Studio (New York and Hollywood branches), in its turn a popularization of Stanislavsky's procedures at the Moscow Art Theatre that is as bald as Nabokov's pun. "One's first love," Ada tells Van, "is one's first standing ovation, and *that* is what makes great artists—so Stan and his girl friend, who played Miss Spangle Triangle in *Flying Rings*, assured me" (p. 426). "Bosh!" answers Van, for Nabokov. "Precisely," continues Ada, "he too [Bosh = Hieronymus Bosch] was hooted by hack hoods in much older Amsterdams, and look how three hundred

Cinematic *poshlost'*: *A Midsummer Night's Dream.*

years later every Poppy Group pup copies him!"—a reference to neo-Boschian psychedelic *poshlost'* as practiced by high counter-culture painters.

The cinema is most susceptible to *poshlost'* when first-rate works of literature are being tailored to fit the needs and demands of a commercial world. Mlle Larivière, "the grotesque governess" in *Ada* who grows rich by rewriting famous works, crafts a tale "about a town mayor's strangling a small girl called Rockette . . . who liked to frolic" (p. 142)—her version of Maupassant's *La Petite Rocque* (1886), and an allusion that simultaneously embraces the pneumatic, high-kicking chorus line at Radio City Music Hall (the Art Deco high temple of American *poshlost'*), formulates a highbrow tourist's murderous fantasy, and choreographs the downward arc of adaptation. "Based on an idea from the Bible," reads the screenplay credit in Cecil B. DeMille's first *Ten Commandments* (1923), while the more exacting scenario of *A Midsummer Night's Dream* (1935) is "By William Shakespeare / With Additional Dialogue By . . ."— his name, alas, escapes this scholar, but he was a professor of English, as one may be reassured to know. A government-financed film travesty of *Hamlet,* based on some ideas in Shakespeare, is produced under academic auspices in *Bend Sinister* (Chapter Seven). Its additional dialogue includes a "Freudian" interlude that prefigures Laurence Olivier's Vienna-oriented version (1948), and Nabokov's parody of such liberties is not idle fun. Film Tsar Goebbels was a pre-McLuhan master of *poshlost,'* and the distortion of *Hamlet* to serve the State, analogous to Communist/Nazi erasures and revisions of the past, recalls the cinematic glorifications of Ivan the Terrible (1944) and Frederick the Great (1942). In *Transparent Things* Mr. R. is more successful but less fortunate than Nabokov's "Spring in Fialta" stand-in, inasmuch as his wife is "having an affair with Christian Pines [= French slang epithet for the male member], son of the well-known cinema man who had directed the film *Golden Windows* (precariously based on the best of our author's novels)" (p. 32). The title *Golden Windows* telescopes the climactic hotel fire in *Transparent Things* and places Hugh Person in the flame-tipped window through which he fails to escape; Nabokov is referring to the book at hand and clearly predicting its fated, unhappy future as a film. Ada's "physics fiction" Time-warp works in the opposite direction, which allows Van's book (an anagram of "Nabokov"), to be filmed within Nabokov's book.

Van's speculative *Letters from Terra*, totally ignored when first published, is transformed by Victor Vitry into a horrific science-fiction farce. *Ada* is an improbable if not impossible book to film, but the screen rights have been optioned to a producer, much to the surprise of many readers. "*Ada* will be enormously difficult to do," grants Nabokov, "the problem of having a suggestion of fantasy, continually, but never overdoing it."[19] Vitry's distortions formulate Nabokov's fears; the director's grandiose effects are blatant, to say the least: "some said [he used] more than a million [extras], others half a million men and as many mirrors. . . . The conception was controversial, the execution flawless" (p. 580). Finding the "historical background absurdly farfetched," Van and Ada consider "starting legal proceedings against Vitry" (p. 581). The disparity between the film's content and its technical competence suggests that Vitry, "the greatest cinematic genius ever to direct a picture of such scope" (p. 580), is a blending of several men—Stanley Kubrick, famous for *2001: A Space Odyssey* (1968) and *Lolita* (1962), marshaling the troops of DeMille, D. W. Griffith, or Abel Gance, director of the monumental silent French film, *Napoléon* (1925): "Look at all those tiny soldiers scuttling along very fast across the trench-scarred wilderness, with explosions of mud and things going *poup-pouf* in silent French now here, now there!" "Three circumstances contributed to the picture's exceptional success," writes Nabokov, taking his measure of contemporary directors and their audiences: "organized religion . . . attempted to have the thing banned"; "in a flashback to a revolution in former France, an unfortunate extra, who played one of the under-executioners, got accidentally decapitated while pulling the comedian Steller, who played a reluctant king, into a guillotinable position"; and "the third, and even more human reason," was the emergence from her "cosmic capsule" of Vitry's naked wife, Norwegian-born Gedda (a literally "liberated" Hedda Gabler), "though, of course, in miniature, a millimeter of maddening femininity dancing in 'the charmed circle of the microscope' like some lewd elf, and revealing, in certain attitudes, I'll be damned, a pinpoint glint of pubic floss, goldpowdered!" (pp. 581-82). She joins a chorus line of sci-fi miniatures extending from *The Lost World* (1925), *The Bride of Frankenstein* (1935), and *The Devil Doll* (1936) to *Doctor Cyclops* (1940), *The Incredible Shrinking Man* (1957), and *Fantastic Voyage* (1966). In addition to suggesting a DeMillean Kubrick, the "brilliant" Victor Vitry (from the French *vitré:* "glazed; of glass") seems especially to mirror the French director Roger Vadim, at one time (c. 1960) engaged to make a film of *Laughter in the Dark*, who bared Bardot his wife in *And God Created Woman* (1956) and later exposed Jane Fonda, his then-blonde wife at that time, in the satirical space opera *Barbarella* (1967). The corruption of *Letters from Terra* is climaxed by an outpouring of consumer goods modeled on the Davy Crockett and Batman crazes of the nineteen-fifties and sixties: "L.F.T. tiny dolls, L.F.T. breloques of coral and ivory, appeared in souvenir shops. . . . L.F.T. clubs sprouted. L.F.T. girlies minced with mini-menus out of roadside snackettes shaped like spaceships" (p. 582).

"Real" works fare no better on Antiterran reels; like M-G-M in its heyday under Thalberg, *Ada*'s producers favor high-toned projects. Chekhov, says Nabokov, is the Russian writer whose works "I would take on a trip to another planet," but he does not survive the ride to Antiterra. Ada appears with her mother, Marina Durmanov, in Chekhov's *Four Sisters* (pp. 427-30), but "It was the (somewhat expanded) part of the nun that Marina acted in an elaborate film version of the play" (p. 427). Marina, writes Ada, "sticks to Stan's principle of having lore and role overflow into everyday life, insists on keeping it up at the hotel restaurants, drinks tea *v prikusku* ('biting sugar between sips'), and feigns to misunderstand every question in Varvarva's quaint way of feigning stupidity." The studio gives its star Method performer "a special bungalow, labeled Marina Durmanova" (p. 333), and "the picture and she received a goodly amount of undeserved praise" (p. 427). Because Ada is poised "at the most delicate moment of [her] career," the printed praise exasperates her. " 'Durmanova is superb as the neurotic nun, having transferred an essentially static and episodical part into *et cetera, et cetera, et cetera*,' " states a pompous reviewer, displaying his ignorance (p. 427). The Russian feminine ending affixed to

Durmanov's anglicized name by both studio and reviewer, doubtless an effort to equal the glamor of
"Karenina," is Nabokov's sly swipe at Hollywood pretentiousness; such small drolleries are overlooked by
most readers, but their loss is not considerable.

The directness and availability of the joke upon
Chekhov is atypical of *Ada*'s procedures. *Ada* is almost two times as long as any previous Nabokov
novel. Although its highly allusive first half constitutes a coherently organized Museum of the Novel
(Austen to *Ada*), an array of the exhausted possibilities any practitioner must now confront, the second half of the book poses too many problems. Where
Lolita and *Pale Fire* are consistently enlivened by the
anatomist's gleanings, *Ada* is often undermined by im-
possibly hermetic and gratuitous encrustations. This
is not true of its treatment of "literary" film adaptations, which reassert Nabokov's hatred of *poshlost'*
and contribute to the anachronistic comedy of its
Time-warp. Nineteenth-century characters drive in
carriages to the cinema, where they drink Cokes, and
Byron and Chateaubriand are especially desirable film
subjects because their incestuous themes mirror *Ada*'s
central story. Ada herself appears briefly in an absurd
"for adults only" movie called *Don Juan's Last Fling*
(pp. 488-89), directed by "the gifted Yuzlik"—Russian for "little Hughes," after Howard himself, who,
among other things, invented the cantilevered bra
and propelled Jane Russell in *The Outlaw* (1943).

Chateaubriand's *René* (1802), rewritten by Mlle
Larivière as the best-selling Book of the Fortnight
Les Enfants Maudits (1887), finally reaches the
screen as another "Painted Western," *The Young and
the Doomed* (1890), starlet Ada's scene cut out, except for a distinct shadow of her elbow—the fate, it
would seem, of all "californized" (p. 199) classics:

[Mlle Larivière] had had two adolescents, in a French
castle, poison their widowed mother who had seduced a
young neighbor, the lover of one of her twins. The author
had made many concessions to the freedom of the times,
and the foul fancy of scriptwriters; but both she and the
leading lady [Marina] disavowed the final result of multiple tamperings with the plot that had now become the
story of a murder in Arizona, the victim being a widower
about to marry an alcoholic prostitute, whom Marina,
quite sensibly, refused to impersonate (p. 424).

Marina has an affair with the film's director, G. A.
Vronsky—named after the dashing officer in *Anna
Karenina* (1876) by way of "Gavronsky," a common
Jewish-Russian name. A good deal has been lost—and
gained—in his transmutation. G. A., as he is always
addressed, California-mogul style, is "elderly, bald-
headed, with a spread of grizzled fur on his fat chest,
[and] was alternately sipping his vodka-and-tonic
and feeding Marina typewritten pages from a folder"
(p. 197).

Tolstoy's shade has thrice been shaken by jejune

Garbo and Gilbert as Anna Karenina and Vronsky in *Love*.

film adaptations of *Anna* (1927, as *Love;* 1935; and 1948), and Nabokov's *jeu* may be of some solace to "old Lyovin," as Van warmly calls him. Although Nabokov has not viewed any of those versions, several unintentionally humorous still-photos have sufficed, especially one of Vronsky (John Gilbert) *en profil*, an aquiline bust all but choking on its collar. "Tell me, have you read Tolstoy?" Axel Rex asks a film star in *Laughter in the Dark*. " 'Doll's Toy?' queried Dorianna Karenina. 'No, I'm afraid not. Why?' " (p. 191). "I would like my readers to brood over my singular power of prophecy," says Nabokov, "for the name of the leading lady (Dorianna Karenina) in the picture invented by me in 1931 prefigured that of the actress (Anna Karina) who was to play Margot forty years later in the film *Laughter in the Dark*."[20] Although it is too soon for their asteroids to have appeared, the cast of *Four Sisters* includes Dawn de Laire and the melancholy Irish actress Lenore Colline, who is "named" after a phrase in Nabokov's parody of a Chateaubriand ballad (p. 138) —another joke that scores against filmdom's international propensity for silly and pretentious screen names. *Four Sisters* is filmed "in Universal City," the actual name of a huge Hollywood studio lot (p. 333), whose existence in *Ada*'s "1889," however, makes it something more than a realistic detail. *Ada*'s fantastic antiworld transmogrifies all American place names save Los Angeles and Hollywood, deemed fantastic enough as they are by a novelist who spent six months there in 1960, adapting *Lolita* for the screen.

Humbert dismisses the Hollywood musical as "an essentially grief-proof sphere of existence wherefrom death and truth were barred" (p. 172). Throughout his fiction Nabokov suggests how the deepest, most personal truths may be trivialized by a concurrence of movie conventions and Stan Slavsky's applied lessons in "drama, despair, hope." The celluloid romances in *Ada* are thus presented as banal versions of the complicated love affairs which have already occurred within the novel's pages. Marina's appearance in a film with a "pair of cheerful youngsters, the 'juvenile' (in movie parlance) on her right, the 'ingénue' on her left," reduces Ada's and Van's relationship to the bland level of Judy Garland and Mickey Rooney in an Andy Hardy romp (p. 252). "Somewhere," continues Nabokov, "safely transformed by [Marina's] screen-corrupted mind into a stale melodrama was her three-year-old period of hectically spaced love-meetings with Demon, *A Torrid Affair* (the title of her only cinema hit)"; and a full catalog of melodramatic screen clichés summarizes the suffering wrought by freedom in *Ada*, Nabokov's critique of Romanticism. *Don Juan's Last Fling* is no idle title.

Insanity, suicide, and prolonged separation, the toll exacted by passion and self-indulgence—and the moral center of *Ada*—are all perceived by Marina and her scenarist as "mere scenery, easily packed, labeled

'Hell' and freighted away" (p. 253). To Marina, existence itself is a chimera or picture-show, a film editor's assortment of technical tricks: "Someday, she mused, one's past must be put in order. Retouched, retaken. Certain 'wipes' and 'inserts' will have to be made in the picture; certain telltale abrasions in the emulsion will have to be corrected; 'dissolves' in the sequences discreetly combined with the trimming out of unwanted, embarrassing 'footage,' and definite guarantees obtained; yes, someday—before death with its clapstick closes the scene" (pp. 253-54). Even the most intimate passages of the autobiographical *Speak, Memory* employ stale movie footage, however fleetingly. On the eve of his beloved father's scheduled duel, fearful young Nabokov "refought all the famous duels a Russian boy knew so well," none of them resembling "the ludicrous back-to-back-march-face-about-bang-bang performance of movie and cartoon fame."[21] Luzhin is deserted by his "chess father," impresario Valentinov, who "disappeared [and found] fresh amusement in the movie business, that mysterious astrological business where they read scripts and look for stars" (*The Defense*, p. 93). A perverter of the imagination, like Axel Rex in *Laughter in the*

"Back-to-back-march-face-about-bang-bang": Lars Hanson and John Gilbert, as old friends reluctantly forced to duel over Garbo in *Flesh and the Devil*.

Dark and Clare Quilty in *Lolita,* his name a play on his heartlessness and the reigning movie idol of the twenties, he re-enters Luzhin's life as Dr. [!] Valentinov of the Veritas [Latin for "truth"; "real life"] Film Company, who offers a befuddled Luzhin a part in a trashy film that would re-stage and trivialize Luzhin's terminated game with Grandmaster Turati. Understanding the offer as a last illusion, a trap meant to inveigle him into playing tournament chess again, Luzhin's "next move" is clear, and he kills himself (pp. 248ff.). A similar counterpoint is effected in *Pale Fire* (1962). John and Sybil Shade are watching television the night of their ungainly daughter's disastrous blind date. Abandoned by her disappointed companion, distraught Hazel Shade throws herself into an icy lake, and the moment of her death is synchronized with the TV preview of *Remorse,* a movie.

> The famous face flowed in, fair and inane:
> The parted lips, the swimming eyes, the grain
> Of beauty on the cheek, odd gallicism,
> And the soft form dissolving in the prism
> Of corporate desire

writes John Shade in his poem *Pale Fire* (ll. 450-54), the watery verbs describing his daughter's fate, the actress' "soft form" in sharp contrast to bedeviled Hazel's desperate search for deathless, elusive truths (the actress, says Nabokov, is Marilyn Monroe, not yet a suicide). In *Laughter in the Dark*, Albert Albinus casts himself into what he had hoped would be a love story, but instead finds himself trapped in a fatal thriller, the blind victim, literally, of cheap romance and his own movie shoot-out, death's clapstick.

Nothing less than history itself is trivialized and effaced by *Ada*'s entrepreneurs, who range from dollmakers to film directors. Although the Vitry-Veen *Letters from Terra* clearly rehearses the first half of twentieth-century history, that fact is completely lost on enthusiastic McLuhanesque audiences so inured to sci-fi conventions that all history, including their own, has ceased to exist (p. 582). Nabokov's is a telling perception, to which this writer can sadly attest, having recently endured a campus film showing that shrewdly paired *The March of Time*'s "The Battle for North Africa" (1942) and *Casablanca* (1943), almost everyone's favorite bad movie. The spectacle of real men dying on newsreel deserts elicited jeers and cheers from the "anti-war" audience; Bogart's and Bergman's war, save for the obligatory "Play it, Sam" applause, enthralled them all. "Strangely enough, that vile script was enacted in reality," says the narrator of "The Assistant Producer" (1943), a White Army Western and spies-and-intrigue thriller based on actual events, and a story that presents history as fiction.[22] If history isn't a nightmare, then it is an open-ended, anti-Aristotelian melodrama, each new terrible twist in the "plot" having already been anticipated by the popular forms that reflect or vulgarly refract modern realities. "Meaning?" asks the narrator-scenarist-impresario, opening the show. "Well, because life is . . . merely that—an Assistant Producer. Tonight we shall go to the movie. Back to the Thirties, and down the Twenties, and round the corner to the old Europe Picture Palace" (p. 75); and throughout the tale, cinematic form and metaphor cohere in a brilliantly projected series of fields of vision, not without humor:

Perhaps he found a haven in Germany and was given there some small administrative job in the Baedecker Training School for Young Spies. Perhaps he returned to the land where he had taken towns singlehanded. Perhaps he did not. Perhaps he was summoned by whoever his arch-boss was and told with that slight foreign accent and special brand of blandness that we all know: "I am afraid, my friend, you are nott nee-ded any more"—and as X turns to go Dr. Puppenmeister's delicate index presses a button at the edge of his impassive writing desk and a trap yawns under X, who plunges to his death (he who knows "too much").

These sentences are from the end of the story, on a page accidentally omitted from all printings after its appearances in *The Atlantic* and Nabokov's *Nine Stories* (1947). "Dmitri loved a series of thriller pictures when he was nine or so [1943, *The Falcon*, says Dmitri], and we would see them at a cinema in Harvard Square," says Nabokov. "The hero [Tom Conway] was a broad-shouldered, handsome American who was always walking into places where things were stacked and stored. They would inevitably crash down upon him, but he would emerge unscathed. The Master Spy, an obese Oriental, had one line, which he used continually on his captives: 'Our methods are simple but *ver-ry* effective.'" Nothing is wasted on the literary anatomist.

There were a dozen or so films in the *Falcon* series, several of which rank with the worst of the forties, and Nabokov—a connoisseur of badness—stored several of its creakiest pieces of furniture for future use. Confronting the curious realities of the nineteen-forties from the cool vantage point of the next century ("Time and Ebb"), Nabokov concludes the middle section of this 1945 story by again evoking *Falcon*-like action glimpsed "on a moon-white screen in a velvet-dark hall": "With a blow of his fist a man sent a fellow creature crashing into a tower of crates. An incredibly smooth-skinned girl raised a linear eyebrow. A door slammed with the kind of ill-fitting thud that comes to us from the far bank of a river where woodsmen are at work" (*Nabokov's Dozen*, p. 161). The eyebrow raised amidst the cinematographic clamor is an index of audience complicity and complacency, the "ill-fitting thud" suggests the cheapness of the enterprise, the image of the woodsmen emphasizes the destructive aura and an authorial shudder. Father Nabokov's good-natured endurance of B-pictures also informs Humbert's unheroic gun-wielding in *Lolita*

as well as the portrait of Gradus, the hoodlum assassin in *Pale Fire*, who receives his assignment from grinning Master Spy Izumrudov in the *de rigueur* spy-movie manner: "No, the [instruction] slip was not for keeps. He could keep it only while memorizing it. The brand of paper (used by macaroon makers) was not only digestible but delicious" (p. 256). The clichés of the thriller combine with the cozy tone ("delicious") to project a contempt for banal death-dealing creatures who would trivialize human existence. "We cannot condone the grossness of [Marina's] soul," writes Van Veen of his "screen-corrupted" mother (p. 252).

Looking back at the forties in the twenty-first century, the aged narrator of "Time and Ebb" laments that Americans

were superficial, careless, and short-sighted. More than other generations, they tended to overlook outstanding men, leaving to us [scholars of the future] the horror of discovering their classics (thus Richard Sinatra remained, while he lived, an anonymous "ranger" dreaming under a Telluride pine or reading his prodigious verse to the squirrels of San Isabel Forest, whereas everybody knew another Sinatra, a minor writer, also of Oriental descent). (p. 157).

Anticipating in method *Ada*'s anachronistic re-creation of famous books, places, films, and people, the allusion to Francis Albert Sinatra is as bitter as it is droll. "The Voice," as he was known in those days, sounded everywhere—juke boxes, stage, screen, and radio—but how many Americans had heard of Sirin or Nabokov?

Although there are exceptions such as Eudora Welty's great story "Powerhouse" (1940), based on Fats Waller, one cannot imagine a writer of Nabokov's generation (he was born in 1899) making positive use of the Andrews Sisters or the alto saxophonist Charlie Parker, as does Pynchon in *Gravity's Rainbow*. Ernest Hemingway (1899-1961) also loved Waller, whose satirical mockery of Pop-songs made him a kind of "literary" performer and a favorite of *littérateurs,* but in Hemingway's *fiction* jazzmen are caricatured (see *The Sun Also Rises,* 1926). "Economics obsessed them [Americans] almost as much as theologies had obsessed their ancestors," says the narrator of "Time and Ebb" (p. 157), and Nabokov is of course not alone in seeing the popular arts as a debasing presence, a readily visible and audible expression of a deadly commercial ethic. The attitude is musically recapitulated by Faulkner (1897-1962) in *Sanctuary* (1931), when he has a jazz band play "I Can't Give You Anything But Love Baby" at the funeral of the gangster called "Red," in a scene equivalent to Wallace Stevens's funerary poem "The Emperor of Ice Cream" (1923). "Now I shall speak of evil as none has / Spoken before. I loathe such things as jazz / . . . [and] Music in supermarkets," writes poet John

"The brand of paper . . . was not only digestible but delicious": a Gradus-like hoodlum in *The Falcon Takes Over* (1942).

Shade in *Pale Fire* (ll. 923-24 and 928). Annotator Charles Kinbote finds them even more loathesome.

Where most literary artists of Nabokov's generation tended to lump together and dismiss all facets of mass culture, gifted composers have more often remained open to "lower" forms of inspiration, which is not surprising, since music is fundamentally pure, content-free: notes on a page, sounds in the air. Nabokov's exact contemporaries Kurt Weill (1900-50) and Bertolt Brecht (1898-56), very active in Berlin during Nabokov's residence there, offer interesting points of reference. Brecht's Marxism, however anarchistic and unorthodox, is of course repugnant to Nabokov, but they shared other Berlin coordinates. Nabokov, c. 1924, contributed cabaret sketches and song lyrics to "a quite fashionable Russian *émigré* night club called '*Sinyaya ptitsa*' ["The Bluebird"], named after Maeterlinck's play," one of the Berlin *émigré* equivalents of the cabarets which fed the imaginations of Weill and Brecht. (Nabokov did it solely for money, and saw perhaps one performance.) *Happy End*, Weill's and Brecht's 1929 musical play, is about Chicago gangsters and Salvation Army girls; the head criminal is called the Governor. Weill and Brecht had not yet visited America. Drawing upon more popular materials than had Brecht's earlier play *In the Jungle of the Cities,* subtitled "A Match Between Two Men in the Giant City of Chicago" (1923), or Franz Kafka's fabular, unfinished *Amerika* (1927), Weill's and Brecht's imaginary land had as its données newspaper stories, pulp fiction, Dos Passos' *Manhattan Transfer* (1925), and Hollywood's romantic, pre-Depression period gangster films (*Underworld,* 1927, and *The Docks of New York,* 1928, both directed by Josef von Sternberg). The English title, *Happy End*, was an explicitly ironic and mordant reference; America, not Germany in 1928, was the land of "Happy Endings," as they are (or were) willed by the conventions of popular culture and historical circumstances. The gusty "Song of the Hard Nut" (= head), a musical caprice in the manner of Chicago jazz, is addressed to hard-boiled American writing and behavior, as it was stylized in the popular arts and in Hemingway and Dos Passos (at the end of *Manhattan Transfer,* Jimmy Herf's hero is a man in Philadelphia who was hit on the "nut" with a lead pipe for wearing a straw hat too early in the season). The effect of the song, however, is ambiguous; Brecht's lyrics are bitter, but Weill's music is an *hommage*, akin to Debussy's *Cakewalk* (1908) and *Minstrels* (1910), Satie's "Ragtime du paquebot" (1917), or, to contrast Nabokov with another grandly allusive Russian *émigré* master of parody and pastiche, Stravinsky's ragtime-influenced *L'Histoire du soldat* (1918), *Ragtime for Eleven Instruments* (1918), *Piano-Rag-Music* (1919), and the four jazz-oriented works he composed in America, where he listened admiringly to Charlie Parker, Art Tatum, and the guitarist Charlie Christian. Humbert

Humbert and Kinbote, the most literate of refugees, must by definition revile popular music, but Stravinsky, a bookish maestro, celebrated *his* arrival with *Tango* (1940), a somber as well as witty Pop number that outdoes Kurt Weill. No lyrics complicate or undermine the composer's affectionate attitude toward his sources. Stravinsky's stirring orchestration of *The Star-Spangled Banner* (1941), never the catchiest of American tunes, is the ultimate *hommage*, an *émigré's* expression of gratitude.

Brecht and Weill curiously anticipate the French directors Jean-Pierre Melville (né Jean-Pierre Grumbach!), François Truffaut, and Jean-Luc Godard, who, thirty years later—also distanced by geographical remove—would absorb American popular materials, but in a totally positive spirit, and transform them into myth and an apolitical *paysage moralisé*. Weill's and Brecht's greatest work, *Rise and Fall of the City of Mahagonny* (1930), is set in another American fantasia, a lawless frontier town that also embodies Berlin. Weill parodies and quotes from many trashy German popular melodies ("That is eternal art," says one of the men of Mahagonny, listening to a maudlin piano solo in scene nine), but the famous "Alabama Song," like "The Song of the Hard Nut," seems to express divergent intentions: Weill's "popular" melody is uncommonly beautiful and haunting, whereas Brecht's lyrics are Tin Pan Alley by way of a kind of pidgin English: "Oh! Moon of Alabama/ We now must say good-bye/ We've lost our good old mama/ And we must have whiskey/ Oh, you know why!" (the song's title and lyrics are in English). Similarly absurd are the lyrics and rhymes of Lolita's favorite song, "Little Carmen" ("And the stars, and the cars, and the bars and the barmen . . .")—Mérimée updated as movie melodrama:

> And the something town where so gaily, arm in
> Arm, we went, and our final row,
> And the gun I killed you with, O my Carmen,
> The gun I am holding now (p. 64).

Brecht believed that pidgin English would become the first international language, and, spoken by bar girls in Saigon, rock-'n'-roll singers in Tokyo, patois-infected teenagers throughout America, and their inarticulate imagos on the screen (*Easy Rider, McCabe and Mrs. Miller*), it very nearly has. "No sweat, man," said a South Vietnamese army deserter to a *New York Times* reporter as they retreated through flaming Hue in the debacle of 1972. "And Junior is clamped on to the telephone calling up a succession of high school girls that talk pidgin English and carry contraceptives in their make-up kit," states Raymond Chandler in *The Little Sister* (1949);[23] born in America but educated in England, he wrote as a displaced person in his own land. The witless lingo of Lolita and her friends is well recorded, an *émigré's* artistic triumph and a true finding that demonstrates the contagious banality of ads, bad movies, and hit songs worthy (if that is the word) of Marxist Brecht.

Nabokov's opinions about movies are at once those of a "classicist" (after Plato—and Arnheim, whom he has never read) and, loosely speaking, a Marxist, as he will be happy to learn. In *Laughter in the Dark,* Albinus is at first "delighted in [Margot's] interest in the cinema and began to unfold a certain favorite theory of his regarding the comparative merits of the silent film and the talkie: 'sound,' he said, 'will kill the cinema straightaway'" (p. 122). "The verbal part of the cinema," continues Nabokov thirty years later, "is such a hodge-podge of contributions, beginning with the script, that it really has no style of its own. On the other hand, the viewer of a silent film has the opportunity of adding a good deal of his own inner verbal treasure to the silence of the picture. . . . I don't even remember if the best Laurel and Hardy are talkies or not. On the whole, I think what I love about the silent film is what comes through the mask of the talkies and, vice versa, talkies are mute in my memory."[24] "And having departed to the sphere of jaunty, quick-talking, self-important con-men with their patter about the philosophy of the screen, the tastes of the masses and the intimacy of the movie camera, and with pretty good incomes at the same time, [Valentinov] dropped out of Luzhin's world," writes Nabokov in *The Defense* (p. 93). Mrs. Luzhin is properly depressed when the guests at a Berlin dance ignore her celebrated husband, an artist in his own right, in favor of the Grosz-like movie producers (p. 195), and Dr. Valentinov's movie offer proves fatal. The cultural implications are clear.

While Humbert's denunciation of Hollywood musicals is not unfair to Alice Faye or clumsy Ruby Keeler, it does not exactly allow for the joy communicated by an Astaire-Rogers or Bill Robinson routine. Humbert's objections are "literary," however; his old world scorn is focused on the genre's corny plots rather than its lyric fantasy, the abstract visual poetry of dance. Nabokov doesn't pretend to be a film critic or historian, and the explicit "criticism" in his stories and novels is always an artistic, thematic necessity. Unlike Borges, who acknowledges the influence of Josef von Sternberg's early gangsters films on his own "hoodlum" stories (see the Preface to *A Universal History of Infamy,* 1935), Nabokov insists, "I'm no *cinéaste!*" His first viewing of Orson Welles's *Citizen Kane* (1941) was in 1972, on Swiss TV. "Extraordinary! A masterpiece. But I think the television version was mutilated by arbitrary cuts." A favorite scene? "Yes, the clutter of the final sequence," but Nabokov said no more about that mute testimony to loss and need, the labyrinth of impersonal possessions also singled out by Borges in his 1945 review of the film.[25] Any other scenes? "It's curious," he answered, "but I don't remember most films very well." "Welles called the 'Rosebud' ending dollar-book Freud. Do you agree?"

inquired the curious guest, a persistent *cinéaste*. Nabokov shrugged his shoulders, and the conversation turned to soccer, an enthusiasm dating back to his playing days at Cambridge; as Ada holds forth on the Nature of Film ("of course, the cinema has no language problems"), "Van swallowed, rather than stifled, a yawn" (p. 427). Asked about the films of Fritz Lang and Josef von Sternberg, Nabokov said, "the names of Lang and Sternberg mean nothing to me," failing to connect the latter director with *Shanghai Express* (1932) and other Dietrich vehicles which he had enjoyed very much. While scripting *Lolita* in Hollywood, the Nabokovs attended a dinner party at David Selznick's luxurious house. Billy Wilder was there, and Gina Lollobrigida, too. "She speaks excellent French," says Nabokov. "It wasn't that good," interrupts Mrs. Nabokov. They were also introduced to a tall, rugged fellow. "And what do you do?" inquired Nabokov. "I'm in pictures," answered John Wayne, smiling through what must have been the worst moment in his long career.

Like Stravinsky, Wittgenstein, and other average movie-goers who relax best at the cinema (Betty Hutton and Carmen Miranda musicals were the philosopher's favorite narcotic), Nabokov has seen more films than he is able or cares to remember. Yet the *catalogue raisonné* of negative images which opened this chapter demonstrates that movies have made an indelible impression where names, titles, and some faces have escaped him; subsequent chapters will suggest that the films of Lang and Sternberg are visible in several books, *Lolita* in particular. M. H. Abrams, Nabokov's colleague at Cornell for a decade (1948-58), recalls how Nabokov entered a living room where a faculty child was watching an old Western on television. Immediately engaged by the program, Nabokov was soon quaking with laughter over the furiously climactic fight scene in a bar. Just such idle moments, if not literally this one, inform the burlesque of the comparable "obligatory scene" in *Lolita*, the tussle of Humbert and Quilty, which leaves them "panting as the cowman and the sheepman never do after their battle" (p. 301).[26] The Pop-inspired killing of Quilty is a crucial scene, and Abrams's reminiscence highlights the truth that nothing is lost on a certain kind of comic writer—the literary anatomist who, while remaining outside popular culture, nevertheless absorbs and utilizes both "high" and "low" materials. *Lolita* is above all a feat of language, a construct whose every sentence has been composed with the exactitude of poetry. Its excellence as a *novel*, however, is predicated on Nabokov's willingness and ability to go beyond the brief summonses of anatomy and extensively convert the kinds of materials he most abhors, the negative images that dot the pages of so many previous works.

Hard research informs several of Nabokov's novels, especially *The Gift*, his veritable dictionary of Russian literature and social ideas. "The Chernyshevski biography, my gift to Fyodor [Chapter Four], was, along with *The Texture of Time* and Shade's poem, the most difficult challenge of my so-called career," he says. Nabokov immersed himself in psychiatric case studies ("I'm a normal man, you know") and commercial movies in behalf of Humbert and Lolita, but *Ada's* movies are almost exclusively the product of secondary sources, as is Veen's work-within-the-work, *The Texture of Time*. "I retire too early at night," says Nabokov, explaining why they rarely go to the cinema anymore. The Nabokovs have seen Fellini's "wonderful 8½, and *La Strada*, too. Excellent, excellent! The film of *Death in Venice*, a mediocre story, was visually most pleasant; the luggage was especially handsome. We detested [Buñuel's] *Viridiana*, a grotesque compote of private parts and Goyaesque borrowings. Why is it so admired?" Those daily walks to the news kiosk, which may turn out to be research trips, allow Nabokov to remain *au courant*—disarmingly so, given his imperious attitude toward so many facets of what he deems to be contemporary nonsense. But because Nabokov the literary anatomist is often amused by odd or campy trivia, his wide-ranging inclusiveness is easily misunderstood. "No, I loathe popular pulp," he told the interviewer who pressed him on the matter of his references to popular culture. "I loathe go-go gangs, I loathe jungle music, I loathe science fiction with its gals and goons, suspense and suspensories [thus Vitry's *Letters from Terra*]. I especially loathe vulgar movies—cripples raping nuns under tables [a mini-burlesque of Buñuel], or naked-girl breasts squeezing against the tanned torsos of repulsive young males. And, really, I don't think I mock popular trash more often than do other authors who believe with me that a good laugh is the best pesticide."[27] Still, drawing upon Gogol's delineation of *poshlost'* in *Dead Souls* (1842) and realizing Flaubert's dream of a vast *Dictionary of Accepted Ideas*, Nabokov does mock "popular trash" more often and more consistently than any other modern author, and some of the best, darkest, and certainly most "moral" laughter in *Lolita* is achieved at the expense of the cinemonkey, expressed in terms uniform with the vision of his *émigré* fiction.

Shirley Temple in *Bright Eyes* (1934).

3
Tristram in Movielove

The Road to *Lolita*

Lolita's greatness as a novel is in part due to the extent to which Nabokov is able to have it both ways, on the one hand involving the reader in a deeply moving yet outrageously comic story, rich in verisimilitude, and on the other distancing him by means of authorial verbal figurations which undermine the novel's realistic base and transform the book into a gameboard.[1] That verisimilitude, as vital to *Lolita* as it is to Nabokov's most blatant artifices, has been taken for granted, especially by the critics who stress Nabokov's artifice at the expense of the more traditional components of his novels. One of these critics will doubtless extend the implications of Humbert's unreliability as a narrator and claim that even Lolita is a fantasized invention, or at best a subjective phenomenon as unreal and unfathomable as, say, the "meaning" of the mock-symbolic centipede in Robbe-Grillet's *Jealousy* (1957). Such a reading would make *Lolita* pointless, for the trickster-conjurer who undercuts the expectations of the old-fashioned reader also happens to be a man committed to certain timeless values, as *Lolita*'s "realism" demonstrates.

Lolita evolved from "Volshebnik" ("The Magician"), a short story written in Russian in 1939, the year before Nabokov emigrated to America. It went unpublished not because of the forbidding subject, but rather, says Nabokov, because his first nymphet "wasn't alive," she possessed little "semblance of reality." "Around 1949, in Ithaca, upstate New York," he began a "new treatment of the theme, this time in English"; the key to his realization of Lolita was to be American popular culture, the *émigré* novelist's sure perception of stimuli that could not fail to affect a normal American girlchild growing up during the

1947-52 period (*Lolita*'s duration). These stimuli and quotidian details were not easily assimilated. "The book developed slowly [1949-54], with many interruptions and asides," writes Nabokov in its Afterword. "It had taken me some forty years to invent Russia and Western Europe, and now I was faced by the task of inventing America. The obtaining of such local ingredients as would allow me to inject a modicum of average 'reality' (one of the few words which mean nothing without quotes) into the brew of individual fancy, proved at fifty a much more difficult process than it had been in the Europe of my youth when receptiveness and retention were at their automatic best" (p. 314). Nabokov strikes a surprisingly native note here, recalling those statements in which our classic nineteenth-century writers bemoaned *their* difficulties in coming to terms with that vast, unfamiliar territory called "America." His problems were obviously more fundamental than those of Hawthorne, Melville, Twain, or James, and Nabokov's finest work of the nineteen-forties testifies to the pain he endured in becoming an American writer by way of *Lolita*.

Viewed from the present perspective of his world fame, Nabokov's massive *œuvre* would seem to have unfolded effortlessly, and the persona donned by the author in prefaces and interviews is not wanting in self-confidence. If one keeps *Lolita* in mind, however, an examination of Nabokov's fiction of the forties proves to be a moving experience in unexpected ways; the middle-aged Nabokov had to start from scratch—to use the slang, the sort of materials the neophyte American writer could not take for granted. Although it doesn't realize the ambitions of the nineteenth-century novel of manners, Nabokov's final Russian novel, *The Gift* (1937-38), had been rich in social detail, German bad manners in particular. He then composed *The Real Life of Sebastian Knight* (Paris, 1938), and the visible world of his first novel in English is as variegated as a lunar photograph or, at best, one of Brassaï's spectral Parisian nightscapes of the nineteen-thirties (empty streets, deserted snowbound parks, skeletal trees shrouded by darkness). "That's not me! I never owned such a hat," said Nabokov in 1972 when he saw the cover of *TriQuarterly*'s special *émigré* issue, a sepia reproduction of Brassaï's eloquent photograph *Avenue de l'Observatoire* (1932), which depicts a lone figure seated on a bench silhouetted against the mist-deployed nimbus of a street lamp. Thematic needs could be said to dictate or justify the barrenness of *Sebastian Knight*'s environment, but Nabokov may have had little choice in the matter. Preoccupied by sentences rather than the transcription of scenery, Nabokov would have each leaf in his new life corrected by Lucie Léon, an *émigré* friend and a member of Joyce's inner circle whose literary English was excellent. After arriving in America in 1940, Nabokov received more stylistic advice on *Sebastian Knight* and then submitted himself to *Ameri-*

can English; the language of Cambridge University would not suit Lolita and Charlotte Haze. Even today, when he uses slang in conversation, he takes delight in the fact that he has expropriated it and worries that he's out of touch with current usage. " 'Square' is very vivid but it's already dated and, as such, quite *corny*," says Nabokov. "Is there any sexual connotation in 'uptight,' " he wonders. Long after *Lolita*'s publication, he was horrified to discover that Humbert calls a flashlight a "torchlight," and the text of *The Annotated Lolita* corrects that lingering Englishism (p. 232), the product of a trilingual childhood.

Nabokov's birth pangs as an American writer are discernible in " 'That in Aleppo Once . . .' " (1943), one of his earliest and best stories in English.[2] Presented in the form of a letter written by a recent *émigré* to America, the story opens,

Dear V.—Among other things, this is to tell you that at last I am here, in the country whither so many sunsets have led. One of the first persons I saw was our good old Gleb Alexandrovich Gekko gloomily crossing Columbus Avenue in quest of the *petit café du coin* which none of us three will ever visit again. He seemed to think that somehow or other you were betraying our national literature, and he gave me your address with a deprecatory shake of his gray head . . . (p. 141).

Old Gekko's name is from the gecko, any lizard of the family Gekkonidae, a nocturnal creature so called from its cry. That cry is also Nabokov's, and the nostalgic quest indulged by Gekko is surely an impulse Nabokov struggled to control and combat, as indicated by his decision to compose in English rather than suffer the obscurity of writing in Russian, the language of the past, for a small audience of scattered *émigrés*. " 'That in Aleppo Once . . .' " does not "betray" the Russian experience, however, retailing as it does the travails of *émigrés* caught up in the German invasion of France; and the title—a tag from *Othello*, one of several in the story—suggests that the putative author will commit suicide, a not uncommon *émigré* fate. "I have a story for you," announces V.'s correspondent (p. 141), employing a narrative trick that formulates a maker's search for new materials. New York City's Columbus Avenue is the first of but two references that would moor the story in space, a dimension that barely exists for the despairing narrator, who records the timeless horrors of the recent past while seated "in the green vacuum of Central Park" (p. 144). A metaphor for Nabokov's own psychic distance from his surroundings, the story's very form suggests flux. An epistolary tale is a refugee, a traveler removed from the scene by air, sea, or rail.

"The Assistant Producer," also written in 1943, reopens "the old Europe Picture Palace" (p. 75), which is exactly that—European. The setting is Paris and the subject is Russian *émigré* political intrigue, by definition a fantastic fiction. Except for the ending, which affords a brief glimpse of Americana (a *Falcon*-like spy thriller and a movie lobby), the story's cinematic form and materials do not depend upon contemporary *amerikanskie* models. "A Forgotten Poet" (significant title!), a story of 1944, retreats even further, to nineteenth-century Russia. Distance of one kind or another prevails in the American tales of the forties, whose English would invariably be checked over by one of Nabokov's American friends.

Nabokov's first effort to fill that "green vacuum" with "local ingredients," to create an eminently American landscape, had already occurred in a 1942 poem, "The Refrigerator Awakes," but the canvas had been significantly small. A nocturnal fantasy, an insomniac's meditation on a refrigerator anthropomorphized into a giant creature mortally tormented by frost and cultural forces, the poem moves from scientific data through various pains and then concludes,

Vladimir, Véra, and Dmitri Nabokov, aged nine, photographed by publisher James Laughlin at Salt Lake City, summer 1943, the year of "Spring in Fialta."

> *Keep it Kold, says a poster in passing, and lo,*
> *loads,*
> *of bright fruit, and a ham, and some chocolate cream,*
> *and three bottles of milk, all contained in the gleam*
> *of that wide-open white*
> *god, the pride and delight*
> *of starry-eyed couples in dream kitchenettes,*
> *and it groans and it drones and it toils and it sweats—*
> *Shackleton, pemmican, penguin, Poe's Pym—*
> *collapsing at last in the criminal*
> *night.*[3]

The poor sentient refrigerator has been crushed by the burden placed on it by powerful advertising; it didn't ask to be made into a god. Nabokov extends it his sympathy by invoking the heroic English Arctic explorer, Sir E. H. Shackleton (1874-1922), whose ship *Endurance* was crushed by ice in 1915. Like the refrigerator, he too died in action, serving his nation. Typically for Nabokov, the resonance of the comparison depends upon special a-literary information; only diffusely present in *Bend Sinister* (1947), such bits and pieces will be beautifully controlled in *Lolita*. Their shared white gleam notwithstanding, the dream kitchenette and Poe's Pym (another Arctic victim) are contrasted in a manner that anticipates the ways in which Humbert will ironically pair literary allusions and popular materials. The "criminal nights" he will spend at particularized motels remain a long way off, however; refrigerators are more manageable for Nabokov in 1942, and the structure of a thirty-nine-line poem serves him well enough, providing a small unit in which to frame and contain his new findings. A very young child takes short steps, especially in an unfamiliar environment.

The commercial weight and contents borne by the refrigerator, a constant pressure on the characters in *Lolita,* are examined more closely in Chapter Three of Nabokov's *Nikolai Gogol* (1944), which leisurely considers *Dead Souls.* "Our Mr. Chichikov," he titles the chapter, and the familiar Pickwickian tone of the possessive locution suggests that past and present somehow cohere, that Gogol speaks to our condition. A dead soul trafficking in dead souls and traveling amongst dead souls, Chichikov the confidence man cloaks his criminality in false charm and rhetoric, the essence of *poshlost'* and American advertising. Nabokov foregrounds his discussion of *Dead Souls* by defining *poshlost'*, choosing most of his illustrations from American ads, magazines, and best-sellers (pp. 66-69); their relevance to *Lolita* is obvious. "She it was to whom ads were dedicated: the ideal consumer, the subject and object of every foul poster," Humbert will say of Lolita (p. 150). By emphasizing *poshlost'*, Nabokov makes Gogol as "relevant" to 1944 as he is to 1974, and the qualifying quotes mark the helplessness of a good word debased by cant usage and current *poshlost'*.

As idiosyncratic and personal as the rest of the Gogol book, these pages are easily misunderstood, particularly by those who would read *Lolita* too readily as a "satire" of America. *Poshlost'* observes no geographic boundaries, as Luzhin's in-laws prove in *The Defense* (1930); their possessions and home furnishings would have appealed to Charlotte Haze and her friends (pp. 119-20). Although he is hardly a hardhat or American Legion type, Nabokov is genuinely troubled that *Lolita* was welcomed by many readers, especially in Europe, as "good news, a satire of America," and he is unsparing in his criticism of some of the post-*Lolita* Black Humorists with whom he is sometimes loosely grouped. "An anti-American book," he says indignantly of *Catch-22* (1961). "And why did he make him [Yossarian] an Armenian? He doesn't *sound* Armenian. Is that some sort of sly racial joke?" asks Nabokov, acutely sensitive to an insidiously subtle form of *poshlost'*; the stationery of The Enchanted Hunters hotel in *Lolita* bears the information "NEAR CHURCHES"—a code sign indicating "Gentiles Only" (p. 263). Nor does Nabokov simply sneer at the laboratory specimens of *poshlost'* he places before us on *Gogol's* dissection table. "The rich *poshlost'* emanating from [such] advertisements . . . is due not to their exaggerating (or inventing) the glory of this or that serviceable article but to suggesting that the acme of human happiness is purchasable and that its purchase somehow ennobles the purchaser" (pp. 66-67). Speaking as a humanist rather than a *déclassé* mandarin snob, he notes that those ads form "a kind of satellite shadow world in the actual existence of which neither sellers nor buyers really believe in their heart of hearts—especially in this wise quiet country" (p. 67). Although Charlotte Haze will epitomize *poshlost'*, she is also its victim, and there are moments when her desperation is revealed, surfacing through the *poshlyi* veneer and suggesting that she too questions the existence of that "shadow world." Her vulgarity withstanding, Charlotte is not an entirely free agent. "Chichikov himself," writes Nabokov, "is

merely the ill-paid representative of the Devil, a traveling salesman from Hades, 'our Mr. Chichikov' as the Satan & Co. firm may be imagined calling their easygoing, healthy-looking but inwardly shivering and rotting agent" (p. 73). Clare Quilty will become *Lolita's* Chichikov, an equally evil and stupid and pretentious dead soul, a homunculus and latter-day swindler who perpetrates *his* mischief at the expense of ladies' lit'ry clubs and movie and theater audiences. Nabokov will affirm *their* souls by routing Quilty, the shadow world's well-paid representative.

In 1944 Lolita's American milieu remains in the middle distance, though Nabokov, in the guise of Gogol's critic, has clearly managed to sharpen his novelistic pencil. At the beginning of Chapter Three he laments that The Reader's Club edition of *Dead Souls* had recently been issued under the title *Chichikov's Journeys, or Homelife in Old Russia*, a change apparently prompted, he states, "by the fear of suggesting gloomy ideas to rosy-cheeked comic strip fans" (p. 62); five years later he created in *Lolita* the most ardent of such fans, and used those strips to his own advantage. Several other images, novelistic in their suggestiveness, anticipate *Lolita* directly. In the course of discussing Gogol's *The Government Inspector*, Nabokov mocks categorical definitions ("tragedy," "comedy") that digest literary masterpieces as "something as readily assimilated as a hot dog at a football game" (p. 55), an isolated and striking "American" detail typical of at least one thousand phenomena and particles so intrinsic to the creative atmosphere of *Lolita* as to defy taxonomic description, paraphrase, or quotation.

Written at the exact midpoint of Nabokov's first decade in America, "Time and Ebb" (1945) attempts to render in fiction *Nikolai Gogol's* American gleanings. A minor story, it is a major signpost and pointer on the road to *Lolita;* the scenery of other future works is also discernible (the college communities of *Pnin,* 1957, and *Pale Fire,* 1962). Where *Gogol* is steeled by a scholiast's distance, "Time and Ebb" achieves its global view of America by virtue of time travel, a familiar sci-fi device. The story's first-person narrator is a ninety-year-old scientist who, writing in the twenty-first century (c. 2024), reminisces about his American childhood of 1945. Paris-born, a war refugee (like Humbert Humbert, his mother died when he was small), the narrator would seem to have arrived in America in 1940 or so, age six—Dmitri Nabokov's age at the time of *his* family's 1940 emigration—and the story's foreground is viewed from a child's perspective, Dmitri's angle of vision. Seated at Saturday movie matinees with young Dmitri or sprawled on the floor with him over the comics pages of the Boston Sunday papers, Nabokov *was* a child again, a sophisticated enough child, by necessity open to experience, observing and remembering all sorts of oddments in his struggle to become an American boy

and a native writer. Central Park, a mere phrase in " 'That in Aleppo Once . . .'," gets its own paragraph in "Time and Ebb," and it is delicately perceived by the narrator's "childish eyes" (p. 159).

Seven years had elapsed since Nabokov had completed a novel—*The Real Life of Sebastian Knight* (1938), whose 1941 publication date is misleading—and "Time and Ebb's" point of view does not succeed in disguising what might advisedly be termed an artistic crisis; time travel, after all, is also a fantasy of escape. "Like other old men before me," writes the nameless narrator, his pen guided by the middle-aged Nabokov, "I have discovered that the near in time is annoyingly confused, whereas at the end of the tunnel there are color and light. I can discern the features of every month in 1944 or 1945, but seasons are utterly blurred when I pick out 1997 or 2012" (p. 156). *Confused* is the signal word, describing the narrator if not his maker, and their task is surely one: to order and re-create the fantastic realism or realistic fantasy of "the past," the nineteen-forties. "You know I do not understand what is advertisement and what is not advertisement," says *émigré* Pnin, responding to an American picture-magazine as though he were a visitor from another planet (p. 60). "But the fact remains that the beings that peopled the world in the days of my childhood seem to the present generation more remote than the nineteenth century seemed to them," says the narrator of "Time and Ebb"

(p. 156), articulating the problems faced by Nabokov, a writer twice displaced by history; the distance provided by the sci-fi form is not sufficient to their needs. A passage that looks forward to *Lolita's voyages gastronomiques* begins with a description drawn from art rather than life, creating the effect of a dream within a dream:

> In a recent and still popular play dealing with the quaint America of the Flying Forties, a good deal of glamour is infused into the part of the Soda Jerk, but the side whiskers and the starched shirt front are absurdly anachronistic, nor was there in my day such a continuous and violent revolving of tall mushroom seats as is indulged in by the performers. We imbibed our humble mixtures (through straws that were really much shorter than those employed on the stage) in an atmosphere of gloomy greed. I remember the shallow enchantment and the minor poetry of the proceedings; the copious froth engendered above the sunken lump of frozen synthetic cream, or the liquid brown mud of "fudge" sauce poured over its polar pate. Brass and glass surfaces, sterile reflections of electric lamps, the whirr and shimmer of a caged propeller . . . (p. 160).

Humbert will find no poetry in Lolita's unpalatable counter culture, but, like the hot dog in *Gogol*, the fine images of the "mushroom seats" and the fan as a "caged propeller" are particularized in the best manner of *Lolita*, where thin-armed girls in their first prom gowns will look like "flamingoes" (p. 188). More often in the 1945 story, however, sweeping generalizations ("They clung to reality . . . ," p. 156) alternate with somewhat belabored descriptions of strange native customs: "In their letters they addressed perfect strangers by what was—insofar as words have sense—the equivalent of 'beloved master' and prefaced a theoretically immortal signature with a mumble expressing idiotic devotion to a person whose very existence was to the writer a matter of complete unconcern" (p. 157). The archness of such observations is instructive; not until *Lolita* would Nabokov be able to delineate American manners and affectations with any ease, as when Headmistress Pratt holds forth on Progressive Education, or Charlotte and her friends smoke and talk, write precious letters and imitate movie folk.

American mass culture of the Flying Forties is variously brought down by the aged narrator. "To those who have been born since the staggering discoveries of the seventies, and who thus have seen nothing in the nature of flying things save perhaps a kite or a toy balloon . . . it is not easy to imagine airplanes, particularly because old photographic pictures of those splendid machines in full flight lack the life which only art could have been capable of retaining—and oddly enough no great painter ever chose them as a special subject into which to inject his genius and thus preserve their image from deterioration," complains the narrator (pp. 162-63), who has earlier remarked how "the 'numberless nebulous pictures' bequeathed us by the drab, flat, and strangely melancholic photography of the past century exaggerate the impression of unreality which that century makes upon those who do not remember it" (p. 156). He is not against technology per se, which by now is trite; rather, he rejects the premises of photojournalism and its awesome sway over pre-television America; his complaint anticipates the influence it now exerts in the form of numberless picture-books that package the nebulous look of history for a vast audience of non-readers.[4] A photomechanical reproduction is a factual notation rather than the essence of truth, an obvious enough statement, but made necessary by the nostalgists, critics, and museum photo curators who, in the wake of *Life*'s demise, uncritically celebrated its cultural contribution to the gross national product. The result of chance or careful setups, an editor's arbitrary selection or an art director's adjustments, few photos are worth a thousand words. Saint-Exupéry's *Wind, Sand and Stars* (1939) has done for the airplane what no photograph *or* painting has ever achieved, just as Mailer's extraordinary evocation of the lunar surface, in *Of a Fire on the Moon* (1970), excelled the pictorial coverage on TV and in *Life*, the magazine that had commissioned him. If they are of people, the pictures mentioned in "Time and Ebb" are *strangely melancholic* and "unreal" because "narrative" photos pose as many questions as they answer: what are the exact circumstances of the picture and its subject? Did that sad person belie the preserved moment two seconds later with a smile? Have those urbanites hurried past that foreground fistfight because Modern Man is Indifferent, or because the first punch was delivered after they had already passed by? Rare indeed is the high-level "candid" photo that can survive the moment and narrate its "story" without benefit of a caption—by definition no reservoir of profundity—and the entrepreneurs of photojournalism aim their lenses low enough; Lolita will study "the photographic results of head-on collisions" and never doubt "the reality of place, time and circumstance alleged to match the publicity pictures of naked-thighed beauties" (p. 167). Wrenched from its context and frozen in space, the photographic image will often communicate only that which the viewer subjectively reads into it, as Humbert will demonstrate in *Lolita*. He cherishes his worn old snapshot of Annabel Leigh, his lost nymphet, and in a sense lives with and dies by that "nebulous picture." By trying to make Lolita conform to it, he reduces her to an image that is dead in every sense of the word; early in the novel, Quilty's hobby is announced as "photography" (p. 33), thereby doubling Humbert's atavistic pursuits. Although Humbert will regret his failure to capture Lolita on film, he ends his narrative by declaring that her immortality depends on "the durable pigments" of art, a shift in attitude that looks back to the mimetic dis-

tinction in "Time and Ebb" between popular photography and a timeless painting infused by individual genius.

Artificial or mechanical means and performances are consistently indicted in the 1945 story. The narrator evokes the drugstore's waitress, "a dapper uniformed girl with a hypertrophied nether lip (that pout, that sullen kiss-trap, that transient fashion in feminine charm—1939-1950)"; the parentheses will topple over in *Lolita*, which focuses fully on numerous transient fashions, revealing them to be anything but skin-deep. Westerns, a source of meaningful fun in

"Nebulous picture": The most intelligent advocates of photography often ask one to read a picture as though it were an essay, a denotative image structured by words, but this extraordinary photograph by Weegee, titled *New York 1942*, refuses any positivistic "reading." The banners bearing U.S. eagles suggest a War Bond rally, but no hard information is provided by any supplementary caption. If a parade is in progress, it certainly doesn't hold the crowd's attention or excite it. The people on the street are strangely contemplative, isolated from one another, adrift. The man on the far right, foreground, is ready to enlist; one only hopes that his young neighbor, who gazes at the camera, will turn out to be 4-F. Does the photo comment on city life, patriotism, or wartime anxieties? What, specifically, are they waiting to *see*? The wide-eyed child in the left foreground would already seem to have witnessed a terrible event. "TIME IS SHORT" proclaim two of the signs, investing the surrealistic scene with "literary" meaning . . . of one's own choice. Is the end of the world upon them, the day of the locust? Perhaps they are merely bored. The strength of Weegee's picture depends on its mystery.

Lolita, are remote and unreal in "Time and Ebb": "Mountain gorges seemed to have been ransacked for echoes; these were subjected to a special treatment on a basis of honey and rubber until their condensed accents could be synchronized with the labial movements of serial photographs on a moon-white screen in a velvet-dark hall" (p. 161). The killing of Quilty, an entire chapter, is derived from a sentence-long fist-fight in this story and the pointed out isolated joke at Sinatra's expense will give way to fully integrated local color in *Lolita*: the "luminous . . . gonadal glow" of juke boxes (p. 136) and "the nasal voices of those invisibles serenading [Lolita], people with names like Sammy and Jo and Eddy and Tony and Peggy and Guy and Patty and Rex" (p. 150). By 1954, Humbert and Nabokov will have lived with them long enough to wax familiar. The distance has been narrowed, and Sammy Kaye (the nasal voices of The Three Kadets), Jo Stafford, Eddie Fisher, Tony Bennett, Peggy Lee, Guy Mitchell, and Patti Page need not be disguised or parodied; a quotidian world has been re-created, and their presence helps to animate it. Rex, however, is a ringer, either an allusion to *Laughter in the Dark*'s Axel Rex—in his own right a Pop entertainer—or a challenge to future scholarship. "'Come and kiss your old man,' I would say, "'and drop that moody nonsense. In former times, when I was still your dream male [the reader will notice what pains I took to speak Lo's tongue], you swooned to records of the number one throb-and-sob idol of your coevals [Lo: "Of my what? Speak English"],' " writes Nabokov (p. 151), in complete control of the materials and language refugee Humbert tries desperately to expropriate in an effort to bridge the distance separating him from Lolita.

As much a literary exercise as a story, "Time and Ebb" suggests that Nabokov was willfully readying himself for An American Subject. "Conversation Piece: 1945," his next story, is well grounded indeed. Originally titled "Double Talk," it records the proto-Nazi sentiments of several figures, including some club ladies who are presented as hateful variants of a Helen Hokinson *New Yorker* cartoon. "The events in the story are actual," says Nabokov, "and I even transcribed some of that dialogue," which may explain why this very American story came so easily to him. In *Bend Sinister*, however, written in 1945-46, he celebrates his recently acquired U.S. citizenship by choosing to revisit and redecorate the dystopian world of *Invitation to a Beheading* (1935-36)—prompted, perhaps, by what those real-life women had taken for granted. Nabokov's Russian roots are once again in the foreground, most literally in *Bend Sinister's* Slavic/Germanic mongrel language, quite appropriate, of course, to the European and totalitarian setting of Padukgrad. Seen in the context of his progress toward *Lolita*, his first American novel thus repre-

sents a kind of regression, a recoil from the challenge implicit in "Time and Ebb" and partially realized in "Conversation Piece: 1945." No critic, however clairvoyant, should be so impertinent as to announce with certitude why a writer composes one book rather than another at a given moment, but *Bend Sinister* does reveal a certain diffidence. Allowing Nabokov his choice of subject (how generous), one may locate that diffidence in the novel's anachronistic American details, its undigested Pop ingredients.

America is specifically invoked early in *Bend Sinister*. Olga, the wife of philosopher Adam Krug, has died at the outset of the novel. "In normal times . . . I would be supplying her picture to American newspapermen" (p. 28), says Ember, Krug's university colleague, who sustains the view of journalism found in "Time and Ebb." When she was alive Olga had "made the horrified Ember persuade Krug to go on [an] American lecture tour" intended to enhance his reputation at home.

Not that the trip itself had been displeasing. Far from it. Although Krug, being as usual chary of squandering in idle conversation such experiences as might undergo unpredictable metamorphoses later on (if left to pupate quietly in the alluvium of the mind), had spoken little of his tour, Olga had managed to recompose it in full and to relay it gleefully to Ember who had vaguely expected a flow of sarcastic disgust. "Disgust?" cried Olga. "Why, he has known enough of that here. Disgust, indeed! Elation, delight, a quickening of the imagination, a disinfection of the mind, *togliwn ochnat divodiv* [the daily surprise of awakening]!" (p. 29).

Nabokov's own imagination at the time of *Bend Sinister* was undergoing the metamorphosis he ascribes to Krug, and Olga's use of indirect discourse recalls the obliquities of "Time and Ebb." Although Nabokov cannot resist letting Krug write down an aphoristic observation or two, notebook jottings toward *Lolita*—"life [in America], that self-conscious stranger, being slapped on the back and told to relax" (p. 30)—he tries not to "squander" his own American experiences in the pages of the present book. Yet several small acquisitions from the trip do manage to sneak into *Bend Sinister*, and they constitute a curious presence.

Because Krug refuses to cooperate with the State he is arrested by the secret police, who are ably assisted by Mariette, a treacherous coquette. After the arrest, a gallant agent tries to help her into her coat before they speed off with Krug in their elegant limousine: "'No—just round my shoulders,' said the debutante. She shook her smooth brown hair; then, with a special disengaging gesture (the back of her hand rapidly passing along the nape of her delicate neck), she lightly swished it up so that it would not catch under the collar of the coat. 'There is room for three,' she sang out sweetly in her best golden-oriole manner from the depths of the car . . ." (pp. 204-5). Mariette's fatuous glamor is well observed, and it looks forward to the women of *Lolita,* but she must be the first Communazi deb—a refugee from the society page, the rotogravure section of a Boston Sunday newspaper, or perhaps an image lifted from the more light-hearted footage of an American newsreel. "Hold it straight, kiddo," grumbles one of the policemen, a bit player practicing his Yankee slang in the wings of *Bend Sinister,* readying himself for an entrance in *Lolita.*

American best-sellers are slipped into *Bend Sinister* in a way that at first seems less obtrusive than the debutante's manner. Ember, "an obscure scholar," is asked to translate into English his *"Komparatiwn Stuhdar en Sophistat tuen Pekrekh* or, as the title of the American edition had it, a little more snappily, *The Philosophy of Sin* (banned in four states and a best seller in the rest)" (p. 28). The event allows Nabokov to sketch in a segment of its landscape of success: "What a strange trick of chance—this masterpiece of esoteric thought endearing itself at once to the middle-class reader and competing for first honors during one season with that robust satire *Straight Flush,* and then, next year, with Elisabeth Ducharme's romance of Dixieland, *When the Train Passes,* and for twenty-nine days (leap year) with the book club selection *Through Towns and Villages*" (p. 28). Read together as one phrase, the italicized titles dispatch the books down a toilet; the passage is complemented by a bathroom shelf containing "A bottle of mineral oil, half full, and a grey cardboard cylinder which had been the kernel of a toilet paper roll. . . . The shelf also held two popular novels (*Flung Roses* and *All Quiet on the Don*)," a blending of famous titles by Remarque and Sholokov, clearly placed there to alleviate the wartime paper shortage (p. 85). This excremental humor, less emphatic than Swift's or Beckett's privy seal of Dublin, recalls Leopold Bloom's use of a page of trashy prose from the prize story in *Titbits*.[5] These toilet jokes, atypical of Nabokov, miss the target because they stop too short; unlike *Lolita*, which boasts Charlotte Haze, the best-sellers in *Bend Sinister* have no readers, and exist in a vacuum. The books might well have had an audience, and at no cost to the European setting. *Flung Roses* is an allusion to *Gone With the Wind* (1936) by way of Dowson's "Cynara," the source of both titles, and it is disappointing that Nabokov didn't dramatize his contempt, inasmuch as he knew from his long residence in Germany that sentimental escapist costume melodramas, the kitschy Teutonic equivalents of *GWTW*, were the principal reading and motion-picture distractions offered in Hitler's Germany. The altered version of *Hamlet* in *Bend Sinister* renders a totalitarian ethos where the book titles remain dormant, a literary anatomist's indulgence. When Humbert evokes the movie version of *GWTW*, though not by name (p. 158), the difference is apparent; in *Lolita* trash will be a thematic necessity, just as the best-sellers on the shelves of Pnin's rented rooms will serve as reflectors of the world around them.

Closest to *Lolita*'s future successful assimilation of Pop materials is *Bend Sinister*'s use of the comic strip. Ember's *The Philosophy of Sin* has also had to compete "for two consecutive years with that remarkable cross between a certain kind of wafer and a lollipop, Louis Sontag's *Annunciata*, which started so well in the Caves of St. Barthelemy and ended in the funnies" (p. 29), an allusion to 1942's number one best-seller, *The Song of Bernadette*, by Franz Werfel, another recent arrival in America; the film version (1943) was even more popular. That concluding image of "the funnies," commonplace enough, will come to life in a subsequent chapter of *Bend Sinister*. Comic strips are not unique to America, of course, and Nabokov didn't need any crash course in the subject; as a boy he had enjoyed his father's books of European comic art, and in *Laughter in the Dark* (1938) he had created a most cruel cartoonist, hatchetman Axel Rex, whose first name also suggests the centrifugal force exerted by popular culture, kingly Rex's dubious province. In *The Gift* (1937-38), also set in the Berlin of the twenties, *émigré* Fyodor ponders "the conscientious student [chess] exercises of the young Soviet composers [which] were not so much 'problems' as 'tasks': cumbrously they treated of this or that mechanical theme . . . without a hint of poetry; these were chess comic strips, nothing more, and the shoving and jostling pieces did their clumsy work with proletarian seriousness . . ." (p. 186). "Mechanical themes" and "flat variants" (p. 186) summarize the aspects of mass culture that lend themselves so well to totalitarian regimes, and in Chapter Five of *Bend Sinister* the comic strip is linked with the Party of the Average Man, as first instituted by dictator Paduk when he was a young student:

In those days a blatantly bourgeois paper happened to be publishing a cartoon sequence depicting the home life of Mr. and Mrs. Etermon (Everyman). With conventional humor and sympathy bordering upon the obscene, Mr. Etermon and the little woman were followed from parlor to kitchen and from garden to garret through all the mentionable stages of their daily existence, which, despite the presence of cozy armchairs and all sorts of electric thingumbobs and one thing-in-itself (a car), did not differ essentially from the life of a Neanderthal couple. Mr. Etermon taking a z-nap on the divan or stealing into the kitchen to sniff with erotic avidity the sizzling stew, represented quite unconsciously a living refutation of individual immortality, since his whole habitus was a dead-end with nothing in it capable or worthy of transcending the mortal condition. Neither, however, could one imagine Etermon actually dying, not only because the rules of gentle humor forbade his being shown on his deathbed, but also because not a single detail of the setting (not even

his playing poker with life-insurance salesmen) suggested the fact of absolutely inevitable death; so that in one sense Etermon, while personifying a refutation of immortality, was immortal himself, and in another sense he could not hope to enjoy any kind of afterlife simply because he was denied the elementary comfort of a death chamber in his otherwise well planned home. Within the limits of this airtight existence, the young couple were as happy as any young couple ought to be: a visit to the movies, a raise in one's salary, a yum-yum something for dinner—life was positively crammed with these and similar delights, whereas the worst that might befall one, was hitting a traditional thumb with a traditional hammer or mistaking the date of the boss's birthday (p. 77-78).

The "z-nap" is a clever touch, but Nabokov's disquisition draws upon a more basic and pervasive comic strip convention; except for *Gasoline Alley* and *Terry* (who stopped growing in 1943), the characters in American strips never age, and poor Orphan Annie was not even allowed to change that one red dress. Etermon is offensive in more far-reaching ways. His very name is a diminution, a corruption of the German *Jedermann,* an abused "Everyman" whose shorn *J* and *n* are linguistically akin to a badly printed comic in which a character's ears have been obliterated by the harsh off-center colors to which the form is restricted. German is the appropriate root inasmuch as the first American comic strips were imitations of nineteenth-century German models (Wilhelm Busch et al.), and the *Gemütlichkeit* ambience of the Etermon strip is a telling German-American hybrid, recalling the transatlantic success enjoyed by Axel Rex. "The strip is invented," says Nabokov, "but the example of *Blondie* helped it along, and Etermon's attire recalls Mutt (as opposed to Jeff), Andy Gump, or Jiggs in *Bringing Up Father:* "the tall collar of celluloid, the famous shirt-sleeve bands and the expensive footgear. . . . [and] washable cuffs with starlike links" (p. 79). "Poster pictures of Etermon showed him smoking the brand that millions smoke, and millions could not be wrong" (p. 78); his iconic stature anticipates Quilty, whose face will stare out of a million ads for Dromes cigarettes, including one posted above "Lo's chaste bed, littered with 'comics'" (p. 71).

Ekwilism, the philosophy of the Party of the Average Man, is worshipped "in the guise of a cartoon-engendered Mr. Etermon" (p. 78), and the mass-produced quality of the strip, with its trite and narrow content, perfectly represents fascistic ideals of conformity. Young Paduk, the future dictator, "deliberately copied the Etermon cartoon in its sartorial sense" (p. 79), just as Lolita and Charlotte will imitate movie stars; which is not to say that America is totalitarian but rather to suggest how Pop culture may work in that direction, dulling consciousness and channeling behavior, containing it as a comic strip would within its flat surfaces, four primary colors, and the parallel serial boxes in which balloons constrain verbal communication. Comics are the only permissible "reading" material in the futuristic world of Truffaut's 1966 film version of Ray Bradbury's *Fahrenheit 451* (1953), but the strips have no balloons and their colors are especially drab; words and hues are *verboten* in a dystopia that extends *Bend Sinister's* Slavic/Germanic *Kulterkammer* and draws upon Godard's "cartoon-engendered" *Alphaville* (1965), whose cast, snap-brimmed hero, and harshly stylized urban setting are patterned on *Dick Tracy.*

Nabokov is not the first modern novelist to employ the funnies in a serious manner. Because Joe Christmas in *Light in August* (1932) is the fatal victim of racial abstractions that deny him color, body, and depth, Faulkner visualizes him as an austere line drawing: profile in silhouette, dangling cigarette, nondescript hat—the iconography of the comic strip, but minus one individualized and expressive touch, be it a caricatured eye, ear, or nose, a cartooned rictus (Smilin' Jack's permanent smile), or a signal void (Orphan Annie's empty eye sockets, Andy Gump's lost chin). *Sanctuary* (1931) is even more explicit and succinct; Popeye's name defines him as a cartoon, an empty outline in place of a moral creature, and Nabokov draws (and quarters) Paduk in a similar way. In Queneau's *The Bark Tree* (1933), the silhouette of Etienne comes to life only when it/he begins to think, a Cartesian cartoon fleshed out in the fashion of the magic-ink-bottle animated cartoons of the twenties

Cinematic chiaroscuro, the major phase: a frame from Milton Caniff's *Terry and the Pirates*, 1945, which in the forties influenced first-rate film directors (Orson Welles, Nicholas Ray). Caniff's lighting is as low-key as any *film noir* of the period, and his draftsmanship is the antithesis of the cartoon models favored by West, Nabokov, et al.

THE "BEAK" HAS A SOURCE OF INFORMATION CLOSE TO PHILIP SHAW

I KNOW SHAW IS LEAVING TOMORROW-- THAT'S OLD STUFF-- I WANT TO KNOW WHAT TIME-- WHAT TIME!

I LISTEN ALL TIME-- MEBBE TONIGHT, I HEAR

Early cinematic chiaroscuro: Alex Raymond's *Secret Agent X-9*, 1935, scenario by Dashiell Hammett, whose hard-boiled dialogue is quite "Hemingwayesque" in its use of repetition. (© 1935 King Features Syndicate) by Max Fleischer, *Popeye*'s creator. Nathanael West went even further than his contemporaries by conceiving *Miss Lonelyhearts* (1933) as "A novel in the form of a comic strip. The characters to be squares in which many things happen through one action. The speeches contained in the conventional balloons."[6] Like Nabokov, Faulkner, and Queneau, West had in mind the clean lines of the silhouette drawing cartooned in bold black and white (*Dick Tracy*), as opposed to the elegant draftsmanship of a Hal Foster (*Tarzan, Prince Valiant*) or the cinematic realism and chiaroscuro subsequently developed in the mid thirties by Alex Raymond (*Flash Gordon, Secret Agent X-9*), Milton Caniff (*Terry and the Pirates*), and Noel Sickles (*Scorchy Smith*). Most of today's comic art, as practiced by highly proficient commercial illustrators, follows their example, and today's cartooned strips (*Peanuts*) are more gentle and idealized versions of earlier caricature (*The Katzenjammer Kids*). Only the "underground" comics revert to that often savage grotesquerie, West's domain in *Miss Lonelyhearts*. Crippled by moral failure or a fatal weakness, rendered grotesque by circumstance and adversity, West's cartoon characters are vividly *seen*, and the impact of this very short novel depends on its comic strip stylization and swift pace, West's creation of an a-novelistic spatial form in which the compact, successive, sharply outlined monochromatic scenes remain in one's mind, a simultaneous visual presence.

"He buried his triangular face like the blade of a hatchet in her neck," writes West of Shrike, the feature editor, effecting a *Dick Tracy tableau vivant* out of newsprint flotsam.[7] "Samuel Spade's jaw was long and bony, his chin a jutting v under the more flexible v of his mouth. His nostrils curved back to make another, smaller, v. His yellow-grey eyes were horizontal. The v *motif* was picked up again by thickish brows rising outward from twin creases above a hooked nose, and his pale brown hair grew down— from high flat temples—in a point on his forehead," writes West's good friend Dashiell Hammett in the opening paragraph of *The Maltese Falcon* (1930), a year *before* Chester Gould created Dick Tracy, another flat geometric face. In Russian Krug means "circle," just another motif on a printed page; and Mr. Everyman, Miss Lonelyhearts, Christmas, and Spade are not the most substantial members of the family of names. Although Spade is a willfully two-dimensional figure, Hammett's stylized surfaces and assemblage of *things* nevertheless suggest much about the quality of Spade's life, his consciousness; and Hammett, who was also a comic strip scenarist (*Secret Agent X-9*), manages this without recourse to traditional forms of exposition. Hammett's unadorned prose and Spade's transparency as a character suggest why the French New Novelists and New Wave film directors have so admired American hard-boiled writing, comic strips, and action films. The flatness which Nabokov dis-

WHAT'S THE IDEA?

I JUST WANTED TO SEE HOW YOU'D HANDLE 'EM ALL AT ONCE.

parages in *Bend Sinister* is to Robbe-Grillet and Alain Resnais an advantage, an aesthetic imperative, the popular equivalent of a "serious" mode whose phenomenology of surfaces eschews analogy, omniscience, depth psychology, and neatly packaged interpretations of behavior, Robbe-Grillet's fallacies of "interiority." When *Giff-Wiff: Revue de la Bande Dessinée*, a journal available in only the best of private libraries, did its 1966 *Dossier Dick Tracy*, Resnais was in charge of the *hommage*, and his direction of Robbe-Grillet's *Last Year at Marienbad* (1961) realizes the diagrammatic or illusionistic anti-realism of *Dick Tracy* and *Mandrake the Magician*. Conjurer Nabokov, a persistent intruder in his own books, greatly admires *Marienbad* ("Brilliant! His novels are worthy

A 1944 Chester Gould drawing that gathers together villains from the 1937-44 period. The creator crouches in the corner, ready to erase his rogue's gallery if Tracy can't handle them, much as Nabokov's firm authorial hand dissolves M'sieur Pierre and Paduk at the end of *Invitation to a Beheading* and *Bend Sinister,* respectively. Director Federico Fellini's appearances in his own films suggest why he admires the artifice of *Dick Tracy,* and collects and studies this strip (and *Flash Gordon,* too). Future oral examinations of candidates for the doctoral degree in popular culture might well ask for a spot-identification of the characters in a drawing such as this one, but only in the section dealing with the classical period. For the answers, see the caption on p. 82. (© 1974 Chicago Tribune–New York News Syndicate) of the Nobel Prize") and would doubtless appreciate the authorial presence evident in a 1944 Gould drawing; but his own use of *Dick Tracy* in *Lolita* is a thematic exigency rather than a tribute. He too eschews depth psychology, but his enthusiasm has its limits, just as his own aesthetic stops short of Robbe-Grillet's extreme position, which reduces humanism to "the old myths of depth."

Although Nabokov insists that he writes with "no moral in tow," his loathing of popular culture is firmly moral and humanistic. *Bend Sinister*, nothing if not an artifice, defines the essential difference between Robbe-Grillet and Nabokov, whose rejection of the State's vision of a homogenized, "cartoon-engendered" Mr. Everyman is expressed in virtually didactic terms. "Actually, with a little perspicacity, one might learn many curious things about Etermons, things that made them so different from one another that Etermon, except as a cartoonist's transient character, could not be said to exist" (p. 78). Nabokov describes several Etermons, their "eyes narrowly glowing" as they variously pursue their humanizing activities: "another Etermon, straight from his shabby office, slips into the silence of a great library to gloat over certain old maps of which he will not speak at home. . . ." p. 79), anticipating the way the hero of *Fahrenheit 451* (the temperature at which books burn) will surreptitiously horde and read those forbidden volumes. "No," concludes Nabokov, "the average vessels

This single frame from a 1938 *Mandrake the Magician* indicates why the Lee Falk–Phil Davis strip was so admired by French practitioners of the *Nouvelle Vague* and *roman*. The flames surrounding Mandrake and the actress are his fabrication—an illusion-within-an-illusion, given the Hollywood setting. Mandrake usually achieved such effects through hypnosis, a state of mind evidently shared by the reader as well as the film director within the frame. *Did* that couple meet last year at Marienbad? *Does* the narrator of Robbe-Grillet's *Jealousy* have anything to worry about? No "objective" point of view mediates or evaluates the visual data, just as we don't actually *see* Mandrake hypnotize the director. (© 1938 King Features Syndicate)

are not as simple as they appear: it is a conjurer's set and nobody, not even the enchanter himself [i.e. Nabokov], really knows what and how much they hold" (p. 79). Nabokov is unsparing of Paduk, however, whose transparent person cannot repulse authorial omniscience. "Although in later years [Paduk's] mimetic adaptation [of Etermon] was no longer consciously pursued . . . [and the] strip was eventually discontinued" (p. 79), the dictator remains a cartoon, a crude stick-figure, a moral joke. "Throughout all his later adventures, in all places, under all circumstances . . . [finally] vested with more power than any national ruler had ever enjoyed, Paduk still retained something of the late Mr. Etermon, a sort of cartoon angularity, a cracked and soiled cellophane wrapper effect, through which nevertheless, one could discern a brand-new thumbscrew, a bit of rope, a rusty knife and a specimen of the most sensitive of human organs wrenched out together with its blood-clotted roots" (p. 80). The comic strip has been developed where *Flung Roses* was merely tossed in.

By bringing a cliché to life in *Bend Sinister* (an accomplishment analogous to the movie-style killing of Quilty), Nabokov took another step toward *Lolita,* whose comic-strip allusions are more fleeting but almost always to the point. The compression of means typical of *Lolita* is glimpsed in the space travel story "Lance" (1952). Rejecting a reader's inclination to pigeonhole the tale as "so-called 'science fiction'"

(p. 200), Nabokov points out that he has left "the question of time" to the "capable paws of *Starzan* and other comics and atomics" (p. 201), a forecast of Van Veen's *Texture of Time* as well as a fusion of *Buck Rogers* (or *Flash Gordon*) and *Tarzan,* which in 1949-50 had introduced into Africa a tribe of monstrous interplanetary visitors. On the road with Lolita, pursued by great thunderstorms and Detective Trapp (Quilty), Humbert suffers real and imagined terrors. He flings open their motel door one stormy night and there, "white-glistening in the rain-dripping darkness . . . stood a man holding before his face the mask of Jutting Chin, a grotesque sleuth in the funnies. He emitted a muffled guffaw and scurried away, and I reeled back into the room . . ." (p. 219). *Dick Tracy* evokes, obviously, the doggedness of Quilty's pursuit, but the brief scene also captures the bizarre spirit and expressionistic style of that strip; framed in the doorway and highlighted by the "crepitating lightnings" (p. 219), the masked figure *is* a Chester Gould drawing. Any concrete allusion, high or low, is a sign rather than a symbol. It suggests more than it specifically invokes by directing us back to what we should already know of Greek mythology, the Bible—or Chester Gould, whose open-ended cast of evil grotesques (Itchy, Shaky, Laffy, Mumbles et al.) complements Humbert's phenomenal vision of a world in which even his car limps and random characters are perceived as grotesques, projections of his shame and guilt and anguish, the "smothered memories" which he characterizes as "limbless monsters of pain" (p. 286). The masked visitor might have been Quilty; he exemplified "Trapp's type of humor," says Humbert—"Oh, crude and absolutely ruthless!"—a good description too of the violence and sadism of Gould's strip, a singular presence in the funnies of the forties. "Somebody, I imagined, was making money on those masks of popular monsters and morons," comments Humbert, expanding the context to include screenwriter Quilty's commercial realm. "Did I see next morning two urchins rummaging in a garbage can and trying on Jutting Chin? I wonder" (p. 219). The allusion to Tracy, more telling than it might at first appear, works so well because Humbert has been able to ransack Lolita's reading material for the appropriate image. Contemplating her accumulation of teentrash, he notes "that repulsive strip with the big gagoon and his wife, a kiddoid gynomide. *Et moi qui t'offrais mon génie*" (p. 256)* declaims Humbert, whose pairing of the *Kerry Drake* strip (a patent imitation of *Dick Tracy*) and that high-toned if bogus quotation compresses his sense of misery and our sense of the two cultures that clash in *Lolita*.

Humbert's scornfulness is not necessarily Nabokov's; as responsive as he is scholarly, Nabokov is often delighted by certain "funnies." "I get that from

---

* "And I was offering you my genius!"—an imitation of a nineteenth-century French Romantic poet such as Alfred de Musset.

LOOSE BOARDS! AN EXIT! SHE WENT TO HER CAR?

Jutting Chin, "white-glistening in the . . . darkness." The villains in the quiz-picture are: (front, left to right) The Brow, The Mole, Pruneface, Flattop (not to be confused with his son, Flattop, Jr., who appeared in 1956), Mrs. Pruneface, Little Face Finney, Mama and The Midget (a married duo); (rear) B–B Eyes (with cigar), The Blank, and 88 Keyes (with cigarette). Star pupils will recognize that The Blank, né Frank Redrum, was the source for a faceless character in *Batman* two years later (1939). (© 1974 Chicago Tribune–New York News Syndicate)

"The ranks of words were again so glowing": a cartoon by Otto Soglow, from *The New Yorker,* 1942. (© 1942, 1970 The New Yorker Magazine, Inc.)

my father, I suppose," says Nabokov, a wide-ranging critic of the cartoon genres. "Too many words," states purist Nabokov of Feiffer's work. "Wanting in draftsmanship," he complains of Steig. "The shmoos were his finest invention," he says of Al Capp and *L'il Abner.* Nabokov the literary anatomist also makes selective use of the cartoons and comic strips whose artistry he admires. No one, he laments in the Foreword to *Speak, Memory* (1966), "discovered the name [in the 1951 first edition] of a great cartoonist and a tribute to him in the last sentence of Section Two, Chapter Eleven. It is most embarrassing for a writer to have to point out such things himself" (p. 15). The tribute is to Otto Soglow, *New Yorker* cartoonist and creator of *The Little King* comic strip: "The ranks of words I reviewed were again *so glowing,* with their puffed-out little chests and trim uniforms . . ." (italics mine; p. 219). "Who will bother to notice," wonders Nabokov in the Introduction to the *Time* Reading Program edition of *Bend Sinister,* "that the urchins in the yard (Chapter Seven) have been drawn by Saul Steinberg" (p. xvii), whose "every curlicue," says Nabokov in conversation, is "invested with poetry." Not even Humbert can resist enjoying one of Lo's favorite strips, a "well-drawn sloppy bobby-soxer, with high cheekbones and angular gestures" (p. 167); the reference immortalizes Harry Haenigsen's *Penny,* a strip quite ignored in surveys of the genre.

Lolita's Americanization of Nabokov also freed him to use such "lower" materials less hermetically, with open affection, and *Pnin* (1957) and *Ada* (1969) demonstrate how these ingredients may emit as much resonance as any literary allusions. An 1871 Sunday supplement of the *Kaluga Gazette* in *Ada* "feature[s] on its funnies page the now long defunct Goodnight Kids, Nicky and Pimpernella (sweet siblings who shared a narrow bed)" (p. 6). Complemented by subsequent allusions to sibling behavior in Chateaubriand and Byron, the reference to an old French comic strip constitutes the novel's first allusion to the incest of Ada and Van. At the end of *Ada*, ninety-seven-year-old Van Veen describes how he "look[s] forward with juvenile zest to the delightful effect of a spoonful of sodium bicarbonate dissolved in water that was sure to release three or four belches as big as the speech balloons in the 'funnies' of his boyhood" (p. 570), a zest that speaks to Henry James's definition of the artist as someone on whom nothing is lost. Nabokov's uninhibited and imaginative responsiveness to the smallest components of the American scene is formulated by Joan Clements when she tries to relax a distraught Pnin by showing him a *New Yorker*-type cartoon picturing a shipwrecked sailor, an unfortunate choice inasmuch as it limns Pnin's own homeless condition:

"Impossible," said Pnin. "So small island, moreover with palm, cannot exist in such big sea."

"Well, it exists here" [said Joan].

"Impossible isolation," said Pnin.

"Yes, but—Really, you are not playing fair, Timofey. You know perfectly well you agree with Lore that the world of the mind is based on a compromise with logic."

"I have reservations," said Pnin. "First of all, logic herself—"

"All right, I'm afraid we are wandering away from our little joke. Now you look at the picture. So this is the mariner, and this is the pussy [he has saved], and this is a rather wistful mermaid hanging around, and now look at the puffs right above the sailor and the pussy."

"Atomic bomb explosion," said Pnin sadly.

"No, not at all. It is something much funnier. You see, these round puffs are supposed to be the projections of their thoughts. And now at last we are getting to the amusing part. The sailor imagines the mermaid as having a pair of legs, and the cat imagines her as all fish."

"Lermontov," said Pnin, lifting two fingers, "has expressed everything about mermaids in only two poems. I cannot understand American humor even when I am happy, and I must say—" He removed his glasses with trembling hands, elbowed the magazine aside, and, resting his head on his arm, broke into muffled sobs (pp. 60-61).

Although the content of the cartoon may have operated subliminally, Pnin's failure to comprehend it has succinctly rendered the stolidity of his mind as well as his temporary misery. Unlike Humbert's pairing of high and low oddments, the cartoon and Lermontov are not juxtaposed ironically; unlike *Bend Sinister*'s use and abuse of Etermon, the cartoon-engendered scene is ultimately sympathetic, though the drawing does serve to reveal something of Joan's silliness.

Bend Sinister's comic strip was a singular success, however, and for the next two years (1947-49), Nabokov assiduously avoided the American scene; the native locale of "Signs and Symbols" (1948), perhaps his best story of the decade, is almost invisible, and its principal accomplishment, a literally stunning trick ending, derives from an earlier story in Russian, "Perfection" (1932).[8] "Is not the setting down of one's reminiscences a game of the same order [as solitaire], wherein events and emotions are dealt to oneself in leisurely retrospection?" asked the narrator of "Time and Ebb" (p. 156), and Nabokov's major project of the late forties—the major product of *his* late forties—was his memoir *Conclusive Evidence* (1951, rewritten in Russian, 1954, and definitively expanded as *Speak, Memory*, 1966). In his Foreword to the 1966 edition, Nabokov says that the original title (= "conclusive evidence of my having existed") unfortunately "suggested a mystery story," a not altogether inappropriate genre (p. 15). An act of discovery rather than a retreat into Russia, *Conclusive Evidence* was the last work whose English he asked a friend to correct—in this instance Sylvia Berkman, his Wellesley colleague; finally at ease with the language, he was

ready to "use" America, whose roads and byways he had traveled each summer in search of butterflies and, as it turned out, *Lolita*. One hundred motel rooms in a score of states had helped to fill the vacuum of " 'That in Aleppo Once . . .'," though his diffidence had not been entirely overcome. Before commencing *Lolita* in 1949-50, he considered writing a novel about Siamese twins; Véra Nabokov dissuaded him—"The subject is too unpleasant!"—and he instead turned to nympholepsy. The discarded idea survives only in the story "Scenes from the Life of a Double Monster" (1950, pub. 1958), where his choice of a foreign setting underscores once more the difficulties he encountered even while composing *Lolita*. At one point, c. 1951, Véra had to rescue the unfinished manuscript from the lawn incinerator of their rented house in Ithaca.

Lolita was well under way in 1952, when "Lance" was published, and the discursive and patently authorial remarks Nabokov makes at the outset of his third "sci-fi" fantasy of the period define what he was then in the process of accomplishing in *Lolita*. Having looked into "science fiction" and rejected it, the narrator of the story notes how the genre's "clichés are, of course, disguised; essentially, they are the same throughout all cheap reading matter, whether it spans the universe or the living room. They are like those 'assorted' cookies that differ from one another only in shape and shade, whereby their shrewd makers ensnare the salivating consumer in a mad Pavlovian world where, at no extra cost, variations in simple visual values influence and gradually replace flavor, which thus goes the way of talent and truth" (p. 201). Anticipating one of the principal metaphors of Pynchon's Pop cosmos in *Gravity's Rainbow*, the allusion to Pavlov suggests that *émigré* Nabokov had now assumed control over the fields of stimuli which would ensnare Lolita, his "ideal consumer." "So the good guy grins, and the villain sneers, and a noble heart sports a slangy speech," continues the narrator (p. 201), assessing those American clichés and anticipating the life Nabokov will invest them with in *Lolita,* where the decade's "slangy speech" will receive its definitive treatment. "I am somewhat disappointed that I cannot make out her features," complains the narrator, speaking of Mrs. Boke, whose son Lance will take the first interplanetary space flight. "All I manage to glimpse is an effect of melting light on one side of her misty hair, and in this, I suspect, I am insidiously influenced by the standard artistry of modern photography and I feel how much easier writing must have been in former days when *one's imagination was not hemmed in by innumerable visual aids,* and a frontiersman looking at his first giant cactus or his first high snows was not necessarily reminded of a tire company's pictorial advertisement" (italics mine; p. 203). A prescient comment, given the fact that more than one American child would be dis-

appointed or bored by the first televised moon landing because they'd seen better adventures on *Star Trek.* The passage as a whole at once looks back to "The Refrigerator Awakes" and "Time and Ebb" and serves to chart Nabokov's own passage in *Lolita,* his outdistancing of sundry difficulties; the italicized phrase describes Lolita and Charlotte, or what Nabokov in *Ada* calls Marina Durmanov's "screen-corrupted mind" (p. 253).

Lolita was completed in the spring of 1954 and quietly published a year and a half later by the uninhibited Olympia Press in Paris. The product of fourteen years of observation, assimilation, and apprenticeship, the *émigré* writer's final citizenship papers, *Lolita* realizes an artistic goal that had been articulated by Nabokov ten years earlier in his discussion of *The Government Inspector:* "The whole play is (somewhat like *Madame Bovary*) composed by blending in a special way different aspects of vulgarity so that the prodigious artistic merit of the final result is due (as with all masterpieces) not to *what* is said but to *how* it is said—to the dazzling combinations of drab parts" (*Gogol,* p. 56). "A painful birth, a difficult baby, but a kind daughter," as Nabokov describes it, *Lolita* offers a dazzling assemblage of vulgar parts, a culmination of negative images, the movies in particular. The American cinema animates *Lolita* to the same extent that it forms Lolita herself and informs Nabokov's moral vision, his critique of mass culture.

Lolita at the Movies

Early in *Lolita*, the narrator recalls how young Humbert Humbert learned the so-called facts of life from "an American kid, the son of a then celebrated motion-picture actress whom he seldom saw in the three-dimensional world" (p. 13); the two dimensions of reel life, to recycle an old pun (as Humbert would), are a most pervasive reality in *Lolita*'s America. Humbert's unfailingly dim view of Hollywood is consistent with his characterization as a displaced European intellectual, a teacher and journeyman scholar whose touchstones are literary and artistic; however humorous it may be, Humbert's juxtaposition of *Kerry Drake* and the French "quotation" summarizes the cultural aspect of his deep misery. And "they call those fries 'French,' *grand Dieu!*" he exclaims (p. 131). Having unsuccessfully searched Europe for his lost Riviera love, "Annabel Leigh," Humbert finds her in America; but it is Lolita, not Humbert, who completes the seduction at The Enchanted Hunters hotel—a Lolita to whom "sex" is a mechanical, matter-of-fact charade. "Lambert Lambert," Humbert tells us, was one of the pseudonyms he considered for his memoir (p. 310), thus invoking the first name of Henry James's innocent ambassador to Europe, seduced by the charms of France. "You talk like a book, *Dad*," says Lolita (p. 116), playing her role in an inversion of James's *Daisy Miller* (1878); and their journey through America—in Jamesian terms a vast Schenectady—ironically reverses yet another nineteenth-century pilgrimage. In *The Innocents Abroad* (1869), Mark Twain tested European cultural artifacts and attractions against his own democratic ideals, and found Rome's Colosseum to be a pile of old rocks. Humbert's is a latter-day mock-grand tour, viewed through the dark prism of obsession and loss. Although he discovers "enormous Chateaubriandesque trees" (p. 147) and "Claude Lorrain clouds" (p. 154) and an "El Greco horizon in Kansas" (p. 155), these landscapes are peopled by creatures foreign to him in more ways than one. "You mean . . . you never did it when you were a kid?" asks Humbert's avatar of Poe's child-bride, kneeling above him at the fateful moment before their first intimacy. "Never," answers the hapless enchanted hunter (p. 135), and throughout *Lolita* his love for her, perversity notwithstanding, is contrasted with an ethic drawn from the two-dimensional realm of "Movielove" (p. 256).

Introduced on the novel's third page by that informative "American kid" and concluded only by Clare Quilty's death almost three hundred pages later, the movie motif functions as an elaborate extended metaphor, a negative image, or what used to be termed an ironic correlative, held in apposition to a veritable avalanche of allusions to the love poets of ancient and modern Europe. By having Lolita examined by a "Dr. Ilse Tristramson" (p. 200), Nabokov punningly compresses the novel's major network of literary allusions. Tristram's lovestruck "sons" are everywhere in *Lolita:* Dante, Petrarch, Ronsard, Belleau, Shakespeare, Goethe, Byron, Keats, Baudelaire, Browning, Verlaine, and Belloc, to name but a few. The principal sources of Humbert's allusive and least elusive quotations, paraphrases, and interpolations are Poe, Mérimée's *Carmen* (1845), and the Latin poets of Rome. Every time he intones "My Lolita" (and he does so on some thirty occasions), he is succinctly evoking Propertius, Horace, or Catullus writing of his faithless Lesbia: *"That* Lolita, *my* Lolita,"* elegizes a more expansive Humbert (p. 67), echoing a donnish translation of Catullus' *"Lesbia nostra, Lesbia illa."* Humbert has earned the right to identify himself with the Old World's poets of love. In the process of writing his American memoir and confession, Humbert the self-styled *"manqué* talent" (p. 17) has become an artist, and joined their company. His allusions are (to paraphrase Eliot) fragments shored against the ruin of a love ethic having nothing to do with pedophilia, Humbert's clinical malady.

Lolita's movie metaphor anticipates one of the signal chapters of Richard Brautigan's *Trout Fishing in America* (1967). Contemplating Hemingway's recent suicide and the vanished Indians and fur traders of Lewis and Clark's virgin land, the narrator remembers a winter he spent as a child in Great Falls, Montana, during World War II, when he saw a Deanna Durbin movie seven times ("Whatever it was about, she sang! and sang!"). Afterwards he sustained a fantasy that he would one day walk down to the frozen Missouri River and find it looking just like a Deanna Durbin movie, something that Meriwether Lewis would never have recognized.[9] Although not always as innocent and blandly wholesome as a Deanna Durbin opus, and surely no virgin land, Lolita's world *is* in many ways a movie, as Humbert is quick to realize. When he first sees Lolita, he parades before her, he says, in "my adult disguise (a great big handsome hunk of movieland manhood)" (p. 41). Shortly afterwards he notices that Lo has clipped an ad from a slick magazine, picturing a "haggard lover," jocosely designated by her as "H. H.," and has "affixed [it] to the wall above the bed, between a crooner's mug and the lashes of a movie actress" (p. 71). But, alas, once they get to know each other better, Humbert must admit that "to the wonderland I had to offer, my fool preferred the corniest movies, the most cloying fudge" (p. 168). "You see," says Charlotte Haze, "*she* sees herself as a starlet; *I* see her as a sturdy, healthy, but decidedly homely kid" (p. 67). Humbert's dream incarnate is of course Lolita; hers is Hollywood. That she will eventually prefer Clare Quilty to Humbert Humbert is the result of her "veritable passion" for Hollywood (p. 172), though no one would suggest that, from her point of view, a distinct moral choice is offered her. When Humbert calls Lolita "Carmencita," he is alluding to both Mérimée's enchantress and filmdom's first vamp, the "Spanish dancer" of the Gay Nineties who dazzled Kinetoscope viewers.

The highlight of Lolita's year-long cross-country tour with Humbert is a visit to Hollywood, where they see "the ugly villas of handsome actresses" (p. 159); observe "the roan back of a screen actress" at an expensive restaurant (p. 157); have a major row "on Third Street, Los Angeles, because the tickets to some studio or other were sold out" (p. 160); and visit Schwab's, the drugstore at which, legend has it, many stars were discovered. Lolita saves Humbert's bribe-money for a trip to Broadway or Hollywood (p. 187), and, in the poem Humbert writes after her disappearance, he lists "Profession: none, or 'starlet'" (p. 257). Ada's teenage "dramatic career" (p. 425) is clearly an abortive realization of Lolita's unfulfilled ambition. "Who is your hero, Dolores Haze? / Still one of those blue-caped star-men?" Humbert wonders (p. 258). She is steeped in Hollywood cosmology, and yearns "to climb Red Rock [in Elphinstone] from which a mature screen star had recently jumped to her death after a drunken row with her gigolo" (p. 212); it is in Elphinstone that Lolita will depart with *her* drunken gigolo, Clare Quilty (p. 249). "The Joe-Roe marital enigma is making yaps flap," notes Humbert, burlesquing a Walter Winchell–type gossip column in a movie magazine (p. 256). Lolita consumes vast quantities of such magazines, reading with "celestial trust" the articles, advertisements, and advice columns in *Movie Love* or *Screen Land* (p. 150), from the tale of "Jill, an energetic starlet who made her own clothes and was a student of serious literature" (p. 141) to the ads that ask her to "Invite Romance by wearing the Exciting New Tummy Flattener. Trims tums, nips hips" (p. 256). *Ada* also satirizes these magazines. The two "unwed" agents of Lemorio (= *l'amour*), a film comedian, have "lived as man and man for a sufficiently long period to warrant a silver-screen anniversary" (p. 513), and a photograph of Ada and Marina on a California patio is featured in *Belladonna*, the Antiterran edition of one of Lo's celestial journals (p. 428). After Lolita's departure, Humbert destroys a great accumulation of such teen trash. "You know the sort," he states confidently. "Stone age at heart; up to date, or at least Mycenaean, as to hygiene. A handsome, very ripe actress with huge lashes and a pulpy red underlip, endorsing a shampoo. . . . Tristram in Movieland. Yessir!" declares Humbert, summarizing his and Nabokov's attitude toward a vision of love distorted and coarsened in the crooked glass of Hollywood (p. 256).

It was "an innocent game on her part . . . in imitation of some simulacrum of fake romance," says Humbert of their first kiss at the hotel (p. 115), but it is a game that encapsules a certain aspect of some forty "innocent" years of American culture, beginning in the child-struck thirties. While there were many child performers in the twenties—Jackie Coogan in Chaplin's *The Kid* (1921), Hal Roach's *Our Gang* comedies, and Mary Pickford, a perennial child star—this curious and very American phenomenon reached its zenith of popularity during the thirties, concurrent with the Great Depression, the first major inroads of progressive education, and the dissemination of Freud's remarks on infant sexuality. Shirley Temple, as everyone knows, was the number one box-office attraction in 1935, displaced a few years later not by Clark Gable but by Mickey Rooney. Few movie-goers under the age of forty have any sense of the pervasiveness of those child performers. Nor would they recognize many of the names of the thirty-five or so famous child stars of the time, featured in film upon film, or the faces of the hundreds of rapidly aging children who poured through the casts of *Our Gang* (reissued on TV as *The Little Rascals*)—with some charm under Hal Roach's supervision, with considerably less at M-G-M—but all part of an open-ended family of tyrannizing tots that, for better or worse, enthralled audiences of all ages until the early forties.

Where film critics and historians have generally ignored the child stars, a certain kind of comic anthropologist has made the most—and least—of them. Nathanael West reduces their collective image in the person of Adore, a hopeful child actor in *The Day of the Locust* (1939). "If it weren't for favoritism," says Adore's mother bitterly, "he'd be a star. It ain't talent.

Mary Pickford, aged twenty-four, in *Poor Little Rich Girl* (1917).

It's pull. What's Shirley Temple got that he ain't got?" (p. 138). Adore appears, "dragging behind him a small sailboat on wheels. He was about eight years old, with a pale, peaked face and a large, troubled forehead. He had great staring eyes. His eyebrows had been plucked and shaped carefully. Except for his Buster Brown collar, he was dressed like a man, in long trousers, vest and jacket" (p. 139), a sad imitation of Freddie Bartholomew's sartorial splendor in *Little Lord Fauntleroy* (1936). The toy is an affecting touch, like Lolita reaching for a comic book from Humbert's wretched conjugal bed, or escaping his claws to go roller-skating. When Adore rolls his eyes back in his head and snarls, his grotesqueries fully communicate the pathos of his situation. "He thinks he's the Frankenstein monster," says his mother, correctly; and she is the manipulative Gothic Doctor's stand-in. Urged by her to perform, he renders "Mama Doan Wan No Peas," expertly imitating a blues singer (Jimmy Rushing's recording with Count Basie?):

> Mama doan wan' no glass of gin,
> Because it boun' to make her sin,
> An' keep her hot and bothered all the day

"The gestures he made with his hands were extremely suggestive" (p. 140), his voice carrying "a top-heavy load of sexual pain" (p. 141). After the applause, "Adore grabbed the string of his sailboat and circled the yard. He was imitating a tugboat. He tooted several times, then ran off" (p. 141).

Adore is a central detail in West's dark painting, an important bit player in a Boschian panorama of grotesques, a landscape of creatures crippled by their dreams of success in the cinema or paradise in California. They had hoped to enter, as it were, the left or central panels of Bosch's *The Garden of Delights* (c. 1500); but in *The Day of the Locust*, as in the right-hand wing of the triptych, monsters finally prevail. At the movie premiere which concludes the novel, Adore indeed becomes a little monster; he hits pathetic Homer Simpson in the face with a stone, and the maddened man, now himself a Frankenstein monster, punches and then stamps on the fallen child actor, precipitating a riot. "A pervert attacked a child," exclaims a woman with "snaky gray hair" (p. 183); her demeanor recalls the blonde woman at the center foreground of Weegee's TIME IS SHORT photograph (see above, p. 70). The ensuing chaos provides West's surrogate in the novel, Tod Hackett, with a completion for his blocked-out painting, *The Burning of Los Angeles,* if not a solution to his blocked sexuality. A cinematic version of the inflamed right panel of Bosch's triptych, Tod's canvas is the ultimate cleansing apocalypse, an artist's moral attack on the cancer of mass culture. The novel ends with Tod carried off in a police car, imitating the siren as loud as he can, paralleling the way Adore imitated a tugboat after performing his song. Tod Hackett has perished too, engulfed by the flames in his painting, his regressive sexuality and impotency ironically counterpointed by the boy's precociously "sexy" delivery and more appropriately childish noises.

Although she is poor, Adore's mother has managed to send him to one of Hollywood's many "talent schools." Less avaricious mothers all across America also squandered their hard-earned savings on behalf of tap-dance lessons for daughters they had cast in Shirley Temple's image. The illegitimate, supposedly mute child named Shirley T. in Eudora Welty's story "Why I Live at the P. O." (1941) yells her first words in "the loudest Yankee voice" the narrator has ever heard: "OE'm Pop-OE the Sailor-r-r-r Ma-a-an!" Leaden feet pound on the upstairs hall. " 'Not only talks, she can tap-dance!' calls [her mother]. 'Which is more than some people I won't name can do.' "[10] The aggressive vulgarity of Shirley T. reflects the mean and empty lives of the adults in the story—the Milky Way bars, casual *amours*, and mindless games (Casino and Old Maid) which sustain them.

Our own unstated figurative desire in response to a lengthy parlor performance by a professional child— *I'd like to kill that kid!*—is fulfilled by Flannery O'Connor, a West disciple, who literally attacks thirties-like "cuteness" in the title story of *A Good Man Is Hard to Find* (1955). The title, of course, refers ironically to the song, though this escapes younger readers and many university teachers. When the family stops at Red Sammy's lunchroom, the mother puts a coin in the nickelodeon, and little June Star goes out onto the dance floor and does *her* Shirley T. tap routine. " 'Ain't she cute?' Red Sam's wife said, leaning over the counter. 'Would you like to come be my little girl?' 'No I certainly wouldn't,' June Star said. 'I wouldn't live in a broken-down place like this for a million bucks!' and she ran back to the table." Readers as cold-blooded as the author may well feel that June Star meets her just reward at the hands of Bobby Lee and The Misfit, who later murder the entire family. An interesting book could be written about the child star phenomenon; the subject clearly deserves something better than the nostalgia-gossip pastiche it naturally invites. As an interlude in cultural history, it is anything but a sweet story.

Because West was an accurate reporter, Adore's mother is a typical figure. Tens of thousands of ambitious mothers besieged the Hollywood studios throughout the thirties, their untalented young properties in tow; few succeeded in placing them—in legitimate pictures, that is. Most of these disappointed stage mothers—and fathers—returned home, but others stayed on and doubtless helped to feed various furtive needs: the pornographic film market and the white slave traffic that flourished in Southern California during the thirties. In *The Day of the Locust* the elegant and cultured Mrs. Jenning, formerly a prominent silent screen star and now a high-priced procuress, shows *Le Prédicament de Marie* to her party guests. It is an "utterly charming" film farce in which all the male members of the household in question pursue buxom Marie, a servant; she in turn has Lesbian designs on the little girl of the family (pp. 74-76). Visiting California in 1941, his second year in America, Nabokov heard rumors of nympholeptic house parties hosted by outwardly solid citizens, the girleens supplied by "an agency" in Los Angeles, and surely these tawdry, darkly resonant tales were not lost on the creator of Humbert Humbert, whose eye for the significantly monstrous is as keen as Nathanael West's. After completing his Hollywood screenplay of *Lolita* (1960), Nabokov was asked to adapt *The Day of the Locust*. It would have been a fitting union: American Black Humor of the sixties, in fiction and film, owes much to *Lolita, Miss Lonelyhearts,* and *The Day of the Locust.*

Hollywood's grotesque and pitiful underground activities had their chaste equivalent in the very movies which had failed to employ those hopeful children, had indeed failed them in every way. The basic pattern for the most bizarre convention of these films was first suggested by a few *Our Gang* skits in the late twenties and then developed by Educational Studios's "Baby Burlesks," a shoddy series of cheaply made one-reelers that presented very young children in burlesques of the most famous adult stars of that era; the spectacle of child stars acting "grown-up" became a predictable, staple ingredient of many subsequent feature films; West's Adore is a transcribed observation rather than a fantastic creation. Shirley Temple's first roles were in the "Baby Burlesks"; the producer, according to his former sub-starlet, would punish naughty performers by putting them in a darkened, primitive ice box (he later served a prison term, but for other crimes). In *The Incomparable More Legs Sweetrick* (1931), Shirley, age three, does a Marlene Dietrich routine; shortly afterwards, in leopard-skin diapers, she played Jane to another toddler's Tarzan; but in *Captain January* (1936), she is out of the freezer forever—a mature star at eight. Cast as Starr, the adopted orphan daughter of bachelor lighthouse keeper Guy Kibbee, and wearing bell-bottomed pants after Ginger Rogers's example in *Follow the Fleet* (1936), Shirley does a whirling, tapping Astaire-Rogers song and dance number with Buddy Ebsen before a gang of his enchanted bachelor chums at The Sailor's Rest. "You can Can-Can at the Codfish Ball" sings Shirley, accentuating each "can" with a vulgar shake of her own. Applauding wildly, the nautical celibates would seem to be measuring her performance against their memories of pants-wearing Dietrich in *Morocco* (1930), Fred and Ginger's "Let Yourself Go" number in *Follow the Fleet,* or Ginger's "I'll Be Hard To Handle" routine in *Roberta* (1935), *her* trousered debut. In a subsequent scene aproned

Kibbee bakes her a birthday cake while comfy Shirley reads smugly, less a daughter than the wifely image in a latter-day women's liberation fantasy. C. Aubrey Smith and his troops and Sikhs are in her sway in *Wee Willie Winkie* (1937), which represents the zenith of Shirley's powers, or so thought movie reviewer Graham Greene in England, much to his and his editors' regrets. Jane Withers, age nine, impersonates Garbo in *Ginger* (1935); in *This is the Life* (1935), Jane's jaunty take-off on Dietrich's white tails and top hat in *Blonde Venus* (1932) achieves a high (or perhaps low) level of mimetic perfection. Playing Garbo and Gable in one of the many *Mickey McGuire* comedies from the early thirties, Shirley Jean Rickert (on loan from *Our Gang*) and Mickey Rooney are two wan and world-weary ten-year-olds, quite distant from *The Adventures of Tom Sawyer* (1876) and from the benign Booth Tarkington and Norman Rockwell children who exist only in our poor memory as the sole models for images of screen mischief. Rooney later played Huckleberry Finn (1939), but too late, since Huck's famous territory ahead, the initiate's dream of an unsullied West, would already seem to have absorbed the young actor and dissipated any vestiges of innocence; however, like Jay Gatsby, who gathered rather than lost illusions, Mickey's movie persona grew more innocent with age. Throughout most of *Strike Up the Band* (1940, directed by Busby Berkeley), Mickey only has eyes for swing music. "How would you feel, losing out to a snare drum?" complains lovestruck Judy Garland to a girl friend. Although Mickey and Judy are cheek-to-cheek by the film's finale, their lips never touch (Gatsby's dream of Daisy is equally chaste); they remain sibling pals to the end.

The willful asexuality of screen adolescents is an interesting contrast to the sexual charades indulged by the same stars when they resembled children. Production codes certainly inhibited the behavior of Mickey and Judy, but, as Leslie Fiedler has argued, adult sexuality in American literature (and, by implication, popular culture) is often rendered as a fearsome responsibility. Shirley Temple's first marriage in 1945 was much publicized, but her fans had been prepared for such a trauma earlier that year by *The Bachelor and the Bobby Soxer*, when Shirley downed her initial screen drink, eliciting newspaper headlines based on the assumption that *Bright Eyes*, *Captain January*, and *Wee Willie Winkie* had been all lollipops and animal crackers.

What seems implicit in even the sunniest of these screen satires is made explicit by the leering, demonic midget, dressed as a child, who lifts the curtain on the girls and winks lasciviously at the audience during Busby Berkeley's famous "Pettin' in the Park" number in *Gold Diggers of 1933*, and who later that year, in *Footlight Parade*'s "Honeymoon Hotel" number, is discovered by Ruby Keeler and Dick Powell under the covers of their nuptial bed ("Cupid is the night clerk / 'Neath the stars above / He just loves his night work / And we just love to love"). Wearing a baby bonnet and nightie, the midget is a mock-ardent bridegroom; forced from the bed, he crawls around the room. Finally ejected, he peers through the keyhole—a lucky witness to the primal scene?—then turns around, and once again winks at the voyeurs seated below him; what they don't see on the screen may be analogous to the rigid censorship of dreams, sterner than the production codes of that era. Equally salacious is a scene in *Stand-In* (1937), which featured Leslie Howard as Atterbury Dodd, a stuffy young banker and efficiency expert, ignorant about films, dispatched to Hollywood by the studio's financial bosses in New York City. An aggressive stage mother, daughter in hand, forces her way into Howard's hotel room. The seven-year-old girl does a seductive song-and-dance routine, much to the embarrassment of Howard, who throws them out; a little girl, he says, should be outdoors, playing in the California sunshine. And when *Our Gang*, having joined M-G-M's star-studded lot, stages a variety show to raise money for a needy neighbor (c. 1939) or, a few years later, does the same thing in behalf of the Red Cross, the female members of the cast vamp *à la* Harlow in an uncomfortably convincing manner, the realism heightened by the fact that theirs is an encapsulated world, a microcosm dominated by little people, if not children.

After W. C. Fields had accepted an assignment in a movie that was also to feature the precocious, scene-stealing Baby LeRoy—a star after nine months on this earth, a has-been at age three—a reporter asked Fields who his co-star would be. "Fellow named LeRoy, says he's a baby," answered Fields.

Whatever the intentions of the filmmakers may have been, these "Movielove" charades assume a distinctive life of their own. The performers are too expert, too talented; little Shirley, her lines and lyrics always memorized perfectly, was known as "one take Temple." When West's tiny Adore sings *his* song, "He seemed to know what the words meant, or at least his body and his voice seemed to know. When he came to the final chorus, his buttocks writhed and his voice carried a top-heavy load of sexual pain. . . . Then he grabbed the string of his sailboat and circled the yard. . . . 'He's just a baby,' Mrs. Loomis said proudly, 'but he's got loads of talent'" (p. 141). Except for the crudest low-budget films, the charades of the child stars seem to complement rather than burlesque adult behavior, as though the performers were adults alchemically reduced in size, as in Tod Browning's sci-fi horror film of the time, *The Devil Doll* (1936). The amorous midgets in the same director's *Freaks* (1932) were also an edifying spectacle to many movie-goers, despite the higher intentions of Browning, if not M-G-M producers and publicists; "THE STORY OF THE LOVE LIFE OF THE SIDESHOW," declared their ads, when

Our Gang's Miss Jean Darling in a 1929 publicity still.

"There is flirtation in the air. It is Harry Spear, all dressed up and making eyes at Mary Ann Jackson," stated the original caption for the 1928 *Our Gang* publicity still. "Greta Garbo and

John Gilbert have nothing on Mary Ann and Harry," reads the studio-prepared caption on the climactic still.

Overleaf:
Boys will be boys: "Chubby" Chaney kisses a Greta Garbo cut-out in the 1931 *Our Gang* two-reeler, *Love Business*, compressing the "Dream Factory" ethic. The film lovers on the left are Thelma Todd and Charley Chase, another Hal Roach comedy team. Pete the dog patiently waits, and little Dorothy De-Bora endures, in the spirit of the Pop song of the time, "Don't Fall Asleep" ("Don't fall asleep and dream you're Gable / Don't fall asleep, I'm young and able . . . Forget the charm of Greta Garbo / And keep your mind on me"). Although *Our Gang* helped set the pattern for such charades, the sequence is uncharacteristic of Hal Roach's Gang productions, which sometimes cleverly mocked the "cuteness" of the standard child-star fare. At M-G-M, however (post-1938), the Gang continually mimed the manner and content of their plastic Metro parents; *The Big Premiere* (1940), *Ye Olde Minstrels* (1941), *Doin' their Bit* (1942), and *Melodies Old and New* (1942) are typical. Even the titles sound "adult."

On preceding page:

Graham Greene seems to have been the first critic to discuss the eroticism of a (chaste) child performer, just as almost twenty years later he was the first *littérateur* to recommend an unknown novel entitled *Lolita*, published in Paris by the infamous Olympia Press. Reviewing *Captain January* in *The Spectator* (August 7, 1936), Greene wrote that "the latest Shirley Temple picture is sentimental, a little depraved, with an appeal interestingly decadent. Shirley Temple acts and dances with immense vigour and assurance [in photo], but some of her popularity seems to rest on a coquetry quite as mature as Miss Colbert's [in *Under Two Flags*] and on an oddly precocious body as voluptuous in grey flannel trousers as Miss Dietrich's" (*Graham Greene on Film* [New York, 1972], p. 92). Greene extended this line of discussion in a review of *Wee Willie Winkie*, remarking on her appeal to the "antique audience" within the film itself and the audience of "middle-aged men and clergymen" without. Published in *Night and Day* (I, October 28, 1937, 31), that review is omitted from the above volume, for certain legal reasons. As a "highbrow," Greene avoided most of the child-star features; *Wee Willie Winkie* was deemed worth a review perhaps because it was directed by John Ford, who had recently been acclaimed for *The Informer*. If Greene had seen more of these films he would have realized that such performances adhered to a convention, and he might have tempered his remarks about perverse intentions and audience response. In any event, lawyers for 20th Century-Fox and Shirley Temple sued for criminal libel (for the court's ruling, see the Appendix to *Graham Greene on Film*), the short-lived magazine folded, and guilty Greene fled England for Mexico, where—thanks to Miss Shirley Temple—he wrote *The Power and The Glory* (1940).

C. Aubrey Smith and Shirley Temple in *Wee Willie Winkie*.

Shirley and friends in *Wee Willie Winkie*.

Demonic Rockwell, or, Tom Sawyer and Becky Thatcher "go Hollywood": Mickey Rooney and Shirley Jean Rickert as Gable and Garbo in a *Mickey McGuire* comedy whose title has not been preserved.

Marlene Dietrich in Sternberg's *Blonde Venus*.

The "child" lifts the curtain on the girls in *Gold Diggers of 1933*.

Jane Withers in *This Is the Life*.

The teasingly translucent curtain in *Gold Diggers* prefigures the more serious voyeuristic games of Hitchcock et al.

"She should be out in the sunshine": Leslie Howard in *Stand-In*.

Freaks was re-released as *Nature's Mistakes*. A midget's marriage to a "normal" woman (Olga Baclanova)
who covets his money also had a certain crowd appeal ("Can a Full Grown Woman Love a Midget?"
asked the ads).[11] Audiences may or may not have had
a perverse taste for miniatures; such generalizations
are risky, and certain "miniatures" were obviously innocent enough: Laurel and Hardy as child stars,
scaled down against huge sets, playing their own
sons in *Brats* (1930)—and more than one baby-sitting
graduate student father, slumped next to a playpen
with a medieval Latin text in his lap, has found himself enjoying an innocuous old *Our Gang* short on TV.
Along with the Busby Berkeley dance extravaganzas,
the child-star feature films were the quintessential
escapist entertainment of the Depression era, and that
context is of course important.[12] Moreover, what is
"cute" to one generation of audiences is often laugh-
able to another.

But viewed today, those movies possess none of the
campy charms of Busby Berkeley; their vulgarity is
eerie and disquieting because it extends beyond the
screen into our own time and our own child-centered
culture of the moment. Humbert's terrible demands
notwithstanding, Lolita is as insensitive as children
are to their actual parents; sexuality aside, she demands anxious parental placation in a too typically
American way, and affords Nabokov an ideal opportunity to comment on the Teen and Sub-Teen

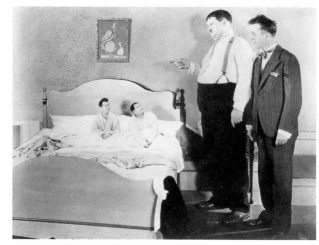

Laurels and Hardys in *Brats*.

The apotheosis of the child, c. 1929: *Our Gang*'s Joe Frank Cobb at his coronation. "Teenybopper is our new-born king," as Sonny and Cher would one day sing ("The Beat Goes On," c. 1967).

Tyranny. It is poetic justice that Lolita should seduce Humbert at The Enchanted Hunters hotel; the irony is obvious, but telling. Nabokov underscores his point with a resonant pun, characteristic of both himself and Joyce. The seduction takes place in the invented town of Briceland (note the *i* rather than *y*). Anyone over thirty-five should recall the popular weekly radio program of the forties, *Baby Snooks*, starring Fanny Brice. A satire rather than a residuum of the cinema's child stars of the thirties, the show featured only Baby Snooks, a sappy but demanding little girl of indeterminate age, who spoke a patois of baby talk and teen jargon, and her helpless, ineffectual Daddums (twice Humbert calls himself this). Year after year the program explored all but one of the various ways the tyrannical Baby Snooks could victimize her poor daddy and hold him in her sway. The town of Briceland is well named. Nabokov's book is Baby Snooks and Daddums in apotheosis.

Lolita is a Baby Snooks who, icon-like, dominates our scene, recalling the kingly image of *Our Gang*'s Joe Frank Cobb; Shirley Temple's reign in the thirties (Sikhs at her feet in *Wee Willie Winkie*, a totem doll in *Bright Eyes*, this chapter's frontispiece); and the film *Waterloo* in *The Day of the Locust*, where "the colors of the Lunenberg battalion, borne by a prince of the family of Deux-Ponts, were captured by a famous child star in the uniform of a Parisian drummer boy" (pp. 133-34), an ironic forecast of Adore's demise in the subsequent, less triumphant mob scene, an entire culture's Waterloo. Born too soon to partake of Woodstock, not to mention Dick Clark's TV *American Bandstand* of the fifties, Lolita and her friends look back to Baby LeRoy, and their cold joyless copulations with indefatigable Charlie Holmes in the bushes at "Camp Q" (= Quilty), by Lake Climax, connect the child star charades of the thirties with the "Movielove" shams of the forties.

To have each cabin at Camp Q "dedicated to a Disney creature" (p. 112) is a far more telling attack on calculated innocence and child-tyranny than, say, Pynchon's similar assault in *Gravity's Rainbow*. His "Zwölfkinder," a little country run by children, is a kind of German Disneyland, with a child mayor, a child city council, and child police.[13] No parent is admitted unless accompanied by a child, and at least one father indulges an incest fantasy at the *kinder*-controlled hotel. The entire sequence owes not a little to *Our Gang*, *The Day of the Locust*, and *Lolita*, obviously, and is even more indebted to John Wyndham's sci-fi novel *The Midwich Cuckoos* (filmed as *Village of the Damned*, 1960), in which a strange race of children threatens to take over the town and, by implication, the world. Because Pynchon, unlike West or Nabokov, savors prolixity, the comic point of Zwölfkinder is later dulled by a little girl's imitation of Shirley Temple, a grunted rendition of "On the Good Ship Lollipop" that echoes West's *Adore*. When the

The apotheosis of the child, 1941, a population explosion and the end of one era: *Our Gang* in a production number from their M-G-M short, *Ye Olde Minstrels*.

girl fails to respond to the obscene requests of the drunken crowd, her "stage-mother" gives her a public spanking drawn from the pages of Sacher-Masoch. The erotic exhibitionistic punishment inspires a wild mob orgy. As happens so often in *Gravity's Rainbow*, the ensuing rampant sadism clouds the issue, and the derivative scene degenerates in every sense of the word, dissipating the satire of Hollywood and Nazi Germany, too. Pynchon's inventiveness and use of detail, brilliantly displayed in his re-creation of wartime London, serves him poorly here, and a catalogue of wanton acts sacrifices art to pathology.[14]

Lolita stands alone among postwar American novels in its uncompromising yet controlled dramatization of the manner in which the iconography of popular culture forms or twists its consumers. Irvin Faust's *The Steagle* (1966) almost succeeds, but its far-ranging allusions (in time and kind) are uncontrolled and finally confusing. The Cuban missile crisis is just cause for his middle-aged professorial hero's regressive mobilization of old Pop fantasies, but the desperate man's post-adolescent immersion in *current* Pop culture—Eddie Fisher and Debbie Reynolds!—is rendered too ambiguously. Faust compromises his character fatally by oscillating between West's or Nabokov's cool posture and that of the riotous movie premiere crowd in *The Day of the Locust* that thinks it has glimpsed Gary Cooper but can't be sure (p. 183). Where *Gravity's Rainbow* frequently waxes nostalgic over the very Pop materials it would seem to be eviscerating, *Lolita* is consistently lucid and unambiguous, authoritative yet never strident. When Pynchon reverses Nabokov's trek through America and utilizes foreign Pop allusions in behalf of realism, as in the London sequences (Ambrose's dance band, Al Bowlly's vocals), the effect of his researches is winning. But his nostalgic, almost elegiac use of American references is often jarring because it contradicts his principal metaphor, which offers Pop as the circumscribing mythology of our hateful technological culture. A Pavlovian field of stimuli has early on ensnared Pynchon's hero, Tyrone (after Power?) Slothrop, stripping away his third dimension and determining his inevitable acquisition of Captain Marvel's identity and mantle, Plastic Man's resilient but clownish persistence. If *Gravity's Rainbow* were a more self-conscious artifice, like G. Cabrera Infante's *Three Trapped Tigers* (1965), a multi-layered Pop construct by way of Sterne, then Pynchon's affectionate and uncritical regard for these materials would be patently authorial and less distractive, a clearly discernible residuum of happy memories existing apart from the terrible events in the fiction.

No one should argue that a writer must be negative on the subject of mass culture, or rage against its immeasurable powers. The characters in Manuel Puig's excellent *Betrayed by Rita Hayworth* (1968) and *Heartbreak Tango: A Serial* (1969) are by definition far more thwarted by their mean culture than is middle-class Lolita or Pynchon's Harvard-educated Slothrop, yet Puig is as tender and compassionate as West, say, is bitter and angry. Although Westian Lonelyhearts columns are interpolated in *Heartbreak Tango*, neither the women nor their needs are seen as grotesque. Nourished by radio soap operas and romance magazines—the Argentinian versions of Gerty MacDowell's sentimental reading material in *Ulysses* —Puig's provincial dreamers are never reduced by authorial parody, the playfully managed serial form that embraces them. The heartbreak in his title is operative as well as funny, a rare achievement in the Pop-oriented novel, which so often patronizes its characters for their gullibility and/or stupidity. Puig, as the very fact of his novels suggests, has escaped his ruinous subject and milieu. Albert J. Guerard's eloquent autobiographical essay "Was Lia de Putti Dead at 22?" (1971) explores more directly a psyche's survival, the man and writer's creative evolution from the boy's indelible, far from unhealthy infatuation with a young screen star in the nineteen-twenties.[15] Most modern fiction, Puig's included, treats such phenomena in a less sanguine manner. Many of the mock-epigraphs which head the episodes in *Heartbreak Tango* are drawn from the silly songs taken seriously by its girls and women. "Blame That Tango" is one of the titles, and Puig does, in his gentle way. Easily misunderstood as camp, the epigraphs also serve as epitaphs, narrowing the distance between Puig and the more relentless writers—West, James M. Cain, Horace McCoy—who have etched acid nightmarish images of people lost to Pop culture.

The iconography of popular culture is not simply a matter of cosmetics and good or willfully bad grooming; it can be psychically crippling, a literally fatal "existential choice." Thurber's timid Mr. Bruhl studies up on his gangster hero, perfects his manner—" 'What's the matta you?' snarled Bruhl [at his wife and friends]. 'Ya bunch of softies' "—and is gunned down in the proper gangland style.[16] Life imitates art, and a cliché suits the subject. As a young hoodlum Joey ("Crazy Joe") Gallo fashioned himself after Richard Widmark's giggling, black shirt–white tie image in *Kiss of Death* (1947); twenty-five years later Gallo died violently in public at his pre-wedding dinner while enjoying a Show-Biz celebrity inspired by *The Godfather*'s success, shot in Technicolor by rival Mafiosi who, among other things, resented Gallo's media-created glamor (a book contract, actor friends, TV interviews). Musical comedy star Jerry Orbach delivered the eulogy at Crazy Joe's funeral. Lecturing on *Madame Bovary* at Cornell in 1953 (*Lolita* was nearing completion), Nabokov emphasized Emma's reading material and dwelt on each cliché. "*Stale romanticism!* Memorize those titles," he would warn in mock-donnish tones, "for they describe her sense of 'reality' (quotes, please, around that word)." ("Describe and evaluate the importance of Emma's reading preferences in *Madame Bovary*. Be specific," read one of the final exam questions.) The Emma Bovary who is poisoned by romantic prose and verse figures throughout Nabokov's *King, Queen, Knave* (1928), whose cardboard characters Franz and Martha also live outside of themselves, as it were, conceiving their love story in terms of a movie or pulp fiction plot. Their plan to toss cuckolded Dreyer from a rowboat parallels the central scenes in Dreiser's *An American Tragedy* (1925) and F. W. Murnau's film *Sunrise* (1927). "A coincidental resemblance," says Nabokov, "but a good one." Martha dies suddenly, *too* suddenly, infected by the cold and corny nature of their Pop murder plot rather than by any medically feasible chill. Her quick demise is also a judgment on the expectations of the old-fashioned reader. The pervasive, debilitating aura of popular culture is examined even more closely in *Lolita*.

The women in *Lolita*, the large as well as the little ones, are a product of the movies they have viewed. "First time I've seen a man wearing a smoking jacket, sir—except in movies, of course," says one of Lo's schoolmates (p. 191). Charlotte Haze, belonging to an earlier era and aspiring to a more European image, has "a shiny forehead, plucked eyebrows and quite simple but not unattractive features of a type that may be defined as a weak solution of Marlene Dietrich" (p. 39).[17] Furtively holding Lolita's hand while Charlotte drives the car, Humbert notices how "the wings of the driver's Marlenesque nose shone, having shed or burned up their ration of powder, and she kept up an elegant monologue . . . and smiled in profile, and pouted in profile, and beat her painted lashes in profile" (p. 53), her version of a stylized performance on the silver screen. "When you wanted me to spend my afternoons sunbathing on the Lake instead of doing my work, I gladly gave in and became a bronzed glamor boy for your sake, instead of remaining a scholar," says Humbert, whose heated verbal attack leaves Charlotte on her knees, shaking her head, clawing at his trousers. "She said I was her ruler and her god" (p. 93), a bit of hyperbole drawn, no doubt, from a popular novel or film. After Charlotte's accidental death beneath the wheels of a car, someone tells Humbert that Lolita's mother "was a celebrated actress killed in an airplane crash" (p. 191), an ironic tribute to her sundry histrionics and a blending of her death, her pale re-creation of Dietrich, and the actual fate of Carole Lombard, their contemporary.

Lolita and her friends, however, naturally draw upon the typical films of the forties and early fifties, and the unnatural vision they present of "corporate desire" (*Pale Fire*, l. 454)—a drab vision of sexuality divorced and dissociated from love, quite different from the very human eroticism communicated in the thirties by a Dietrich or a Harlow, or funned by Mae West. Although the stellar names are not given in the

Erotic comedy of the thirties: Mae West (above) in *Klondike Annie* (1936), burlesquing Anna May Wong—and the "Oriental" exotica of Dietrich. Tallulah Bankhead in *The Cheat* (1932, left), and Garbo as Mata Hari (p. 40). "I'm an Occidental woman in an Oriental mood for love," sings Miss West.

Joan Crawford in *Humoresque* (1947).

text, Lolita and her friends would have had as their female exempla the icy narcissistic perfection of Lana Turner, the porcelain features of Hedy Lamarr, the vacuous glamor of Linda Darnell or Rhonda Fleming, the plastic gambols of Betty Grable or Virginia Mayo, the grotesque "sexy" posturings of Jane Russell (*The Outlaw,* 1943) or Jennifer Jones (*Duel in the Sun,* 1947). There are exceptions, of course: Ingrid Bergman, too ladylike to enter this discussion, and Rita Hayworth, beauty redeemed by talent, both of them *hors de concours;* Bette Davis and Joan Crawford, "emasculators" who inevitably paid for their indomitable willfulness; Katherine Hepburn, a liberated sister who escaped such punishments; and Joan Bennett, Ida Lupino, Gloria Grahame, and Lauren Bacall, whose cool, tough, and sardonic acting styles looked back to the thirties, to Lombard, Hepburn, Jean Arthur, Ginger Rogers, Barbara Stanwyck, Rosalind Russell, Irene Dunne, and Myrna Loy—all clearly women, as opposed to objects, their performances often enlivened by wit, even when the films were not comedies. But Lolita and her friends derive their inspiration, such as it is, from the waxen mannequins of the subsequent decade, and the sexuality of these children, whether innocently mimed or mechanically performed, represents yet another charade; to grow up too quickly is perhaps never to grow up at all, and it is an old American story.

A comprehensive emblem for this aspect of *Lolita*

is a *trompe l'œil* painting by the American surrealist Man Ray, titled *Observation Time—The Lovers* (1932-34), picturing a huge pair of female lips filling a cloud-stippled sky as they float miraculously above a landscape.[18] Although the lips suggest two lovers coupling, their disembodied state simultaneously charts the distance separating love from lovemaking. Current college audiences admire Bogart in *The Maltese Falcon* (1941) because he doesn't seem to confuse the two and can turn in Mary Astor to the police. "That's cool, man," murmured at least one student, perhaps unaware that scenarist-director John Huston had shrewdly omitted Hammett's concluding scene, which reveals Sam Spade as a desperate, shoddy man, spurned by secretary Effie and seated at his desk, shivering. A week after seeing *The Maltese Falcon,* the same audience laughed derisively at Dana Andrews's unabashedly romantic, unconsummated love for Gene Tierney in *Laura* (1944), suggesting that sexual freedom is a mixed blessing. "You never did *it* when you were a kid?" asked Lolita (my emphasis), sounding a very contemporary note.

In his diary Humbert remarks his realization that he could kiss Lolita with impunity. "I knew she would . . . even close her eyes as Hollywood teaches" (p. 50). As a "modern child, an avid reader of movie magazines, an expert in dream-slow close-ups, [she] might not think it too strange" if "the glamorous lodger" were to take a few liberties, reasons Humbert

(p. 51), quite correctly, as he learns shortly in the most prolonged and explicitly sexual passage of *Lolita* (pp. 59-63). Their sprawling tomfoolery on the couch soon sends an unconcerned Lolita onto his active lap, and culminates three pages later with "the last throb of the longest ecstasy man or monster had ever known" (p. 63). "And nothing prevented me from repeating [the] performance," says Humbert (p. 64), but he doesn't repeat it; Lolita has gone out with a friend to another performance—a movie, naturally.

The movies viewed by Humbert and Lolita constitute a veritable survey course in the popular American product. In his diary Humbert notes that, on the previous evening: "Warm dusk had deepened into amorous darkness. The old girl [Charlotte] had finished relating in great detail the plot of a movie she and L. had seen somewhere in the winter. The boxer had fallen extremely low when he met the good old priest (who had been a boxer himself in his robust youth and could still slug a sinner)" (p. 47)—a paraphrase which conjures up images of John Garfield and a priestly Spencer Tracy or Pat O'Brien (*Fighting Father Dunne,* 1948). Amorous Humbert is not above taking advantage of a movie's aura, but at a "matinee in a small airless theatre crammed with children and reeking with the hot breath of popcorn," Gene Autry arouses but cannot assist an anxious Humbert:

The moon was yellow above the neckerchiefed crooner, and his finger was on his strumstring, and his foot was on a pine log, and I had innocently encircled Lo's shoulder and approached my jawbone to her temple, when two harpies behind us started muttering the queerest things— I do not know if I understood aright, but what I thought I did, made me withdraw my gentle hand, and of course the rest of the show was fog to me (p. 173).

American sites become movie sets: Humbert and Lolita visit "Antebellum homes with iron-trellis balconies and hand-worked stairs, the kind down which movie ladies with sun-kissed shoulders run in rich Technicolor, holding up the fronts of their flounced skirts with both little hands in that special way, and the devoted Negress shaking her head on the upper landing" (p. 158), Hattie McDaniel or Butterfly McQueen fluttering after Vivien Leigh in *Gone With the Wind* (1939). Sometimes a trite turn in the unfolding of Humbert's own story suggests to him the hack scenarist's easy solution: "With people in movies I seem to share the services of the machina telephonica and its sudden god," laments Humbert, in regard to the manner in which an irate neighbor's phone call interrupts "a strident and hateful" argument with Lo, allowing her to run out of the house and escape for the nonce (p. 207). Yet given the number of movies inflicted upon Humbert, it is remarkable that he isn't plagued by a myriad of movie spectres:

We took in, voluptuously and indiscriminately, oh, I don't know, one hundred and fifty or two hundred programs during that one year, and during some of the denser periods of movie-going we saw many of the newsreels up to half-a-dozen times since the same weekly one went with different main pictures and pursued us from town to town. Her favorite kinds were, in this order: musicals, underworlders, westerns. In the first, real singers and dancers had unreal stage careers in an essentially grief-proof sphere of existence wherefrom death and truth were banned, and where, at the end, white-haired, dewy-eyed, technically deathless, the initially reluctant father of a show-crazy girl always finished by applauding her apotheosis on fabulous Broadway. The underworld was a world apart: there, heroic newspapermen were tortured, telephone bills ran to billions, and, in a robust atmosphere of incompetent marksmanship, villains were chased through sewers and storehouses by pathologically fearless cops (I was to give them less exercise). Finally there was the mahogany landscape, the florid-faced, blue-eyed roughriders, the prim pretty schoolteacher arriving in Roaring Gulch, the rearing horse, the spectacular stampede, the pistol thrust through the shivered windowpane, the stupendous fist fight, the crashing mountain of dusty old-fashioned furniture, the table used as a weapon, the timely somersault, the pinned hand still groping for the dropped bowie knife, the grunt, the sweet crash of fist against chin, the kick in the belly, the flying tackle; and immediately after a plethora of pain that would have hospitalized a Hercules (I should know by now), nothing to show but the rather becoming bruise on the bronzed cheek of the warmed-up hero embracing his gorgeous frontier bride (pp. 172-73).

"The prim pretty schoolteacher arriving in Roaring Gulch":
Millard Mitchell and Helen Wescott in *The Gunfighter* (1950).

"The shivered windowpane," with a vengeance: *Jesse James*
(1939), a rerun favorite of the nineteen-forties.

Villain Ralph Morgan in the *Gang Busters* serial.

If Humbert has viewed typical naturalistic "story" musicals of the forties and fifties (daughter Kathryn Grayson or Jane Powell versus papa Lewis Stone), as opposed to reruns of the best lyric *dance* fantasies of the thirties, then he is correct, though it doesn't matter: his remarks are in character and are not always consistently those of Nabokov, who admits to having actually enjoyed a few Technicolor Westerns—"for their limpid landscapes"—and at least one gangster movie, genus *film noir* (more on which later). By definition hostile, Humbert's film criticism is not altogether unfair: the chase through underworld sewers mocks a convention abused by first-class directors (Fritz Lang's *While the City Sleeps*, 1956) as well as grade-C hacks (the acrid *Gang Busters serial*, 1942, and the *Falcon* series, which Nabokov viewed regularly with his young son Dmitri, c. 1943). Most important, that spectacular frontier fistfight looks forward to Humbert's considerably less acrobatic Western-style tussle with his cornered shadow, Clare Quilty (p. 301), while the staging of Quilty's death—a grand vaudevillian version of the movie gunplay of *King, Queen, Knave* and *Laughter in the Dark*—easily outdoes the "robust atmosphere of incompetent marksmanship" of any previous "underworlder." It is fitting and thematically consistent that Humbert's nemesis, the novel's most sinister presence, is in fact a specter from the movie world, who indeed pursues Humbert and Lolita from town to town with a far greater tenacity than those newsreels.

"My dear sir," Quilty tells Humbert, who is bent on destroying him, "stop trifling with life and death. I am a playwright. I have written tragedies, comedies, fantasies. I have made private movies out of *Justine* and other eighteenth-century sexcapades. I'm the author of fifty-two successful scenarios. I know all the ropes" (p. 300). Prior to checking out of The Enchanted Hunters hotel, Humbert has observed "a fellow of my age in tweeds" (Quilty) staring at Lolita as she sat in the lobby, "deep in a lurid movie magazine" (p. 140), and Humbert will later learn that Quilty's enticements, akin to Valentinov's overtures to Luzhin, included an offer to take her to "Hollywood and arrange a tryout for her, a bit part in the tennis-match scene of a movie picture based on a play of his —*Golden Guts*—and perhaps even have her double one of its sensational starlets on the klieg-struck tennis court. Alas, it never came to that" (p. 278). Quilty's unkept promise and its pornographic alternate at once represent a debasement of the novel's most wondrous scene, Humbert's own unrealized movie of it, and the enchantments of art cherished by Nabokov, who makes foul Quilty the victim of his irony, his scorn, and, in Part Two, Chapter Thirty-five, something even more lethal.

Shortly before she departs with Quilty, Lolita and Humbert play a tennis game which, to Humbert, is "the highest point to which I can imagine a young creature bringing the art of make-believe, although I daresay, for her it was the very geometry of basic reality" (p. 233). Admittedly "susceptible to the magic of games" (p. 235), Humbert and his creator in this scene (pp. 233-36) come as close as they ever do to depicting Lolita's ineffable charms, from her "gaspingly young and adorable apricot shoulder blades . . . lovely gentle bones, and . . . smooth, downward-tapering back" (p. 233), to the infinite grace of her game:

The exquisite clarity of all her movements had its auditory counterpart in the pure ringing sound of her every stroke. The ball when it entered her aura of control became somehow whiter, its resilience somehow richer, and the instrument of precision she used upon it seemed inordinately prehensile and deliberate at the moment of clinging contact. Her form was, indeed, an absolutely perfect imitation of absolutely top-notch tennis—without any utilitarian results. . . . I remember at the very first game I watched being drenched with an almost painful convulsion of beauty assimilation. My Lolita had a way of raising her bent left knee at the ample and springy start of the service cycle when there would develop and hang in the sun for a second a vital web of balance between toed foot, pristine armpit, burnished arm and far back-flung racket, as she smiled up with gleaming teeth at the small globe suspended so high in the zenith of the powerful and graceful cosmos she had created for the express purpose of falling upon it with a clean resounding crack of her golden whip.

It had, that serve of hers, beauty, directness, youth, a classical purity of trajectory, and was, despite its spanking pace, fairly easy to return, having as it did no twist or sting to its long elegant hop (pp. 233-34).

Humbert savors all the qualities of her game, which produce in him the "delirious feeling of teetering on the very brink of unearthly order and splendor" (p. 232): "the polished gem of her dropshot" (p. 235); the ease with which, "despite her small stature, she covered the one thousand and fifty-three square feet of her half of the court" and "entered into the rhythm of a rally"; the way "her overhead volley was related to her service as the envoy is to the ballade"—that is, as the concluding, summary postscript is to the stanza of the poem (p. 234).

By explicitly employing the vocabularies of poetics and music to describe the poetry of her play, Nabokov brings to mind Johan Huizinga's remarks on the "nature and significance of play." "Inside the play-ground an absolute and peculiar order reigns," writes Huizinga in *Homo Ludens* (1944). Play "creates order, *is* order. Into an imperfect world and into the confusion of life it brings a temporary, a limited perfection. Play demands order absolute and supreme. . . . The profound affinity between play and order is perhaps the reason why play . . . seems to lie to such a large extent in the field of aesthetics. . . . The words we use to denote the elements of play belong for the most part to aesthetics, terms with which we try to describe the effects of beauty." Humbert's key words and phrases complement Huizinga's statement: "elegance"; "balance"; "instrument of precision"; "rhythm"; "classical purity"; "unearthly order." Play, concludes Huizinga, "is invested with the noblest qualities we are capable of perceiving in things: rhythm and harmony."[19] On the tennis court, Lolita occupies a sphere whose innate harmonies are artistic, musical, timeless. "She would wait and relax for a bar or two of white-lined time before going into the act of serving," writes Nabokov in the sentence which opens the description of her game (p. 233). "At match point, her second serve, which . . . was even stronger and more stylish than her first, would strike vibrantly the harp-cord of the net" (p. 235). Humbert now realizes how, among other things, his own discordant coaching had failed Lolita,

not only because she had been so hopelessly and irritatingly irritated by every suggestion of mine—but because the precious symmetry of the court instead of reflecting the harmonies latent in her was utterly jumbled by the clumsiness and lassitude of the resentful child I mistaught. Now things were different, and on that particular day, in the pure air of Champion, Colorado, on that admirable court at the foot of steep stone stairs leading up to Champion Hotel where we had spent the night, I felt I could rest from the nightmare of unknown betrayals within the innocence of her style, of her soul, of her essential grace (p. 235).

Their game is interrupted, however, by two new tennis players (Quilty's friends), Bill Mead and Fay Page ("Maffy On Say"), who is, inevitably, an actress (p. 236). For Humbert the game is in several senses over; Quilty will soon spirit Lolita away. When Humbert is called to the telephone, Quilty himself appears, and forms a new game: "From the . . . terrace I saw, far below, on the tennis court which seemed the size of a school child's ill-wiped slate, golden Lolita playing in a double. She moved like a fair angel among three horrible Boschian cripples" (p. 237).

Early in the novel, Humbert says, "If I close my eyes I see but an immobilized fraction of her, a cinematographic still, a sudden smooth nether loveliness, as with one knee up under her tartan skirt she sits tying her shoe" (p. 46; Lolita's pose recalls any of several paintings of "nymphets" by Balthus). As he describes her tennis, he can only mourn his failure to preserve that Champion scene: "Idiot, triple idiot! I could have filmed her! I would have had her now with me, before my eyes, in the projection room of my pain and despair! . . . That I could have had all her strokes, all her enchantments, immortalized in segments of celluloid, makes me moan with frustration. They would have been so much more than the snapshots I burned!" (pp. 233, 234). Like Valentinov's filmic re-creation of Luzhin and Turati's extraordinary chess game, Quilty's "movie picture" *Golden Guts* would clearly have been something less splen-

did, at best a trivialized version of Humbert's magical vision—and at worst the lurid reality of Quilty's cinematic plans, which ironically underscores the corruptness of at least one scenarist. Instead of Hollywood, Lolita briefly endures Quilty's Duk Duk Ranch, where he tries to enlist her services in one of his pornographic home movies. Lolita "refused to take part because she loved him, and he threw her out" (p. 278).

The two contrasting movies "double" one another, as do Humbert and Quilty, and wordplay underscores their relationship: "That absurd intruder had butted in [to the game] to make up a double, hadn't he, Dolly?" says Humbert, punning unintentionally (p. 238). "There are no 'real' doubles in my novels," protests Nabokov, who loves *Dr. Jekyll and Mr. Hyde*. Yet his own practices in this area are in the spirit of Gogol's *The Nose*, a comical variant of the Gothic theme in which the vagrant proboscis, resisting definition like ethics itself, refuses to stay put and behave as it should. Although the Humbert-Quilty relationship finally parodies the neatly divisible Good and Evil selves in a Poe or Dostoevsky *Doppelgänger* fiction,[20] the doubling of their films is straightforward and singularly unambiguous. Moral and aesthetic perspectives cohere, as ideally they should: the scenarist's sexuality, dissociated from love and naked in every way, degrades its objects, while the artist's obsession, transformed by love and humanized by language, rescues its subject, and, one would hope, the readers who had anticipated in *Lolita* "the copulation of clichés" (p. 315). Nabokov is for once didactic, and Humbert's tennis "movie," preserved only in prose, is a sensuous recording of visual and aural delights.

That Champion scene is not Humbert's sole cinematic revery, venture, or game. During the course of *Lolita* the reader should be able to see Humbert's obsessional lust metamorphose into genuine love, a redeeming feature absent from Stanley Kubrick's 1962 movie version. But Nabokov recognizes that no less than Charlotte and Lolita is the reader a product of the best-sellers he has read, the poor films he has seen; the considerable distance between narrator and author is narrowed when Humbert toys with such readers. Humbert's and Lolita's first kiss was "an innocent game on her part" (p. 115), but the perverse game that is played with the reader is wise and serious indeed. To insure that readers understand *Lolita* as a novel about love (insofar as one can say that any complex work of art is finally "about" one discernible, reducible element), Nabokov structures it as a kind of anti-pornographic novel and film: only the first *thirteen* chapters of Humbert's "confession," allegedly written in prison, are truly erotic, and the trickster's signal number is a reader's unlucky omen. Patterned on the 1933 introductory materials provided *Ulysses* by Morris L. Ernst and Judge John M. Woolsey, the Foreword by John Ray, Jr., Ph.D., allows for the

book's "controversial" nature—a titillating prospect— but the *coitus interruptus* suffered by young Humbert and his girleen on the Riviera also augurs poorly for common readers (p. 15). Humbert is soon rehearsing (all too succinctly?) his shoddy, unsatisfactory encounters with nymphet-like prostitutes in Paris:

an asthmatic woman, coarsely painted, garrulous, garlicky, with an almost farcical Provençal accent and a black mustache above a purple lip, took me to what was apparently her own domicile, and there, after explosively kissing the bunched tips of her fat fingers to signify the delectable rosebud quality of her merchandise, she theatrically drew aside a curtain to reveal what I judged was that part of the room where a large and unfastidious family usually slept. It was now empty save for a monstrously plump, sallow, repulsively plain girl of at least fifteen with red-ribboned thick black braids who sat on a chair perfunctorily nursing a bald doll. When I shook my head and tried to shuffle out of the trap, the woman, talking fast, began removing the dingy woolen jersey from the young giantess' torso; then, seeing my determination to leave, she demanded *son argent*. A door at the end of the room was opened, and two men who had been dining in the kitchen joined in the squabble. They were misshapen, bare-necked, very swarthy and one of them wore dark glasses. A small boy and a begrimed, bowlegged toddler lurked behind them. With the insolent logic of a nightmare, the enraged procuress, indicating the man in glasses, said he had served in the police, *lui*, so that I had better do as I was told. I went up to Marie—for that was her stellar name—who by then had quietly transferred her heavy haunches to a stool at the kitchen table and resumed her interrupted soup while the toddler picked up the doll. With a surge of pity dramatizing my idiotic gesture, I thrust a banknote into her indifferent hand. She surrendered my gift to the ex-detective, whereupon I was suffered to leave (pp. 25-26).

The interlude is purposefully reminiscent of the "raw life" offered in cheap French *policiers,* old American pulp fiction (remember *Spicy-Adventure?*), and, to move higher in a Darwinian manner, the postwar Italian "neorealistic" cinema (also parodied in *Pnin,* p. 86). Humbert is humanized by his pity, but what of the readers whose gross appetites have only been stirred by the grotesque *mise-en-scène?* That enticing "theatrical curtain" and the procuress's "trap" describe Nabokov's principal sleight-of-hand trick in *Lolita.* By surrendering *son argent,* Humbert escapes, but the reader who wants to see more has had his expectations parodied by Nabokov. "I do not know if the pimp's [photo] album may not have been another link in the daisy chain," says Humbert (p. 26); it is definitely one of several sexual "visuals" that are promised but then withheld. Instead of an accelerating novel-length crescendo of explicitly sexual scenes, each topping the previous ones as to novelty and brio, the subsequent bits and pieces from Humbert's tantalizing diary (pp. 42-57) only set up the reader-viewer for the next chapter, which concludes the arousing aspects of *Lolita.* The remainder of Hum-

bert's narrative is diminuendo, a word that lends itself to an obvious but relevant pun.

"I want my learned readers to participate in the scene I am about to replay," says Humbert (p. 59), inviting the audience into his peepshow for the lap scene. Casting the reader as voyeur, Humbert carefully sets up and unreels the sequence as though he were like Quilty a scenarist and filmmaker, a *metteur-en-scène:* "Main character: Humbert the Hummer. Time: Sunday morning in June. Place: sunlit living room. Props: old, candy-striped davenport . . . Mexican knickknacks," and a prop named Lolita (p. 59). "Pity no film has recorded the curious pattern, the monogrammic linkage of our simultaneous or overlapping moves," he parenthetically remarks about their good-natured struggle for possession of a magazine (p. 60), prefiguring a similar, more urgent regret he will voice further on in regard to the unfilmed tennis scene (p. 234). The "simultaneous moves" of Humbert's orgasmic grappling with the unconcerned child seated on his lap (p. 63) constitute the most overt "sex" exhibited in *Lolita* and an anti-climax, considering what does not happen later. Unlike Quilty, Humbert will never again produce such a scene. "And nothing prevented me from repeating a performance that affected her as little as if she were a photographic image rippling upon a screen and I a humble hunchback abusing myself in the dark," says Humbert (p. 64), anticipating the kinds of pleasures available to any audience of one of Quilty's "underground" pornographic films; the image of the hunchback adumbrates Nabokov's use of the grotesque, the manner in which Humbert, the self-styled ape and hairy spider, expresses his moral recoil from his repugnant obsession. The performance is not replayed, of course; the procuress's curtain has been lowered for the duration of the novel, the pimp's album will remain firmly closed, and the groupings and gropings filmed by Quilty at Duk Duk will remain in the can, to use a movie man's argot.

Quilty "was a complete freak in sex matters, and his friends [at the Duk Duk Ranch] were his slaves," says Lolita (*How so? How so?* we wonder). As for the movie: "Oh, weird, filthy, fancy things. I mean, he had two girls and two boys, and three or four men, and the idea was for all of us to tangle in the nude while an old woman took movie pictures," Lolita tells Humbert (p. 279). Poor girl; he had promised her a part in *Golden Guts*, his Hollywood tennis opus. Pity too the reader who wants to see Quilty's Duk Duk film; it is not "shown" in any further detail. The action (so to speak) at Nabokov's Duk Duk is mainly linguistic, as it is throughout most of *Lolita; duk,* as gentle scholars know, is an obscene Persian word for copulation. Nabokov has effected an infinite regress of broken promises, and those interstices must be filled in by the reader, whose Duk Duk footage is not necessarily artistic. The shaping of Humbert's pain and one's sense of the bliss of eroticism and the burden of obsession in no way depend upon sexual exhibitionism. Tennis replaces copulation in Humbert's pages, tracing the course of *his* transcendence, at least. No wonder Nabokov made public his horrified reaction to William Woodin Rowe's enthusiastic dissection of the sexual "symbolism" in Nabokov's work, Lolita's wondrous tennis game in particular: " 'Wickedly folded moth' suggests 'wick' to Mr. Rowe, and 'wick,' as we Freudians know, is the Male Organ. 'I' stands for 'eye,' and 'eye' stands for the Female Organ. Pencil licking is always a reference to you know what. A soccer goal hints at the vulval orifice (which Mr. Rowe evidently sees as square). . . . No less ludicrous is his examination of Lolita's tennis and his claim that the tennis balls represent testicles (those of a giant albino, no doubt)," writes Nabokov,[21] an enraged Humbert firing pointblank at an academic Quilty or John Ray, Jr. In the *Lolita* screenplay (1960), Dr. Ray is scheduled to talk to a women's club "on the sexual symbolism of golf" (p. 15).

Movie-maker Quilty also doubles, quite clearly, the desires of those disappointed "learned readers" (p. 59) who, ignoring Humbert's sorrowful warning—"I have only words to play with!" (p. 34)—had nevertheless hoped for the replaying of a good many "sexy" scenes. Teasingly located at the start of the affair, but never repeated, these explicit passages and scenes formulate the reader-viewer's voyeuristic prurience. On *Lolita*'s last page, his fictive life ebbing, Humbert's voice becomes strangely distant and authorial: "And do not pity C. Q. One had to choose between him and H. H., and one wanted H. H. to exist at least a couple of months longer, so as to have him make you [Lolita] live in the minds of later generations" (p. 311). Quilty, then, might have been the author, and one wonders how many readers, denied further access to Humbert's diary, have unconsciously wished that Quilty *had* narrated *Lolita*, and that his movie had formed the body of the narrative, the bodies *in* the narrative. "The mirrors of possibility cannot replace the eyehole of knowledge," writes Nabokov in "The Assistant Producer" (1943), his most cinematic fiction.

Nabokov's trope limns what has always been the cinema's basic or base appeal, the vantage point which allowed unspoiled audiences of *Suspense* (1912) to share and enjoy the prowler's keyhole view of a nursemaid and child, a perspective reversed when the "baby" looks through the keyhole in *Footlight Parade*'s "Honeymoon Hotel" sequence. The pornographic peepshows that grace current "Adult Entertainment" parlors are only an extension of the first American box-office hit, *The May Irwin–John C. Rice Kiss* (1896), Vitascope's fifty feet of torrid film known

From *Suspense*.

May Irwin and John C. Rice in *The Kiss*.

simply as *The Kiss,* drawn from the stage play *The Widow Jones* and condemned by contemporary clergymen as "a lyric of the stockyards." "HOW THE PUERTO RICAN GIRLS ENTERTAIN UNCLE SAM'S SOLDIERS" declared a Mutoscope ad, c. 1895 ("Drop Payment in Slot—Keep Turning Crank to the Right"). The Mutoscope appears in *Ulysses,* after Bloom, a humble cuckold, has abused himself in the semi-darkness, provoked by the image of another nursemaid, Gerty MacDowell, who is lame. "A dream of wellfilled hose. Where was that?" wonders Bloom. "Ah, yes. Mutoscope pictures in Capel Street: for men only. Peeping Tom. Willy's hat and what the girls did with it. Do they snapshot those girls or is it all a fake?"[22] Joyce's sense of cinema is both prescient and historically precise. The exploding fireworks which mark and mock Bloom's orgasm, Joyce's visual equivalent of Gerty's Pop reading material, anticipate a latter-day movie cliché. The sartorial, fetishistic touch refers to *Willy's Hat* (1897), a Mutoscope offering deemed too racy for regular release ("men only"); and Joyce would expect his readers to remember that the original Tom, who peeked at Lady Godiva, was struck blind for his "crime." Joyce's psychology is accurate, too, for the voyeur's excitement is in part predicated on the discovery, shame, and punishment he would risk and endure. Far from being a mere display of ingenuity, the lengthy parody of Gerty's trash-infested sensibility establishes the poor quality of the pin-up on display, a joke at Bloom's expense; Gerty's limp is a resonant metaphor. Bloom notices her affliction only after he has masturbated and the stationary, exhibitionistic object has come to life, risen, stepped out of his frame (or screen) and limped away into the encroaching night. "O!" he thinks, and the exclamation point is as expressive as Joyce's succinctness. "Poor girl!" The quotient of her humanity complicates the situation, the one-way circuit of voyeurism: "Glad I didn't know it when she was on show."[23]

Mack Sennett, whose fortune was not built on slapstick alone, transported this peep-show ethos to the conventional movie house, but with a crucial difference: his Bathing Beauties, a passel of *September Morns* (or animated *poshlost'*), cavort alone on the screen in Sennett's cleverly respectable bourgeois version of the strip-tease. In his most representative Bathing Beauty scenes (c. 1918) there are no males present to break the dream-free circuit of audience identification and participation. The dark eyes of Sennett's garlanded nymphs are fixed on the audience: they smile and wave at our fathers and grandfathers, and invite them in for a swim. They disrobe, they gambol, they splash (children, don't laugh at their suits). Out of the sea, they change their clinging wet togs behind a coyly curtained blanket—*Gold Diggers of 1933* updates the image, *Lolita* uses it too—or peel behind a large striped beach umbrella, which begins to spin, faster and faster, its vortex filling the screen, an abrupt comic distancing that reasserts the gestalt's flat, rectangular surface and reminds our somnolent dreamy forebears that screen eroticism is artifice. The girls cease (if not refuse) to be objects, and the audience—Bloom's brothers or cousins—must readjust its sights. Sennett's teasing is humorous, naive, but it anticipates the more complicated procedures and perceptions of sophisticated artists such as Joyce.

Max Beerbohm's well-known caricature of Henry James at a keyhole (c. 1910) may have been correct about the passional life of the author of *The Sacred Fount* (1901), but it missed the point by localizing a general condition. Except, possibly, for the Soviet Union and the People's Republic of China (where socialist realism remains puritanical), movie-going, if not reading, is by definition voyeuristic, and Nabokov's assaults on audience expectations have several contemporary analogues. The voyeuristic protagonists of Alfred Hitchcock's *Rear Window* (1954), *Vertigo* (1958), and *Psycho* (1960), a trilogy of sorts, perversely complement and comment upon audience psychology—the deep needs and desires that may or may not be fulfilled in darkened theaters. "These new films are not like the old ones," complains the murderous narrator of Julian Symons's *The Players and the Game* (1972). "Though I liked *Psycho*, that was good. The shower cabinet, the blood running away. And there is one called *Peeping Tom*, which sounds as if it should be good"—a reference to Michael

The audience as voyeur: James Stewart in *Rear Window*.

The screen world: the courtyard set in *Rear Window*.

Powell's 1960 film, whose homicidal photographer is an all too explicit manifestation of the dark undertones of *Rear Window* and *Vertigo*.[24]

Rear Window, the center of the "serious" or "moral" Hitchcock as first put forth by Claude Chabrol and Eric Rohmer in their *Hitchcock* monograph (Paris, 1957), is by far a more obviously telling and nastier film than *Psycho* or *Vertigo* because James Stewart is presented as a "normal" fellow. A news photographer with a broken leg, he eases his boredom by spying on the activities of his neighbors in the apartment building across the courtyard. Because James Stewart is after all James Stewart (fresh from his triumphs in Anthony Mann-ly Westerns), the audience is slow to recognize the character as a Peeping Tom. By profession a passive witness, an invader of privacy, a dispassionate recorder of mayhem and misery (the apartment is decorated with his photographs of violent events), Stewart is psychically as well as physically immobilized; he recoils from his fiancée, Grace Kelly, preferring the variegated scenes caught in his telescopic viewfinder. If his point of view represents the audience's perspective, then the apartment world into which he peers is, as has been suggested, a correlative for the screen world; each window reveals— and conceals—a *donnée* for a feature film, from Honeymoon Farce to Murder Melodrama. When the wife-murderer across the yard learns of Stewart's presence and invades his apartment, Hitchcock is attacking an audience as well as an actor. "What do you want of me?" asks the killer (Raymond Burr), with surprising poignancy, as he looms in the doorway, and Stewart defends himself with the tools of his trade: flashbulbs. What, indeed, *do* readers and viewers really want?

Because his needs and fears and traumas are so complicated, one hesitates (briefly) before claiming that James Stewart's role in *Vertigo* is also an extension or reflection of an audience's experience. Formerly a detective (a professional voyeur), Stewart has retired from the police force because of acrophobia (fear of heights). Hired by a wealthy former friend to shadow his stylish blond wife Madeleine (Kim Novak), the sexually passive Stewart falls in love with her from afar, despite the fact that Madeleine appears to be a suicidal schizophrenic (only recently, thanks to R. D. Laing, has this become attractive). At first Stewart's behavior may not seem strange; as in *Rear Window*, Hitchcock quietly casts Stewart against his usual screen persona and the audience's sense of Our Jimmy's affecting shyness. His infatuation with a glamorous but cold image—they have not yet spoken—is an emblem of the one-way circuit of screen eroticism, however electric; it is no accident that Stewart, a dangerous somnambulist, continually drives on the wrong side of a two-lane highway. When he follows Madeleine to a cemetery, Hitchock's fog filter creates an explicitly dreamlike ambience, analogous to the film-viewing experience itself.

Kim Novak is literally a performer within the film: Madeleine is only pretending to be the wife, and her neurosis and "suicide" midway through the movie are staged in behalf of a plot to murder the real wife, with Stewart as the gulled witness. After Stewart rescues Madeleine from a "suicide attempt" in the bay, he takes her home, undresses the unconscious woman, and puts her to bed. He doesn't call her "husband" immediately; like an audience, or an onanist, he wants the image for himself. But Hitchcock denies the audience any view or suggestion of Stewart's deportment in that crucial scene; her underwear, however, is prominently displayed (after what fact?), and the audience's frustration is equal to Stewart's furtive needs, underscored by his coy first conversation with Madeleine after she regains consciousness, all perversely managed by Hitchcock. Barbara Bel Geddes, who pines for Stewart, designs brassieres; and empty brassières, rather than breasts, are featured in the first half of *Vertigo*, as a psychological *mise-en-scène* and a booby-trap for viewers who had expected to see more of Kim Novak.

Some time after her seemingly successful suicide, Stewart meets Madeleine's "double," Judy, a common red-haired working girl, played by Novak, of course, whose garish crimson lipstick clashes with her

Symbolic action on the set of *Vertigo:* Hitchcock manipulates Judy (Kim Novak).

cheaply dyed hair. Their new relationship is stranger yet, and *Rear Window*'s "What do you want of me?" resounds. Voyeurism is replaced by fetishism and, as Hitchock told Truffaut, "a form of necrophilia."[25] Performance is once again the operative word: Judy must pretend not to know Stewart, who pretends she is Madeleine and literally directs *her* performance in that role. Like another sick man, Humbert by name, who tried to re-create a live creature in the image of a dead girl (his lost Riviera love), Stewart remakes Judy in Madeleine's image (clothes, hair, *no, not that way; please stand over there*). Novak's woodenness as an actress is for once an asset; Stewart and his scheming friend variously create her to suit their needs, just as Hollywood—mogul Harry Cohn in particular—tried to make poor Kim Novak into Rita Hayworth when the latter refused to perform. The mental sets formed by screen eroticism are rigid enough, for Stewart prefers coolly contained Madeleine to Judy's beguiling bra-less state, a telling touch predicated on one's having perceived the earlier fetishistic details (breasts as *things,* an American tale familiar to all adolescents disguised as men). Stewart's transformation of Judy's common but sensual vitality into a vision of his dead love (a glamorous but illusory being) telescopes and comments upon the psychology of audience fantasizing, the process through which women become "Kim Novak" (or whatever) by virtue of cosmetics and/or their partners' cranial cinema, producing a dead love indeed. Stewart overcomes his acrophobia but loses the girl, in a meaningfully terrifying scene: Madeleine/Judy plunges from the bell-tower in a lethal re-enactment of her mock-suicide; illusions *are* reality in their ability to destroy us, as Humbert proves.

"What do you want of me?" is a question asked by any popular entertainer. Of late audiences have enjoyed Technicolored orgies of gore, as *Ada's* "canny" film director Victor Vitry demonstrates by retaining the pleasing footage of the accidental decapitation in his movie version of Veen's *Letters from Terra* (p. 581). Hitchcock's *Frenzy* (1972) is structured with such needs in mind. In the opening scene an attentive London crowd (an audience), dapper director Hitchcock among them, swiftly abandons a pompous, knighted government propagandist in order to peer down at a naked female corpse afloat in the Thames. A graphic and grisly on-screen rape-murder whets appetites further, but when the most important and sympathetic victim is lured to the killer's apartment, Hitchcock literally closes the door in the audience's face. With an excruciating slowness, the camera tracks silently away from the door, down the staircase, through the building's front door, and into the street. The effect on the frustrated viewer-voyeur is truly stunning: the killer's teasingly inscrutable window and the prosaic, disquieting façade of the building mask—and reveal—far more than the vicious-

ness of one psychopath. Because *Frenzy* is not *Letters from Terra* or Sam Peckinpah's *Straw Dogs* (1971), Hitchcock's screen is a *tabula rasa* for the nonce, onto which the audience must project *its* vision of violence, if that is its pleasure. "The Master of Suspense" (a dreadful, misleading cliché) highlights the audience's moral suspension. Anthony Perkins's motel peephole in *Psycho* is a signal image: the absence of *erotic* on-screen violence after the famous shower murder of Janet Leigh (in itself a deceptive, teasing *tour de force* of film cutting, analogous to the "sex" exhibited early in *Lolita*), manipulates the audience in unexpected ways.

Where *Psycho* ends with a psychiatric explanation, *Frenzy* stops short with an impersonal image of the crime itself, rather than a dramatization of the expected violent confrontation between betrayed friend and cornered criminal, thus denying a frenzied audience its "catharsis" (to employ the controversial, muddy term of the apologists for screen violence—a catch-word whose meaning classicists now hotly dispute). Reversing the previous tracking movement away from the door, the final shot is a close-up of the empty steamer trunk intended for the latest corpse, a *tabula rasa* of another sort—an empty anti-ending, a refusal to explain human behavior definitively. This suggests that Hitchcock (or scenarist Anthony Shaffer) has learned from Hitchcock's disciple Chabrol's *Landru* (1962), in which the wife-murderer's motives remain mysterious, in film-fiction as well as life; from novelist-theorist-filmmaker Robbe-Grillet; or from Nabokov, whose *Eye* (1930, the Russian title, *Soglyadatai*, means "the spy"), *Despair* (1936), *The Real Life of Sebastian Knight* (1941), *Lolita* (1955), and *Pale Fire* (1962) parody the classic detective tale, the rational genre which supposes that "clues" will lead one to the truth (in the fullest sense) and that once the criminal is identified the closed little world of the story will be rid of malevolence and mystery. These two words describe the universe of the thriller in literature and film, as well as G. K. Chesterton's "The Absence of Mr. Glass" (1914), the important Father Brown shaggy-dog detective story that, by mocking the locked-room mystery cycle created by Poe ("Murders in the Rue Morgue," 1841), prefigures the techniques which reverse the Conan Doyle/Agatha Christie formulas. Witness *The Erasers* (1953), Robbe-Grillet's novel-length upending of *Oedipus Rex,* the first detective tale. Or the way the hapless detectives at the end of John Hawkes's *The Lime Twig* (1961) set out through the rainy gloom to discover "the particulars of this crime"—which is impossible, since the literal murderer is a horse, and the truly killing factor, sexual revery, cannot be outlawed. Or the disappearance of the cornered title criminal at the anti-ending of *The French Connection* (1971—*Point Blank,* 1967, revisited and simplified); he escapes, however illogically, because he is, finally, an evil force rather than an individual man. Or *Lolita,* whose magically resilient incarnation of evil, Detective Trapp (Quilty), also resists bullets, refusing to surrender to the reader his or killer Humbert's ultimate *raison d'être* or literary "meaning."

Not by chance did Hitchcock, one-time employer of Thornton Wilder and Raymond Chandler, telephone Nabokov from London during the winter of 1970, before he had signed Shaffer to turn Arthur La Bern's *Goodbye Piccadilly, Farewell Leicester Square* into *Frenzy.* "Yes, *of course* I know who you are, and I admire your work," Nabokov told Hitchcock, whose modest self-introduction was predicated on the assumption that a "highbrow" artist—another active child of 1899—would be ignorant of his existence. Hitchcock wanted Nabokov to do an original screenplay, but Nabokov declined because he was committed to *Transparent Things* (1972), a ghost story and eschatological thriller that employs many of the devices of the "suspense" and "mystery" genre and ends violently, with the principal question—*what,* after death?—left unanswered. "Actually, I've seen very little Hitchcock," says Nabokov, "but I admire his craftsmanship. I fondly recall at least one film of his, about someone named Harry" (*The Trouble with Harry,* 1955). Why did Hitchcock think to ask him for a scenario, ten years after Nabokov's sole screen effort for Kubrick? "Oh, his *humour noir* is akin to my *humour noir,* if that's what it should be called," answered Nabokov. "Perhaps there are other reasons, too. I don't know. Do you?"

A "hole" early in the narrative line of Robbe-Grillet's *The Voyeur,* published the same year as *Lolita* (1955), anticipates *Frenzy* (and, in a way, *Vertigo*) by also omitting the crucial scene in which a young girl has been tortured and murdered by, it would seem, a strange, itinerant traveler named Mathias. The vexing ellipsis is psychologically consistent with a psychopath's mental erasures or evasions, but since a sadistic killer is by definition no longer a voyeur, Robbe-Grillet's title may well allude to those readers who feel cheated by that "hole." No such complaints may be made about Robbe-Grillet's most cinematic performance, *Project for a Revolution in New York* (1970). Revolting in many ways, a vertiginous projection of very private needs in public places, Robbe-Grillet's scenario extends the idea of audience manipulation by monstrously developing the keyhole perspective of the bonneted midget in *Footlight Parade*'s "Honeymoon Hotel" number, leaving *The Kiss, Suspense,* and even *Psycho* far behind. "The first scene goes very fast," writes Robbe-Grillet in the opening paragraph. "Evidently it has already been rehearsed several times: everyone knows his part by heart"—everyone, that is, except the reader, whose part can be played in a number of ways. The other parts are drawn from the stock footage of detective thrillers and the greasy pages of pulp fiction and what paperback blurb-writers call "Modern Erotic Classics" (mad medicos, mysterious implementa, dames in chains). Foreign film distribution rights are sold, the narrator's house is outfitted with concealed movie cameras, and violent political, criminal, and sexual fantasies are activated before our eyes. A range of shifting masks—or serial selves—reveals, qualifies, and withdraws forbidden fields of vision and terrible, definitive self-knowledge. The "go-between" (as he is called) in all these underground activities is ubiquitous Ben-Saïd; at one point he enlists the narrator in criminal activity. A protean, Quilty-like presence and potential cameraman at the Duk Duk Ranch, Ben-Saïd also appears as the reader's agent: a near-sighted and bald little locksmith-voyeur, kit in hand, to whom all keyholes are "orifices," the central link in an unholy alliance between author, characters, and readers. Private eyes all, they are ill equipped to perceive what they think they have seen, but, as in *Lolita* and *Frenzy,* perhaps shocked into self-knowledge by the sense imposed on them of what they had hoped to see.

Chabrol dramatized this process in *A Double Tour* (1959, freely translated as *Leda* for its American release). In one intimate scene, the audience watches the bikini-clad maid walk languorously around her bedroom; the pleasure is ours as well as hers; she is the granddaughter, as it were, of one of Sennett's nubile Bathing Beauties. When the camera moves

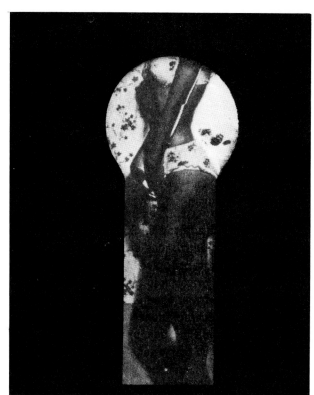

From *A Double Tour.*

back to frame her in the keyhole and then cuts to outside the door, where she is also being viewed by the family's son (who is among other things a murderer), one may feel uncomfortably crowded, trapped and compromised—unassailable evidence that critic-director Chabrol, unlike Truffaut, has truly appropriated *auteur* Hitchcock's course.

Hitchcock's most apt pupil, however, is Brian De Palma, whose bloody *Sisters* (1973) extends the voyeuristic concerns of *Rear Window*, *Vertigo*, and *Psycho*, yet is interesting enough to stand on its own considerable merits. *Sisters* is a teasing title inasmuch as there is only one, a homicidal schizophrenic Siamese twin whose sibling died after the operation which separated them. The machinations of the plot do not lend themselves to brief paraphrase, but the film's opening sequence, involving a TV game show called *Peeping Toms*, summarizes the argument here. Based on the *Candid Camera* premise, the program's logo is a giant keyhole. Television, newspapers, and magazines share the brunt of the director's assault on the persistent and insatiable needs of an audience. Readers have a "morbid fascination" with Siamese twins, says a *Life* magazine journalist in *Sisters*, and a film-within-the-film's documentary footage about the history of such "freaks" cleverly feeds that fascination, which proves to be fatal: the doctor who operated on the twins and is obsessed with the surviving sister is killed by his own maddened creation, the object of his darkly troubled desires. An accessory to crime and a voyeuristic presence in the early part of the film, the sinister doctor is clearly intended to be an evil twin in his own right, the activated alter-ego of the viewer, who may not be too willing to see the resemblance. Blindness, the fate of the legendary Peeping Tom, is De Palma's controlling metaphor, and the conclusion of *Sisters* offers an anti-ending in triplicate: a police detective, a reporter, and a private eye are variously frustrated and immobilized, cut off from "the truth" even as the criminal is apprehended.

By structuring *Claire's Knee* (1970) as an anti-thriller, Eric Rohmer (Chabrol's co-author of *Hitchcock*) also suggests that Hitchcockian suspense techniques are not divorced from content, as some critics have maintained. Rohmer's erotic comedy is composed of public parts: talk, narcissistic posturing, un-realized promises of sexandviolence (Claire's sullen, jealous boy friend), spurious suspense (*When will our hero grab the knee, and what will happen then?*), more talk, inaction, anti-climax. *That's all? That's what we've waited for this long?* complained several trapped red-blooded consumers, unwilling to recognize or accept eroticism as a state of mind (its principal locus of reality, alas). *Claire's Knee* is of course a droll title. Like Dr. John Ray's foreword to "Lolita, or the Confession of a White Widowed Male"—taken seriously by many readers—it serves as a mock come-on, a morally resonant parody of "sexy" movie titles and randy publicity campaigns.

In a witty 1948 essay on *The Outlaw* (which aco-lytes Chabrol and Rohmer surely read), André Bazin views its "technique of provocation" as Howard Hughes's "outrageous trick" on the audience as well as on the censor who had long delayed the film's re-lease. Bazin points to the disparity between its posters —Jane Russell with lifted skirts and generous décol-leté—and the film itself: breasts alone, but not even at their best, a decorous handkerchief placed wherever too much cleavage might show, creating a neutralized zone akin to *The Voyeur*'s narrative gap, Hitchcock's *tabula rasa*, Claire's isolated knee. "It was the censor-ship that turned it into an erotic film," states Bazin. Cinematographer "Gregg Toland must have had great fun lighting the throat of Jane Russell, scrupulously focusing on that milk-white patch barely hollowed by a shadow, whose mere presence had the frustrated spectators dithering with resentment,"[26] the same dis-appointment as that suffered by those readers, learned and otherwise, who put down *Lolita* because of Hum-bert's willful reticence. "FINALLY, at last, after a 3 year delay, you can *see*," proclaims a famous *Outlaw* ad and poster, as though a miracle were in the offing.

Like Hitchcock, Robbe-Grillet, Rohmer, and Chabrol at their best (Howard Hughes is not yet an *auteur*), Nabokov carefully sets up his audience for severe letdowns, drawing too on its previous training, its indiscriminate immersion in trash, a helpless condition inasmuch as trash and *poshlost'* are everywhere —a subliminal presence, an invisible virus. Supremely self-conscious literary artists have been done in by base materials. Robbe-Grillet's *La Maison de rendezvous* (1965) aspires to transmute the exotica of pulp fiction yet reads like Sax Rohmer revisited, a chic rearrangement of cheap furniture, and Hitchcock typifies the ways in which our best popular artists have unconsciously succumbed to *poshlost'*. "Dali is really Norman Rockwell's twin brother kidnapped by gypsies in babyhood," writes Nabokov in *Pnin* (p. 96), and Dali's overwrought dream-decor is in part responsible for the blatantly "Freudian" nature of Hitchcock's *Spellbound* (1945)—as opposed to the director's no less Freudian but brilliantly realized incest nightmare, *Shadow of a Doubt* (1943), whose excellence is in part due to scenarist Thornton Wilder's sure hand and on-the-scene advice. Nabokov, however, has been able to exercise tight control, injecting his doses of trash sparingly as preventative medicine employed to the advantage of the work and its game with the reader.

"This is only a game," says Humbert (p. 22). "We're all playing games," says the mad narrator of *The Players and the Game*, a perfect example of the way popular genres (crime thrillers, sci-fi) have self-consciously expropriated "highbrow" modes. "Do you know who I am?" asks Symons's narrator. "I'm Bela Lugosi." No, says his companion ("Bonnie Parker"), he is Dracula. "She was absolutely right. . . . Dracula's played a different game, a sex game, with other people, but here sex does not come into it."[27] This describes *Lolita*'s tantalizing "sex game" with "other people" (its readers), foreplay but no coitus, a game that allows Nabokov to highlight his major themes: the limitations of language, the nature of love and loss, and the deathly *cul-de-sac* of nostalgia—a theme especially relevant to our present condition. Maurice Sendak's large collection of Mickey Mousiana suggests that nostalgia may be an energizing and creative force, but in most cases the cult of nostalgia is an index of contemporary despair and desperation. Recent magazine articles on "nostalgia" collectors have featured several unintentionally terrifying photographs. One pictured a Lana Turner devotee seated in a windowless room, a Gothic playpen whose walls and ceiling were completely papered with Lana images; another exhibited the premier Mickey Mouse collector in his attic retreat surrounded by every Mickey icon and toy known to man or boy—nostalgists snug in the regressive morgue or womb of popular culture, "drunk on the impossible past" (to quote Humbert).

Reunited at last with a pregnant, veiny-armed, far

from nymphic Lolita, Humbert realizes "that I loved her more than anything I had ever seen or imagined on earth, or hoped for anywhere else" (p. 279). After interpolating the lyrics of "Little Carmen" early in the novel, Humbert had parenthetically added his own conclusion: "Drew his .32 automatic, I guess, and put a bullet through his moll's eye" (p. 64). When wan Mrs. Schiller (Lolita) conclusively refuses to return to Humbert, "I pulled out my automatic—I mean this is the kind of fool thing a reader might suppose I did" (p. 282). Only the literal-minded reader who has in mind Humbert's hints and the denouement of *Carmen,* or, more likely, the reader nurtured on a lifetime of "Little Carmens"—of pulp fiction, Pop songs, and "Movielove" melodramas—would believe, in spite of everything Humbert has said, that he would nonetheless kill *this* Lolita, *his* Lolita. Humbert's biting rhetorical trap has dispatched that reader to Quilty's party, *Lolita's* purgatory, a way station for the trash-afflicted reader and indiscriminate movie-goer who believes that sentimentalized violence, predictable by virtue of Pop conventions, is truly the heart's revenge. "It never even occurred to me to [shoot her]," adds Humbert. " 'Good by-aye!' she chanted, my American sweet immortal dead love," he elegizes, no longer a Horatian poet *manqué.* Experiencing a pain and despair far removed from the "grief-proof sphere of existence" of his Hollywood, he drives away "through the drizzle of the dying day,

with the windshield wipers in full action but unable to cope with my tears" (p. 282).

Quilty's is obviously a prophetic hobby; his "private movies" at the Duk Duk Ranch limn yet another genre, one that became public enough a decade after *Lolita's* American publication. Had Quilty survived, he might easily have become such an *auteur* as the director of the recent X-rated *Homo on the Range* ("All-Male Ranch Movie" read the marquee at Chicago's Bijou, 1972), or *Ada's* "brilliant" Victor Vitry, or Russ Meyer—or, worse yet, one of those directors who pretentiously couple their imaginative combinations of characters in the soft-focus, slow-motion name of art. Asked for his opinion of director Tony Richardson's 1969 film version of *Laughter in the Dark,* Nabokov addressed himself to this subject:

I was appalled by the commonplace quality of the sexual passages. I would like to say something about that. Clichés and conventions breed remarkably fast. They occur as readily in the primitive jollities of the jungle as in the civilized obligatory scenes of our theatre. In former times Greek masks have set many a Greek dentition on edge. In recent films, including *Laughter in the Dark,* the pornograpple has already become a cliché though the device is but half-a-dozen years old. I would have been sorry that Tony Richardson should have followed that trite trend, had it not given me the opportunity to form and formulate the following important notion: theatrical acting, in the course of the last centuries, has led to incredible refinements of stylized pantomime in the presentation of, say, a person eating, or getting deliciously drunk, or looking for his spectacles, or making a proposal of marriage. Not so in regard to the imitation of the sexual act which on the stage has absolutely no tradition behind it. The Swedes and we have had to start from scratch, and what I have witnessed up to now on the screen—the blotchy male shoulder, the false howls of bliss, the four or five mingled feet—all of it is primitive, commonplace, conventional, and therefore disgusting. . . . The lack of art and style in those paltry copulations is particularly brought into evidence by their clashing with the marvellously high level of acting in virtually all other imitations of natural gestures on our stage and screen. This is an attractive topic to ponder further and directors should take notice of it.[28]

Nabokov might also have said that the new freedom on the no-longer-silver screen is rampant *poshlost'*, or posh lust, as Humbert might say, and in *Ada*, published shortly after the release of Richardson's film, Nabokov mocks both literary adaptations and the screen's nude freedoms. Ada appears in *Don Juan's Last Fling* as the gypsy girl whom the dashing Don rescues, somewhat anticlimactically:

The Don rides past three windmills, whirling black against an ominous sunset, and saves her from the miller who accuses her of stealing a fistful of flour and tears her thin dress. Wheezy but still game, Juan carries her across a brook (her bare toe acrobatically tickling his face) and sets her down, top up, on the turf of an olive grove. Now they stand facing each other. She fingers voluptuously the jeweled pommel of his sword, she rubs her firm girl belly against his embroidered tights, and all at once the grimace of a premature spasm writhes across the poor Don's expressive face. He angrily disentangles himself and staggers back to his steed (p. 489).

Ubiquitous, versatile Quilty—lecturer, pornographer, and playwright ("I have been called the American Maeterlinck")—clearly anticipates a wide range of current types, from highbrow aestheticians of trash to starlets on TV talk shows ("I'd only undress if the story called for it and it was, like, dignified, you know?"). Clare Quilty is clearly expendable.

In addition to concluding the novel's main parodic themes,[29] the killing of Quilty (Part Two, Chapter Thirty-five) also lays to rest the movie motif. Searching for Quilty's "ancestral home [on] Grimm Road" (p. 293) the night before the execution (Chapter Thirty-four), Humbert drives along "a narrow winding highway," past a "series of short posts, ghostly white." In front of him, "like derelict snowflakes, moths drifted out of the darkness into my probing aura. At the twelfth mile, as foretold, a curiously hooded bridge sheathed me for a moment and, beyond it, a white-washed rock loomed on the right . . . I turned off the highway up gravelly Grimm Road. For a couple of minutes all was dank, dark, dense forest. Then, Pavor Manor, a wooden house with a turret, arose in a circular clearing. Its windows glowed yellow and red" (p. 294). Nabokov's description clearly cries out for an illustration by Gustave Doré or Moreau, or, even better, Charles Addams. At the end of the brief chapter, after "casing" Quilty's manor, Humbert passes a drive-in cinema: "In a selenian glow, truly mystical in its contrast with the moonless and massive night, on a gigantic screen slanting away among dark drowsy fields, a thin phantom raised a gun, both he and his arm reduced to tremulous dishwater by the oblique angle of that receding world,—and the next moment a row of trees shut off the gesticulation" (p. 295). The raised gun foreshadows Quilty's death and looks back twenty-three years to a like moment in *Laughter in the Dark* (p. 20), the prefiguration of Albinus's fate. Both gesticulations mimic the devices of bona fide thrillers. In James M. Cain's *Double Indemnity* (1936), for example, insurance agent Walter Huff intends to base a murder alibi on his presence at *Gun Play*, a movie whose title predicts his own death and the unexpected gunplay which ruins his plan—and him. Unlike that in *Laughter in the Dark* and, of course, *Double Indemnity*, the gunplay in *Lolita* is comical. That gigantic screen, as ludicrous as it is "mystical," serves as a summary image, a kind of tombstone for Quilty, who dies, as it were, as he has lived, receding into the world he has created, reduced by parody. "I could not help seeing the inside of that festive and ramshackle castle in terms of 'Troubled Teens,' a story in one of her magazines, vague 'orgies,' a sinis-

ter adult with penele cigar, drugs, bodyguards," says Humbert (pp. 294-95).

Your Home Is You is one of Charlotte Haze's essential volumes, and Pavor (= Latin; "fear" or "panic") Manor is the mock-Symbolic obverse of her Good Housekeeping Seal of Approval. House-wrecker Nabokov funs many of the familiar, staple ingredients found in Gothic novels from Walpole's *The Castle of Otranto* (1764) to Bram Stoker's *Dracula* (1897). A thunderstorm accompanies Humbert on the way to Grimm Road, but when he reaches Pavor Manor, "the sun was visible again, burning like a man"—a nod to the opening scene of F. W. Murnau's *Nosferatu* (1922)?—"and the birds screamed in the drenched and steaming trees," like the horror-film cockatoos in *Mad Love* (a 1935 Hollywood version of *The Hands of Orlac*) and *Citizen Kane*'s seaside Gothic jungle (1941), a "Germanic" import twice removed inasmuch as that jungle is back-projected footage from *Son of Kong* (1933), an analogue to Kane's monstrous ego. "The elaborate and decrepit house seemed to stand in a kind of daze, reflecting as it were my own state," says Humbert, invoking Poe's crumbling House of Usher (p. 295).

Miasmic Pavor Manor's portentous ambience and disarrayed innards burlesque a number of other structures: a "symbolic" medieval setting in Maeterlinck, or one of Quilty's own Maeterlinck- or Lenormand-influenced plays; Hollywood's prefabricated, *poshlye*

"The house was like a spectre": the conventional, crumbling German Expressionist castle as depicted in *Chronicles of the Grey House* (1925), a House Horrible ideal for numberless Hollywood films.

houses of horror, or their source, German Expressionist melodrama as produced at the famous UFA studio. "I detested the heavy-handed German Gothic cinema," says Nabokov, a Berlin resident for fifteen years (1922-37).

We saw many of those films in the twenties—all trash except for the one about the downfall of a very grand doorman [Emil Jannings in Murnau's *The Last Laugh*, 1924]—and *The Hands of Orlac* [1925, directed by *Dr. Caligari*'s Robert Wiene]. That was wonderful, with Veidt and Fritz Kortner, whom I met in London after he had bought an option on my *Camera Obscura*. By then an exile from Nazi Germany, Kortner was a gifted artist and a very homely man—ideal for those films!—whose homeliness disappeared when you were with him, dissolved by the delightfulness of his person. I remember perfectly certain scenes in *Orlac*: the nocturnal train crash in which the concert artist [Veidt] loses his hands—steam, smoke, infernal confusion—and the "executed" murderer's unexpected return, his broken neck bolstered by a terrible brace, his face masked, mechanical claws in place of the hands that have been grafted onto Orlac's maimed limbs. That was wonderfully macabre and bizarre.

Nabokov seems unaware of the degree to which *Orlac* influenced Hollywood's sci-fi and horror films of the early thirties. "But most of those German films were awful, and imitations of them are even worse," adds Nabokov, whose conversations are as forceful as his formal, carefully written out published interviews.

His book of interviews and articles is titled *Strong Opinions* (1973).

The Germanic *Stimmung* ("mood") of *The Last Laugh, The Hands of Orlac,* and other German films distinguished by their chiaroscuro (if not their plots and performances) is visually evident in many of Nabokov's novels, from *Mary* (1926) and *Laughter in the Dark* (1938) through *Lolita.* Nor has he been completely immune to the contents of those "awful" films. *The Golem* (1914, 1920), *Homunculus* (1916), and Fritz Lang's *Metropolis* (1927) are the most famous of a cycle of German films that dealt with the creation of a synthetic being. Maria, the beautiful human-like robot who is graced by artificial flesh in *Metropolis,* is the most perfect of such creatures, and Martha, in Nabokov's *King, Queen, Knave* (1928), is her unnatural sister. Throughout the novel her husband Dreyer negotiates mysteriously with a nameless Inventor in regard to the production and possible merchandising of automated store mannequins. Rather than employ the homunculus idea for thrills and chills, or as a critique of science, Nabokov uses it as an ironic foil. The Inventor does not exhibit samples of his automatons until almost the end; in essence, however, they have been present all along, in the persons of the novel's morally dead characters (all of whom are German). When the Inventor produces the female robot of the species, it doesn't work properly,

Conrad Veidt in *The Hands of Orlac.*

which is logical as well as just, since Martha herself is an imperfect robot. Alienated from organic creativity, morbidly fearful of childbirth (her contraceptive implementa are a horrific presence), movie fan Martha will never beget an heir or, on Nabokov's part, a *Son of Martha* sequel. She expires rather than dies, a spent machine akin to the destructive but finally self-annihilating automatons of medieval legend, nineteenth-century Gothicism, and the horror/sci-fi films which were then so popular on the German screen. That Nabokov would later mock the horror-film does not vitiate its contribution to *King, Queen, Knave;* and even if he did accept the other myths and mechanisms of the horror genre, he could not employ them too straightforwardly in *Lolita* because they would be inconsistent with the novel's parodies of popular culture. "His head was hanging down beside her head," writes Cain (b. 1892) in *Double Indemnity,* describing how Phyllis carries the body of her murdered husband. "They looked like something in a horror picture," but the realist stops short with a simile.[30] Perhaps only a much younger writer, weaned on such films, can take the genre seriously enough to transform it into an elaborate metaphor for contemporary history. Pynchon's *Gravity's Rainbow* and Brock Brower's *The Late Great Creature* (1972) realize this end, though Peter Bogdanovich anticipated them both in *Targets* (1968) by

linking Boris Karloff with a lunar suburbia and the Texas sniper, horrors that refuse to be contained by laws or local movie screens.

Humbert frequently employs horror-film effects which would be blatant or ridiculous on any screen: "And less than six inches from me and my burning life, was nebulous Lolita! After a long stirless vigil, my tentacles moved towards her again, and this time the creak of the mattress did not awake her. I managed to bring my ravenous bulk so close to her that I felt the aura of her bare shoulder like a warm breath upon my cheek. And then, she sat up, gasped, muttered with insane rapidity something about boats, tugged at the sheets and lapsed back into her rich, dark, young unconsciousness," reminisces Humbert of his first night with Lolita at The Enchanted Hunters hotel (p. 132), a sequence that brings to mind the restless Sleeping Beauties of American remakes such as *Mad Love* and *The Cat and the Canary* (1939), laboratory examples of the ways in which the macabre can quickly shade into absurdity. The best American horror films of the forties—*I Walked with a Zombie* (1943), despite its title, and *The Seventh Victim* (1943)—produced by Russian-born Val Lewton (Nazimova's nephew), allowed audiences to *imagine* their phantasms, employing poetic suggestion rather than gross makeup and/or Gothic trappings. Pavor Manor broadly mocks the latter genre: Quilty's

Left:

"The black trains roared past, shaking the windows of the house; with a movement like ghostly shoulders shaking off a load, heaving mountains of smoke swept upward, blotting out the night sky. The roofs burned with a smooth metallic blaze in the moonlight; and a sonorous black shadow under the iron bridge awoke as a black train rumbled across it, sending a chain of light flickering down its length. The clattering roar and mass of smoke seemed to pass right through the house as it quivered between the chasm where the rail tracks lay like lines drawn by a moonlit fingernail and the street where it was crossed by the flat bridge waiting for the next regular thunder of railway carriages. The house was like a spectre you could put your hand through and wriggle your fingers. Standing at the window of the dancer's room, Ganin looked out onto the street: the asphalt gleamed dully, black foreshortened people walked hither and thither, disappearing into shadows and re-emerging in the slanting light," writes Nabokov in *Mary* (p. 95), employing the Max Reinhardt lighting effects one associates with countless German films of the period, the chiaroscuro and awesome machines of *Metropolis*, the well-named *Asphalt* (1928) and *The Hands of Orlac*, whose train wreck Nabokov still vividly remembers. Thirty years later, describing Humbert's first night with Lolita (p. 132), Nabokov re-creates that very Germanic *Stimmung*.

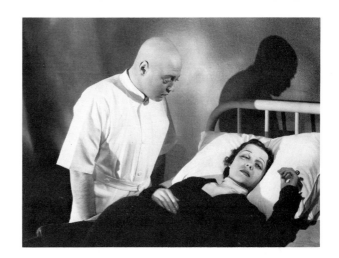

Right, top:

"I managed to bring my ravenous bulk close": Refugee Peter Lorre as Dr. Gogol (!) and Frances Drake as Yvonne Orlac in *Mad Love*, the foolish American remake of *The Hands of Orlac*. The "Gothic" shadows (if nothing else) are authentic inasmuch as director Karl Freund had been the cameraman on several famous German films, including Murnau's *The Last Laugh* and Lang's *Metropolis*.

Right, bottom:

"After a long . . . vigil my tentacles moved towards her again. . . . And then she sat up [and] gasped": Paulette Goddard in *The Cat and the Canary*.

"steaming trees" recall the unsubtle atmosphere provided by Universal Pictures's busy fog machines in their Sherlock Holmes series of the forties (*The Scarlet Claw*, 1945) and horrid horror films such as *The Wolf Man* (1941), direct descendants of the Gothic films abhorred by Nabokov. *The Wolf Man* expropriates the setups of *The Student of Prague* (1926), and the sources of its silly pastiche of *Doppelgänger* conventions—E. T. A. Hoffmann and Poe's "William Wilson"—are in turn parodied in *Despair* and *Lolita*. "And the bathroom doubled as my study. Here is the *Doppelgänger* theme for you," says Nabokov, reminiscing about their cramped *émigré* accommodations in Paris.

Humbert's self-loathing is often visualized in the metamorphic man-into-monster images of the popular cinema—"And a metamorphosis is a thing always exciting to watch," writes Nabokov in *Gogol*, referring to etymological phenomena (p. 43).[31] "I am lanky, big-boned, wooly-chested Humbert Humbert, with thick black eyebrows and a queer accent, and a cesspoolful of rotting monsters behind his slow boyish smile," says Humbert (p. 46), who also characterizes both himself and Quilty as "apelike"; describes himself rushing along a suburban street like Stevenson's evil "Mr. Hyde" ("My talons still tingling, I flew on," p. 208); and who assumes, wrongly, that a photographer at The Enchanted Hunters has immortalized "the bared teeth of Humbert Humbert sidling between the bridelike lassie and the enchanted cleric"

Left:
A heavy-handed Gothic *Doppelgänger* about to strike Conrad Veidt in the second of three versions of *The Student of Prague* (1926). Left, bottom: That uplifting setup is repeated by Claude Rains fifteen years later in *The Wolf Man,* the Germanic setting moved to "Wales." Lon Chaney, Jr., is the werewolf ("lanky, big-boned, wooly-chested, with thick black eyebrows") and Evelyn Ankers is his victim (a "purplish spot on her naked neck"?).

"Talons still tingling": Max Schreck, the "fairy tale vampire" of *Nosferatu.*

(p. 129). "Nothing could have been more childish than . . . the purplish spot on her naked neck where a fairy tale vampire had feasted," notes Humbert at their honeymoon hotel on the night that he first possesses Lolita (p. 141). Although Nabokov's cosmetic effects are more subdued, "werewolf" Humbert is kin to hirsute Lon Chaney, Jr., in *The Wolf Man,* a Beauty and the Beast saga somewhat less artful than Nabokov's version of the fairy tale[32] or Jean Cocteau's more faithful re-creation (1946) with Jean Marais as the Beast. Humbert's talons, like all movie talons, *Orlac*'s mechanized version included, have grown out of the impressive claws wielded by Max Schreck in the first Dracula film, *Nosferatu,* a potential ad for false fingernails that has served as a touchstone for subsequent horror-film directors. These abundant and comical movie effects all point toward Quilty, *Lolita*'s homunculus, and it is fitting that the two enchanted hunters in Nabokov's Grimm tale should finally confront one another in the mock-Gothic Manor, where the novel's principal parodies are united. More specifically, the manner in which Quilty is executed, in both senses of the word, parodies the hack scenarist's stock-in-trade, so loved by Lolita, her friends, and her mother.

"The archetypal American is a killer," asserts D. H. Lawrence in his *Classic Studies in American Literature* (1922), and refugee Humbert tries to play the role as Quilty, among others, might have written it.

Hastily outfitted for the scene by George Raft's or Humphrey Bogart's haberdasher at Warner Brothers (raincoat, black suit, black shirt, but, alas, no tie, p. 297), Humbert has carefully readied his .32 caliber automatic. "I had inherited it from the late Harold Haze [Humbert has explained earlier], with a 1938 catalog which cheerily said in part: 'Particularly well adapted for use in the home and car as well as on the person'" (p. 218), a blurb worthy of a National Rifle Association newsletter. Naturalist Nabokov abhors hunting and its equation with a "masculine" ethic. "I read [Hemingway] for the first time in the early forties," says Nabokov, "something about bells, balls and bulls, and loathed it. Later I read his admirable 'The Killers.' . . ."[33] Acting like a full-blooded American, Humbert had roamed the woods with John Farlow, "an admirable marksman, [who] with his .38 actually managed to hit a humming bird, though I must say not much of it could be retrieved for proof —only a little iridescent fluff. A burley ex-policeman called Krestovski, who in the twenties had shot and killed two escaped convicts, joined us and bagged a tiny woodpecker—completely out of season, incidentally. Between these two sportsmen I of course was a novice and kept missing everything, though I did wound a squirrel . . ." (p. 218). Humbert has kept Haze's weapon in a box, "loaded and fully cocked with the slide lock in safety position, thus precluding any accidental discharge. We must remember," he

adds, "that a pistol is the Freudian symbol of the Ur-father's central forelimb" (p. 218). Nabokov's parody of "phallic symbolism" is aimed at the American mystique about guns. "'You lie here,' I whispered to my light-weight compact little chum [his gun], and then toasted it with a dram of gin" (p. 218); thus Humbert joins the company of those earlier American heroes who anthropomorphized their weapons, from Fenimore Cooper's Natty Bumppo talking to his rifle in *The Pioneers* (1823) to Hemingway's Santiago engaged in a one-sided conversation with his fishing gear in *The Old Man and the Sea* (1952).

Humbert heads for Pavor Manor, Chum—as he now calls his gun—"aching to be discharged" (p. 294). He has treated him all too lovingly. "Such a thorough oil bath did I give Chum that now I could not get rid of the stuff. I bandaged him up with a rag, like a maimed limb, and used another to wrap up a handful of spare bullets" (p. 295). Following Quilty upstairs and striving for the efficiency of, say, Lee Marvin, killer Humbert "gingerly unwrapped dirty Chum, taking care not to leave any oil stains on the chrome —I think I got the wrong product, it was black and awfully messy. In my usually meticulous way, I transferred naked Chum to a clean recess about me and made for the little boudoir" (p. 297). Humbert had imagined Quilty as wielding that familiar gangster icon, a "penele cigar" (p. 295)—a very masculine adjectival coinage. Quilty, however, soon reveals "the

"Why can't you be more like Gregory Peck": Peck, bartender Karl Malden, and Skip Homeier in *The Gunfighter*. The celluloid *machismo* scorned by Nabokov is treated most seriously by Borges, as befits a fact of daily life in Argentina. Humbert is amused by "the pinned hand still groping for the dropped bowie knife" in a Western (p. 173), but in "The Tango" (1958), a poem, Borges elegizes "A mythology of knife thrusts / Slowly dying in oblivion: / A *chanson de geste* lost / In sordid police reports. . . . Made of time and dust, man lasts / Less long than the libidinous melody. . . ." Eschewing philosophy, Puig's *Heartbreak Tango* (1969) finds these lingering songs far less appealing, their libidinousness all too deathly.

melancholy truth" about himself—impotency—and, says Humbert, "his condition infected me, the weapon felt limp and clumsy in my hand" (p. 299). Pathetic Chum performs poorly at first, clicking helplessly, then sending, "with a ridiculously feeble and juvenile sound," a bullet into "the thick pink rug, and I had the paralyzing impression that it had merely trickled in and might come out again" (p. 299).

Humbert had earlier hoped to achieve the perfect crime that had eluded wife-murderer "G. Edward Grammar" (pp. 289-90), an actual crime based on a newspaper story, but an invented name based on Edward G. Robinson. The initial pages of the Pavor Manor chapter toy with another well-established grammar, upending the clichéd American conjunction of manhood, sexuality, and guns that is celebrated in our literature and lore and in countless Westerns and thrillers such as *Gun Crazy* (1949), an early salute to Bonnie and Clyde; *The Gunfighter* (1950), with its "virginal" ingenue killer (Skip Homeier); and *The Fastest Gun Alive* (1949), an epic of failed and compensatory masculinity in which shopkeeper Glenn Ford, the son of a famous marshal, is a fancy marksman but no killer, pretending to be a "fast gun" now in retirement (with six spurious notches on his gun butt). Ford sneaks away from his childless wife to shoot by himself, caresses his firearm in a most tender way, gazes at it diffidently, has it admired by a young boy (an obligatory moment in many Westerns of the period), exhibits it proudly to disbelievers in a saloon, and finally tests it against grizzled old Broderick Crawford, who has become a fast gun because his wife ran away with a gambler, or so Crawford's sidekick explains, an orthodox Freudian diagnostician of 1885. "No matter how fast you are there's always somebody faster" (the cuckold's perception), intones a blind man, cast as tragedy's chorus or seer, an all-seeing Tiresias at the outset of the film—as myth meets *poshlost'* on the frontier. The policeman's wife in *On Dangerous Ground* (1951) languorously straps on his revolver for him with a kiss and says how much she'll miss him while he's out on night patrol. Recent films do not bother with innuendo. In *Hit Man* (1972), hoodlums surprise the hero in bed, naked save for an outsized shotgun, which he fires from the loin at an improper angle, the ultimate in "symbolism" until some X-rated trick photography can produce a literally blazing phallus, prefigured years ago by *Ulysses* and the roman candles of *Fireworks* (1947), Kenneth Anger's one-reel Fourth of July homosexual revery, which in turn is funned by the Riviera fireworks that accompany Grace Kelly's and Cary Grant's embrace in Hitchcock's *To Catch a Thief* (1955). "That's all I got between me and them, between me and the whole world," says Rico (Edward G. Robinson) of his gun in *Little Caesar* (1930), the archetypal gangster film, whose "little" is operative; Robinson, like tough guys

"MAGIC TO A BOY," stated the original caption on this M-G-M publicity still, which shows Glenn Ford being idolized by young Chris Olsen in *The Fastest Gun Alive*. Nabokov's parody is also factually grounded; Chum is only a .32, more likely to be feeble, "impotent," and inaccurate than .38 or .45 caliber weapons.

The fastest gun alive? An obligatory moment in the "Freudian" Western or thriller. The tradition is kept alive by *Bonnie and Clyde* (1967) and *The Wild Bunch* (1969), where one gunman (Strother Martin) seems to experience an orgasm while awaiting his target.

Raft, Cagney, and Bogart, is a short man, as good Freudians or Jungians should note. (In *Symbols of Transformation*, 1927, Jung discusses the "smaller than small and bigger than big" shape-shifting of the libidinal hero.) " 'Say! [Quilty] drawled (now imitating the underworld numbskull of movies), 'that's a swell little gun you've got there. What d'you want for her?' " (p. 299).[34] Chum is a male, as Humbert has said, and envious Quilty's pronoun, prefiguring the "feminine 'ahs!' " of his death struggle (p. 305), is an apt choice, a carefully planted "Freudian slip."

The slangy sense of that cliché, lending itself to a jejune pun (picked up by The Freudian Slips, a female rock group), quite literally describes *Johnny Guitar* (1954), which starred Joan Crawford as a saloon owner named Vienna (appropriate city) in a baroque testing of the Western's mythology, a good-natured send-up of *Belle Starr* (The Bandit Queen, 1941) and Dietrich's role as the outlaw den mother in *Rancho Notorious* (1952, possibly Fritz Lang's worst American mistake). "I've never seen a woman who was more like a man," one of her bartenders says of Vienna, who, in an extension of the Dietrich–Una Merkel brawl in *Destry Rides Again* (1939), symbolically completes that most enviable "Freudian" transformation by shooting it out with Mercedes McCambridge at the end of the film, in what one hopes is intended as a parody akin to the way in which Quilty will bite the dust.

After Quilty cheerfully tries out his bad French, Humbert asks him whether he wants to be executed sitting or standing. "Ah, let me think. . . . It is not an easy question" answers Quilty (p. 300), as "feminine" and nonplussed as the debonair, thespian "heavy" (Beatrice Lillie!) in a fine, little-known Hollywood silent comedy, *Exit Smiling* (1926). Fitfully awakened to the peril, Quilty lurches and sends Chum "hurtling under a chest of drawers" (p. 300). They wrestle for the weapon in the style of "the obligatory scene in the Westerns of [the reader's] childhood":

Our tussle, however, lacked the ox-stunning fisticuffs, the flying furniture. He and I were two large dummies, stuffed with dirty cotton and rags. It was a silent, soft, formless tussle on the part of two literati, one of whom was utterly disorganized by a drug while the other was handicapped by a heart condition and too much gin. When at last I had possessed myself of my precious weapon, and the scenario writer had been reinstalled in his low chair, both of us were panting as the cowman and the sheepman never do after their battle (p. 301).

After pausing to read aloud his own death sentence in the form of Humbert's poem ("poetical justice," Humbert calls it), Quilty is variously impatient ("This pistol-packing farce is becoming a frightful nuisance"), conciliatory, and remarkably athletic. Although an "underworlder" denouement is more within the reach of handicapped Humbert, his diligent tar-

Edward G. Robinson, "stung by a hornet" in *Little Caesar*. "Physically, the conventional moving-picture gunman is a copy of [the colossal Monk Eastman], not of the pudgy, epicene Capone," writes Borges in "Monk Eastman, Purveyor of Iniquities" (1933, collected in *A Universal History of Infamy*). The lore of American crime and the mythology of our frontier, culled from history books as well as films, inform several of Borges's (non-parodic) tales. The Pop appeal of fabulous criminals is keynoted by his "The Widow Ching, Lady Pirate" (in *A Universal History*), which celebrates the documented exploits of the female pirate on whom Milton Caniff based his Dragon Lady (1938). But subsequent Borges stories are akin to Nabokov's send-ups of the popular detective tale and thriller ("Emma Zunz," 1949, whose concluding "solution" only establishes the mystery).

Left, top:
"That's a swell little gun you've got there": Franklin Pangborn (left) and Bea Lillie, the "villain" in *Exit Smiling*'s play-within-the-film, a mock-melodrama. Lillie calmly disarms him.

Left:
Dummies Ken Maynard and Charles King wrestle for possession of their Chum.

get practice serves him poorly. Shooting bullets rather than blanks, revived Chum only manages to send Quilty's black rocking-chair into a zestful, panic-stricken "rocking act," its owner flashing into the music room to play several vigorous chords on the piano, "his nostrils emitting the soundtrack snorts which had been absent from our fight." But Humbert's next bullet propels Quilty "from his chair higher and higher, like old, gray, mad Nijinski, like Old Faithful, like some old nightmare of mine, to a phenomenal altitude, or so it seemed, as he rent the air" with a velocity and comic trajectory that easily outdistance all the hurtling and caterwauling figures in the "obligatory scenes" of Hollywood thrillers (p. 304). With one hand "pressed to his brow" and the other "clutching his armpit as if stung by a hornet, down he came on his heels and, again a normal robed man, scurried out into the hall" (p. 305). More bullets find their mark, yet "bloated" Quilty manages to "trudg[e] from room to room, bleeding majestically," the bravura comedy burlesquing, among many things, the river of rhetoric and gore that runs from the Elizabethans to Mickey Spillane (p. 305). One of the most comical scenes in modern literature, it is as deeply serious as it is funny: Humbert's guilt is not to be exorcised so easily; "false" *Doppelgänger* Quilty, and all that he represents, *is* slow to die. He finally expires "in a purple heap" (p. 307), the color of his prose, as evidenced by his play, *The Enchanted Hunters* (pp. 202-3).

"This . . . was the end of the ingenious play staged for me by Quilty," declares Humbert as he departs the Horror House and walks "with a heavy heart" through "the spotted blaze of the sun" (p. 307), lighting effects by UFA or RKO Pictures, where many German refugee technicians were employed in the forties.

Watching Lolita's stylish game in Champion, Colorado, Humbert had imagined her a "real girl champion," "acting a girl champion in a movie" (p. 234), a remarkable forecast of Quilty's plans for her, as yet unknown to Humbert. Quilty has in turn anticipated Humbert, since the stage version of Quilty's *Golden Guts* (p. 278), however trashy it may be, would seem to predate the tennis scene and Humbert's own "movie" of "golden Lolita" (p. 237) and "the clean resounding crack of her golden whip" (p. 233). These coincidences extend far beyond Nabokov's conception of Quilty as Humbert's horrific alter ego and mock-Double. When Quilty first appears in person, on the darkened, pillared porch of The Enchanted Hunters hotel, and is about to engage Humbert in the verbal sparring that prefigures their eventual fight (p. 129), Humbert recalls how he "could not really see him but what gave him away was the rasp of a screwing off, then a discreet gurgle, then the final note of a placid screwing on" (p. 128), as though a doll or puppet were being assembled in the wings, a homunculus was coming to life in the artist-alchemist's workshop

(a foreground reality in *King, Queen, Knave,* where the Inventor's auto-mannequins fail to work but the author's moral dummies run all too smoothly). Nabokov's are the sounds of an antic Dr. Frankenstein at work in Pavor Manor's horror-movie basement laboratory.

Trailing his "fiend's spoor" (p. 249) across the "crazy quilt" landscapes of America (pp. 154 and 309), Humbert notices how the license plates of four of Quilty's rented cars had "formed interrelated combinations (such as 'WS 1564' and 'SH 1616,' and 'Q32888' or 'CU 88322') which however were so cunningly contrived as to never reveal a common denominator" (p. 253). The letters and numerals on Quilty's first two plates offer Shakespeare's monograms and dates of birth and death, an ironic emblem, while the letters on the second set of licenses refer to Quilty and his nickname "Cue." Their numerals include "32," a mirrored allusion to the April 23rd birthday Nabokov shares with Shakespeare and Shirley Temple, and add up to a quietly telling fifty-two. Humbert and Lolita spend fifty-two weeks together on the road, there are that many lines in Humbert's poem to her (pp. 257-59), and Quilty is the author of fifty-two successful scenarios. In his Foreword to *Lolita,* John Ray, Jr., Ph.D., states that Lolita, Quilty, and Humbert, our putative and extraordinarily perceptive author, have all died in '52 (p. 6). There are fifty-two cards in a deck, and the author of *King,*

Queen, Knave draws many more from his sleeve, superimposing on his quotidian world numerical and verbal *figura* that recall the more blatantly stylized chess squared landscape—or landscaped chessboard—of *Through the Looking-Glass* (see Tenniel's drawing in Chapter Two). Queneau structured *The Bark Tree* as a series of mathematically exact units, Robbe-Grillet has been known to measure the visible world in terms of inches, and has said that nothing is more fantastic than precision. "I have only words to play with!" declares Humbert, speaking for his maker and numerous contemporary writers, from Beckett and Borges to Barthelme and Barth, who recognize that the prose artist can no longer hold the mirror up to nature with the certitude of yore. The book is a book, and "reality" is—

Akin to hundreds of such involuted inlays and patterned elements distributed throughout the novel, waiting to be perceived by the re-reader, the "coincidences" in *Lolita* serve to reveal "the common denominator," the manipulative hand of card-sharp, conjurer, puppeteer Nabokov, who somehow manages to stage the tennis scene in "Champion," and who pulls the strings most blatantly in fantastic Pavor Manor, where all of the novel's carefully achieved realism is suspended, and "the two literati" are sent against each other in a fight between "two large dummies, stuffed with dirty cotton and rags" (p. 301), ruled over by Nabokov the artist and judge, who passes sentence on a bad writer, Movielove's champion. The killing of Quilty thus serves poetical justice, if no other, and murder, along with parody, becomes an act of criticism, more suited to art than life.

Harold Lloyd in *Safety Last.*

4
Positive Images

There is surely implicit in Quilty's death scene a lesson for recent film and TV directors who, in the wake of the James Bond movies (in *their* turn a vulgarization of Hitchcock's excellent *North by Northwest*, 1959), would hope to spoof violence but instead end by demeaning and dehumanizing their audiences. If it is unfair to ask of visual modes what verbal structures can of course stage or suggest more easily, then at least scenarists and directors might submit themselves to one of the principal wellsprings of twentieth-century comedy. That lesson *can* be learned in the anarchic school of earlier American screen comedy, and Nabokov the movie-goer and youthful gagwriter has absorbed its curriculum, as has Stanley Kubrick, or at least the Kubrick who directed *Lolita* (1962) and *Dr. Strangelove* (1963).

"In Europe," Nabokov says,

I went to the corner cinema about once in a fortnight and the only kind of picture I liked, and still like, was and is comedy of the Laurel and Hardy type. I enjoyed tremendously American comedy—Buster Keaton, Harold Lloyd, and Chaplin. . . . However, today's Little Man appeal has somewhat spoiled Chaplin's attraction for me. The Marx Brothers were wonderful . . . [and] Laurel and Hardy are always funny; there are subtle, artistic touches in even their most mediocre films. Laurel is so wonderfully inept, yet so very kind. There is a film in which they are at Oxford [*A Chump at Oxford*, 1940]. In one scene the two of them are sitting on a park bench in a labyrinthine garden and the subsequent happenings conform to the labyrinth. A casual villain puts his hand through the back of the bench and Laurel, who is clasping his hands in an idiotic reverie, mistakes the stranger's hand for one of his own hands, with all kinds of complications because his own hand is also there. He has to choose. The choice of a hand. . . . My favorites by Chaplin are *The Gold Rush* [1925], *The Circus* [1928], and *The Great Dictator* [1940]—especially the parachute inventor who jumps out of the window and ends in a messy fall which we only see in the expression on the dictator's face.[1]

Chaplin's poetry, celebrated elsewhere by Hart Crane, e. e. cummings, and James Agee, informs young Fyodor's own prose-poetry in *The Gift* (1937-1938): "in the flower beds around them rippled pale, black-blotched pansies (somewhat similar facially to Charlie Chaplin)" (p. 326). Earlier in the novel, set in Berlin c. 1925, Fyodor had observed that "over the entrance to a cinema a black giant cut out of cardboard had been erected, with turned-out feet, the blotch of

a mustache on his white face beneath a bowler hat, and a bent cane in his hand" (p. 174)—only a local color detail, but emblematic in its scale, recalling the tribute to Chaplin in *Pnin* (p. 80) and the resonance of his image in the first chapter of Agee's *A Death in the Family* (1957).

It is not by chance that Nabokov should single out Laurel and Hardy's labyrinth or the parachute inventor's fall. "One likes to recall," he writes in *Gogol*, "that the difference between the comic side of things, and their cosmic side, depends upon one sibilant" (p. 142), and the inventor's "messy" disappearance complements fifty years of Nabokov's own creative researches, his unflinching contemplation of the void. "In the early twenties in Berlin—1924, perhaps, since I was not yet married—I got well paid for cabaret sketches for the *émigré* night club 'Sinyaya ptitsa,' or 'Bluebird,'" says Nabokov, recalling the period before he had written any novels and was turning from lyric poetry to short fiction and verse drama. He had recently composed *Smert'* ["Death"], a short two-act "Byronic" play set in 1806 at Cambridge University, and *Dedushka* ("The Grandfather"), another untranslated play of 1923, which also confronts the nature of death. The five-act "historical" verse drama of 1924, *Tragediya gospodina Morna* ("The Tragedy of Mister Morn"), extends the theme of death,[2] but none of these plays are comic, and that sibilant marks a wide gap. One sees it narrowed in Nabokov's commercial sketches. "There were a number of things I had entitled 'Locomotion,'" he says.

One sketch was a little on the *Candid Camera* lines, long before *Candid Camera*, of course (a program I loved, incidentally). It was situated on a railway platform. You saw a porter with a red nose trundling his luggage cart containing a very large trunk, very badly closed. At one point the trunk flew open and a skeleton half flopped out of the trunk but he merely pushed it back with his foot and went on his way. Then there was the sketch in which a wildly hirsute man visited a barber. The actor portraying the customer was a small chap, whose real head, concealed inside his collar, was topped by a dummy head, its face partially concealed by thick long whiskers and very long hair. The barber cut and cut, and when the man was finally shaved and shorn, only a tiny head remained, like the knob of a post with very big ears. In "The Chinese Dragon" [the title in English is a pun on *"chai,"* the Russian word for "tea"], a sequence of Chinese disappeared in a dragon's open mouth. Another Bluebird "Locomotion" had a Venetian background and presented a blind man going along the bank of a canal, taptapping with his cane. Visible were the edge of the canal and the moon reflected in the water. The blind man got nearer and nearer and at the very last moment, when he was practically at the brink, his foot already raised, he took out a handkerchief, blew his nose, turned and went back, taptapping. (No, no, Alfred, don't say it; that tapping is not a reference to the blind stripling's leitmotif in Joyce's *Ulysses.*) These "Locomotions" took about five minutes, there was music and songs explaining and commenting on the action. I wrote the lyrics of the songs, too. I think I saw only one performance. As I said, they paid well. But all this is not really very interesting, is it?

It *is* interesting, of course. As comic archetypes, these sketches bring to mind Samuel Beckett's works and the athletics of a play such as Jerzy Grotowski's *Akropolis* (1964), whose concentration camp inmates disappear one by one into a box, the reverse of the stream of circus midgets who tumble out of a little car. Nabokov's reduced hairy man also recalls *The Barbershop* (1934), one of W. C. Fields's four Mack Sennett shorts—especially the scene in which a monstrously fat man (padded, of course) with a long beard comes into the shop to use the steam room. The barber, Fields, forgets about him, and when he finally rescues him from the locked steam bath, and the great clouds of steam have cleared away, we see that the fat man has shrunk, has melted into a little fellow, suspended inside huge, blimplike trousers. Sennett and Fields certainly didn't pick up ideas in Berlin *émigré* cabarets of the twenties. The Bluebird "Locomotions" may well be archetypal, but they are far more interesting for the ways in which their themes and procedures anticipate works Nabokov would write years later: the various farcical elements of *Invitation to a Beheading* (1938), *The Waltz In-*

vention (1938), and *Ada* (1969); Quilty's death scene and the most darkly comical aspects of *Pale Fire* (1962).

One of the central themes, or actions, of *Pale Fire* is a kind of fully orchestrated "Locomotion": the activities of the Shadows, that regicidal organization of stooges, whose antics recall the Keystone Cops, and the Shadows' loathsome, bumbling, but lethal agent, assassin Gradus—Death as the common, rigid vulgarian (see pp. 151-54). Always dressed in brown and blessed with a "chimpanzee slouch" (p. 277), excremental Gradus is a failed "Jack of small trades" and everything else. "Mere springs and coils produced the inward movements of our clockwork man. He might be termed a Puritan" (p. 152). "He was not interested in sightseeing or seasiding. He had long stopped drinking. He did not go to concerts. . . . Sexual impulses had greatly bothered him at one time but that was over. After his wife . . . had left him (with a gypsy lover), he had lived in sin with his mother-in-law until she was removed, blind and dropsical, to an asylum for decayed widows." His attempts to castrate himself only lead to a "severe infection" (pp. 252-53). "Our 'automatic man'" (p. 279) "worship[s] general ideas and [does] so with pedantic aplomb" (p. 152), lynches the wrong people (p. 112), moves his lips "like wrestling worms" while he pores over newspaper ads (pp. 274-75), speaks, "mediocre French" and "worse English" (p. 199), gets

Easy, Gradus, hold your fire: Paul Guilfoyle (left) and Ben Welden as "our 'automatic man,'" in *The Missing Corpse* (1945).

"Slapsie" Maxie Rosenbloom as a Gradus-like hoodlum in a forgotten and forgettable gangster film.

lost on the road to Lex (= "law"), and at the end of *Pale Fire* fights to control the diarrheal "liquid hell inside of him" (p. 282) as he rushes to relieve his gun on an unintended victim. When he writes out "their client's alias," Gradus's Shadow superior "shak[es] with laughter (death is hilarious)" (p. 256). Agent Gradus, an anti–James Bond Super-Op figure, evokes the image of the inept, dumb, and easily frightened hoodlum who voraciously consumes candy bars and comic books when he's not bumping off the wrong guy, getting himself locked in bank vaults, or failing with the girls—a role played for laughs in many grade-B gangster films of the forties, particularly in the *Falcon* series so dear to at least one Nabokov. Most strikingly visualized as a vaudevillian bat- or birdman villain from an old movie or animated cartoon (like the Penguin in *Batman*), Gradus is a "grotesque . . . cross between bat and crab" (p. 150), a jet-age Angel of Death "avail[ing] himself of all varieties of locomotion—rented cars, local trains, escalators, airplanes—[though] somehow the eye of the mind sees him, and the muscles of the mind feel him, as always streaking across the sky with black traveling bag in one hand and loosely folded umbrella in the other, in a sustained glide high over sea and land" (pp. 135-36)—"rising, soaring, desecrating the sky" (p. 264). "I was the shadow of the waxwing slain," writes John Shade in the opening line of that veritable aviary, *Pale Fire*. ". . . Infinite foretime and /

The Penguin, "availing himself of all varieties of locomotion,"
Batman, 1946.

A bat man (not to be confused with *the* Batman, né 1939) attacks Clyde Beatty in *Darkest. Africa* (1936), the first Republic serial.

Infinite aftertime: above your head / They close like giant wings and you are dead" (ll. 122-24). Akin also to the birdlike harbingers of doom that fly through the hellish skies of Bosch, Brueghel, Callot, Goya, Blake, Fuseli, Meryon, Ensor, and Baskin, or the figure of Mephistopheles (Emil Jannings), whose black cape shrouds the sky and town in Murnau's *Faust* (1926), Nabokov's iconographic personification of Death casts its vast shadow across the entire novel—its creations, creator, and readers—extends forward over *Ada* and *Transparent Things*, and reaches back to include *Speak, Memory, Invitation to a Beheading, Despair, The Eye, Bluebird,* and the three verse dramas. "The Tragedy of Mister Morn" introduces in turn a king who has been exiled from an imaginary land, a figure who appeared again in several of Nabokov's Russian works, emerging with final, mad tragicomic splendor in *Pale Fire.*

"Death," the untranslated drama, is well titled, but Nabokov's is no morbid preoccupation. Student Van Veen achieves "a brilliant ascendancy" among his peers by mastering the "knack of topsy-turvy locomotion on his hands" (p. 81), bettered only by Nabokov, whose *Ada* reverses Time and rearranges geography. Early in the novel, Van describes the phases of Aqua Veen's disintegration, "every one more racking than the last; for the human brain can become the best torture house of all those it has invented, established and used in millions of years, in millions of lands, on millions of howling creatures" (p. 22). Those howls are audible throughout *Ada*, even in Ardis, since death exists in Arcady too. But it is fourteen-year-old Van's hazardous equipoise that best expresses the spirit of Nabokov's most transcendent performances: "Not the faintest flush showed on his face or neck! Now and then, when he detached his organs of locomotion from the lenient ground, and seemed actually to clap his hands in midair, in a miraculous parody of a ballet jump, one wondered if this dreamy indolence of levitation was not a result of the earth's canceling its pull in a fit of absentminded benevolence" (p. 82). Van's is the brio of gravity-defiant Oliver Hardy in *Hog Wild* (1930). Remaining atop a ladder as he and it are swept away by hapless Laurel's rampaging car, Ollie braves the underpasses and traffic and doffs his bowler to the startled passengers in an open-topped bus.

Nabokov's less daringly locomoted blind man of 1924 partakes of perhaps the most compelling of cosmic sight gags, a balancing act that is as funny as it is bracing, performed again and again by the masters of American screen comedy: Chester Conklin, his eyes widened by terror as the Keystone Cops' auto teeters on the brink of a canyon (c. 1918); blindfolded Charlie Chaplin skating around the rim of a balcony in *Modern Times* (1936), his gasp and retreat when he removes the cloth, a moment perfected earlier in *The Gold Rush* (1925), when he starts out

Vladimir Nabokov, Berlin, 1922, aged twenty-three, shortly after his father's assassination.

the door and realizes that the storm-driven cabin is tottering over a cliff; nonplused Buster Keaton suspended in various fearful postures—at an oblique angle in the ship's rigging of *The Love Nest* (1923), over the edge of a waterfall in *Our Hospitality* (1923), from a window in *College* (1927)—or perched high in a thin cyclone-torn tree in *Steamboat Bill, Jr.* (1928), what Nabokov in *Transparent Things* calls "the silhouette of human panic" (p. 28); Oliver Hardy on top of a leaning, wavering tower of piled chairs in *Fra Diavolo* (1933); or Laurel and Hardy encased in cylinders of cement in *Our Relations* (1936), seesawing furiously on the edge of a wharf like two crazed metronomes, or contending with a gorilla as they haul a piano across a crumbling Alpine suspension bridge in *Swiss Miss* (1938), a scene that ends with Hardy dangling by his hands above the gorge. Their perilous scrambling on the superstructure of a new skyscraper in *Liberty* (1929) was a patent imitation of the most famous of such scenes, in Harold Lloyd's *High and Dizzy* (1920) or *Safety Last* (1923, repeated by him in *Feet First*, 1930); in *The Defense* (1930), a still photo from one of those Lloyd films, lying on Valentinov's table amid other shots of "frightened women and ferociously squinting men," suggests to ex-Grandmaster Luzhin his means of suicide: "a white-faced man with lifeless features and big American glasses [was] hanging by his hands from the ledge of a skyscraper—just about to fall off into the abyss" (p. 247). Reading a Soviet chess book in *The Gift*, Fyodor "began to enjoy quietly a study in which the few white pieces seemed to be hanging over an abyss and yet won the day" (p. 187), a forecast of the outcome of "Lik" (1938), composed immediately after completion of *The Gift*. Although the ailing actor appears in "a play of the nineteen-twenties called *L'Abîme* ('The Abyss')," it is his enemy who suffers that plunge and commits suicide on the story's last page. "No wonder one peers over the parapet into an inviting abyss," writes distraught Kinbote in *Pale Fire;* he will survive only long enough to complete his edition (p. 220). Fyodor meets the respected *émigré* novelist Shirin (= Russian for "breadth" or "width," *not* Sirin), author of *The Hoary Abyss,* who is "blind like Milton, deaf like Beethoven, and a blockhead to boot" (p. 327). In search of treacherous Margot in *Laughter in the Dark*, blind and doomed Albinus gets out of the elevator and "moved forward and stepped with one foot into an abyss—no, it was nothing, only the step leading downstairs. He had to keep still for a moment, he was quivering so" (p. 287). Asked in 1970 to characterize his memory, Nabokov answered, "I am an ardent memorist with a rotten memory; a drowsy king's absent-minded remembrancer. With absolute lucidity I recall landscapes, gestures, intonations, a million sensuous details, but names and numbers topple into oblivion with absurd abandon like little blind

The Keystone Cops' auto, poised rather than "Grouching" at the brink.

Harold Lloyd (left) in *For Heaven's Sake* (1926).

Mack Swain and Chaplin in *The Gold Rush*, their cabin wavering over the abyss.

Buster Keaton in *College*.

Keaton in *The Love Nest*.

Keaton in *Our Hospitality*.

Charley Chase, ten stories up.

Laurel and Hardy in *Hog Wild*.

Laurel and Hardy's *Liberty* draws upon Harold Lloyd, but his *Feet First* coincides with the same year's *Hog Wild*.

Harold Lloyd in *Safety Last*.

Luzhin's drop out of time in *The Defense* is most suggestively glossed by *Safety Last*, which probably provided the model for his suicide.

"No wonder one peers over the parapet into an inviting abyss," writes Kinbote. Buster Keaton has two alternatives.

Laurel and Hardy test Shirin's *Hoary Abyss* in *Liberty*.

Lloyd takes the plunge in *Safety Last*. An awning saves him—the safety net of comedy that is beyond Luzhin but not Nabokov.

men in file from a pier."[3] Cincinnatus in *Invitation to a Beheading* ends a chapter by writing (in the book-within-the-book) how he stepped from his window-sill onto the elastic air, and Nabokov literally leaves him transfixed in mid-air, a moment which not only telescopes the novel's main theme, its confrontation of death and dying, but is also strikingly similar to the way the blind man in Nabokov's "Locomotion" tests the void and teases the viewer.[4] "Yes, yes. A family group. I had not made those connections," said Nabokov, when several of these parallels were pointed out to him.

Nabokov's locomotive comedy is most free-wheeling in *Invitation to a Beheading*, the anti-utopian fantasia written in Berlin in 1935, an atypical refraction of contemporary German and Russian realities, the mammoth prison-society of Stalinist spies, informers, and interrogators best documented in Robert Conquest's *The Great Terror* (1968), Nadeszhda Mandelstam's *Hope Against Hope* (1970), and Solzhenitsyn's *Gulag Archipelago* (1973). Like many of Nabokov's works, *Invitation to a Beheading* draws upon and revivifies a diversified popular genre which Nabokov has been all too willing to disparage. For more than forty years he has employed, with varying success, the themes, modes, and conventions of science fiction: time travel ("The Tragedy of Mister Morn," 1924, and "Time and Ebb," 1945); automata (*King, Queen, Knave,* 1928); invisibility, immortal-

ity, identity transfer, and telekinesis (*The Eye,* 1930); the fantastic invention or infernal machine (*The Waltz Invention,* 1938, which can be compared with Alexey Tolstoy's *The Death Box,* 1927, rev. 1937); teleportation ("The Visit to the Museum," 1939); space and time travel ("Lance," 1952); and psychic phenomena ("The Vane Sisters," 1959). Nabokov's sci-fi strain culminates in the "physics fiction" that is *Ada* (1969). Antiterra's startling geographic boundaries are the result of Nabokov's version of the "What if—?" mode of sci-fi, the story that is based on an imaginary and dramatic reversal of history, a very old idea that also served Queneau well in *The Blue Flowers* (1965). Nabokov's 1968 dismissal of science fiction's "gals and goons [and] suspense and suspensories" is a strong but dated opinion; the best sci-fi writers had abandoned space operas in favor of futuristic dystopias even before Sputnik had turned speculative fantasies into lunar realities (see Pohl's and Kornbluth's *The Space Merchants,* 1953, in which "space" also refers to advertising).

What *is* Nabokov's favorite work of science fiction? "*The Tempest* [1611], of course," he answers, having never seen the film version (*Forbidden Planet,* 1956); *Ada*'s oblique allusions to Cyrano de Bergerac's *A Voyage to the Moon* of 1656 (p. 339), Jules Verne (pp. 5 and 334), and H. G. Wells's *The Invisible Man* of 1897 (pp. 133 and 203) locate Nabokov's sympathies in epochs earlier than his own. "A small map

. . . might be quite thickly prickled with enameled red-cross-flag pins, marking, in her War of the Worlds, Aqua [Veen's] bivouacs," the sanatoriums that contain her howling disintegration (p. 19). Did Nabokov have in mind the final pages of Wells's *The War of the Worlds* (1898), when the silence of devastated and darkened London is disturbed by the terrible last lamentations of those mammoth invaders from Mars, toppled by lowly bacteria? "Yes," says Nabokov, "I can still hear those creatures."

"A writer for whom I have the deepest admiration is H. G. Wells," continues Nabokov. "I could talk *endlessly* about Wells, especially his romances: *The Time Machine* [1895]; *The Invisible Man; The War of the Worlds*, of course; *The First Men in the Moon* [1901]; and *The Country of the Blind* [1904, expanded in 1939]," which is about the travails of the only man with sight (= spiritual isolation) in a land of sightless people. Cincinnatus is Nabokov's version of this by now stock figure who has undergone countless sci-fi permutations: The Last Man in the World. Cincinnatus even calls himself this (p. 95). That he is not permitted the full companionship of the Last Woman, a familiar twist in the trashiest of sci-fi (prose and film), is thematically important and consistent with his very human fears, which include sexual inadequacy and failure. Where Wells employs blindness, Nabokov divides his population, unevenly enough, between opaque (= sentient) and transparent (dehumanized) people. The futuristic world beyond Cincinnatus's prison is mapped with care. "Progress" has been made in transportation, city planning, child care, education, journalism, library science, literature, and, of course, in the relationship between executioner and victim. As in all anti-utopian fiction, the culture of the past is obsolete; Cincinnatus once worked in a doll workshop making figurines of Pushkin and Tolstoy, those shams from "poetical antiquity," "the mythical Nineteenth Century" (p. 27). Poetry has been replaced by photojournalism because its truths, however limited, can be retouched so easily. "Photo-horoscopes" parody the pic-biographies of the German photojournals that were to give birth to *Life* (1936), extending the implications of their source by projecting the subject's future in line with the photographic distortion or simplification of his past— "a parody of the work of time," a Luce pun before the fact (pp. 170-71). Color photos in newspapers (unknown in 1935), as well as public killings in Thriller Square, are distractive treats welcomed by almost everyone; black-snouted news photographers crowd around the execution platform. "The perpetual fountain at the mausoleum of Captain Somnus [= the tomb of consciousness-denying Lenin] profusely irrigates with its spray the stone captain, the bas-relief at his elephantine feet and the quivering roses" (p. 74).

Critics have subdued their natural professional in-

clination to relate *Invitation* to Huxley's *Brave New World* (1932), Warner's *The Aerodrome* (1941), or Orwell's *Nineteen Eighty-Four* (1949), but the generic (though not aesthetic) kinship is strong and clear. It may not be apparent immediately because Nabokov eschews the reportorial exposition (see Vonnegut's *Player Piano*, 1952) and tendentious moralizing (see Heinlein's *Stranger in a Strange Land*, 1961) one often finds in admonitory utopias, and *Invitation*'s farcical action and tone make it unique. Its "map" is filled in gradually, through an accretion of vivid touches and precise, painterly details—a futuristic, Dürer-like landscape glimpsed through a partially opened window. Dystopia, moreover, is only part of the story, as it were, in *Invitation to a Beheading* (as well as *Bend Sinister*, its brother). *Invitation* is also a novel of consciousness (old-fashioned as that may sound), which should suggest why Nabokov, in his Foreword to the American edition, does not welcome any comparisons with "G. H. Orwell or other popular purveyors of illustrated ideas and publicistic fiction" (p. 6). The Penguin paperback edition of *Invitation*, thanks to an extraordinary coincidence, is number "1984" in their series.

Véra Nabokov witnessed the first nocturnal book-

Vladimir, Véra, and Dmitri Nabokov (b. 1934), Berlin, summer 1935.

burnings in the streets of Berlin, and while her husband wrote the first draft—"in one fortnight of wonderful excitement and sustained inspiration," a "spectacular exception" to his usual snail's pace—the searchlights from Nazi *fêtes* illuminated the wintry sky, stage lighting for the Nabokovs' second *Götterdammerung*. "At Véra's cousin's flat," recalls Nabokov, "we heard Hitler's voice from rooftop loudspeakers," but in Cincinnatus's prison world, great dictators are figuratively and literally reduced in size; "Who is Mussolini?" asks the "Nabokovian" novelist Udo Conrad in *Laughter in the Dark* (p. 215), and Nabokov's untranslated story "Istreblenie Tiranov" ("Tyrants Destroyed"), written in Berlin in 1936, provides a Swiftian coda to *Invitation* by suggesting that derision is the best weapon. "When we left Berlin for good in '37, I was worried that the German authorities would discover that manuscript in our baggage," says Nabokov. "'It's about Stalin,' I would have told them, but they didn't find it. They had their translators—the Nazis couldn't read Russian, of course, and perhaps not German, either."

Sentenced to die because he alone has retained his sentience, or opacity, Cincinnatus must contend with the omnipresent M'sieur Pierre, his executioner. "Life is a long lesson in death and dying," said Socrates, and near the end of *Invitation to a Beheading*, "the deputy city director" jumps up on the execution platform to announce to the townspeople a new furniture exhibit: "I also remind you that tonight, there will be given with sensational success the new comic opera *Socrates Must Decrease*," a précis of the novel and the State's intentions (p. 220). Some of the other comic operas of the period are the Marx Brothers' *A Night at the Opera* (1935); the Ritz Brothers' *The Firefly* (1938, from Rudolf Friml's opus); and Laurel and Hardy's *Fra Diavolo* (*The Devil's Brother*, 1933, a burlesque of François Auber's operetta), *Babes in Toyland* (1934, based on Victor Herbert's operetta), and *The Bohemian Girl* (1936, a take-off on Michael Balfe). René Clair's futuristic *A Nous la liberté* (1931) has its own "operatic" flourishes: the guards wear anachronistic royal costumes and Clair's forlorn little prisoner, who is employed as a toymaker, gradually joins the other prisoners, who sing with surprising joy —the kind of joy that Cincinnatus, a former toymaker, will experience at the end of the book. "I loved the French films of René Clair," says Nabokov, "a new world, a new trend in cinema,"[5] of which *Invitation to a Beheading* is a whirling, slapstick extension: *The Shape of Things to Come* (H. G. Wells's formulations of 1933) submitted to a comic sensibility—a prototypical dystopia, such as Zamiatin's *We* (1920), worked over by Laurel and Hardy, the Marx Brothers, Lloyd, Langdon, or Keaton.

Whether or not film comedy has influenced Nabokov (and to what degree) is not the primary issue here. "Influence," of course, is a troublesome, controversial,

Imprisoned Louis (Raymond Cordy) in *A Nous la liberté.*

and mysterious business; that comedy, after all, drew on the traditions of *commedia dell'arte,* of music hall and vaudeville. Unlike Joyce, however, the youthful creator of the Bluebird sketches was no devotee of the popular stage, and classic film comedy stands alone as a visible source of Nabokov's inspiration, if sources are a source of critical enlightenment. Nabokov's enthusiasm for screen comedy notwithstanding, *he* is not about to reduce the chemistry of creation. Would that he had been as forthright and considerate of his critics as Ionesco or the exiled Cuban novelist G. Cabrera Infante, a *cinéaste* and scenarist who is happy to reveal the motive force behind his wildly funny *Three Trapped Tigers* (1965), a summa of movie allusions and a Marxian romp quite uncharacteristic of the Castro regime. "Nothing was closer to my purpose in *Three Trapped Tigers* than the philosophy of life expressed by the Marx Brothers," Cabrera Infante told interviewer Rita Guibert (see her *Seven Voices,* 1971). Ionesco has somewhere said that the greatest influence on his plays has been the Marx Brothers, and when, in *The Chairs* (1952), the Old Man reluctantly impersonates the month of February, the stage direction reads, *"He scratches his head like Stan Laurel"—that's* the kind of textual evidence the critic of Nabokov would welcome.

To see Nabokov's affinities with Laurel and Hardy et al. is perhaps to read *Invitation to a Beheading* less solemnly, to find new pleasure; except for Robert

Alter's brilliant essay on Nabokov's conjunction of art and politics (*TriQuarterly* 17, Winter 1970), its critics have offered little help. "Spiritual affinities have no place in my concept of literary criticism," declares Nabokov in the Foreword to the American *Invitation to a Beheading*, but the present occasion provides at least one instance where, "for better or worse, it is the commentator who has the last word," as Kinbote writes in *his* Foreword.

Although Laurel and Hardy frequently share the same bed (*Their First Mistake*, 1932), and don women's clothing (*Another Fine Mess*, 1930), who would be so obtuse as to term them homosexual or transvestite? Their asexual or pre-sexual comedy recalls the earlier pantomime of child-man Harry Langdon as *The Soldier Man* (1926) who is distracted by the udders of a cow. Laurel and Hardy's own lactic slapstick is developed fully in *Their First Mistake*. The boys adopt a baby for Mrs. Hardy (Mae Busch), who has meanwhile left Ollie to file for divorce. They take care of the child, and the film ends with Stan, instead of the baby, draining the delicious bottle that has been handed to him by an equally somnolent Ollie. A year later they made a brief, unbilled appearance as guest babies in *Our Gang's Wild Poses* (1933), and in *Saps at Sea* (1940), Stan reads *Mother Goose* to Ollie. When they appear as their own children in *Brats* (1930) and behave very much like their "adult" selves, Ollie and Stan are defining the essentially

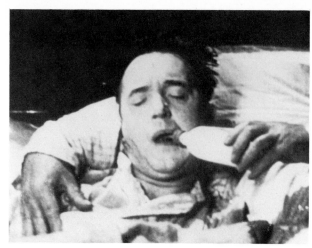

Stan Laurel in *Their First Mistake,* an understated title. The deprived baby is asleep on the left side of their bed.

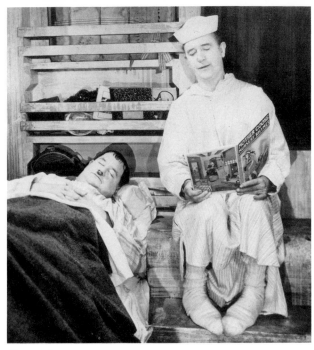

Saps at Sea.

Brats enjoy the natural province of play.

Lloyd in *Dr. Jack*. The worried mother appears older.

childlike (as opposed to childish) nature of their comic world; Harold Lloyd's *Dr. Jack* (1922) would feel at home there. The childlike exploration of being and nonbeing that is so touching in *Invitation to a Beheading* is also present in many Laurel and Hardy films, and its deep appeal is not lost on children. In *Saps at Sea,* Stan picks a banana from a fruit bowl, sits down, and casually peels it, only to find another unpeeled banana beneath the skin. He flips the peel away, strips the banana again, and the same thing happens: another somewhat smaller unpeeled banana. After patiently performing this operation a few more times, with the same results, Stan peels it for what will be the last time, for it turns out there is no fruit there; his hand is now empty. He blinks his eyes and, shrugging his shoulders, blithely tosses the nonexistent banana away. My son watched it with me on television, when he was four, and found this scene hilarious. "What did he have, Richard?" I asked him. "He had a wonderful nothing," he answered.

Maurice Sendak was quite right to transport his dreamy child to a wondrous kitchen staffed by three Oliver Hardys, who whip up a fine doughy mess, a launching pad for the boy's triumphant flight to the top of the Empire State Milk Bottle (*In the Night Kitchen,* 1970, written and drawn by Sendak while his father was fatally ill). Winsor McCay's *Little Nemo in Slumberland* (created in 1905), a precursor of Sendak's fantasy and screen comedy's "children,"

ventures even further. Nemo is a confident dreamer who, unlike Laurel and Hardy, always escapes his nightmares—roused by his father or mother. Cincinnatus is of their party, and Nabokov himself finally plays the role of father, a one-man rescue team. On the opening page, unsteady Cincinnatus is "like a child who has just learned to walk." A jailer embraces him like a baby and easily lifts him down from his table (p. 29), and at the execution M'sieur Pierre treats him like a child at bath- or bedtime: "We shall first of all remove our little shirt" (p. 221). Fittingly enough, young Emmie, the ballerina, is the first to take Cincinnatus backstage, enabling him to perceive that he is part of an artifice, someone else's grand design, a "game" whose outcome is difficult to foresee; "Terra Incognita" is the title of a 1931 Nabokov tale whose mortally ill narrator, witnessing a fight to the death, thinks "that this was all a harmless game, that in a moment they would get up and, when they had caught their breath, would peacefully carry me off. . . ."[6] "Let them be. . . . After all, they are both children," says M'sieur Pierre, unable to recognize childhood as the natural province of the most profound kinds of play (p. 166). The idea, the fact of growth through play is developed with elegance and deceptive simplicity. Is Cincinnatus's name an allusion to one or both of the Cincinnatuses of Roman history? At least one critic has stressed this connection. "No," answers Nabokov. "I simply liked the sound of 'Cin-Cin' "—the childish, reductive diminutive by which his keepers often address him. If not children, all the characters are clearly shams, waxen dummies, animated authorial toys. "I know that the horror of death is nothing really, a harmless convulsion—perhaps even healthful for the soul—the choking wail of a newborn child or a furious refusal to release a toy" (p. 193), writes Cincinnatus in the book he is rushing to complete, a book within the book that will release *him*.

"We play, we die," exclaims the desperate narrator of " 'That in Aleppo Once . . .' " (1943),[7] and *Invitation to a Beheading*, staged on one of Huizinga's playfields of the mind, poetically investigates the possibilities. "The fortress must have suffered a mild stroke," writes Nabokov at the beginning of the last chapter (p. 213); the choice of *stroke* (rather than "quake") emphasizes the cranial setting. M'sieur Pierre brings Cincinnatus a checkerboard, a box, and a punchinello doll, signal authorial gifts no less than the childlike, rhythmic prose that seems to scan—Death as an iamb:

"You've had company?" [Pierre] inquired politely of Cincinnatus when the director had left them alone in the cell. "Your mama visited you? That's fine, that's fine. And now I, poor, weak little M'sieur Pierre, have come to amuse you and amuse myself for a while. Just see how my Punch looks at you. Say hello to uncle. Isn't he a scream? Sit up, there, chum. Look, I've brought you lots of entertaining things. Would you like a game of chess first? Or cards? Do you play anchors? Splendid game! Come, I'll teach you!" (p. 137).

"My Punch looks at you," says M'sieur Pierre, adumbrating Cincinnatus's appeal to the reader as well as the authorial toy's insubstantiality as "Character," to borrow one of the four subheadings in Robbe-Grillet's important 1957 essay "On Several Obsolete Notions" (included in his *For a New Novel*, 1963). *Look at the Harlequins* is the title of Nabokov's new novel (1974), one more reminder that the idea of performance is crucial to him. Music and mime, circus stunts and stage props, and playthings too numerous to name prevail throughout *Invitation;* Dr. Leavis would certainly not call *this* a "novel." Yet "my Punch" also underscores the book's central paradox, the manner in which a fantast may deny or withhold verisimilitude at the same time that he responsibly refracts the historical moment and moves us deeply by engaging and easing our very real fears. Although doomed Cincinnatus is "already thinking of how to set up an alphabet" which might humanize his dystopian world (p. 139), a lesson-plan which a Leavisite might well applaud, it is the artifice of dance which most conspicuously humanizes the artificial world of the novel at hand. "Come, I'll teach you!"

Recalling one of Harpo Marx's enchanting, impromptu harp recitals (in *A Night at the Opera*, or *A Day at the Races*) or any one of several Laurel and

Hardy soft-shoe routines (*Pardon Us*, 1931, as escaped convicts; *The Music Box*, 1932; *Bonnie Scotland*, 1935; *Way Out West*, 1937), the cast of *Invitation to a Beheading* occasionally forgets the furious business at hand and breaks into a spontaneous dance or song:

Rodion the jailer came in and offered to dance a waltz with him. Cincinnatus agreed. They began to whirl. The keys on Rodion's leather belt jangled; he smelled of sweat, tobacco and garlic; he hummed, puffing into his red beard; and his rusty joints creaked. . . . The dance carried them into the corridor. Cincinnatus was much smaller than his partner. Cincinnatus was light as a leaf. The wind of the waltz made the tips of his long but thin mustache flutter, and his big limpid eyes looked askance, as is always the case with timorous dancers. . . . At the bend in the corridor stood another guard, nameless, with a rifle and wearing a doglike mask. . . . They described a circle near him and glided back into the cell, and now Cincinnatus regretted that the swoon's friendly embrace had been so brief (pp. 13-14).

Nabokov acknowledges that his title alludes to Weber's *Invitation to the Waltz*—as well as Baudelaire's *L'Invitation au voyage* (see p. 94)—and the entire cast's subsequent, more frenzied prancing (p. 156) anticipates the grand finale of Fellini's *8½* (1963). In order to escape the ship's crew in *Monkey Business* (1931), another animated Punchinello, Harpo by name, takes refuge in a children's Punch and Judy show. Harpo thrusts his head through the little theater's curtain, clips a puppet's body to his collar, and "freezes." The captain cannot determine which of the three puppets is real. Along with Harpo's autistic, soundless aria in *A Night at the Opera*, that brilliant sequence best recapitulates Nabokov's dreamlike mode, his operatic puppet show; the beautifully controlled, accelerating rhythms of the action are also akin to *Petrushka* (1911), another playful Russian's positively resolved puppet show. "We shall all dance, we shall all die," says Martha on her deathbed in *King, Queen, Knave* (p. 271). *The Waltz Invention* is doomsday, and its old generals (Gump, Bump, Dump, Hump, Lump, Mump, Rump, and Stump), each of whom plays two other roles as well, generate a ceaseless Marxian locomotion.

Unlike the three movie-mad compulsive jokers in Cabrera Infante's extraordinary novel, Nabokov's characters do not discuss the Marx Brothers, who nevertheless seem to have left their marks (as Cabrera's fellows would say) on the pages of the *Invitation*. Recalling *A Night at the Opera*, Nabokov dwelled on "the opera, the crowded cabin, which is pure genius. I must have seen that film three times!"[8] He lovingly rehearsed the cabin scene in detail, the stream of people piling in, delighting particularly in the arrival of the manicurist. Nabokov's first, perhaps unconscious, tribute to the scene occurs midway through *Invitation to a Beheading*. Cincinnatus' wife,

A Night at the Opera.

Marthe, a Laurel and Hardy shrew, crams her entire family into his cell for a visit, including all their furniture:

How they lumbered in! Marthe's aged father, with his huge bald head, and bags under his eyes, and the rubbery tap of his black cane; Marthe's brothers, identical twins except that one had a golden mustache and the other a pitch-black one; Marthe's maternal grandparents, so old that one could already see through them; three vivacious female cousins, who, however, were not admitted for some reason at the last minute; Marthe's children—lame Diomedon and obese little Pauline; at last Marthe herself, wearing her best black dress, with a velvet ribbon around her cold white neck, and holding a hand mirror; a very proper young man with a flawless profile was constantly at her side (pp. 98-99).

More furniture, household utensils, a tricycle, "even individual sections of walls continued to arrive," as do a lawyer, a cat, M'sieur Pierre, and "the director" (p. 104). Responding to the now cozy environment, one of Marthe's brothers, a distinguished singer, bursts into song as "everybody began talking simultaneously. '*Mali é trano t'amesti!*' Marthe's brother sang full voice," in corrupt, Marx Brothers Italian (p. 103). Nabokov mocks the stilted Italian of *Il Trovatore*, the Marx Brothers' main target. Although the phrase is a syntactical mishmash, there is sense in Nabokov's nonsense. *Mali* is the plural of "evil," *é trano* a re-created *é strano* ("it's bewildering"), and *t'amesti* a nonexistent form that approximates the imperfect subjunctive "you loved you"—parodic evocations of overused operatic tags and a compressed description of Cincinnatus's isolation. The packed Zemblan jail in *Pale Fire* (p. 144) outdoes both this scene and its *Night at the Opera* precursor (repeated by the Marxes in *Room Service*, 1938).

Assisted by the jailers Rodion, Rodrig, and Roman (Nabokov's Three Stooges), M'sieur Pierre, the lethal "operatic woodman" (p. 171), has all the sartorial panache of Laurel and Hardy in *Fra Diavolo*. Dressed for the execution "in a pea-green hunting habit," the pea-green hat graced with a pheasant feather, "attractively rouged M'sieur Pierre bowed, bringing together his patent-leather boot tops, and said in a comic falsetto: 'the carriage is waiting, if you please sir. . . . Off to do chop chop.'" (p. 207). But Pierre's farce comes apart at the execution, and he fares even worse than the impresario of *A Night at the Opera*, who, briefly locked in a closet, is spared the early sounds and sights of the opening night debacle: the orchestra's segue from *Il Trovatore* to "Take Me Out to the Ball Game," Harpo's Tarzan-like swoops through the scenery, and so forth. An equestrian match for the Marx Brothers' game-winning gladiatorial horse-drawn garbage cart in *Horse Feathers* (1932, a burlesque of *Ben-Hur*, 1926), the skinny old nag pulling the ancient "scarred carriage" breaks into a miraculous gallop and flies by the eager crowds

M'sieur Pierre's sartorial elegance: Laurel and Hardy and Dennis King in *Fra Diavolo,* an invitation to a hanging.

Harpo Marx in *Horse Feathers.*

Harry Langdon, ill at ease in *Long Pants* (1923). Buster belies *his* pair in the final moments of *Sherlock, Jr.,* when he turns to the film-within-the-film for amatory instructions. The hero kisses his girl, and Buster does the same, but when hero and heroine next appear with babies, perplexed Buster can only shrug his shoulders. The regressive sexuality of screen comedy, and Kafka and Beckett too, is encapsulated by Langdon in *His Marriage Vow* (1925) when he assumes a fetal position on the floor of the nuptial chamber.

(p. 217). Like Harpo Marx amuck, Stan Laurel as his target, "a person in Turkish trousers came running out of a cafe with a pail of confetti, but, missing, sent his vari-colored blizzard into the face of a cropped fellow who had just come running from the opposite sidewalk with a bienvenue platter of 'bread and salt'" (pp. 217-18). As vulnerable as Chaplin and as innocent or pre-sexual a "lover" as Harry Langdon, or Laurel and Hardy, or Keaton in *Sherlock, Jr.* (1924), cuckolded and threatened Cincinnatus nevertheless resists the circus they would make of death and all life. At the last possible moment at least one Cincinnatus refuses to play his part in *Socrates Must Decrease,* and—like the Showman in *Petrushka* or Gradus in *Pale Fire*—impotent, unlucky M'sieur Pierre is mocked and defeated.

Journeying to the execution, Cincinnatus copes with his "implacable fear," "even though he knows perfectly well that the entire masquerade is staged in his own brain" (p. 213), that he is playing out his part in an authorial dream, the psychological phenomenon that allows a creative sleeper to perceive his nightmare as an "unreal" drama and calmly confront and control it on a new dream-level; his sexual inadequacies and humiliations are equivalent to fears of death, in Nabokov's reversal of the Elizabethan pun on "die." Impotency is also equated with artistic failure, the respective desires to complete the novel and the book-within-the-book. In *Speak, Memory,* Nabokov's first love and initial efforts at verse are cojoined in a sensuous and painterly celebration of a brilliant landscape (pp. 212-13). As a free man (the phrase is used advisedly), Cincinnatus had been in charge of a kindergarten of bastards, his wife's included, but Pierre is hardly his superior: he has called Marthe "mama" (p. 137) and failed with his Jocasta off-stage (p. 199), just as he will at the chopping block, duplicating his other losing games (chess and dice, pp. 144-46). The head of "one Cincinnatus" is on the block, counting loudly as Pierre's ax begins its arc, when suddenly "the other Cincinnatus" (spirit, soul?) joyfully gets up and looks around (p. 222), like ghostly Petrushka's triumphant appearance above his limp straw body (definitively performed by Nijinsky), or Buster Keaton roused from the nightmare that has placed him on a hangman's scaffold in *Convict 13* (1920), or the moment in *Sherlock, Jr.*, when movie projectionist Keaton, falling asleep on the job, divides himself and departs from his body by means of a technical trick (a superimposition on a double exposure). Buster's dream double leaves the projection booth, scrambles over the orchestra pit, and climbs into the film-within-the-film to rescue the heroine. Cincinnatus moves in the opposite direction, toward the author and his readers, easily achieved in a verbal infinite regress. As the creaking set and setting of Nabokov's most limpidly structured artifice come unglued, Cincinnatus slowly descends from the plat-

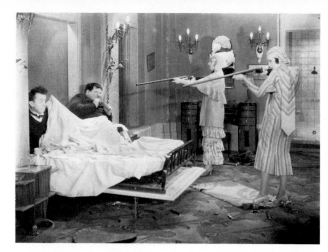

Another sexual nightmare: Laurel's and Hardy's unsatisfied wives aim their "Freudian" weapons in *Be Big* (1930), an ironic double entendre that may be unintentional. "I've got my gun and I've never missed yet!" says Mrs. Hardy in *Sons of the Desert* (1933), whose title alludes to Laurel and Hardy's fraternal organization, an all-male utopia in the American grain. When Vivien Oakland literally rides Stan in *Scram* (1932), his humiliating posture follows the lead of Leopold Bloom, on whose bare back gambols Bella Cohen (Circe) in the dreamy Nighttown section of *Ulysses*.

The apotheosis of a weakling: Lloyd in *The Freshman*.

The comic rhythm and velocity of *Invitation to a Beheading*'s end: Chico, Groucho, and Harpo *Go West* (1940).

form, "a spinning wind" whipping all sorts of debris and falling scenery past him (pp. 222-23), recalling the most extraordinary and moving scene in all Keaton: Buster standing alone in the street while a cyclone rips apart the town of *Steamboat Bill, Jr.* With no warning, the wind-loosened front wall of the two-story building behind him collapses on its unseeing victim, and Buster, playing Everyman as stationary target, disappears from view. The settled timber reveals Buster, still on his feet, motionless, unmoved, facing the camera, standing in the fallen wall's life-saving open window. He walks away, but after a glance over his shoulder and a classic double-take, he races away in terror, the gale in pursuit. Cincinnatus, however, has outdistanced fear—"By myself," he has said, several times, as the awful moment drew near—and his triumph is akin to Harold Lloyd's apotheosis of a weakling in *The Freshman* (1925), who zigzags his way through crashing tacklers to score the game-winning points, leaving in his wake a field littered with bodies. Pierre has been dispatched and grotesquely reduced by crushing debris and authorial magic, just as Stravinsky's Showman is chased off by the two trumpets' dissonant fanfare. Cincinnatus is finally as indomitable as a Marx Brother on the move, and at "the end" of the novel—a renewal and in the best sense a beginning—he strides through the chaos of Thriller Square "in that direction where, to judge by the voices, stood beings akin to him" (p. 223), gathered by Nabokov into Yeats's "artifice of eternity."

The diminution of the hairy man in Nabokov's Bluebird "Locomotion" not only anticipates Fields's *The Barbershop*, it pinpoints one of the most nightmarish of sight gags: physical dismemberment, displacement, or metamorphosis, the human equivalent of the "empty" banana routine in *Saps at Sea*. In *Blockheads* (1938), war veteran Laurel absent-mindedly "loses" a leg, a surreality that gets him into considerable trouble and tests the compassion of others, a theme the film shares with Kafka's *Metamorphosis* (1912). *Going Bye Bye* (1934) ends with Laurel and Hardy having had their legs twisted around their necks by a vengeful criminal, while another figurative threat is literally carried out by the ship captain in *The Live Ghost* (1934), who twists Laurel's and Hardy's heads back to front, as in one of Marc Chagall's early Russian caprices; in *Way Out West*, Hardy's neck is stretched three feet (by trick photography, most likely). The Three Stooges (vulgarized Laurel and Hardy) suffer similar indignities, their bones or savagely tweaked noses creaking and crackling like stripped engine gears, gross textbook examples of Bergson's definition of comedy ("the mechanical encrusted upon the living"). Occasionally the boys will bark like dogs, a Darwinian descent reversed in the *Speaking of Animals* shorts of the forties, in which crudely cartooned lips are superimposed on "talking" creatures; "Animals is de cwaziest

peoples!" was always narrator Lew Lehr's closing tag in Fox Movietone News's *Dribble Puss Parade*, a dreadful imitation of that series. Fear may be at the center of the universal fascination with freak shows ("Move along, kid," said four-hundred-pound Baby Irene in 1944 after my chubby friend had stared for fifteen minutes) and the human oddities offered for view in Ripley's *Believe It or Not* and its movie short version, *Strange As It Seems*, as well as the perverse appeal of the cautionary German children's book *Struwwelpeter*, *Plastic Man* comic books, horror film metamorphoses and sci-fi miniaturism, and the amusement park funhouse mirrors which allow us to transform ourselves temporarily into monstrous sight gags and to view our safe return to "normalcy." How fortunate we are! "A metamorphosis is a thing always exciting to watch," writes Nabokov in *Gogol* (p. 43).

Authenticity and existence are also at stake in the best involuted *Bugs Bunny* animated cartoons of the forties and fifties, which, according to their chief animator, Chuck Jones, often drew their inspiration from Keaton, Laurel and Hardy, and the Marx Brothers. "I loved that Bunny," says Nabokov, "he was so different from those sentimental Disney creatures, except for the Duck, who endured real trouble. Was the Bunny Disney's?" Scholars may recall a *Bugs Bunny* cartoon (Warner Brothers, c. 1943) in which there is a running battle between the rabbit and the artist, whose visible hand alternately wields a large gum eraser and a drawing pencil, terrible weapons which at one moment remove the rabbit's feet so that he cannot escape, and at another give him a duck's bill so that he cannot talk back,[9] not unlike the lot of the characters in *Invitation to a Beheading*, where, however, the creator—if not *the* Creator—is ultimately more sympathetic. On the way to "do chop-chop," dreamer and dream (or Yeats's inseparable dancer and dance) grow more distinct, and lucidly self-conscious Cincinnatus "suddenly understood that everything had in fact been written already." He only needs time to finish writing *his* book: "I ask three minutes—go away for that time or at least be quiet—yes, a three-minute intermission—after that, so be it, I'll act to the end my role in your idiotic production" (p. 209). "You can't kill me. You ain't got time. This is the end of the picture," says the helpless sheep to the knife-wielding wolf that has strapped him to a platter in the animated film *No Mutton fer Nuttin'* (1944).[10] Earlier in the novel, "cartooned" Cincinnatus has been taken apart and reassembled at will; and his rusty-jointed jailers have interchangeable parts, in both senses of the phrase.[11] Literal-minded source hunters, seeking links in the chain, should be told that Professor Nabokov, lecturing at Cornell, delighted in a similar resolve in *Ulysses* (1922): Bloom's vision of ghostly Virag, his suicide father, metamorphosed into a garrulous birdman, the grotesque Nighttown equivalent—and rejection—of Bloom's morbid and crippling diurnal mourning. Virag unscrews his head, tucks it under his arm, and exits. "Quack!" is the disembodied bird-head's first and final word;[12] similar moments in popular culture insist on the archetypal persistence of such projections, nightmares considered at arm's length.

The epilogue to *Freaks* (1932) reveals that the aroused denizens of the sideshow have demonically transformed Cleopatra, the trapeze *artiste* and instigator of their local miseries, into a hen-woman who is exhibited in her own sideshow box, squawking unintelligibly. That denouement is given a somewhat lighter treatment in the following year's *Dirty Work* (1933), which finds chimney sweeps Laurel and Hardy serving a mad scientist who has just discovered a rejuvenating formula and turned a duck into an egg. Helpmate Laurel accidentally knocks Hardy into a vat containing the elixir. A chimpanzee shortly emerges, wearing Hardy's bowler hat; "I have *nothing* to say!" states the indignant chimp. Badly beaten up by his wife in *Thicker than Water* (1935), Hardy is taken to the hospital. Laurel is forced to donate blood, but too much is taken and the transfusion process is reversed. The incredibly complicated comic business ends with Laurel and Hardy having exchanged roles (by virtue of make-up, dubbing, and clothes), Stan playing the "shrunken" Ollie. "Here's *another* fine mess you've gotten me into!" he says, borrowing Hardy's most famous line. Sweet vengeance is similar in Nabokov and Lewis Carroll. In the course of their escape from prison in *Liberty*, Laurel and Hardy crush a burly, pursuing policeman in an elevator, reducing him to a midget. At the end of Queen Alice's riotous party in Chapter Nine of *Through the Looking-Glass* (1872), "the Red Queen, whom she considered as the cause of all the mischief . . . had suddenly dwindled down to the size of a little doll, and was now on the table, merrily running round and round after her own shawl. . . . "I'll shake you into a kitten,'" says Alice, and she does (Tenniel's drawings illustrate the metamorphosis beautifully). When last seen in *Invitation to a Beheading*, Pierre is in the care of "a woman in a black shawl," who is "carrying the tiny executioner like a larva in her arms" (p. 223). "Death be not proud, though some have called thee / Mighty and dreadful, for, thou are not so," wrote Donne in an earlier address to the executioner; Nabokov's lighter toned *Invitation* is no less serious. " 'The thought, when written down, becomes less oppressive,'" states Cincinnatus in his book-within-the-book (p. 194), a concise statement too of the permanent appeal of Laurel and Hardy, whose comic response to the terrible exceeds the context and conscious intent of light entertainment: "I have *nothing* to say!"

Priglashenie na Kazn' (*Invitation*'s Russian title) was serialized in 1935-36 in three issues of the most distinguished *émigré* journal, the Paris-based *Sover-*

mennye Zapiski (*Contemporary Annals*), and in 1938 was published in book form by Berlin and Paris *émigré* presses. After *Lolita*'s success (1958) created a market for Nabokov's hidden *œuvre*, *Invitation to a Beheading* was the first book to be translated (1959, dateline "Oak Creek Canyon, Arizona"). By 1971, with the American publication of *Glory* (1932), Nabokov had completed the Englishing of his nine *émigré* novels, but he opens his Foreword (dateline Montreux) with a bibliographical catalog that is more somber than triumphant. "He who cares to scan the list [of novels] given below should mark the dramatic gap between 1938 and 1959," declares Nabokov, referring to the *émigré* and American editions of *Invitation*. The gap is dramatic in several ways, not all of them happy.

The Nabokov family moved to Paris in 1937, and the following year represents the apogee of the writer's "Russian career." He had recently completed *The Gift, The Waltz Invention, The Event,* and several of his best stories (datelines Paris, Cap d'Antibes, Mentone, and Marienbad), and published *Soglyadatay* (*The Eye*), a collection of fictions. Never insensitive to auguries of the future, Nabokov had already begun to exercise a polyglot author's options, though *writing* in your second or third language is no blithe experience, especially in early middle age. At the end of 1936, he had translated *Despair* for a London publisher—"This was my first serious attempt," he says,

"to use English for what may be loosely termed an artistic purpose"—and in Paris he wrote in French as well as Russian: "Mademoiselle O" (now Chapter Five in *Speak, Memory*) and what he calls "a very difficult" critical article on Pushkin for the prestigious *Nouvelle Revue Française*. "Paulhan [Jean Paulhan, its editor] wanted to know who had helped me," says Nabokov, with justifiable pride. Contemplating Hitler's rapid adjustments of the map of Europe and the fact that his wife Véra is Jewish, Nabokov chose to compose his next novel in English. *The Real Life of Sebastian Knight* was written in their 1938 apartment "on rue Saigon, between the Etoile and the Bois . . . in a large sunny bathroom [which] doubled as my study," and was published three years later in America. In 1939 he traveled to England to seek an academic position, but there were no offers; later that year, Nabokov's mother died in Nazi-occupied Prague (his father, murdered by Russian monarchist assassins in 1922, is buried in what is now East Berlin). Refusing to surrender an *émigré* writer's sole legacy, his language, he began composing another Russian novel, *Solus Rex*. (Its title—"The King Alone"—was in Roman, not Cyrillic type. A chess gambit by way of a traditional stage direction, the title telescopes authorial solitude.) Chapter One, "Ultima Thule," is a narrative addressed to a dead woman. A long section from the book was the lead contribution in the last issue of *Sovremennye Zapiski* (1940), whose editor,

Ilya Fondaminsky—"a saintly and heroic soul who did more for Russian *émigré* literature than any other man," eulogizes Nabokov in *Speak, Memory* (pp. 286-87)—was soon to perish in a German death camp, as did Nabokov's brother in 1945. On May 28, 1940, Nabokov, his wife, and young son sailed for America and a new life in English (that bibliographical gap), leaving behind *Solus Rex* and the German and French chapters of the Russian emigration.

> Beyond the seas where I have lost a sceptre,
> I hear the neighing of my dappled nouns,
> soft participles coming down the steps,
> treading on leaves, trailing their rustling gowns

Nabokov was to write in "An Evening of Russian Poetry" (1945),[13] commemorating a loss that choreographers, composers, and musicians in exile did not have to overcome, since they had at their fingertips an international language (Balanchine; Stravinsky; Rachmaninov, who kindly offered Nabokov an ancient cutaway to wear for his first lecture at Stanford University's 1941 Summer Session; and Dmitri Tiomkin, whose Oscar-winning scores, concurrent with

Solus Rex: Vladimir Nabokov at Wellesley College, c. 1941. The mural in the background ("For Purple Mou—") celebrates *America the Beautiful,* written by Katherine Lee Bates, a Wellesley Professor of English.

Nabokov's Americanization through *Lolita,* included *High Noon,* 1952, and *The High and the Mighty,* 1954, mordant titles in the context of the plight of the *émigré* writers). At the end of *Pale Fire,* Kinbote says of Shade and his poem, "I even suggested to him a good title—the title of the book in me whose pages he was to cut: *Solus Rex;* instead of which I saw *Pale Fire,* which meant nothing to me" (p. 296).

With German armies circumscribing France, the winter and spring of 1940 was a fearful time. Anyone who has negotiated and survived the bureaucratic labyrinth of Nansen passports and exit visas knows that *émigré* confusions, anxieties, and terrors are well recorded in Nabokov's epistolary tale "'That in Aleppo Once . . .'" (1943, dateline Boston)—the "Refugee Blues" W. H. Auden attempted to express in *Another Time* (1940). Nabokov's title, a phrase from *Othello* supplied by the narrator, suggests that one more despairing *émigré* will soon take his own life. A brief respite was offered the Nabokovs by a Parisian showing of *Ninotchka*—the only Garbo film, according to Nabokov, that is not doomed by "its corny scenarios and overwrought players." Her first American comedy cast Garbo as an inhumanly humorless and glacially business-like Soviet agent dispatched to luxurious Paris. *Ninotchka* contains several biting sequences analogous to the blended Communazi phenomena of *Invitation to a Beheading* and *Bend Sinister,* not surprising when one notices that its director was Ernst Lubitsch and its scenarists included a Viennese Jewish refugee named Billy Wilder. When the three male Soviet agents go to the station to meet Garbo (they don't expect a woman), one spies a bearded fellow with a proletarian knapsack. "That must be the one!" "Yes," says another, "he looks like a comrade!" They follow him, but before they can greet the "comrade," he is met by a German girl. The two exchange the Nazi salute: "Heil Hitler!" Nabokov recalls with a not entirely apolitical delight the ways in which the three Soviet agents, ensconced in their hotel's Royal Suite, quickly succumb to "capitalistic" pleasures. The scene he remembers most vividly, the film's most famous interlude, is the thawing of Garbo by Melvyn Douglas. Seated together in a carefully chosen "working-class" restaurant (a cozy atmosphere for seduction), suave Douglas tries to force Garbo to laugh by telling a series of stupid jokes. She remains unmoved until, in his frustration and fury ("You have no sense of humor! *None!* No humor!"), he leans excitedly on his flimsy table, which topples over, sending him and everything else crashing to the floor. The restaurant quakes with classless mirth. Garbo struggles to maintain her composure, but suddenly a laugh bursts through the stolid mask, and she too roars with uncontrollable laughter. It is a wondrous moment. Remembering the scene thirty years later, Nabokov also rocks with laughter, as he must have done in 1940, when laughter in the dark, to borrow a phrase, was as rare as it was necessary. Joyous as well as haunting, *Invitation to a Beheading* offered its contemporary audience the same opportunity, but its form and affirmative tone seem to have confused almost as many readers as were sustained. Although *Lolita* is the novel for which Nabokov feels the greatest affection, *Invitation* is the performance which he esteems above all others.[14]

Whether baffled or impressed by the novel, *émigré* critics were correct in their complaints that the "Kafkaesque" *Invitation to a Beheading* was "un-Russian" and belonged to some "foreign" tradition; their heated remarks curiously echo the previous decade's attacks on the "neoclassical" Stravinsky's "traitorous" departure from *l'âme slave* (the Slavonic spirit). Prattle about "influences" and "traditions" aside, the novel's affinities with screen comedy seem clear, and they constitute a brightly lit exit sign, or beam of light, in Nabokov's dark cinema. "A wonderful movie could be made of *Invitation to a Beheading*," says Nabokov, and, in a sense, it has been done.

Quilty's long death scene represents a return to earlier movie madness, and its violent pratfalls and verbal vaudeville have countless visual analogues in Laurel and Hardy's theater of cruelty. In *County Hospital* (1932), immobilized Hardy is abruptly hoisted from his bed and suspended by his broken leg when the doctor falls out the window and clings to the pulleys of Ollie's traction. Far more savage is the climax

Laughter in the dark, a 1940 necessity: Garbo and Douglas in *Ninotchka*.

to *Them Thar Hills* (1934), which builds slowly toward the inevitable orgy of destruction. "Bend down," says Hardy's tormentor, who then proceeds to douse his trousers with gasoline. Hardy retains his composure and gazes plaintively at the camera, as if to say, "Bad form to resist or run," an example of "grace under pressure" never imagined by Hemingway. "Got a match?" the man asks Laurel, who sweetly obliges, and flaming, gout-afflicted Hardy hops about wildly, finally jumping into a well that contains liquor discarded earlier by hastily departing bootleggers. The terrible explosion catapults Ollie into the air, "higher and higher, like old, gray, mad Nijinski . . . to a phenomenal altitude," as Humbert says of Quilty (p. 304), whose gravity-defying acrobatics also evoke images of Keaton's amazing Veen-like feats in films such as *Sherlock, Jr.*, where he pole-vaults from a roof into the back seat of the villain's speeding car and is propelled through an open window after a ride on the handlebars of a motorcycle. The Three Stooges demonstrate the persistence of this kind of comic mechanism. At the end of *Idle Roomers* (1944) they are trapped with a gorilla in an elevator that wildly hurtles up, up, and away, but not, unfortunately, into orbit. At certain moments Humbert's own violent action would seem to have been choreographed by the Buster Keaton who outruns the entire metropolitan police force in *Cops* (1922), or the anti-Sisyphus who runs, leaps, and dodges down a hillside to escape an avalanche of one thousand rocks in *Seven Chances* (1925), or the aging Keaton whose acrobatics dazzled Parisian music-hall audiences in 1953: "I see myself following [wounded Quilty] through the hall, with a kind of double, triple, kangaroo jump, remaining quite straight on straight legs while bouncing up twice in his wake, and then bouncing between him and the front door in a ballet-like stiff bounce, with the purpose of heading him off, since the door was not properly closed" (p. 305). Their violent *pas de deux* is executed with precision as well as gusto; the accelerating velocity of the chase, its zaniness, its realization of a range of dream-like impossibilities all further suggest that, besides its burlesque of "underworlders" and other targets, the scene is also staged in the style and spirit of the unsentimental film masters whom Nabokov admires most—Keaton, of course; the Marx Brothers; and Laurel and Hardy, "who are my favorites," says Nabokov.

The comedy of Humbert's erratic markmanship is exceeded only by the magical resiliency of Quilty, who, like Oliver Hardy *in extremis*, accepts with uncommon gentlemanly grace the violence performed upon his ample person:

Suddenly dignified, and somewhat morose, he started to walk up the broad stairs, and, shifting my position, but not actually following him up the steps, I fired three or four times in quick succession, wounding him at every blaze; and every time I did it to him, that horrible thing to him, his face would twitch in an absurd clownish manner, as if he were exaggerating the pain; he slowed down, rolled his eyes half closing them and made a feminine "ah!" and he shivered every time a bullet hit him as if I were tickling him, and every time I got him with those slow, clumsy, blind bullets of mine, he would say under his breath, with a phoney British accent—all the while dreadfully twitching, shivering, smirking, but withal talking in a curiously detached and even amiable manner: "Ah, that hurts atrociously, my dear fellow. I pray you, desist. Ah—very painful, very painful, indeed . . . God! Hah! This is abominable, you should really not—" His voice trailed off as he reached the landing, but he steadily walked on despite all the lead I had lodged in his bloated body—and in distress, in dismay, I understood that far from killing him I was injecting spurts of energy into the poor fellow, as if the bullets had been capsules wherein a heady elixir danced (p. 305).

Capturing as it does the immunities often enjoyed by Hardy (bricks bouncing off his head in *Dirty Work*), the passage recapitulates the "heady elixir" of comedy offered to a movie audience more susceptible to pain then Ollie, a trusting child who can't believe that anyone would want to hurt *him*. Growing larger before Humbert's eyes, as in another one of Laurel and Hardy's sight gags involving grotesque physical distortion (*They Go Boom*, 1929, in which cold-sufferer Ollie is inflated further by an inhalator), "bloated" Quilty trudges through Pavor Manor, "bleeding majestically," as invincible as Rasputin.

"Grace under pressure": Laurel and Hardy in *Blockheads*.

Chimney-sweep Hardy awaits the final brick in *Dirty Work*.

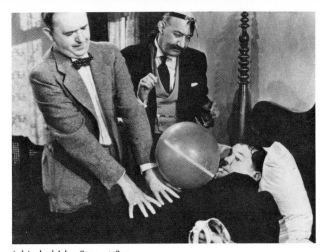

A big bubble, *Saps at Sea.*

" 'Get out of here, get out of here,' he said coughing and spitting; and in a nightmare of wonder, I saw this blood-spattered but still buoyant person get into his bed and wrap himself up in the chaotic bedclothes," regressive Laurel and Hardy's unsafe haven in numerous films. Humbert "hit him at very close range through the blankets, and then he lay back and a big pink bubble with juvenile connotations [= the Lolita they have both "consumed"] formed on his lips, grew to the size of a toy balloon, and vanished" (p. 306), in a manner not unlike the explosive interlude in *Saps at Sea,* when Dr. Finlayson attempts to cure bedridden Hardy, suffering from a nervous collapse, by having him inflate a large toy balloon. Minutes later "Quilty of all people had managed to crawl out onto the landing, and there we could see him, flapping and heaving" (p. 307)—Nabokov's version of Laurel and Hardy's lovely "Locomotion" at the end of *Hog Wild.* Crushed between two streetcars, their miraculous car still runs, if only in a circle, like some crazed infernal machine. Even Quilty's slow death, its thematic "meaning" aside (the persistence of evil, however banal), is consistent with the spirit that is underscored by the second syllable of Ada—"*da*"!—when it is pronounced correctly in the Russian way. "Yes!"—an echo of Molly Bloom's chorus of musical *yeses,* comedy's soaring, affirmative note, sustaining us above the hoary abyss contemplated by Keaton and Lloyd, Laurel and Hardy, Kinbote and

Luzhin, Shirin and Nabokov. "The [Alpine] gondola [containing Hugh Person and Armande] would have gone on gliding forever in a blue haze sufficient for paradise had not a robust attendant stopped it before it turned to reascend for good," writes the author of *Transparent Things* (p. 54), bringing to mind the closing moments of *The Balloonatic* (1923), when the canoe bearing Buster Keaton and his girl sails over the edge of a waterfall and floats through the air, suspended by love and (as the camera moves back, visual surprise) the more literally supportive balloon —which deflates our sentimental metaphor.

The Nabokovs' arrival in America in June 1940, on a ship peopled mainly by Jewish refugees, was of course a joyous occasion. Their most vivid memory of the event is a scene characteristic of Nabokov's art: two Immigration Service officials (formidable to any traveler, but especially to *émigrés*), discovered Dmitri Nabokov's boxing gloves in the family's baggage. The inspectors grabbed the gloves, each donned one, and they began to spar together—a Laurel and Hardy introduction to the promised land, a magical reversal of *Pack Up Your Troubles* (1932). "Velcome to Amer–r–rika!" said a friend-of-a-friend, in a thick, unintentionally comical German accent, greeting the Nabokovs after they had passed through Immigration's portals. Five years later, in Boston, Nabokov became an American citizen. On their way to the citizenship exam and ceremony, Nabokov's sponsor, Michael

Hardy about to be knocked out in *Pack Up Your Troubles*.

Karpovich, a staid Harvard professor and former consular official, told the apprentice American, "No joking, *no* joking, *please!*" "Oh, a *professor!*" said the Immigration official upon meeting the candidate. A solemn Nabokov began the oral exam. "Name the American presidents," which Nabokov did, unerringly. He was next told to read aloud from a standard text which began, "The child is bold." "*The child is bald,*" declaimed Nabokov, soon to purchase new eyeglasses. "You can't read English," said the official, "he is *bold.*" "No, no," argued Nabokov. "Why should the poor little child be 'bold'? He is very young. It should read *'bald.'*" "You're right, I never thought of that," said the official, and, save for the mortified Karpovich, everyone laughed. Nabokov taught for almost two decades in America, where he quietly launched several books composed in English, causing only minor ripples. With no fanfare whatsoever, the Paris-based Olympia Press brought out *Lolita* in 1955. Three years later it was published in America and, as John Shade writes in *Pale Fire*, "Hurricane Lolita/ Swept from Florida to Maine." "A painful birth, a difficult baby, but a kind daughter," *Lolita* enabled Nabokov, at sixty, to resign his professorship. Part of a fortune lost in 1919 had been restored exactly forty years later, the rubles miraculously converted to dollars, and the Nabokovs soon moved again, first to Hollywood to script *Lolita,* and then to Switzerland in 1960. Nabokov's last public appearance at Cornell was as featured speaker at the 1959 Festival of Contemporary Arts, before an audience of four or five hundred, which included Deane W. Malott, president of Cornell. The subject: "On Censorship." Lecturing on recent Soviet literature, rather than *Lolita*, Nabokov constructed socialist realism's ideal love scene, Boy Meets Girl at the Factory (or was it a farm? witnesses disagree, legends grow)—the boy and girl standing next to each other but never touching since they are manning their machines and have a work quota. Their dialogue was a parody of Party jargon, a distillation of the clichés of four decades. Nabokov played both roles, his entire body vibrating violently as he delivered, in a terrible machine-induced stutter and stammer, their banal and hapless endearments. All witnesses agree that Nabokov made his exit from academe on a tumultuous sea of laughter.

Edward G. Robinson
in *The Woman in the Window*.

5
Dark Cinema

The End of the Road

"If you want to make a movie out of my book, have one of these [criminal] faces gently melt into my own, while I look," says Humbert, studying the "Wanted" posters in the post office at Wace (p. 224). It seemed incredible to Nabokov in 1954 that such a film might be made, yet it is not surprising, if only for one reason. Nabokov is an intensely visual writer—"I see in images, not words," he says—and his work abounds in images and scenes that are cinematic by design. "Houses have crumbled in my memory as soundlessly as they did in the mute films of yore," he writes in *Speak, Memory* (p. 95),[1] but in *Lolita* he favors more sinister effects and an iconography which bring to mind more recent films. Describing his tormented first conjugal night with Lolita, Humbert recalls how, after all the hotel guests "were sound asleep, the

avenue under the window of my insomnia, to the west of my wake—a staid, eminently residential, dignified alley of huge trees—degenerated into the despicable haunts of gigantic trucks roaring through the wet and windy night" (p. 132). Nabokov's *mise-en-scène,* his prose equivalent of deep-focus, creates a veritable dark cinema here, for the most evocative aural and visual descriptions in *Lolita* are in the manner of classic nineteen-forties *films noirs,* with their oppressive rain-washed nightscapes and their desperate, driven men—seemingly decent people who have irreparably committed themselves to their dreams, passions, or obsessions, and are suddenly criminals, their respectable selves dissolved into the "Wanted" poster imagined by Humbert. His thin guise of bourgeois normality, maintained by a series of judiciously chosen masks ("Teacher," "Husband," "Father," "Neighbor," "Jokester"), links Humbert with the central characters in several *films noirs*, particularly some of the non-gangster roles played by Edward G. Robinson. But Humbert's affinities with *noir* characters are obvious enough, and any extended comparison would reveal differences as well as similarities; he is more a rhetorical than a visual figure. A comparison of *film noir* with the quotidian world of *Lolita* and Kubrick's version of it is far more rewarding because it provides another instance in which the accomplishments of high and popular art may be considered in the very same terms.

Because the *film noir* is not a genre,[2] its properties cannot be defined as readily or exactly as those of, say, the Western. It is a kind of Hollywood film peculiar to the forties and early fifties, a genus in the gangster film/thriller family. The taxonomic tag first introduced by French *cinéastes* of the fifties is appropriately imprecise: *film noir* is a matter of manner, of mood, tone, and style, though its cultural attitudes are concrete enough, its psychological appeal quite direct. Although the most memorable of early *films noirs*—*Shadow of a Doubt* (1943), *Laura* (1944), *The Woman in the Window* (1944), *Double Indemnity* (1944)—variously penetrate the masks of middle-class probity, many other *films noirs* are in the outlines of their plots indistinguishable from traditional gangster films or thrillers (thus *The Killers*, 1946, and *Gun*

Crazy, 1949). *Scarlet Street* (1945), a domestic tragedy, and *The Big Heat* (1953), ostensibly a big city crime and corruption melodrama, both directed by Fritz Lang, suggest that a capacity for betrayal and violence is human rather than "criminal," and the expressive low-key lighting of the two films establishes a consistent tone. What unites the seemingly disparate kinds of *films noirs*, then, is their dark visual style and their black vision of despair, loneliness, and dread—a vision that touches an audience most intimately because it assures them that their suppressed impulses and fears are shared human responses. It is no wonder that these old movies "hold up" so well today, and that at least one young movie-goer of the forties should have found them strangely comforting. *Out of the Past* (1947) is a title that at once encapsulates the elements of loss, nostalgia, and anxiety as common to the *film noir* as they are atypical of what Humbert terms the "grief-proof sphere" of Hollywood. Masked as genre entertainments, the finest *films noirs* are "escapist" works only in the sense that they consistently avoid and challenge the sentimentality, piety, and propaganda, the programmed innocence and optimism of most Hollywood films of the period.

The best and most influential *film noir* directors and technicians were German or Austrian refugees. Although F. W. Murnau and other directors susceptible to dollars had introduced the Germanic style in

The mask of probity: In *The Woman in the Window*, a representative *film noir*, Edward G. Robinson plays a very solid citizen, a professor of psychology. When his wife and children leave the city for a summer holiday, the lonely middle-aged man picks up a beautiful woman (Joan Bennett), but no classroom has prepared him for the ensuing events: he murders a man (albeit in self-defense), is the victim of blackmail, and would seem to have committed suicide until we discover that most of the film has been his dream. Although the ending is hardly original and has been severely criticized, its psychological reality is totally convincing and quite moving; poor man, even in his dreams he doesn't get to kiss the girl. Freud's *Beyond the Pleasure Principle* has gone to his head. Left: Robinson says good-bye to his wife (Dorothy Peterson) and children. The boy is Bobby Blake, an *Our Gang* graduate who was to star in the film version of *In Cold Blood*. The still on p. 194 pictures Robinson upon his return to Bennett's apartment, ready to dispose of the corpse.

their Hollywood productions of the late twenties, refugee directors such as Fritz Lang, Billy Wilder, Robert Siodmak, Max Ophuls, Otto Preminger, and Curtis Bernhardt transformed the "look" of the American cinema of the forties and early fifties. Happily enough, a good deal of their more Gothic baggage did not survive the move to Hollywood, and the blatant devices of Expressionism, which many of these directors had abandoned long before Hitler's advent, persisted mainly in American horror films. Characteristic of their *films noirs* is the more refined and poetic *Stimmung* (mood) of the German cinema, which utilized mannered lighting, rather than bizarre sets, to render the "vibrations of the soul."[3] The chiaroscuro of this *Stimmung* might seem to have been perfected in Hollywood by Sternberg's famous cycle of Dietrich films (1930-35), but their campy charms were decidedly non-Germanic, and their exotic settings were the fantasias of their creator rather than a refraction of familiar American surroundings, the solidly located domain of even the most stylized *films noirs* of the refugee directors. Nor is the chiaroscuro of the American films of these directors simply an indulgence of techniques left over from the heyday of the UFA studio. It is instead the cinematic expression of stark and sorrowful and pessimistic attitudes that had been confirmed if not heightened by the exigencies of their own historical circumstances. Often effected more elegantly than it had been in Germany (here, perhaps,

Is this still from a German film, 1924? No, it is Hollywood, 1944, from refugee director Siodmak's *Phantom Lady*. Ella Raines here visits her unjustly imprisoned boss.

the Sternberg influence), this melancholic visual style is also informed by a mordant eye for the kind of cultural details that had been overlooked by most native American directors. If some of their later American work would seem slack (Preminger), careless (Lang), or casually cynical (Wilder), it may well be because their films of the forties and early fifties had profited from the fact that, like *Lolita* (as opposed to *Ada*), they were the product of an artist's exhilarated response to a radically new culture. "I read a lot of newspapers [after my arrival in America], and I read comic strips—from which I learned a lot. I said to myself, if an audience—year in, year out—reads so many comic strips, there must be something interesting in them. And I found them very interesting. I got (and still get today) an insight into the American character, into American humour; and I learned slang. I drove around in the country and tried to speak with everybody. I spoke with every cab driver, every gas station attendant—and I looked at films."[4] The speaker might be Nabokov, describing how he prepped for *Lolita;* actually, it is Fritz Lang, rehearsing his own Americanization.

That Lang and Nabokov should have responded so similarly to the lies and trivialities of the popular arts is only surprising if one believes that directors only pander to their audience, that movies are incapable of criticizing mass culture. A movie screen is the ideal space on which to project such a critique. Although the studio-oriented Lang worked more quietly than the *noir* directors of the late forties and early fifties, who often filmed on location, his effects are sardonic enough, and truly subversive. "A Boy Scout is never scared," says the scout to the newsreel camera in *The Woman in the Window* after he has discovered the body of the man whom Edward G. Robinson has murdered and dumped in the woods; Lang, the director of *Metropolis* (1927) and *Spies* (1928), of *M* (1931) and *The Testament of Dr. Mabuse* (1932), finds the chubby boy's ethic less than amusing. Similarly *Lolita's* Camp Q extends "The Girl Scout's Motto": "My duty is—to be useful," says the nymphet. "I am a friend to male animals" (p. 116). When a terrified Robinson turns on the radio to hear any news about the murder, he must endure an interminable "Castola Rex" laxative commercial; an equally unbearable and grimly humorous tension is created in Lang's *Scarlet Street*. Hen-pecked Robinson, a frustrated painter, cowers while his monstrous wife listens to *The Happy Home Hour* or *Hilda's Hope for Happiness*, her favorite soap opera. Robinson's own hopes rest with Kitty (Joan Bennett), but her initial appearance in the film augurs poorly for their future. Clad in a transparent plastic raincoat, she is less a woman than a piece of packaged goods, though it is Robinson who will be consumed. "Yipe" and "Jeepers," her constant verbal tics, render what Humbert terms Lolita's "eerie vulgarity," and the gimcrackery

Dan Duryea, Joan Bennett's boyfriend in *Scarlet Street,* recovers from a hangover in her first apartment, before cashier Edward G. Robinson embezzles from his company and sets her up in real style (right).

Fritz Lang directs Joan Bennett and Robinson in his *Scarlet Street.* Robinson's ice-pick murder of her will be reflected in the mirror, a device also used by Lang in *The Woman in the Window* and *The Big Heat.* The infinite regress of funhouse mirrors at the end of Orson Welles's *Lady from Shanghai* (1949) is the ultimate in baroque mirror effects, which are as typical of Nabokov as they are of *film noir.* "There was a double bed, a mirror, a double bed in the mirror, a closet door with mirror, a bathroom door ditto, a blue-dark window, a re-flected bed there, the same in the closet door," says Humbert of his and Lolita's first conjugal chamber, at The Enchanted Hunters hotel (p. 121). No mere decoration, *noir* mirrors mag-

nify the circumscribing nature of crime and obsession, and by affixing a semblance of Robinson's name to a middle-class murderer noted by Humbert (the case was drawn by the author from a newspaper story), Nabokov evokes something of *The Woman in the Window* and *Scarlet Street:* "Gee, Ed, that was bad luck—referring to G. Edward Grammar, a thirty-five-year-old New York office manager who had just been arrayed on a charge of murdering his thirty-three-year-old wife, Dorothy. Bidding for the perfect crime, Ed had bludgeoned his wife and put her into a car . . ." (p. 289).

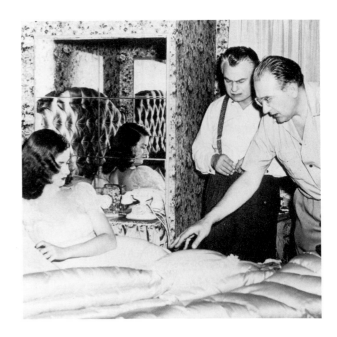

of Kitty's bedroom, a typical *noir* construct, anticipates Charlotte Haze's happy home.

Throughout *Scarlet Street* Kitty's vulgarity is counterpointed by the soundtrack's rendition of her favorite number, "Melancholy Baby." The song, always a
joke to musicians, is no romantic descant here; like
the "nasal voices" of the crooners adored by Lolita
(p. 150), and *her* tops in pops ("Little Carmen"), it
underscores the dreariness of mass culture. Many
films noirs use music in a similar fashion. A juke box
dominates the opening and closing scenes of *Fallen
Angel* (1945), directed by Otto Preminger, and the
cheapness of waitress Linda Darnell's dreams is defined by "Slowly," the corny tune she continually demands. An animating if not animate object, that juke
box is the cultural center of Preminger's small town,
and its contents and "gonadal glow" (to quote Humbert) are an incessant, oppressive presence in the
films of the refugee directors; their soundtracks, frequently orchestrated by other recent arrivals from
Europe, stress the cloying qualities of standard songs
in a manner reminiscent of the Berlin musical caprices
of Brecht and Weill. "Always" is used ironically in
Robert Siodmak's black *Christmas Holiday* (1944),
and a jarring rhumba arrangement of "Dark Eyes" is
offered as Circe's song in the nightclub scene of the
same director's *Criss Cross* (1949). Projected by a
distant radio, the eerie and haunting strains of "Tangerine," the narcissist's anthem ("Yes, she [Tanger-

ine] has them all on the run / But her heart belongs
to just one—Tangerine"), drift through the claustrophobic final scene of Wilder's *Double Indemnity* as
Fred MacMurray confronts, murders, and is himself
mortally wounded by his double-crossing accomplice,
Barbara Stanwyck; *belles dames sans* any *merci* are a
constant menace in *films noirs*. Ella Raines's grotesquely "glamorous" get-up in Siodmak's *Phantom
Lady* (1944) finds its musical equivalent in the ca-
cophonous and uncontrolled jazz performed by Elisha
Cook's band, and the lovely melody of "I'll Remember
April" is linked with a murder. In *Touch of Evil*
(1958), directed by Orson Welles, the most Germanic
of American stylists, rock 'n' roll is clearly Lucifer's
music. Played on the radio at top volume to cover up
a motel crime, its shattering decibel count is fitting
because *Touch of Evil* is the culmination of *film noir*.
Its 1958 release coincides with the appearance of
Lolita and of *The Americans*, the epochal book of
documentary photographs by Robert Frank, another
transplanted and mobile European with sharp eyesight, whose cross-country discoveries virtually exhausted the field of *noir* documentary—save, perhaps,
for the subsequent rear-guard probings and perceptions of Garry Winogrand (caged animals), Diane
Arbus ("freaks" at ease, unguarded), and Lee Friedlander (ominous or cryptic self-portraits). Crises of
society and self merge in the foreground of *Touch of
Evil*, which was filmed in that graveyard of American

aspirations, Venice, California—a tawdry and decaying remnant of an eccentric millionaire's attempt to re-create architecturally Europe's glorious past. "A sudden burst of sunshine seemed to illumine the Statue of Liberty, so that he saw it in a new light," writes Kafka in his fantasized *Amerika,* a description too of the way Robert Frank, *films noirs,* and *Lolita* illuminate familiar American settings and circumstances. By shooting juke boxes from a low perspective, Frank accentuated their massiveness, exaggerated their height, and the "gonadal glow" of his mock-monumental icon of romantic illusion and false hope highlights the somnolent faces of adolescents throughout *The Americans.*

When the *film noir* went outdoors, its vision of America became more severe, a sci-fi forecast of the future, as dictated by the realities of Southern Californian locations. Doutless everyone knows that almost every otherwise idyllic American community now has its own prototypical Southern Californian commercial street, with its motel or motor court, its discount stores and garish Da-Glo signs, its gas stations festooned with the competing banners of a price war, its glass and chrome quick-service lunch counters and its pseudo-ethnic eateries, unpalatable in every way, their bizarrely designed buildings topped by an enormous plastic pizza or sombrero. But not everyone knows the degree to which the *film noir's* view of roadside America anticipates *Lolita* and the

Orson Welles in *Touch of Evil.* Venice, a part of Los Angeles, served Welles as a kind of vast *objet trouvé.* The infernal or fallen world of his film is smartly glossed by actual signs awaiting the arrival of Welles's cameraman—"Hotel Ritz" (a run-down place), "Jesus Saves," "PARADISE." Subsequent attempts to blend dark "documentary" footage and a story line pale next to *Touch of Evil.* The characters in films such as *The Savage Eye* (1959) and *Zabriskie Point* (1970) are found objects too, clichés or signs created to support the directors' solemn, attenuated "messages."

Black Humor *Lolita* would beget in the sixties. These films in turn have their literary precursors: West's *The Day of the Locust* (1939), and, more importantly, since their findings were less freakish, the hard-boiled California writers such as James M. Cain and Raymond Chandler, whose education and residence in England made him a kind of internal *émigré* when he returned home. Their unremitting and gloomy depiction of a commercial culture is especially telling inasmuch as their stories and novels were, like movies, offered as light genre entertainments, often enough in the pages of popular or pulp magazines such as *Liberty* and *Black Mask*. It is not surprising that several works by Cain and Chandler readily became excellent *films noirs,* though some literary critics, following Edmund Wilson's lead in *The Boys in the Back Room* (1941), continue to hold this fact against the hard-boiled school.

Like West and, subsequently, Nabokov, Cain didn't have to invent the bizarre phenomena pictured in his novels. "The Victor Hugo," described in *Mildred Pierce* (1941) as "one of the oldest and best of the Los Angeles restaurants,"[5] is an actual place, as is *Lolita*'s "zoo in Indiana where a large group of monkeys lived on [a] concrete replica of Christopher Columbus' flagship," an allusion that finally puts Evansville, Indiana, on the literary map (p. 160). Viewers who dismiss as an obscene invention the funeral of Gloria Swanson's pet monkey in Wilder's *Sunset Boulevard* (1950) have doubtless never visited the elaborate tombstones erected in Forest Lawn cemetery to commemorate the beloved pets of movie stars. The "Drop Inn" and "U-Bet Market," details from *Mildred Pierce*'s California of 1931, look forward to a crescendo of cute commercial names in *Lolita,* including the "U-Beam" motel. Little Veda Pierce, a child of the cinema, realizes Lo's daydreams of celebrity; she gets her big break on "the Hank Somerville (Snack-O-Ham) program," singing on the same bill as the Krazy Kaydets.[6] Cora, the *femme fatale* of Cain's *The Postman Always Rings Twice* (1934), is called "a California Bar-B-Q slinger," and the novel's original title, *Bar-B-Q,* marked her little eatery as a cul-de-sac on the road to success. Cain, an unjustly neglected writer, does not exaggerate or catalog his observations, or sentimentalize them, as Kerouac did his in *On the Road* (1957). Cain's images of a man-made topography are caught with the cold clarity of his contemporary, the distinguished documentary photographer Walker Evans, whose mordant and strangely dramatic pictures of signs, empty rooms, and worn architectural façades surely affected the cinematographers of *film noir* as much as they influenced still photographers such as Robert Frank, who may also have learned from free-lancer Weegee (Arthur Fellig), a "technical adviser" on several *films noirs* (1948-52).

Witness the hard-edged visual style of *Double In-*

demnity, one of the first *films noirs* to use actual Los Angeles locations. The furtive, initial rendezvous of Barbara Stanwyck and Fred MacMurray was filmed in Jerry's Market on Melrose Avenue in Hollywood; the neat and antiseptic surroundings mirror the dispassionate manner in which they plot her husband's murder. A close-up of Stanwyck, her eyes shrouded by dark glasses, positions her expressionless white face against a pyramid of baby food boxes, whose multiple cherubic images (which anticipate the design of a Warhol silkscreen c. 1964) radiate the life that the childless woman would deny, reducing *her* to a flat image—a Pop Art *Death's Head, L.A.* (as yet unpainted). The signs, ads, tourist attractions, and commercial products in *Lolita* are found objects, too. "A great user of roadside facilities, my unfastidious Lo would be charmed by toilet signs—Guys-Gals, John-Jane, Jack-Jill and even Buck's-Doe's" (p. 155); Humbert's observations are as true as the extraordi-

Interior detail, West Virginia Coal Miner's House, a photograph by Walker Evans, 1935. "You can always shop to advantage . . ." advises the bottom border of the graduation sign, a confident assertion and assumption that ironically underscores the poverty of the (unsmiling?) coal miner. "The Lord will Provide," reads the placard on the wall of a run-down, disarrayed farm house in an Evans photo of 1932. Santa Claus is a (soda) Pop icon and *objet trouvé* rich in potential ironies, as Robert Frank proved twenty years later in his photograph *Ranch Market—Hollywood.*

Barbara Stanwyck and Fred MacMurray in a scene from *Double Indemnity* that was filmed at a Hollywood supermarket in 1943.

nary findings of Weegee's uncompromising Speed Graphic camera. The signs on the shabby toilet doors documented in Weegee's *Naked Hollywood* (1953), harshly illuminated by his flashbulb technique, complement Humbert's *préciosités de la route:* "King," "Queen"; "Neptune," "Mermaid"; "Man," "Woman." If the motel "instructions pasted above the toilets [in *Lolita*] . . . asking guests not to throw into its bowl garbage, beer cans, cartons, [and] stillborn babies" (p. 148) exhibit a certain unpoetic license on the author's part, they nevertheless have an authentic ring and are corroborated by the "real" *mises-en-scène* of Robert Frank and of *films noirs* from *Double Indemnity* through *Touch of Evil,* where a blind woman sits by a sign that announces, "If you are mean enough to steal from the blind Help Youself." "WE DELIVER" "MORE FOR LESS" read the run-on twin signs on the rear wall of Jerry's Market, a happy accident that ironically frames the two lovers, whose murderous insurance swindle will cost them their lives.

Double Indemnity (1944) is perhaps the high point of the first period of *noir.* Directed by Billy Wilder and adapted by scenarists Raymond Chandler and Wilder from a short novel by James M. Cain (1936), it is the result of a signal conjunction of talent. The film changes the novel considerably, and improves it by making MacMurray a less cynical and more Average American who is unwilling to kill, if only at first—

one of several subtle shifts that draw upon the actor's light comedy screen persona and emphasize the viral nature of materialism.

"America was promises," declared Archibald MacLeish in the thirties, and the *film noir* records the erosion of the fabled open American road. A generation that has suffered through the Vietnam war, Watergate, and the ecological crisis quite rightly "reads" these films in the dark light of the moment. But meretriciousness and deceit did not yet appear to be the law of the land in 1954, when *Lolita* was completed, and Nabokov justifiably laments the way it "was welcomed, particularly by left-wing Europeans," as an "anti-American book." *Lolita*'s tone is far too complicated for its attitudes to be reduced so flatly. Reviewing the itinerary of the 27,000 miles he spent on the road with Lolita in 1947-48, Humbert says that "our

Ranch Market–Hollywood, c. 1956, a photograph by Robert Frank from *The Americans.* Another Frank photo depicts a department store display of plastic flowers and crosses, a crowded mini-graveyard topped by the sign, "REMEMBER YOUR LOVED ONES 69¢." The harshest "found" ironies are documented by Weegee, the preeminent chronicler of urban violence and crowd prurience. His *Naked City* collection (1945) includes an accident scene—wide stream of blood in the gutter, battered corpse, discreetly covered save for its feet by newspapers that transform the sidewalk into a makeshift morgue. A marquee above the rapt bystanders announces, "IRENE DUNNE in 'JOY OF LIVING' / also 'DON'T TURN THEM LOOSE.'"

long journey had only defiled with a sinuous trail of slime the lovely, trustful, dreamy, enormous country" (pp. 177-78). One could argue that *Lolita* belies Nabokov's conscious intentions, yet the *émigré* novelist's gratitude as well as his naturalist's sense of wonder and beauty do shine through the narrator's "satirical" observations. The American continent in *Lolita* is not about to be consumed by hell-fire or sink into the slime of Judgment Day, as it is in *The Day of the Locust* and *Touch of Evil;* Nabokov's contempt is aimed at the manipulators who would homogenize, despoil, or corrupt the "enormous country," with its "trustful" inhabitants. "The disappointment I must now register . . . should in no wise reflect on the lyrical, epic, tragic but never Arcadian American wilds. They are beautiful, heart-rendingly beautiful, those wilds, with a quality of wide-eyed, unsung, innocent surrender that my lacquered, toy-bright Swiss villages and exhaustively lauded Alps no longer possess," says Humbert (p. 170), and Lolita personifies an innocence that was surrendered in advance of Humbert's foul assaults. A "tender charm" nevertheless manages to linger about the "tragic" nymphet, a casebook victim of Pop culture whose youth has been claimed and denied by two armed forces. Although Nabokov may not share the extreme pessimism of the *film noir, Lolita*'s definitive indictment of a corrosive mass culture is very much in the spirit of *film noir.*

Humbert is no "underworlder" fan, yet his research-oriented creator seems to have absorbed something of the atmosphere and visual style of *film noir* and profited too from the example of its compact yet trenchant *mises-en-scène*. Nabokov doesn't remember many film titles, but he does admire Murnau's *The Last Laugh* (1924)—a wellspring of *noir* style—and is not unaware of *film noir*, as I discovered inadvertently during a visit to Switzerland. Returning from a walk (November 1972), Nabokov and I entered the dimly lit bar of the Montreux Palace Hotel. Standing at the bar, he ordered a scotch, and I asked for a well-known aperitif which was not in stock. "Good!" said Nabokov, "that's no drink for a man." Our rather tight-fitting overcoats still on, we began a three-way badinage with the barman on the unavailability of that aperitif. "We're like Hemingway's killers," observed Nabokov, speaking out of the corner of his mouth in mock-gangster fashion. Pointing to his wide-brimmed gray fedora, placed in gentlemanly fashion on a bar stool, Nabokov said, "I should return it to my head, no?, and heighten the realism. I loved 'The Killers' and the [initial] film version, too [1946, directed by refugee Siodmak]: the first scene in the diner was superb, each detail so exact, the unappetizing kitchen in which the killers, working with frightening dispatch, truss together those innocent men. The scene in which the fellow [Burt Lancaster] awaits his fate in a tawdry, shadowy rented room was excellent, too. But the remainder of the film

Charles McGraw and William Conrad in *The Killers.*

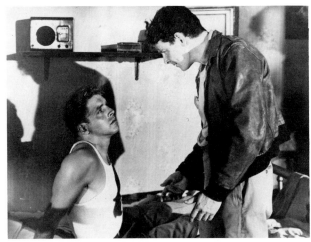

Nick Adams (Phil Brown) warns the Swede (Burt Lancaster) in *The Killers*. A moment later Nick departs, concluding Hemingway's direct contribution to the Hellinger-Siodmak version. *The Killers* is never discussed by critics interested in the literature-into-film process, doubtless because of its "lowbrow" gangster ordonnances and the fact that only seven or eight of its 107 minutes are faithful to Hemingway's ten-page story (a truly faithful feature-length version would have been slow-paced indeed). But the new material, thanks to the film's brilliant narrative structure, realizes the spirit of Hemingway's entire *oeuvre*, his long lesson in death and dying. After the stoical Swede is murdered in his room, insurance investigator Edmond O'Brien explores the dead man's past. Eleven convoluted flashbacks, covering an eleven-year period, define the Swede's entrapment by McFate (as Humbert would term it). The flashbacks chart successively smaller and smaller units of time, rendering the tenuousness of the Swede's hold on life. The audience suffers the tragic action, too—the closing circle, the narrowing duration of movie time that speaks to their death sentence as well as his. This aspect of the film allows it to transcend the more conventional, entertaining components of its post-Hemingway plot, and suggests why the author himself admired this "loose" version of his classic story.

added a good deal to Hemingway, didn't it? Gangster stuff . . . [Nabokov grimaces] . . . more conventional, but very well done. I did the screenplay of *Lolita* in order to guard it against such liberties. What did Hemingway think of them?" According to his biographer, Carlos Baker, *The Killers* "was the first film from any of his work that Ernest could genuinely admire."[7] Its compelling *noir* qualities seem literally to have overshadowed any objections to those considerable "liberties," which are not entirely scorned by Nabokov, either, his grimace notwithstanding. The killing of Quilty parodies some of that "gangster stuff," of course, but the death-dealing dark sedan which rushes through the black night of *The Killers*, one of several fateful vehicles in the film version, prefigures Humbert's paranoid vision of an endless American road coursed relentlessly by an automotive "McFate," a "Proteus of the highway" (p. 229).

The commercial success of *The Killers* prompted its producer to advertise his *Brute Force* (1947) as a sequel. "MARK HELLINGER TELLS IT THE 'KILLERS' WAY!" declared the pre-*auteur* lobby posters, which for once did not lie or exaggerate. Featuring the same actor (Lancaster) and directed by Jules Dassin, *Brute Force* is the most *noir* of all prison movies because it focuses on personal obsession as well as violent action. To compare it with *Lolita* is more than a stab in the dark. Humbert, writing his "confession" in prison, describes how he returned alone to The Enchanted

Hunters, the scene of the crime, three years after Lolita's disappearance, five years after their stay there. Having given up all hopes of tracing her and her "kidnaper," he tried to recapture the past in "autumnal Briceland" (p. 263). Leafing through a "coffin-black volume" of the 1947 *Briceland Gazette*, he noted that *Brute Force* and *Possessed* were to come to the two Briceland theatres the week following his "honeymoon" sojourn with Lolita (p. 264). One would assume that Nabokov had culled these fitting titles from a newspaper ad or an uninviting theatre marquee. "No, no," he says, "I saw both films, and thought them appropriate for several reasons. But I don't remember why . . . *so* many years have passed. Was one a prison picture? I guess I should have said more about them." Indeed yes.

John Milton was able to assume that his narrow seventeenth-century audience shared the same education and would "get" the classical and biblical allusions that now necessitate crowded footnotes. The modern writer, as opposed to unemployed scholiasts, is not so fortunate. *Lolita*'s most important literary allusions, to Poe and *Carmen*, can be recognized by a reasonably well-educated reader, but the meaning of more commonplace materials may be lost, since one generation's popular culture is another's esoterica. When Marianne Moore collected in a book her poem "Hometown Piece for Messrs. Alston and Reese," a tribute to the 1955 World Series victory of the Brook-lyn Dodgers, she glossed it with two pages of "learned notes" explicating what was then obvious (see *O to Be a Dragon*, 1959). Now that those players and their feats have vanished into legend, along with a demolished Ebbets Field, her once humorous notes assume a new utilitarian logic. Billy Wilder used only the melody of "Tangerine" in *Double Indemnity*, and the effect, a kind of aural shorthand, is more subtle than if he had allowed words; like Milton, he could assume that his audience knew the lyrics of a recent hit song. But Pynchon's allusion to "Tangerine" in *Gravity's Rainbow*, that massive Pop inversion of Milton's method, is meaningless to anyone in Pynchon's audience who hasn't had the benefit of a democratic nineteen-forties education.[8] *Brute Force* and *Possessed* are cases in point. Some of *Lolita*'s first readers (1955) may have remembered those 1947 films, but their functional thematic relevance is now as obscure as the storied background of one of Milton's players.

Humbert, who cherishes the tattered photo of his lost Riviera love, has much in common with the prisoners of *Brute Force*, whose female cellmate is also an inanimate object, a pinup picture that provokes their own sexual fantasies. That it should be a composite portrait of the kind of actresses admired by Lolita is a fortuitous coincidence. Humbert's dreams of vengeance upon Quilty never equal *Brute Force*'s image of the stool pigeon being driven under a steam

hammer by convicts wielding blowtorches, but that fate might well have entered Humbert's terrible musings. *Possessed,* an excellent *film noir* directed by refugee Curt Bernhardt, is more immediately appropriate. Joan Crawford plays a neurotic nurse whose hopeless and obsessive love for Van Heflin drives her into a loveless marriage with widower Raymond Massey. When Heflin pursues her new stepdaughter, Crawford slowly goes mad, has terrifying hallucinations, and finally murders Heflin. Discovered wandering about Los Angeles, she is institutionalized. The plot and chiaroscuro speak to the condition of Charlotte, destroyed by Humbert's diary, and obviously apply to Humbert, too, who repairs to a madhouse a year after Lolita's departure.

Brute Force and *Possessed,* the allusions that got away, are a small matter to be sure, yet they do underscore the problems occasioned by any allusive matter, high or low. It is safe to say that *Lolita* nevertheless survives, as does the analogy with *film noir,*

Howard Duff and Burt Lancaster as convicts in *Brute Force.* The following is excerpted from the caption prepared by the Universal-International publicity department: "John Decker, one of Hollywood's most renowned artists, painted this composite picture from the faces of Ella Raines, Yvonne DeCarlo and Ann Blyth. The striking painting is used as a calendar which hangs in a prison cell in 'Brute Force.' Burt Lancaster, Hume Cronyn and Charles Bickford portray 'the men on the inside.' . . . Nose and middle portion of the calendar face are the features of Yvonne; portrait's hairline is Ella's and the lips and lower portion of face were sketched from the features of Ann Blyth. The three girls appear briefly as 'The women on the outside' in 'Brute Force' "—and their composite portrait unintentionally embraces the Frederick's-of-Hollywood ethos, the duplication process undertaken by countless American females.

Joan Crawford in *Possessed.*

Left:
The stool pigeon (James O'Rear) dies in *Brute Force*, in perhaps the most sadistic sequence in forties *film noir.*

buoyed perhaps by Nabokov's remarks about *The Killers.* The acute observation of roadside America typified by *The Killers* and the Germanic *Stimmung* of *film noir* are everywhere in the novel, if not the film version.

That mood is, in a word, *noir.* Nabokov had employed German lighting tricks in a few scenes of *Mary* (1926), but the "endless night" of Humbert's despair called for open-air nocturnal effects, and they are sustained in the best style of *Double Indemnity, Sunset Boulevard, They Live by Night* (1949), and other *films noirs* that were not fettered by the restrictions of indoor shooting. "She had entered my world," says punster Humbert, "umber and black Humberland," the shadowland of memory and desire (p. 168). As in many *films noirs,* Humbert's nightmare is suffered in the broad daylight of everyday surroundings. "The elms and the poplars were turning their ruffled backs to a sudden onslaught of wind, and a black thunderhead loomed above Ramsdale's white church tower when I looked around me for the last time," says Humbert as he sets off to claim Lolita at Camp Q after Charlotte has been killed (p. 105). Reminiscent of the train engine smoke that casts symbolic if unnatural black clouds over the quiet sunny town at the outset of Hitchcock's *Shadow of a Doubt,* that "black thunderhead" will pursue Humbert and Lolita through the novel. It is Clare Quilty's leitmotif, introduced early on by the title of his play, *The Lady*

Who Loved Lightning (p. 33), which also serves as one of a hundred detective-story clues that reveal Lo's inspirational intimacy with Humbert's shadow, "Detective Trapp" (Quilty). "I am not a lady and do not like lightning," Lolita tells Humbert, referring to that play (p. 222); the "prehistorically loud thunder" which rolls above them all that night announces the proximity of Quilty and his mistress Vivian Dark-bloom (an anagram of Vladimir Nabokov), who appear the next evening at a performance of their play (p. 223). Its "self-conscious light effects" are Gothic enough, but Humbert's weather report is consistent with Nabokov's cinematic effects; crucial scenes in *Lolita* are inevitably marked by rain, as in numerous *films noirs* of the period, which give the impression that a steady monsoon deluged America from 1944 to 1954. The seduction at The Enchanted Hunters occurs on a "soggy black night" (p. 128), rain marks Humbert's unhappy reunion with Dolly Schiller (p. 282), and the thunderstorm which accompanies him to Quilty's Pavor Manor heralds a downpour of effects which are "Germanic" in only the worst sense (p. 295).

Humbert is as threatened and tormented by machines as he is by thunder: "And sometimes trains would cry in the monstrously hot and humid night with heartening and ominous plangency, mingling power and hysteria in one desperate scream" (p. 148). The aura of "steam, smoke [and] infernal con-

"How many small dead-of-night towns I have seen! . . . neon lights flickered twice slower than my heart," says Humbert after his reunion with Lolita has failed. In a few moments, he is "weeping again, drunk on the impossible past" (p. 284). Above: Cathy O'Donnell and Farley Granger find no safe haven in *They Live by Night*. The "No Parking" sign is emblematic of the impossible past and future both.

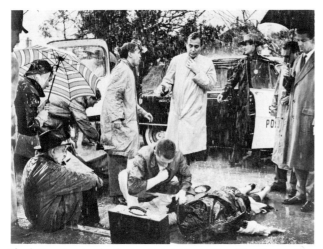

Charlotte Haze's death in Kubrick's *Lolita*. Mr. Beale, the driver, is seated on the left while his son apologizes to Humbert (James Mason), who feigns shock and sorrow.

fusion" which Nabokov recalls so vividly from the train wreck in *The Hands of Orlac* (see p. 140), also survives in *films noirs* such as Raoul Walsh's *White Heat* (1949), *Brute Force* (with its images of careening, enflamed vehicles), and the same director's *Thieves' Highway* (1949). Dassin's nightmarish visualization of the rampaging and roaring trucks combated by a weary driver (Richard Conte) might well be glossed by Humbert's descriptions of his own fearful nocturnal locomotions or roadside insomnia: "At night, tall trucks studded with colored lights, like dreadful giant Christmas trees, loomed in the darkness and thundered by the belated little sedan" (p. 155). Humbert's forlorn car introduces a dramatic *noir* image that looks back to *The Killers*, and is far more concrete than "mood."

Along with Robert Frank and *Lolita*, film noir established a contemporary iconography of the American road that forced its natives to see their environment with a new acuity. The concept of iconography, once the sole province of art historians stolidly limning the religious symbolism of Old Master paintings, has sometimes been applied rather loosely by *cinéastes*. Although the *film noir* tends to inspire open-ended definitions,[9] it does possess a pattern of imagery recurrent enough to form an iconography as coherent and recognizable as the "underworlder" relics burlesqued in Quilty's death scene (cigars, guns, black clothes). The awe and respect with which Americans regard their cars surely warrants the grand designation "icon," and the iconography of the car is central to *Lolita,* *film noir,* and *The Americans.* Quilty's tireless pursuit, his "cycle of persecution," is made more harrowing by the constantly shifting rainbow profusion of his rented vehicles: Aztec Red, Campus Green, Horizon Blue, Surf Gray, Crest Blue, Chrysler's Shell Gray, Chevrolet's Thistle Gray, Dodge's French Gray, and so forth (pp. 229-30).

> Where are you riding, Dolores Haze?
> What make is the magic carpet?
> Is a Cream Cougar the present craze?
> And where are you parked, my car pet?

asks Humbert in the amusingly bad poem he composes in a Quebec sanatorium after her disappearance (p. 258). The car hues are very funny, but "I didn't invent them," says lepidopterist Nabokov, who cruised the country each summer in a series of secondhand cars chauffeured by Véra. "I borrowed those colors from commercial manuals on cars obtained in Ithaca, New York, circa 1952." Readymade satire aside, the cars in *Lolita* are ultimately no simple joke. The car that solves one of Humbert's most vexing problems by running over Charlotte is literally the *deus ex machina* of *Lolita* (p. 99), and the laughter evoked by cars, or Quilty's pursuit, is invariably dark. The tone of *Lolita*'s automotive world is defined perfectly by Robert Frank's photograph of a beloved car whose covering is at once as protective as a caul and as final as a shroud.

Humbert's own car, a "Dream Blue Melmoth" (p. 229), is a different sort of borrowing, a more than merely amusing allusion to Maturin's interminable Gothic novel *Melmoth the Wanderer* (1820). Piled high with his "car pet"'s comic books, movie magazines, and clothing, their wandering Melmoth *is* a Gothic enclosure, and its cramped conjugal area is as repugnant as Edward Kienholz's grim lover's-lane Pop Art construct *Back Seat Dodge-38* (1964). Locked together in a succession of motel rooms, Humbert and Lolita are captives of each other, and the claustrophobic interior of the Melmoth best renders their terrible mutual isolation, which makes Humbert seem as alone during the first trip West as he will be on the second after she has left him and the car becomes a natural setting for his solitary confinement. The Melmoth recalls many *films noirs* and the vagabond cars which serve as home and haven, death chamber or prison cell, all set in motion against the lonely landscapes of urban and rural America. In *Out of the Past* (1947), for example, Robert Mitchum is never at rest or at ease, is never pictured in his house or apartment; where *does* he live?, one wonders. A car seems to be his sole possession, and it is there that he confesses his past to Virginia Huston (through flashbacks). This setup is repeated in the final scene,

Covered car—Long Beach, California, a photograph by Robert
Frank from *The Americans*.

femme fatale Jane Greer in Miss Huston's place, the confessional booth transformed into a death cell; they both die violently inside the vehicle. Like the car in the opening sequence of *The Big Heat* or the glossy corpse-bearing Packard fished out of the water at the end of *The Big Sleep* (1946), Mitchum's car becomes a coffin.

The equation of cars with violence is obviously not new, but distinctions should be made, for the *film noir* did in fact expand and enrich the iconography established by the gangster films of the thirties. Except in Lang's *You Only Live Once* (1937), a precursor of *They Live by Night* and *Bonnie and Clyde*, the gangster's car functioned in narrow, expected ways: as an *arriviste* gang lord's "status symbol"; a chase or getaway car; an expedient place from which to fire a machine gun. But *film noir* personalized that violence, removed those cars from a patently criminal ambience and serviced them in average filling stations, which made the fated action more immediate. By drawing upon wartime realities, *film noir* quite literally drove its dark themes homeward. A five-year moratorium on the production of cars had domesticated the American auto, had made it into a familiar worn figure, a member of the family whose own nutritional needs were also subjected to rationing. Postwar car advertising, touting the millennial arrival of new models, took advantage of that famine, as did *film noir*. Melmoth, as Humbert calls it, as though it

Back Seat Dodge-38, by Edward Kienholz (Tableau, 240 x 144 x 66).

U.S. 285, New Mexico, a photograph by Robert Frank from *The Americans.* Dorothea Lange's photograph, *U.S. 54 in Southern New Mexico,* the cover illustration and frontispiece of *An American Exodus* (1939), is virtually the same picture as Frank's, with two crucial differences: her highway is caught in daylight, in a horizontal composition more relaxed than Frank's vertical framing, and the clearly visible arid fields on either side of her road complement the book's sub-title, *A record of human erosion in the thirties.* Lange documents their environment in behalf of social legislation, but Frank's decision to shoot at night transforms a potential factual observation into metaphor or symbol, the expression (or dark confirmation) of a psychological state. Nabokov is no reformer, yet Humbert's camera eye is fixed on both of these highways.

Robert Mitchum and Virginia Huston in *Out of the Past.*

"Malevolent curiosity": Farley Granger, on the run in *They Live by Night,* will not stop to enjoy the "Holliday Hot Shots" at the Meadowbrook.

The motivating force of vengeance in *The Big Heat:* Glenn Ford, a police detective drawn from the breakfast table by the sound of an explosion, is unable to rescue his wife (Jocelyn Brando), the victim of the bomb intended for him.

were a person, is said to limp, and its owner grotesquely anthropomorphizes cars in a manner which befits their violent temperament: "A big black glossy Packard had climbed Miss Opposite's sloping lawn at an angle from the sidewalk . . . and stood there, shining in the sun, its doors open like wings," he writes of Charlotte's killer, Bosch by way of *The Big Sleep* (p. 99).

Menaced by Quilty's mirage-like protean car(s) and the "malevolent curiosity" of highway patrolmen sworn to uphold the Mann Act (p. 173), Humbert fearfully navigates "the nightmare of crisscross streets . . . in factory town[s]" (p. 221) as well as the truck-dominated open roads. The brutal realities of the highway, a distraction welcomed by Lolita, are observed with the somber detachment of a documentary or news photographer (Robert Frank or Weegee): she "silently stared, with other motorists and their children, at some smashed, blood-bespattered car with a young woman's shoe in the ditch (Lo, as we drove on: 'That was the exact type of moccasin I was trying to describe to that jerk in the store')" (p. 176). Her callousness is as consistent as what Professor Nabokov might have termed "the car theme" in *Lolita*. "She and the dog saw me off," says Humbert, describing his unhappy departure from Dolly Schiller's house. "I was surprised (this is a rhetorical figure, I was not) that the sight of the old car in which she had ridden as a child and a nymphet, left her so very indifferent. All she remarked was it was getting sort of purplish about the gills" (p. 282). The fishy attribute invests it with a cold-blooded life appropriate to her incarceration in Melmoth, that durable witness to crime and misery:

> My car is limping, Dolores Haze,
> And the last long lap is the hardest,
> And I shall be dumped where the weed decays,
> And the rest is rust and stardust

writes Humbert in the concluding stanza of his "maniac's masterpiece" (p. 259). Despite its "lurid rhymes," it accurately prefigures the last scene in *Lolita,* the end of the road for Humbert.

After killing Quilty, Humbert drives across open country. "Since I had disregarded all laws of humanity, I might as well disregard the rules of traffic," writes Humbert, explaining why he then crossed to the left side of the highway. "In a way, it was a very spiritual itch. Gently, dreamily, not exceeding twenty miles an hour, I drove on that queer mirror side. . . . Cars coming towards me wobbled, swerved, and cried out in fear. . . . Then in front of me I saw two cars placing themselves in such a manner as to completely block my way. With a graceful movement I turned off the road, and after two or three big bounces, rode up a grassy slope, among surprised cows, and there I came to a gentle, rocking stop," as helpless as a bar-bound *film noir* hero/victim (pp. 308-9). The forward motion of the narrative has stopped, too, a conclusion analogous to the end of another mordant grand tour of the country, Frank's *The Americans.* Its closing image pictures a young woman and a boy, their faces blank from fatigue, huddled in the front seat of a cluttered car parked by the side of a bleak highway in Texas. "I was soon to be taken out of the car (Hi, Melmoth, thanks a lot, old fellow)," writes confessor Humbert, a more resilient traveler, who capers in prose for a putative judge and jury (p. 309). "And while I was waiting for them [the police and the ambulance people] to run up to me on the high slope, I evoked a last mirage of wonder and hopelessness," another moment along the highway during which Humbert had realized the enormity of the loss suffered not by him but by Lolita. Eloquent and straightforward, in no way undercut by parody, the long passage (pp. 309-10) constitutes the "moral apotheosis" promised by silly Dr. John Ray, Jr. (p. 7). It also represents a "mirror side" reversal of the reader's assumption that the "spiritual itch" of morality is beyond Humbert. Released from his obsession by love, Humbert will be removed from Melmoth and transferred from his mobile cell to a real one, where, as the reader knows from Ray's Foreword, he has already died of a coronary thrombosis (p. 5). Many *films noirs* are also narrated by dead or dying men (*Laura,* for example, *Double Indemnity,* or *D.O.A.,*

1949, whose hero, Edmund O'Brien, has been slipped an antidote-proof poison), a narrative device which undercuts the old-fashioned idea of "story" by revealing its outcome. What remains is the unfolding of a terrible, fated action, the fleshing in of the outlines of human pain and panic.

Nabokov's account of the novel's origin, which may even be true, offers a moving and signal metaphor. "The first little throb of *Lolita*," he writes in its Afterword,

went through me late in 1939 or early in 1940, in Paris, at a time when I was laid up with a severe attack of intercostal neuralgia. As far as I can recall, the initial shiver of inspiration was somehow prompted by a newspaper story about an ape in the Jardin des Plantes [zoo] who, after months of coaxing by a scientist, produced the first drawing ever charcoaled by an animal: this sketch showed the bars of the poor creature's cage (p. 313).

Refugee Humbert, the "aging ape" writing from prison, whose impossible love figuratively connects him with that imprisoned animal, learns the language and records his "imprisonment," and his book is the "picture" of the bars of the poor creature's cage, visualized literally by a device borrowed from the cinema. Numerous directors and cinematographers have enjoyed the prison-bar chiaroscuro created by light projected through the slats of lattices or venetian blinds. The device is far less blatant than even the best stills might suggest, since they are isolated, frozen moments of a *moving* picture. Horizontal or oblique angles are favored because vertical shafts of light and shadow would be too obviously prison-like. When they are employed dramatically and economically as a metaphor for entrapment or a clue that all is not well in the seemingly calm world of the film, the barred shadows are truly iconographic. If they are merely indulged to interrupt the visually boring surface of a wall, as in routine TV thrillers, the results will only be interesting to students of interior decoration. The pathological jealousy suffered by the effaced narrator in Robbe-Grillet's *Jealousy* (1957), keynoted throughout the novel by blinds and their shadows, underscores the literary possibilities of this film convention, and the title in French (*Jalousie* = venetian blind) punningly emphasizes a point reinforced by the cover photo on the American paperback edition of the dour author peering out behind the prison bars formed by the jalousies.

Although it is impossible to say who first introduced this device, it is clearly present in the films of German (Wiene, Murnau) and "Germanic" (Stroheim, Hitchcock, Sternberg) directors of the twenties and early thirties. By the mid forties it was omnipresent in American movies, the consistent signature of *noir* stylists in the wake of Murnau, whose *Last Laugh* (1924) records the decline of an old man (Jannings) whose identity is dependent upon his "status" as a Prussian-style doorman at a Berlin grand hotel. Unable to unload heavy trunks with his former aplomb, Jannings is stripped of his rank and demoted to washroom attendant; a heavy *noir* rainfall has augured *his* fall. The film was supposed to end with Jannings slumped in his mirror-lined cell, a condemned man sealed off by the striped shadows of a debilitating humiliation. (The subsequent epilogue, a "happy ending" foisted on the film by its producer, is as unconvincing as similar gratuities in Twain and Dickens.) Sternberg's *Shanghai Express* (1932), starring Dietrich as Shanghai Lily ("the white flower of the Chinese coast"), sustains Murnau's expressive visual. The shimmering bars of light that transform the corridor of the train into another prison cell are a visual correlative for the *femme fatale*'s spell and the various deceptions that lock each character into himself. Nabokov greatly admires "the wonderful stylized chiaroscuro" of these two films, and his is not empty praise. The most illuminating iconography of *The Last Laugh* and *Shanghai Express*, a dominant presence in *film noir*, also flickers from the pages of *Lolita*.

Humbert's first night with Lolita contains vintage *noir* footage:

The door of the lighted bathroom stood ajar; in addition to that, a skeleton glow came through the Venetian blind from the outside arclights; these intercrossed rays pene-

Emil Jannings in *The Last Laugh*. This kind of chiaroscuro underscores the paradoxical nature of cinematic "realism." The product of patently artificial lighting, the prison bars are nevertheless realistic because they suggest a mental set, the character's separation from an open, natural environment.

Marlene Dietrich and Warner Oland in *Shanghai Express*.

trated the darkness of the bedroom and revealed the following situation.

Clothed in one of her old nightgowns, my Lolita lay on her side with her back to me, in the middle of the bed. Her lightly veiled body and bare limbs formed a Z. She had put both pillows under her dark tousled head; a band of pale light crossed her top vertebrae.

I seemed to have shed my clothes and slipped into pajamas with the kind of fantastic instantaneousness which is implied when in a cinematographic scene the process of changing is cut; and I had already placed my knee on the edge of the bed when Lolita turned her head and stared at me through the striped shadows (p. 130).

She had wanted to go to the movies that evening (p. 118), a request realized ironically by the unreeling of the "seduction scene," with its baroque *noir* mirrors (p. 121) and "striped shadows," its campy horror-film close-ups ("my tentacles moved towards her again," and so forth, p. 132). Nabokov's camera follows Humbert to and from the bathroom: "I re-entered the strange pale-striped fastness where Lolita's old and new clothes reclined in various attitudes of enchantment" (p. 133). As bewitching as anything worn or shed by Shanghai Lily, they are also a convict's clothes. Toward the end of the novel, Humbert recalls some "fabulous, insane [sexual] exertions that [had] left me limp and azure-barred" from the silvery neon lights outside their room (p. 287), and the cinematographic effect, which looks back to The En-

Edward G. Robinson instructs his psychology class in the opening scene of *The Woman in the Window*. The neat outline on the blackboard of Freud's "Divisional Constitution of Mental Life" speaks to the psychological validity of his chaotic dream, while the prison-bar shadows of the blinds define his sense of middle-class entrapment and forecast the criminal outcome of his abortive libidinal fling.

A more literal use of the prison metaphor marks the next-to-last scene of *Scarlet Street*. Dan Duryea has been arrested for the murder committed by Robinson, who, in the following sequence, deranged by guilt, is tormented by the flickering prison bars projected by a neon sign. "Azure-barred" forever, he runs out into the night.

Venetian blinds have their say throughout *Double Indemnity*. When Fred MacMurray first visits Barbara Stanwyck at her house, the prison-bar shadows on the rear wall suggest that her interest in insurance is more than routine. Four or five crucial scenes are keynoted by those shadows, including the final murder sequence (left), accompanied by "Tangerine."

"Lolita . . . stared at me through the striped shadows": James Mason and Sue Lyon at The Enchanted Hunters hotel, whose barred shadows also reflect *films noirs* such as *Laura*, *Fallen Angel*, *Shadow of a Doubt*, *Strangers on a Train*, *The Postman Always Rings Twice*, *Mildred Pierce*, *Criss Cross*, *Cry of the City*, *An Act of Murder*, and *Macao*.

chanted Hunters, suggests the extent to which Humbert is imprisoned in "the pale-striped fastness" of obsession. Kubrick's version of the seduction scene is faithful to Nabokov's *film noir* visuals, and the movie's opening close-up of Humbert painting Lo's toenails, repeated in a subsequent scene, is also *noir* enough. A direct allusion to the same ritual of enslavement as managed by Fritz Lang in *Scarlet Street,* it at first seems to suggest by way of *hommage* that Kubrick's *Lolita* will self-consciously attempt the definitive *film noir*. Although Kubrick improved upon Nabokov by having Charlotte die in the rain, a very *noir* scene, the most curious and disappointing aspect of his *Lolita* is that it finally chooses not to follow the main roads traversed by *film noir*.

Joan Bennett and Edward G. Robinson in *Scarlet Street.*

Mason and Sue Lyon in *Lolita.*

The Making of *Lolita*

Kubrick's *Lolita* project was from the start circumscribed if not doomed by the censorship standards of 1959-60, the period during which he and scenarist Nabokov planned their film, released in 1962. "I would fault myself in one area of the film," Kubrick told interviewer Gene Phillips in 1970. "Because of all the pressure over the Production Code and the Catholic Legion of Decency at the time, I wasn't able to give any weight at all to the erotic aspect of Humbert's relationship with Lolita; and because his sexual obsession was only barely hinted at, it was assumed too quickly that Humbert was in love. Whereas in the novel this comes as a discovery at the end. . . ."[10] Kubrick's *Lolita* is akin to a film of *Moby-Dick* that would omit all harpoons, if not the whale itself, and the director's candor is understandably restrained. The considerable fault he acknowledges is but one of several compromises aimed at the censors.

Although the initial close-up of Lolita's pedicure suggests degradation, its effect is considerably softened by the soundtrack's romantic music; and the first full view of Sue Lyon in her bikini is far too pleasing. Most everyone agrees that she looks too old, a blossomed seventeen. "Have the reviewers looked at the schoolgirls of America lately?" demurred Pauline Kael in her lively, favorable review (a minority report). "The classmates of my fourteen-year-old daughter are not merely nubile: some of them look badly used. . . . and [they] have *figures*,"[11] which is exactly why Sue Lyon would never have passed Humbert's muster. She manages to embody Lolita's Pop-conditioned "eerie vulgarity," but her womanly body undercuts the clinical and criminal aspects of Humbert's obsession. Nymphets are children, need we be reminded, and shortly before Lo's disappearance in the novel, Humbert is alarmed by unseemly changes in her measurements. Kubrick assumed (rightly?) that no censor would accept a narrow-hipped and flat-chested nymphet of four feet ten, or Humbert's extended definition of "their true nature which is not human, but nymphic (that is, demoniac)" (p. 18), bolstered by a catalogue of nymphets in history and literature (p. 20). In Nabokov's screenplay, Humbert offers his learned explanation as a lecture to the stupefied members of a women's club. He loses control, starts screaming, and faints. Fearful that the censors would respond similarly, Kubrick omitted any definition of nympholepsy. His Humbert has no clinical symptoms or history, and James Mason's "crush" on Sue Lyon seems quite normal, at worst the by-product of one more professorial *crise de quarante*.

The most dramatic shift in the film, which also occurs in Nabokov's scenario, is Humbert's killing of Quilty in the *opening* scene. John Ray's Foreword may have purposefully "spoiled" the story by revealing Humbert's death, as in the beginning of *Double Indemnity* when a dying Fred MacMurray announces, "I didn't get the money and I didn't get the woman" —or the second scene in *The Killers*, in which the Swede (Lancaster) is murdered in his room. Both sequences are followed by convoluted flashbacks which fill in the histories of those finished lives, much to the advantage of the films in question. But Kubrick and Nabokov reverse this effect by killing a clown rather than their "hero," which seems to transform *Lolita* into a thriller, however bizarre; Humbert's own death is not mentioned until the very end, denying the film any sense of a fated action. James M. Cain disliked the well-made *film noir* version of his *Mildred Pierce*

(1945), probably because it too transplanted a corpse from a concluding scene to the beginning of the film, thereby transforming Cain's critique of the success ethic into a murder mystery that is only solved when the ensuing flashback circles around to that foreground crime. "Four Years Earlier" reads the screen title which follows Quilty's death, and as the film proceeds, in one long flashback, the Big Question on the audience's mind is *why exactly did Humbert kill Quilty?* The shrewd and drastic structural change disarms and distracts the audience by emphasizing what Humbert considers to be the least of his crimes. His obsession sacrificed to censorship, his principal identity is now that of murderer, an "improvement" predicated on the assumption, certainly debatable theoretically, that a killer is more acceptable than a pervert, which proved to be correct in actuality. The censors accepted *Lolita*. Might not Kubrick have been more daring and risked a condemnation from the Catholic Legion of Decency? The question is academic, and, as Nabokov says in the Foreword to the published version of his screenplay, one cannot deny that "infinite fidelity may be an author's ideal but can prove a producer's ruin" (p. xiii).

Lured by "a considerable honorarium" and the hope of giving *Lolita* "some kind of [cinematic] form which would protect it from later intrusions and distortions," Nabokov journeyed to Hollywood in 1959. At a meeting with Kubrick and producer James B.

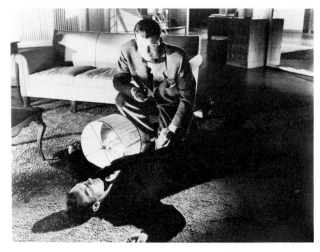

Jack Carson discovers the corpse of Zachary Scott at the outset of *Mildred Pierce*. The *noir* lighting is typically low-key.

Harris, Nabokov "was told that in order to appease the censor a later scene should contain some pudic hint to the effect that Humbert had been secretly married to Lolita all along." A week later the Nabokovs left for Europe. In his Foreword to the screenplay, Nabokov explains how, one evening in Lugano, long after he "had ceased to bother about the film," he suddenly "experienced a small nocturnal illumination, of diabolical origin, perhaps, but unusually compelling in sheer bright force, and clearly perceived an attractive line of approach to a screen version of *Lolita*. I regretted having had to decline the offer and was aimlessly revolving bits of dream dialogue in my mind when magically a telegram came from Hollywood urging me to revise my earlier decision and promising me a freer hand" (pp. vii-viii). By mid-March 1960, the Nabokovs were ensconced in a rented Hollywood villa, and work on the screenplay was underway. "Kubrick and I . . . debated in an amiable battle of suggestion and countersuggestion how to cinemize the novel" (p. ix). They agreed that Quilty's death should come first, that Part One of *Lolita* would be stressed. Kubrick introduced Tuesday Weld to Nabokov, who exercised his veto: "a graceful ingenue but not my idea of Lolita" (p. ix). Six months later, at their final meeting, Kubrick showed Nabokov several photos of "demure" Sue Lyon, "who, said Kubrick, could be easily made to look younger and grubbier for the part of Lolita for which he already had signed her up" (p. xi). Having completed his responsibilities, Nabokov and his wife sailed for Europe. The 1961 production of the film proceeded without them.

Although Nabokov received sole screen credit for *Lolita*'s scenario, the situation is rather complicated. After three months of work, Nabokov delivered a four-hundred-page screenplay to Kubrick, who understandably refused this new version of *Greed*, explaining that it would take seven hours to run. Nabokov then wrote a considerably shorter version, of which Kubrick used only about twenty per cent. The *Lolita* screenplay which McGraw-Hill finally published in 1974 is not an exact replica of Nabokov's second attempt. While preparing it for publication in 1970 (legal problems delayed its appearance) Nabokov made further revisions, rearranged and dropped scenes, and of course kept certain interludes deleted by Kubrick. Given Kubrick's directorial methods—ad hoc and improvisatory—it is doubtful if a reliable and complete shooting script is even available, and Nabokov's first version is hidden forever. The *auteur* critics who celebrate Kubrick's "consistent vision" avoid these problems of authorship, and either don't know—or refuse to report—that Quilty's wonderful ping pong game was Peter Sellers's idea. How many other inspired moments arose this way? Did Kubrick use material from Nabokov's *first* version, or sequences omitted from the published screenplay? And is it true, as rumor has it, that Calder Willingham also did a treatment of *Lolita*? These circumstances and rhetorical questions demonstrate why film scholarship is a messier area than *cinéastes* will admit, and suggest too why an ambitious discussion of "The Making of *Lolita*" (as that study might unhappily be titled) would be a blessing as mixed as the film itself. Perhaps a few comments may be safely hazarded.

Nabokov's first and last screen assignment is by no means an unqualified success, but it was deemed professional enough to bring him the offer to adapt *The Day of the Locust*. "I considered it," says Nabokov, "but the book's short chapters were too disjuncted; I could not visualize them as a unit. It would have been too difficult a task." He was able to "cinemize" *Lolita* with surprising dispatch because it was not his initial effort at "screen writing." His story "The Assistant Producer" (1943) is cinematic by design, and "The Potato Elf" (1924), the best of his youthful tales, is unconsciously cinematic, as Nabokov recently discovered in the course of translating it: "Although I never intended the story to suggest a screenplay or to fire a script writer's fancy, its structure and recurrent pictorial details do have a cinematic slant."[12] *Lolita*, a baroque verbal structure, has its cinematic slant, too, and the "stage directions" in Nabokov's screenplay underscore that slant by quoting directly from the novel's most pictorial passages, or referring to specific pages for the appropriate *mise-en-scène*.

Yet the screenplay is not a close adaptation of the novel; Nabokov worked hard to find cinematic equivalents for its prosier components. The screenplay stands on its own and includes the following variety of effects and materials, most of which were omitted by Kubrick:

1. *Scenes rejected from the final draft of the novel and reinstated in the screenplay.* Humbert arrives in a taxi at the charred-out, roped-off ruins of the Mc-Coo house. A crowd of bystanders cheers him as he grandly alights from the cab. Bewildered Mr. McCoo conducts Humbert on a grotesque guided tour of his non-existent "lovely home"; an encyclopedia is the holocaust's most resilient survivor (pp. 32-33). Charlotte Haze's home is Humbert's second choice. Some of Quilty's dialogue is adapted from a scene at a women's club early in the first draft of *Lolita*, omitted in the novel because, says Nabokov, "Quilty had to be a shadow until almost the end." Quilty's presence is all too conspicuous throughout the screenplay.

2. *Materials from the novel, completely transposed.* Dr. Ray serves as narrator, and, in addition to new expository material, bits and pieces of his Foreword sound through the screenplay (as voice-over). Kubrick's Dr. Zemph is the only "clinician" in the film. The references to Poe sustained in the screenplay (pp. 16-18, 71, 121) are more obvious than the bits and pieces in the novel, and an allusion to "Baskerville Cottages" (p. 117), replacing the novel's "Shirley

Holmes" (p. 66), succinctly foreshadows the way Detective Trapp will hound Humbert. The screenwriter holds in check the literary anatomist's impulse toward elaboration, easing the demands he customarily makes upon a reader. But allusions to the painter "Lewis Ruskin" and to the inhibited passional lives of two Victorians (pp. 113 and 143) parallel rather than transpose the matter of the parent text. With his eye on a film budget scenarist Nabokov scales down the wide range of tourist attractions readily available to the camera eye of the novel. Humbert: "I think I've never seen such iridescent rocks." Lolita: "I think iridescent rocks stink" (p. 139).

3. *Scenes composed almost entirely of dialogue, unlike anything in the novel.* Humbert is a teacher, yet there is very little in the novel about his life at Cantrip College. There is more academic satire in the screenplay, akin to the fun in Nabokov's previous novel, *Pnin*, and his next venture, *Pale Fire*. A wonderful scene at Lolita's prom (pp. 56-58) reunites Charlotte and Quilty, who dimly recalls that she had a daughter: "Ah, of course: Dolores, the tears and the roses." "And tomorrow she'll be having a cavity filled by your uncle," says Charlotte, referring to Dr. Ivor Quilty. "I know," answers Quilty, "he's a wicked old man." Kubrick had the sense to retain Quilty's "poetic" recollection and Charlotte's double entendre, but the leering rejoinder was (rightly?) dropped, along with some very funny dialogue. Most of the double entendres which critics have labeled as Kubrick's are drawn from the screenplay, as when Charlotte, employing the hard sell, offers her lush garden and cherry pies to hesitant Humbert at the moment when he first sees Lolita (p. 40). "Was my garden the decisive factor?" Charlotte quickly asks her new roomer, who of course does not mention the spicy cherry pie—a genteel *émigré's* belated verbal discovery.

4. *Self-conscious visuals which serve to remind the viewer that the fiction-film is artifice.* As the screenplay opens, Lolita (Mrs. Dolly Schiller) is heard on the soundtrack, talking to Humbert about Quilty: "He's got a house there, a regular old castle (*rustle of rummaging*). There was a picture of it somewhere (*flip-flip*). Yes, here it is." A "brief still" is indicated, and then Pavor Manor comes alive on the screen; the sun rises and a world starts to move (p. 1). Death is marked similarly by stop-action techniques. After Charlotte is run over, a small crowd gathers. "A photographer from the Traffic Division is taking a picture," instructs the scenario. "In a projection room it is shown to a bunch of policemen by an instructor with a pointer," who then recapitulates the entire scene, using diagrams (p. 87). As he returns to the still picture, it too "comes to life," resuming the action at the accident scene (p. 88). Screenwriter "Vivian Darkbloom" (to use Nabokov's alias in *Lolita*) has shown his hand, but it is an unnecessary presence to

Kubrick, who tactlessly casts a woman in the anagrammatic role. Quilty's mistress is virtually invisible in the novel, as befits a scrambling of the author's name. "Her" silence speaks to Humbert's claim that he has "only words to play with!" Kubrick discarded the opening gambit of the screenplay because he is not about to suggest that he has only images to play with.

5. *A number of excellent visuals, many of which capture the essence of Nabokov's high-spirited prose.* When Humbert receives Charlotte's inane letter, declaring her love for him, he reads it aloud, "with ironical asides": "In one SHOT, he is dressed as a gowned professor, in another as a routine Hamlet, in a third as a dilapidated Poe. He also appears as himself"; the disguises are clearly an effort to visualize the subject if not the specific text of literary parody (p. 73). After reading the letter, "he goes into an awkward and grotesque jig (in striking contrast to his usual mournful and dignified demeanor). Dancing, he descends the stairs" (p. 74); the choreographed action, recalling Quilty's dance of death in the novel, is equivalent to the rhetorical arabesques and grotesqueries of Humbert's narrative persona. He then calls Lolita at Camp Q to tell her he is marrying Charlotte: "Now both parties are visible in a montage arrangement, with the camp's various activities illustrated at the corners as in a publicity folder," a visual compression of an entire chapter (p. 75). The seduction scene at The Enchanted Hunters indicates "*Various Rooms*": "The CAMERA glides from room to room at dawn, with some of the guests still fast asleep. The purpose of these shots is to construct a series of situations contrasting with the atmosphere in Room 342. The movement of the CAMERA reveals the following scenes, all of very brief duration" (p. 111). Ten shots follow. "I was very proud of that sequence," Nabokov told me in 1971, after I had read the typescript he had recently readied for publication.

Despite their imaginativeness, Kubrick dropped all of these visuals, which may account for Nabokov's modest sense of his own accomplishment. "Oh, it's really a stage play, it's not very visual," he said in 1971, as though he had accepted the verdict implicit in Kubrick's *Lolita*—the director's decision to use some of Nabokov's dialogue but little else. Nabokov was genuinely surprised when I argued in his favor, particularly in behalf of the several comic interludes which, like *Invitation to a Beheading* and Quilty's Laurel and Hardy death scene, reflect Nabokov's love of classic screen comedy. Keaton would have relished and no doubt happily realized several of these set pieces, and one of them clearly echoes Chaplin. In the novel, young Humbert's mother accidentally dies in a parenthetical throwaway phrase ("picnic, lightning," p. 12), but screenwriter Nabokov visualizes "*A Mountain Meadow—thunderhead advancing above sharp cliffs*": "Several people scramble for shelter, and the first big drops of rain strike the zinc of a lunchbox. As the poor lady in white runs toward the pavilion of a lookout, a blast of livid light fells her. Her graceful specter floats up above the black cliffs holding a parasol and blowing kisses to her husband and child who stand below, looking up, hand in hand" (p. 4), a comic version of the last moments of Cocteau's *Beauty and the Beast* (1946), when the two lovers, locked in an embrace, are lifted into the clouds to live happily ever after—a paradise which beastly Humbert will never enjoy. The screenplay also describes how one of the drawers of Humbert's desk in Charlotte's house should "come out by itself in a kind of organic protractile movement, disclosing a photograph of Humbert's first love in a Riviera setting" (p. 65); the magical action, powered by the spell exerted by Humbert's past, recalls the way animated things pursue Keaton, Chaplin, and Laurel and Hardy. Humbert shows Lolita the photo of Annabel Leigh: "Same snapshot, same setting, but now in the photograph the chair next to Annabel is occupied by young Humbert, a moody lad. Morosely, he takes off his white cap as if acknowledging recognition, and dons it again" (p. 66). The metamorphosing picture parallels the constantly shifting surfaces of Keaton's involuted *Sherlock, Jr.,* while young Humbert's polite but illusion-shattering gesture evokes Groucho's direct address to the audience as well as the opening of René Clair's *The Flame of New Orleans* (1941). "Has anyone in the audience ever seen a wedding dress floating down the Mississippi?" inquires Clair's narrator (voice-over). "Open [the door], please, we're late for the opera," and a liveried servant bows to the narrator and the audience. Lolita herself posits farcical incongruities. "Here, on that beach, you see the angels envying [Annabel] and me," says Humbert, pointing to a white-garbed couple. Lolita: "That's not angels. That's Garbo and Abraham Lincoln in terrycloth robes" (p. 66). Chaplin's version of a summit meeting helps to elevate a sequence at Dr. Ivor Quilty's office. Clare Quilty discovers Lolita seated in his uncle's dentist's chair, and pumps it "up and backwards with his foot. . . . There should be a fantastic blend of an Amusement Park wobblecar and a flying machine. Summer clouds and sun stripes glide by. Lolita soars, Lolita solos," says the scenarist; this interlude, which is not included in the published screenplay, recalls the wonderful barbershop scene in *The Great Dictator* wherein the competitive, megalomaniacal despots (Chaplin and Jack Oakie) have their chairs cranked up skyward. "You're right," says Nabokov. "Kubrick should have filmed those vivacious 'visuals.'"

Nabokov was disappointed when he saw the film at its New York premiere, "mainly because it demonstrated that I had wasted six months of my time." Unlike those writers who almost automatically revile the filmed versions of their novels or scenarios, Nabokov is amazingly good-natured about the experience, partly because he has not been embittered by long servitude in Hollywood (like Fitzgerald, John O'Hara, Dorothy Parker, Lillian Hellman, et al.). He knows, moreover, that a writer's time is never completely wasted, as hack scenarist West proved with *The Day of the Locust*. The idea for *Pale Fire* was in its chrysalis stage; and although Nabokov's butterfly-hunting in the Hollywood hills was fairly unproductive, his field observations of Hollywood starlets, agents, and producers were labeled and filed for future use in *Ada* (see Chapter Thirty-two, the Hollywood swimming pool scene). The Nabokovs dined with Gina Lollobrigida and John Wayne, David Selznick and Billy Wilder, "a worldly, cultivated man." Their gossip and shop talk was not lost on the novelist: *Ada's* absurd lessons from Stan Slavsky recall the way Marilyn Monroe was at that time being coached within an inch of her life by a well-known "Method" practitioner. At one gala party the Nabokovs met the actress, and the spectacle of her frantic, open pursuit of her French leading man may have influenced Nabokov's portrait of *Ada's* insatiable star Marina Durmanov, whose actor/gigolo Mexican lover (p. 197) is unworthy enough to belong in *Hollywood Babylon* (1965), Kenneth Anger's dark sexual history of the community.

Ada does make considerable fun of screen adaptations, but Nabokov himself speaks kindly of Kubrick and his *Lolita:* "a great director, a first-rate film."

"The four main actors deserve the very highest praise," Nabokov told a *Playboy* interviewer in 1963. "Sue Lyon bringing that breakfast tray or childishly pulling on her sweater in the car—these are moments of unforgettable acting and directing. The killing of Quilty is a masterpiece, and so is the death of Mrs. Haze."[13] Nabokov has not always been so sanguine about such matters. The first edition of his *Nikolai Gogol* (1944) included a still from the excellent Soviet film version of *The Overcoat* that depicted the awesome cloak and Akaky Akakyvich, the humble clerk. The publisher's utilitarian caption is garnished by a parenthetical "Author's comment: 'I would not mind including the picture of the "overcoat," but by all means let us omit the man, who does not look like Ak. Ak. at all'" (p. 142). Two decades later, however, a mellowed Nabokov withholds any complaints that Miss Winters does not look like the "Marlene Dietrich type" described in the novel. Nor does he complain that the movie's Charlotte is in several ways broader than his, her cultural pretensions telegraphed for a mass audience that might have missed the thrust of his quieter observations.

Nabokov is so gracious about Kubrick's efforts because he no longer entertains any illusions about the business of making movies, *auteur* theory notwithstanding. "By nature I am no dramatist," he writes in the screenplay's Foreword.

I am not even a hack scenarist; but if I had given as much of myself to the stage or the screen as I have to the kind of writing which serves a triumphant life sentence between the covers of a book, I would have advocated and applied a system of total tyranny, directing the play or the picture myself, choosing settings and costumes, terrorizing the actors, mingling with them in the bit part of guest . . . prompting them, and, in a word, pervading the entire show with the will and art of one individual—for there is nothing in the world that I loathe more than group activity, that communal bath where the hairy and slippery mix in a multiplication of mediocrity (pp. ix-x).

Only a handful of contemporary directors approach that tyrannical ideal (Bergman, Fellini), and Nabokov's riposte at once summarizes both the literary community's attitude toward Hollywood and the literature-oriented film critic's hostility toward auteurism, which posits the existence of a directorial style despite the inroads of "group activity."

Nabokov didn't get a chance to direct *Lolita,* of course, but his experience in adapting it is reason enough for his magnanimous attitude toward Kubrick. The opening scenes of Nabokov's screenplay are too static, too talky (Dr. Ray in particular, p. 3), and its world is often almost benign; he had seen for himself that he couldn't entirely "lick the book," as they say in Hollywood of a controversial, challenging "property." The verbal texture of *Lolita,* its rhetoric of desperation and mock-confession, is a far cry from the transparent prose and crisp dialogue of Dashiell Hammett or the sardonic idiom of Raymond Chandler's Marlowe, which lend themselves so well to screen adaptation. The sombre realism of John Ford's version of *The Grapes of Wrath* (1940) improves upon Steinbeck because it omits the novel's sentimental rhetoric and portentous symbolism by returning to Steinbeck's original source of inspiration, his 1938 documentary "photo-story" assignment from *Life.* Ford's cinematographer, Gregg Toland, based his setups on these and Farm Security Administration pictures—on life rather than art. Adaptations of novels such as *Lolita, The Sound and the Fury* (1957), and *Ulysses* (1967) take the opposite course. Perhaps not even the most stylized of productions could have solved the basic aesthetic problem of *Lolita,* a novel whose effects depend on a richly rhetorical first-person narrator. "[Lolita] complained of a painful stiffness in the upper vertebrae—and I thought of poliomyelitis as any American parent would. Giving up all hope of intercourse . . ." (p. 242)—translate *that* tonal shift, typical of the rhetorical trapdoors that constantly keep the reader off balance. The scenarist's dialogue may not equal Humbert's novelistic voice, his crucial indirect discourse (and intercourse), but Nabokov's most fantastic visuals come close, and it is a pity Kubrick didn't include them.

Kubrick may have been reluctant to use them because he was still committed to a naturalistic visual style. In spite of its surreal qualities, his wonderfully funny opening scene is fundamentally conservative, and the macabre slapstick is safely grounded, more verbal than visual. Kubrick is unwilling to risk the bravura "Western-style tussle" described in the novel, and his Quilty dies discreetly behind a painting. *Lolita* is the turning point in Kubrick's evolvement from a naturalistic cinema (*Paths of Glory,* 1957, *Spartacus,* 1960); after *Lolita,* his films were fantastic as well as futuristic: *Dr. Strangelove* (1963), *2001* (1968), *A Clockwork Orange* (1971). Kubrick and fantast Nabokov got together too early in the director's career. One wishes he could have filmed *Lolita* in 1970.

Although Kubrick dropped Nabokov's comical and Chaplinesque visuals, he did include his own *hommage* to earlier screen comedy. Chaplin's tussle with the wall-bed in *One A.M.* (1916) informs Humbert's and the night porter's equally funny struggle with the collapsible cot at The Enchanted Hunters, but the slapstick is distractive—another sop for the censors?—and the tone is wrong; for all its ironies, the seduction sequence is ultimately no laughing matter, no Busby Berkleyan "Honeymoon Hotel." This scene best illustrates the problems faced by *Lolita*'s adapters, and screenwriter Nabokov acknowledges that it was his most troublesome challenge: "Long before, in Lugano, I had adumbrated the sequence at The Enchanted Hunters hotel, but its exact mechanism now proved tremendously difficult to adjust so as to render by the transparent interplay of sound effects and trick shots

both a humdrum morning and a crucial moment in the lives of a desperate pervert and a wretched child" (p. x). As excellent as James Mason is in this scene, the scenario and director fail to communicate Humbert's delicately balanced tonal oscillations, the original scene's splicing of lust and despair, its verbalization of the pain at the center of all the playfulness and parody, all of which may elude the film medium:

Every now and then, immediately east of my left ear (always assuming I lay on my back, not daring to direct my viler side toward the nebulous haunch of my bed-mate), the corridor would brim with cheerful, resonant and inept exclamations ending in a volley of good-nights. When *that* stopped, a toilet immediately north of my cerebellum took over. It was a manly, energetic, deep-throated toilet, and it was used many times. Its gurgle and gush and long afterflow shook the wall behind me. Then someone in a southern direction was extravagantly sick, almost coughing out his life with his liquor, and his toilet descended like a veritable Niagara, immediately beyond our bathroom [Quilty]. And when finally all the waterfalls had stopped, and the enchanted hunters were sound asleep, the avenue under the window of my insomnia, to the west of my wake—a staid, eminently residential, dignified alley of huge trees—degenerated into the despicable haunt of gigantic trucks roaring through the wet and windy night.

And less than six inches from me and my burning life, was nebulous Lolita! After a long stirless vigil, my tentacles moved towards her again, and this time the creak of the mattress did not awake her. I managed to bring my ravenous bulk so close to her that I felt the aura of her bare shoulder like a warm breath upon my cheek. And then, she sat up, gasped, muttered with insane rapidity something about boats, tugged at the sheets and lapsed back into her rich, dark, young unconsciousness. As she tossed, within that abundant flow of sleep, recently auburn, at present lunar, her arm struck me across the face. For a second I held her. She freed herself from the shadow of my embrace—doing this not consciously, not violently, not with any personal distaste, but with the neutral plaintive murmur of a child demanding its natural rest. And again the situation remained the same: Lolita with her curved spine to Humbert, Humbert resting his head on his hand and burning with desire and dyspepsia (p. 132).

The *film noir* vista beyond Humbert's window is cinematic enough, but no camera could capture the "warm breath" of Lolita's shoulder, and those horror-film "tentacles" resist the naturalistic style favored by Kubrick. They might have been realized as a hallucination, though such an effect would be intrusive unless fantasy had figured consistently throughout the film (as, say, in Polanski's *Repulsion,* 1965). Only a literal equivalent suits Kubrick's style, and the excellent shock-cut from Charlotte's garden to the drive-in theatre uses actual footage from *The Curse of Frankenstein* (Peter Cushing as the monster, 1957). But no visual quotation or metaphor or setup can fully project the special richness of Humbert's voice, the short but vertiginous distance between his sorrowful memory of her "plaintive murder" and his alliterative

frippery, "desire and dyspepsia." Tough-minded members of the jury might argue that confessor Humbert is dissembling, but the passage is instructive. What, then, asks Kinbote, *is* the "password"? "Pity," answers John Shade (p. 225), and neither Sue Lyon nor James Mason's tamed Humbert elicit it too often.

Kubrick is at his best, and nearest to the spirit of Nabokov and Keaton, when he is able to blend farce and terror. Peter Sellers accomplishes this brilliantly in the role of Quilty. Whenever Sellers is on the screen, the film is "Nabokovian" in its own right. The celluloid Quilty also dons two disguises: a police conventioneer at The Enchanted Hunters, and Dr. Zemph, a thick-accented German child psychologist allegedly employed by Lolita's school—the Kubrick-Sellers version of the self-styled "private member of the Public Welfare Board" (Quilty) who interviews Humbert at length on the telephone in Nabokov's screenplay (pp. 164-69). Humbert discovers him in his living room one night. Seated stiffly in the semi-darkness, his eyes masked by glittering thick glasses, Dr. Zemph transposes some of Headmistress Pratt's dialogue from the novel and convinces Humbert that Lolita should participate in the school play, Quilty's own *The Enchanted Hunters.* A Gothic Dr. Ray and an Ur–Dr. Strangelove, Zemph is as terrifying as the leering, flat-voiced conventioneer who has already confided to Humbert, breathlessly, "I'm not suspicious but other people think I'm suspicious especially when I stand around on street corners. One of my boys picked me up the other week, he thought I was too suspicious."

The reviewers who objected to these phantoms because they're not in the book misunderstood *Lolita* and the essential problem of adaptation; fidelity to all the events in a novel is no criterion of excellence, nor an index of success. Although Kubrick's *A Clockwork Orange* closely follows Anthony Burgess's text, it nevertheless upends the writer's Christian humanism; the director's violence-prone Alex is too charming an actor. The film version of *Ulysses* honors Joyce's plot at the same time that it casts too manly an actor as the vulnerable, wilting Bloom. Quilty's lethargic slow-motion Lindy at the school prom isn't in the novel, but its unnatural rhythms faithfully render his resiliency: so bloodless a dancer will also be difficult to kill. "I'm not with anybody, I'm with you," conventioneer Sellers tells James Mason at the hotel, summarizing Quilty's role as comic *Doppelgänger*, a grotesque projection of Humbert's criminal self. "Is 'mask' the keyword?" asks Humbert in the novel (p. 55), and the serial selves portrayed by Sellers answer the question affirmatively. Willfully charming, sinister, and hysterical, a creature who gets what he wants by means of rhetoric, his Quilty *is* Nabokov's prose, and Sellers might well have played Humbert, too. "Wonderful idea!" agrees Nabokov.

Quilty's death scene in the film is appropriately ver-

"She is suffering from acute repression of the libido of her natural instincts. . . . You, Dr. Hombard, zhould unveto zat girl's partizipazion in ze school play": Quilty as Dr. Zemph (Peter Sellers) persuades Humbert to change his strict ways. The low-key lighting of the scene, atypical of Kubrick's *Lolita*, derives from *film noir* and the parent text. After Humbert and Quilty conclude their eerie colloquy on the pillared porch of The Enchanted Hunters, the nameless man "struck a light, but because he was drunk, or because the wind was, the flame illumined not him but another person, a very old man, one of those permanent guests of old hotels—and his white rocker. Nobody said anything and the darkness returned to its initial place" (p. 129), Kubrick's point of departure at the outset of the interlude with Dr. Zemph.

bal. Like Humbert, he finally has only words to play with, and Kubrick serves him well. Scenarist Nabokov curiously reduced the scene to less than one page. The "silent shadowy sequence . . . should not last more than one minute" states the novice screenwriter, unable to imagine a visual treatment of the movie-style killing; except for the rocking chair that is activated by a bullet (a moment drawn from the novel), the death sequence is not funny (p. 2). Kubrick and Sellers masterfully realize the spirit of the original scene, and hack writer Quilty succumbs in a sea of clichés equal to the clutter of his Pavor Manor. "My motto is Be Prepared," says Quilty, producing an extra ping pong ball from his sleeve. Unable to return Humbert's weak serve, he says, "It's not really who wins, it's how you play." "I want to die like a champion," he states, pulling on a pair of boxing gloves as the bullets start to fly. Quilty's dialogue quickly sketches the variegated "Boschian cripples" that populate the novel: "One guy had a bat instead of a hand," recalls sportsman Quilty; "I got nice friends, use 'em for furniture, one guy looks like a bookcase," he gasps as Humbert reloads his gun. These word-pictures resolve a casting problem that could have turned *Lolita* into Tod Browning's *Freaks*.

Quilty rushes about the room, but his death scene omits the comic balletic violence of the novel. Nabokov's unwillingness or inability to "cinemize" the chapter may well have been instructive, and the director, a writer for the nonce, takes his cue from the scenarist. Instead of staging the "Western-style tussle," Kubrick has Sellers employ a caricatured Western drawl while reading aloud from Humbert's poem; it's possible that Sellers, a veteran of the madcap B.B.C. radio "Goon Shows" (1951-60), may have improvised some of this comic business. "Cain't read, never did none of that book larnin'," protests Quilty, purposefully horsing around. The future director of *A Clockwork Orange* is unwilling to spill blood—gore is not always funny—and the non sequiturs of dark verbal slapstick suffice: "Gee, right in the boxing gloves," marvels Quilty as Humbert's first bullet smashes a vase. "My leg'll be black and blue tomorrow," complains Quilty after a bullet has finally found its mark. Kubrick forsakes the long chase and death bed sequences of the novel, and compresses Quilty's agony. The wounded man seeks refuge behind an eighteenth-century portrait painting of a delicate young girl (imitation Gainsborough?) and is dispatched by the bullets that neatly riddle her face, Kubrick's sole metaphor for the two nympholepts' abuse of Lolita.

The director's strategy in this scene is intelligent as well as strangely prescient. He then recognized that a stylized spoof of violence, unless it is clearly an arabesque (like the hoodlum/private eye dance parody in *The Band Wagon*, 1953), may risk more than it accomplishes by charming and morally disarming an audience, allowing it to enjoy the spectacle, whatever the director's intentions—as happens in the "Singin' in the Rain" sequence of *A Clockwork Orange* (see Pauline Kael's definitive critique, which draws blood[14]). Quilty's off-camera death throes—"That hurt!"—observe the classical proprieties without compromising the audience or the brilliantly realized comedy. We laugh aloud—at the death of a painting. To open *Lolita* with this scene is more than a structural and thematic blunder; it's so good that the remainder of the film becomes an anti-climax, posing an obvious question: why wasn't Humbert allowed to evoke some dark word-pictures of his own?

James Mason's Humbert is generally a lovestruck lamb of a fellow, though now and then he realizes the delirious range of the first Humbert's emotions. Witness the horror that crosses his face when Charlotte informs him that the urn he is holding contains the ashes of the late Mr. Haze, whose memorial shelf recalls *Sunset Boulevard;* or the diabolical laughter which Charlotte's love letter inspires; or the way in which he sits in a steamy bath after her death, stupified equally by his unexpected luck and the glass of Scotch which floats under his nose. Memorable too is his shrill argument with Lolita after he has abruptly dragged her home from the cast party of *The Enchanted Hunters.* "You creep . . . *I hate you!*" shrieks the costumed enchantress, for once demoniac, whose grotesque eye make-up, realized in the decadent style

"What's this, the deed to the ranch?": Quilty tries to read Humbert's poem, a parody of Eliot's "Ash Wednesday," though the object of Sellers's burlesque—the comic sidekick of "B" Westerns (Al St. John, Gabby Hayes)—is more likely to be recognized by a mass audience.

Right, top and bottom:
At home with Lolita after her performance in *The Enchanted Hunters.*

of her well-named Beardsley School, expresses the aura of bewitchment rarely present in the film. Attempting to describe what it was like to live without her, Humbert writes: "the general impression I desire to convey is of a side door crashing open in life's full flight, and a rush of roaring black time drowning with its whipping wind the cry of lone disaster" (pp. 255-56). Kubrick completely omits this three-year period of anguish and aimless pursuit, but Humbert's discovery that she has disappeared from the hospital fully realizes the spirit of that passage. While Lolita convalesces, a feverish Humbert waits in their darkened motel room, tossing and twisting in bed until a massive quilted bolster has covered his head. A mysterious predawn phone call sends him to the hospital; she is gone, he *has* been Quilted. As Humbert runs down the dimly lit corridor—stumbling, coughing, screaming—the "rush of roaring black time" and "the cry of lone disaster" come to life on the screen.

As in Dr. Zemph's spectral interlude, the excellence of these scenes is partly attributable to their Germanic *Stimmung*. Their dark tonalities are exceptional, however; most of the film is poorly served by high-key lighting, the stylistic signature of M-G-M, which helped finance the venture. It is no small irony that the novel should turn out to have employed the chiaroscuro and iconography of *film noir* more expressively than the film version. Roadside America, the *least* challenging aspect of the adaptation process, is barely evident in Kubrick's *Lolita*. It too was the victim of censorship, albeit indirect. To avoid harassment and make use of blocked overseas funds, *Lolita* was filmed in England. This explains why, except for some nondescript stock footage, the American landscape is absent from *Lolita*. But it doesn't explain why Kubrick didn't do more to remedy the situation. A lone California-based cinematographer could have quietly accumulated and mailed Kubrick the requisite footage of motels, gas stations, signs, and the nightscapes which confirm the desperate situation of Humbert and Lolita. Back-projection and other studio tricks would have accomplished the rest, certainly to the advantage of Kubrick's curiously limp car scenes, which possess little of the drama of similar sequences in *film noir*, Robert Frank, and Nabokov's *Lolita*. Nor should indoor shooting have been out of the question: studio-bound *films noirs* such as *The Killers* created excellent "outdoor" scenes, while the less realistic, more stylized streets of *The Woman in the Window* and *Scarlet Street* suggest an alternate route consistent with scenarist Nabokov's desire to "control the flow of the film from motel to motel, mirage to mirage, nightmare to nightmare" (p. x). Charlotte's house is wonderfully done (and done-in), but the interiors of motels do not suffice. Moreover, says Nabokov, "Kubrick put a TV set in their motel rooms—that's wrong! They were utterly alone."

Kubrick also fails to take advantage of the smaller realistic components of *Lolita* and *film noir*. The nymphet's movie culture is virtually absent from the film, as is its aural equivalent, through no fault of Nabokov's; his screenplay had included a corny Pop song titled "Lolita, Lolita, Lolita"—no doubt the flip-side of "Little Carmen," Lo's "fave" in the novel.

> Because it's a maddening summer,
> Because the whole night is in bloom,
> Because you're in love with a strummer
> Who brings his guitar to your room (p. 127).

Kubrick omitted this new song, and didn't replace it with the possible alternatives. Bob Harris's "Lolita theme" is too romantic, and Nelson Riddle's soundtrack is far too lush. The "nasal voices" of the "invisibles" who serenaded Lolita would have been perfect; Peter Bogdanovich used their actual recordings on the soundtrack of *The Last Picture Show* (1971), an excellent example of how a handful of Kubrick's juniors have recently taken full advantage of Pop materials. The effect of 1951 songs in a 1971 film is elegiac, but in 1961 those songs were the property of an uncherished past. Rock 'n' roll had recently sent "Jo and Eddy and Tony and Peggy and Guy and Patty" into limbo (p. 150), and if Kubrick had utilized Eddie Fisher's "Wish You Were Here," Jo Stafford's "You Belong to Me," and Tony Bennett's "Cold Cold Heart" —instant pastoral in Bogdanovich—the results would have been ideally sardonic, equal to *Scarlet Street's* "Melancholy Baby" and *Double Indemnity's* "Tangerine." Paradoxically enough, displaced and cultured Europeans such as Lang, Wilder, and Nabokov seem to approach Pop more confidently than Kubrick, the self-educated artist (an American archetype) whose ambition to make Important Pictures may actually alienate and isolate him from "vulgar" sources of inspiration. The staid and sophisticated behavior of the kids in Kubrick's prom scene suggests that the director is the foreigner—or, perhaps, hasn't done the homework which made Nabokov's *Lolita* possible.

Kubrick is but one of several filmmakers who, in the wake of the cinema's new respectability and the director's star status, would rescue the form from the allegedly base context of popular culture. Kubrick's first three feature films, *The Killing* (1956) in particular, were in the *noir* tradition, but his *Lolita* unfortunately strives after a supposedly higher form. Although *Sunset Boulevard* and *Touch of Evil* had already demonstrated that *film noir* could brilliantly accommodate what would soon come to be called Black Humor, Kubrick's *Lolita* suggests that he felt compelled to choose one of two roads. His production bypasses many of the appropriate properties of *film noir,* the putative low road, in favor of a more "literary" mode whose comedy—broader than Nabokov's— is most akin to the fashionable Black Humor of Joseph Heller and Terry Southern, Kubrick's collabo-

rator on the *Dr. Strangelove* scenario. *Lolita's* opening allusion to *Scarlet Street,* repeated toward the end of the film, may well be a declaration of independence rather than an *hommage.* Two other sly visual allusions, in-jokes for the *cinéastes,* reinforce the valedictory idea. The shooting of the painting evokes the moment in Nicholas Ray's *Party Girl* (1958) when gangster Lee J. Cobb fires into a large picture of Jean Harlow, while Humbert's bathtub whiskey alludes to tippler Edward G. Robinson's similar posture in *Key Largo* (1948), directed by John Huston, whose *Asphalt Jungle* (1950) had influenced Kubrick's own heist thriller, *The Killing,* and employed the same star (Sterling Hayden). These allusions constitute a telegram from England, where Kubrick even now resides: NO MORE HOLLYWOOD GENRE FILMS OR PERIOD PIECES FOR ME STOP. "I am Spartacus, set me free," says Quilty at the outset of *Lolita* as he rises from a chair to unwind a toga-like dustcloth from his unathletic body. The joke refers to Kubrick's previous venture, where he had served as Kirk Douglas's directorial slave, and announces that the *auteur* is now on his own, for better or worse.

Camera Obscura

Kubrick's allusion to *Spartacus* would seem to place him in the camp of Nabokov, the most well-armed of self-conscious artists, a *performer* in the tradition of

Cervantes, Sterne, Diderot, Melville, Claude Mauriac, Carroll, Joyce, Queneau, Robbe-Grillet, Beckett, Borges, and Bugs Bunny. Although they need not be rehearsed here,[15] the numerous a-novelistic components of Nabokov's novels are as self-referential as the rear-wall mirror that magically captures the image of Van Eyck in his *Arnolfini Wedding* (1434). Cinematic effects allow Nabokov to show his hand, if not always his face. "Close-up, close-up!" commands *Bend Sinister*'s puppeteer, a director for the nonce, and his cinematographer obliges with a zoom-shot of the "moon-white monstrously padded shoulder" that lurks in "the farewell shadows of the porch" (p. 59). More bravura shots are conditionally posited: "Photographed from above, [Paduk and Krug] would have come out in Chinese perspective, doll-like, a little limp but possibly with a hard wooden core under their plausible clothes—one slumped at his desk in a shaft of grey light . . . and the secret spectator (some anthropomorphic deity, for example) surely would be amused by the shape of human heads seen from above" (p. 148). A succession of rapidly withdrawn visuals in the final two chapters serve to reveal the mind behind the hand-held camera, the spirit of a "secret spectator" who both shares and transcends the unamusing terrors experienced by Adam Krug.

The "anthropomorphic deity" is the nucleus of every Nabokov performance, the shifty successor of "the stage manager whom Rex had in view" in *Laughter in the Dark*—"an elusive, double, triple, self-reflecting Proteus" (p. 183)—the same fellow who, sans mask or make-up, had moved among his players in the last two chapters of *King, Queen, Knave*. Tormented by the murder plan that has gone amiss, Franz's gaze is drawn toward

The foreign girl in the blue dress [who] danced with a remarkably handsome man in an old-fashioned dinner jacket. Franz had long since noticed this couple; they had appeared to him in fleeting glimpses, like a recurrent dream image or a subtle leitmotiv—now at the beach, now in a café, now on the promenade [and in the person of several anagrams]. Sometimes the man carried a butterfly net. The girl had a delicately painted mouth and tender gray-blue eyes, and her fiancé or husband, slender, elegantly balding, contemptuous of everything on earth but her, was looking at her with pride; and Franz felt envious of that unusual pair, so envious that his oppression, one is sorry to say, grew even more bitter, and the music stopped. They walked past him. They were speaking loudly. They were speaking a totally incomprehensible language (p. 254).

As Franz walks back to the hotel the next morning, he is overtaken by that "puzzling foreign couple":

They were both in beach robes and walked rapidly, rapidly conversing in their mysterious tongue. He thought that they glanced at him and fell silent for an instant. After passing him they began talking again; he had the

"A remarkably handsome man . . . slender, elegantly balding": Vladimir Nabokov, Berlin 1926, age twenty-six, hairline slightly receding the year before he began *King, Queen, Knave*.

Nabokov, in action at Le Boulou, Pyrénées Orientales, France, photographed by Véra Nabokov in the spring of 1929. He had just begun to write *The Defense*, and this landscape is described in the Foreword to the translated edition.

Alfred Hitchcock (with book) in *Blackmail*.

impression they were discussing him, and even pronouncing his name. It embarrassed, it incensed him, that this damned happy foreigner hastening to the beach with his . . . lovely companion, knew absolutely everything about his predicament and perhaps pitied, not without some derision, an honest young man who had been seduced and appropriated by an older woman. . . . The flimsy paper he had lost fluttered along the promenade, settled, fluttered again, and slithered past the happy couple. . . . What happened to it next is not known (pp. 258-59).

The passage at once teases the premises of omniscience and laughs at the fallibility of perception; the final phrase is a very Gogolian locution. Franz would have to read the novel at hand to see how little he is pitied by that man, an eavesdropper in his own right, whose image recalls Hitchcock's less glamorous presence in *Blackmail* (1929), the first of *his* walk-on appearances. Martha, Franz's dreadful partner, dies suddenly that night, dispatched by the moralist in the beach robe. If it is disturbing to learn that Franz plans to attend "the premiere of the film *King, Queen, Knave*" (p. 261), this is because it suggests, as Borges says of the play within *Hamlet*, "that if the characters of a fictional work can be readers or spectators, we, its readers or spectators, can be fictitious."[16]

The self-conscious effects in the *Lolita* screenplay are clearly derived from these involuted visuals, as is a sequence based on the assumption that authorial anagrams are not always deciphered by a movie audience. Humbert and Lolita have lost their way on a dirt road in a canyon and seek directions. Lolita says, "Ask that nut with the net over there," a character identified as "The Butterfly Hunter. His name is Vladimir Nabokov." The following fast-paced action and dialogue are indicated:

A fritillary settles with outspread wings on a tall flower. Nabokov snaps it up with a sweep of his net. Humbert walks toward him. With a nip of finger and thumb through a fold of the marquisette, Nabokov dispatches his capture and works the dead insect out of the netbag onto the palm of his hand.

HUMBERT   Is that a rare specimen?

NABOKOV   A specimen cannot be common or rare, it can only be poor or perfect.

HUMBERT   Could you direct me—

NABOKOV   You meant "rare species." This is a good specimen of a rather scarce subspecies.

HUMBERT   I see. Could you please tell me if this road leads to Dympleton?

NABOKOV   I haven't the vaguest idea. I saw some loggers (*pointing*) up there. They might know (pp. 127-28).

"Yes," says Nabokov, "I was going to play the part.

"Ask that nut with the net over there": Nabokov, Switzerland, c. 1962. (Photo by Horst Tappe)

In one *Bugs Bunny* cartoon of the forties, Bugs and his house have been quarantined because of an epidemic of rabbitytis, a highly contagious disease. "Look out there in the audience," says Bugs's nemesis, embittered by the bunny's enforced security. "That woman, that man with the tomato. They've got rabbitytis. No folks, you'd see red and yellow spots before your eyes. Then they'd begin to swirl around. Then, everything would go black," all of which occurs on the screen, ending the cartoon. "We do this to him all through the picture," says the tortoise, turning to the audience in another *Bugs Bunny* cartoon, and Disney's feature-length *The Three Caballeros* (1945) pulls out all stops, imitating Keaton's *Sherlock, Jr.,* by way of *Bugs Bunny.* Donald is shown watching a film-within-the-film. When an image is projected upside down, the narrator intrudes and says "let's turn the theater over." Nabokov does something similar with a slide projector in *Speak, Memory* (Chapter Eight), though the Disney influence remains minimal. Donald and a parrot enter a pop-up book to visit Baião, where actual singers and dancers materialize. Illusory Donald, a cartooned figure, realizes his fantasy, a real woman, and Aurora Miranda tweaks him under the bill (above). This photo is for the benefit of *cinéastes* who believe that Godard alone invented such games.

There's a precedent, of course." Hitchcock? "No, I had in mind Shakespeare, as the ghost in *Hamlet.* Kubrick loved the idea. I wonder why he changed his mind."

Kubrick thwarted Nabokov's thespian career because, unlike Godard or the early Truffaut, he is a self-effacing technician who keeps his camera invisible. Four or five allusions in the course of his two-and-a-half hour *Lolita* are nothing compared to the widely allusive artifices of Godard, who also casts his favorite directors as themselves: Sam Fuller in *Pierrot le fou* (1965) and Fritz Lang in *Contempt* (1963), where he is directing a film of no less a work than the *Odyssey,* and is assisted by Jean-Luc, a humble apprentice in his own film. Godard also appears in *Breathless* (1959), as does director Jean-Pierre Melville—who plays Nabokov![17]

Kubrick may have thought that an appearance by Nabokov would have been frivolous and self-indulgent, a criticism often leveled at involuted novels and films. If Kubrick had read *Conclusive Evidence* (now titled *Speak, Memory*), or read it carefully, he might have been more sympathetic. The tender if not obsessive nostalgia that is so central to Nabokov's vision, nowhere better evidenced than in his memoir, is ultimately no substitute for a viable life in the present, and among other things, *Lolita* is a devastating criticism of the reflexive attempt to move out of time, a parody of the psychological pastoral—Nabokov's own answer to *Conclusive Evidence,* his previous book. As Humbert says, "I was weeping again, drunk on the impossible past" (p. 284). Nabokov's presence in *Lolita,* novel or film, is quite justifiable, and very affecting: the multiple perspectives provided by a self-conscious work bring the viewer/reader closer to the mind of the artist, our totem figure, the "anthropomorphic deity" who in practice best embodies the fears and needs and desires of the race, and its unceasing efforts to confront, order, and structure the chaos of "reality." "Jan Van Eyck was here," reads the inscription above the mirror in the *Arnolfini Wedding,* announcing with no uncertainty that the artist is a spiritual and psychological participant in the ceremony. Hitchcock's dramatic walk-on in *I Confess* (1953), literally his most Catholic film, argues against any complaints of "gimmickry" and suggests that this popular artist is personally involved with the dark themes of his entertainments, the demons which he —unlike his characters or audience—can master through form.

Fellini, Bergman, and Lindsay Anderson have also appeared in their own films, and still photographers are now doing it, too; Lee Friedlander's haunting collection, *Self Portrait* (1970), is comprised of shots in which the photographer catches his own shadow or mirror-reflected image in Robert Frank–like settings. Orson Welles best realizes the possibilities of the self-conscious cinema because his most impressive "natu-

Hitchcock in *I Confess.*

Ray Milland and Marlene Dietrich in *Golden Earrings*.

"You're a mess, honey": Marlene Dietrich in *Touch of Evil*.

ralism" is so patently the product of camera-work, and the director does not restrict himself to a walk-on or delegate a surrogate (like Mastroianni as Fellini in 8½). Welles's *Touch of Evil* is a dark film that embraces two traditions. "Have you forgotten your old friend?" sheriff Hank Quinlan (Welles) shyly asks Tanya (Marlene Dietrich), the proprietress of a shoddy brothel. "You're a mess, honey," says Marlene to Orson, one old friend addressing another, and this colloquy between a former movie queen of the thirties and the swollen remains of the ex-Boy Wonder of Hollywood is strangely moving. Her point is well taken, and she in turn accepts the mess director Welles has made of *her*, burlesquing *Golden Earrings* (1947), the disastrous "comeback" movie that, in reviewer Bosley Crowther's words, had made "a greasy ragamuffin of her."[18] Growing old is no joke, but self-parody is an exorcism.

Touch of Evil is self-conscious in many ways. Janet Leigh, its female lead, tells rackets boss Akim Tamiroff that he looks like a poor version of a movie gangster, a cheap Little Caesar, but instead of being angry, he responds by burlesquing Edward G. Robinson. "What has this to do with me?" she asks a hoodlum, as though she has strayed onto the wrong set and, bemused by evil, has not yet realized that her role broadly mocks and brutalizes her screen and fan magazine persona of the All-American Girl, fifties variety. Leigh is named Susan, after Citizen Kane's second wife and Welles's one triumph, just as the melancholy sound of Tanya's pianola evokes the past and Hank Quinlan's happier days. Joseph Cotten's cameo role as an old man also looks back to *Kane,* and the cameo performances of Zsa Zsa Gabor and Mercedes McCambridge mordantly comment on their screen personae and personal lives. "This quirkish casting . . . damages the film's realistic mood," says Charles Higham in *The Films of Orson Welles* (1970). He is right, but wrong in his complaint; the best self-conscious works—from *Tristram Shandy* to Mauriac's *The Marquise Went Out at Five* (1962)—are multiform units. "O Jamesy let me up out of this," thinks Molly Bloom, addressing her "director," who has cast his disparate selves as Dedalus and Mr. Bloom—has everywhere shown his hand but never his face.[19]

The *auteur* who performs as his own actor (Renoir, Welles, Truffaut) reminds the audience that identity is an artistic construct, however antic or imperfect, and that role-playing, rather than character, may be our stock in trade, our sole means of survival. "Yes, okay, it's fiction, but it has brought me closer to what is real," says Maoist Véronique at the end of Godard's *La Chinoise* (1967), articulating the kind of truth that is not always self-evident to critics of the involuted novel or film.

Unlike the most lifelike of paintings, which are canvases framed on a wall, and unlike poems or plays which contain their artifice on a page or a stage, cin-

Palisades Parkway, New York 1966, a photograph by Lee Friedlander from his *Self Portrait;* the absence of a hyphen in the title underscores his intentions. Friedlander may have stopped by this parkway in order to document his attitude toward (arid? conformist?) suburbia, but his literally dark self-portrait, typically elliptical and disturbing, questions the efficacy of his mission, the processes of his art. Is the photographer a colossus, a master of the scene and subject, or is he a monster whose arbitrary selections beget distortions of reality? Do the mechanical elements of his craft control *him,* reduce the depth of his findings, the dimensions of self-expression, thereby producing visual conundrums rather than clear statements? Van Eyck was explicit enough, and actor-*auteur* Welles makes his point, but where *does* the self figure in a photo? The personal mark cast on this picture recalls those anonymous victims of the cataclysms at Pompeii and Hiroshima whose shadows were burned onto floors and walls.

Camera obscura: "1. *Optics.* A darkened chamber having an aperture (usually provided with a lens) through which light from external objects enters to form an image on the surface opposite. It originally took the form of a large room whose occupants viewed the image as thrown upon a white screen. In smaller form it is used for making drawings or for taking photographs. 2. A dark chamber or room" (from *Webster's Unabridged Dictionary,* 2d ed.).

ema is the preeminent illusionistic art. Rarely does a novel equal the way in which the most routine of movies can suspend our disbelief, engage our trust, immerse us in its world. The self-conscious film and novel take advantage of this situation. The dizzying inversions and distancing effects of a Godard or a Nabokov creatively destroy the trust engendered by the rise of so-called realism, and in its place re-create their versions of the first dark cinema, the camera obscura of the Renaissance. In the original dark chamber, the image was inverted, but by refusing to provide the corrective retinal mirror of the portable camera obscura, self-conscious art examines the nature of perception and challenges the reader/viewer to question his own poor device, everyman's camera obscura. The cranium is a lonely projection booth, and it is appropriate that Nabokov's first attempt at a cinematic fiction should have been titled *Camera Obscura.*

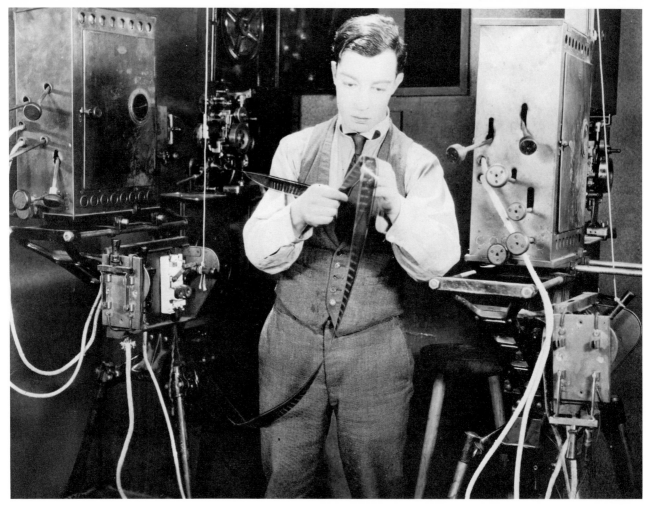

Buster Keaton in *Sherlock, Jr.*

6
Form and Metaphor: Exit Smiling

History (which, like certain film directors, proceeds by a series of abrupt images) now puts forward the image of a danger-filled saloon, located—as if on the high seas—out in the heart of the all-powerful desert.

Borges, "The Disinterested Killer Bill Harrigan" (1935)

These [sixteenth-century] accounts, true as they may be, are too picturesque in my opinion. They're the westerns of History.

Mauriac, *The Marquise Went Out at Five*

Everyone is in the dark as far as popular culture is concerned, unaware of the degree to which it has affected our attitudes and our daily performances. This holds true for writers as well as for the denizens of Frederick's of Hollywood. Nabokov's independence and imperious self-awareness make him a representative figure, ironically enough; like it or not, he too has absorbed and appropriated many cinematic properties. "Cinematic" is a term loosely employed these days to describe visual and aural techniques that extend back to Chaucer; Walter Scott, an action direc-

tor before the fact, called himself "a master of motion." The early masters of the cinema learned from literature (Griffith, Eisenstein), and the cycle is now in reverse. Numerous modern writers have, by intention or osmosis, made use of the film's grammar and syntax, its compression of narrative means. Dos Passos, Hemingway, Fitzgerald, West, Cain, Hammett, Agee, Robbe-Grillet, Pynchon, Malcolm Lowry, Cabrera Infante, and Graham Greene, to name but a few, have all gone to school at the movies. "I don't think my style as a writer has been influenced by my work for the cinema. My style has been influenced by my going to the cinema," says Greene, a former movie critic and scenarist. "*It's a Battlefield* [1934] was intentionally based on film techniques, and it was written before I did any film scripts. It is my only deliberate attempt to tell a story in cinematic terms."[1] Unlike Greene, Nabokov would of course never characterize himself as "a film man," yet his *Camera Obscura* (1932) anticipates Greene by two years. Pirandello's novel, *Shoot!: The Notebooks of Serafino Gubbio, Cinematographic Operator* (1926), a nightmarish inversion of Keaton's *Sherlock, Jr.* (1924), had already tendered the cinema as a metaphor of dehumanization, and J. D. Salinger's 1961 Preface to "Zooey" (1957) would declare that "what I'm about to offer isn't really a short story at all but a sort of prose home movie,"[2] an exaggerated claim, as it turns out, but an excellent description of Delmore Schwartz's great story, "In Dreams Begin Responsibility" (1939). Nabokov's "The Assistant Producer" (1943), a rare amalgam of form and metaphor, is, along with Schwartz's story, the most successful of all attempts to tell a story in cinematic terms.[3]

Camera Obscura is by no means a spontaneous "cinematic" creation. The black and white stylization of decor and dress in *King, Queen, Knave* (1928), a dazzling visual performance, adumbrates similar effects in *Camera Obscura* as well as films such as *Dinner at Eight* (1933). "People thought it was all a capital stunt, circus publicity, or the shooting of a picture," writes Nabokov of the dwarf's fatal sprint at the end of "The Potato Elf" (1924), whose eight brief sections employ a scenario-like rhythm. Fred "collapse[s] in slow motion" as the story concludes.[4] The nasty, lascivious narrator of "The Dashing Fellow" (c. 1932), a distant relative of Humbert, undresses his potential pick-up with "our crystalline lens," a possessive eye that assumes the reader's prurience and anticipates the voyeuristic games of *Lolita*.[5] The girl is an actress named Sonja Bergmann, an ironic nod toward the tender refinement personified by Elisabeth Bergner, the Jewish Grace Kelly of the pre-Hitler German cinema, who opened *her* emigration by starring in *Catherine the Great* (England, 1934). Martin's nocturnal fantasy in *Glory* (1932) passes through three stages—"outline," "rough draft," "filmed scene" (quoted above, p. 37)—and *Camera Obscura,* Nabokov's next novel, builds on all of these effects and devices and introduces Dorianna Karenina, whose bisexuality alludes to the rumors about two glamor queens of the period.

"I wanted to write the entire book as if it were a film," says Nabokov. "Because color films barely existed in those days, I decided to render the seven main colors the way that tinctures in heraldry are rendered by means of lines or dots placed in this or that way. That scheme proved to be much too ambitious and very soon I was putting in the bright

FOR ALFRED

FAN

Dupe negative with optical effect

IRIS

LINEX MOVIOLA DIAGONAL WIPE

FROM VN montreux

NOV. 13 1972

colors of stained glass windows. I remember the girl's red dress (it's not a symbol, of course), and the man's purplish suit in the last scene. The bright colors are a compromise, though the scenes and dialogue do manage to follow a cinematic pattern. The scene of the accident I saw vividly as a film [Chapter Thirty-two]. On the whole it was a general idea. I wasn't thinking of the form of a screenplay; it's a verbal imitation of what was then termed a 'photoplay.'" Nabokov's stated intentions provide neat critical guidelines.

Camera Obscura's thirty-eight chapters, a large number for a medium-length novel, convincingly imitate a rapidly paced series of short-takes. Most of them are set indoors and omit from their *mises-en-scène* all but the most essential details. Except for certain "suspense techniques," objects and scenery do not compete for the viewer's attention; the main focus is on the three principal players. Unlike Brecht's and Weill's crowded portraits of the period, or Isherwood's *Berlin Stories* (1935/1939), the local color is minimal; allusions to Garbo and Conrad Veidt and fleeting satirical thrusts at surrealist art, movie producers, and Hindemith's music locate the action—

From the author's copy of the *émigré* edition of *Camera Obscura,* inscribed in seven colors by Nabokov. The Cyrillic lettering on the wing of the larger butterfly proffers the name of book and writer, an advertising gimmick that has not been sufficiently utilized.

Berlin, c. 1928—but never at the expense of the novel's dark mood, its world of furtive yearning, betrayal, and terror. Director Nabokov exerts the tight control of a Fritz Lang, whose long-running *M* (1931) was concurrent with *Camera Obscura*'s release and distribution in the *émigré* conclaves of Paris and Berlin. "It was a bright windy day in April," writes Nabokov. "On the sunlit wall of the opposite house the fast shadow of smoke ran sideways from the shadow of a chimney. The asphalt was drying patchily after a recent shower, the damp still showing in the form of grotesque black skeletons as if painted across the width of the road,"[6] and one expects Peter Lorre to walk through the scene and cast an anxious look over his shoulder. Nabokov's nocturnal setups also evoke the Berlin chiaroscuro of UFA productions, but the basic bright colors in which everything else is "filmed," so different from Nabokov's customary wide range of painterly hues, nicely approximate the limited palette of a primitive color film and help set off a more vivid visual moment or epiphany at the end of both versions of the Englished *Camera Obscura*.

The novel was translated from the Russian by Winifred Roy and published in England in 1936. Nabokoff-Sirin, as the London edition calls him, was not satisfied with the results. After *Camera Obscura* was accepted for American publication, he vastly revised Miss Roy's translation—"not quite successfully," he says. The new version, published as *Laughter in the Dark* (1938), follows the main outlines and intentions of *Camera Obscura* but incorporates countless significant changes, including a splendid new opening:

> Once upon a time there lived in Berlin, Germany, a man called Albinus. He was rich, respectable, happy; one day he abandoned his wife for the sake of a youthful mistress; he loved; was not loved; and his life ended in disaster.
>
> This is the whole of the story and we might have left it at that had there not been profit and pleasure in the telling; and although there is plenty of space on a gravestone to contain, bound in moss, the abridged version of a man's life, detail is always welcome.

The first phrase places the reader in the timeless realm of the fairy tale and indicates that enchantment, entrapment, and illusion will prevail in a story that is over before it has even begun. Young Margot Peters, whom Albert Albinus will pick up at the Argus cinema, does indeed cast an evil spell, and his curious name—changed from *Camera Obscura*'s Bruno Kretschmar[7]—implies that the distanced action is not contained or determined by any geographic space. "Please, don't touch anything," shouts Albinus when Margot visits him in his daughter's nursery. "But she was already holding a purple plush elephant," writes Nabokov (p. 61), and its owner dies shortly thereafter, as will Albinus, of course. Margot's subsequent telephone call to Professor Grimm is signal (p. 169). The initial paragraph suggests that Albinus's tale has been told more than once. Its baldly stated action is also a scenarist's précis of a potboiler written for profit rather than pleasure, and both versions of *Camera Obscura* mimic the conventions of a thriller: assumed names; clandestine meetings; swift cars; violent catastrophes; anti-climactic surprises which mock suspense techniques;[8] a concluding gun shot; a network of fateful coincidences, coordinates marking the labyrinth in which Albinus is locked. "He had come in at the end of a film: a girl was receding among tumbled furniture before a masked man with a gun. There was no interest whatever in watching happenings which he could not understand since he had not yet seen their beginning" (p. 20), a preview of his "end."

Laughter in the Dark's cast inhabits a cinematic plot equal to their own shortsightedness, banality, or corruption. Usherette Margot entertains a "vision of herself as a screen beauty in gorgeous furs being helped out of a gorgeous car by a gorgeous hotel porter under a giant umbrella" (p. 30). She falls "in love with the life that Albinus could offer her—a life full of the glamour of a first-class film with rocking palm trees and shuddering roses (for it was always windy in filmland)" (p. 118). Axel Rex is a caricaturist and occasional counterfeiter of Old Master paintings whose considerable talents are available to the highest bidder in marks, francs, or dollars. His

devilish name in *Camera Obscura,* Robert Horn, also alludes to W. G. Horner, the inventor of the Zoetrope ("wheel of life"), a nineteenth-century forerunner of the animated cartoon, and Horn's transatlantic career, if not character, parallels that of Emile Cohl (1857-1938), a gifted French newspaper caricaturist and animator who also made cartoon shorts in New York. Margot is a cartoon in her own right, a picture postcard *fräulein.* When Albinus's wife was pregnant, he "dreamed of coming across a young girl lying asprawl on a hot lonely beach" (p. 17), a wish fulfilled by Margot's subsequent appearance, "spread-eagled on the sand"—a "perfect seaside poster" (p. 112) who demonstrates that Albinus's long history of erotic daydreams (p. 15) is as second-rate as his abilities as an "art critic and picture expert." One night, "as he was giving his learned mind a holiday and writing a little essay . . . upon the art of the cinema," a "beautiful idea came to him": the production of animated colored cartoons based on Old Master paintings (p. 8).[9] The idea is not even his own. It is based on a phrase from a book by his acquaintance Udo Conrad, the novel's stand-in for Nabokov, who has in turn been inspired by the first of Disney's *Silly Symphonies, The Skeleton Dance* (1929)—an animated interpretation of Saint-Saëns's *Danse Macabre*—or Oskar Fischinger's German cartoon, *Brahms's Hungarian Dance* (1931). Albinus takes his idea to a Berlin film producer. "We could begin by something quite simple

. . . a stained window coming to life, animated heraldry," Albinus explains, alluding to Nabokov's original visual scheme. "I'm afraid it's no good," answers the producer. "We can't risk fancy pictures" (p. 10). Albinus then enlists the services of Axel Rex, and is soon entangled in a semi-classic triangle.[10] "I have no one in the world but you," Albinus tells Margot (p. 44), employing the stock dialogue of the romantic genre in which starlet Margot will dismally fail. Things go from bad to worse (as unoriginal Albinus might say), and, as we already know, "his life ended in disaster." There *is* "profit and pleasure in the telling," as in a Graham Greene thriller, and the welcome "details" on the space of Albinus's novel-length "gravestone" transcend its mean beginnings.

Nabokov does not agree. "It's my poorest novel," he says. "The characters are hopeless clichés." But isn't that part of their characterization? "Yes, perhaps, but I 'succeeded' all too well. They are clichés nonetheless, except for the novelist [= V. N.]. He's all right." If Nabokov were conversant with critical jargon, he would doubtless say that he had been guilty of "the fallacy of imitative form" (e.g., attempting to render chaos or boredom and producing a chaotic or boring work). One need not agree with Nabokov, who is surely correct on one point: his imitation of the "silver ghost of romance . . . that special brand of romance" (p. 40) was so successful that *Camera Obscura*, unlike his other *émigré* novels, was immediately translated into four languages and optioned to a movie producer. At last count it had been translated fourteen times, more than any novel save *Lolita*. An author isn't altogether responsible for the terms on which he is admired or accepted, but the "universal appeal" of *Laughter in the Dark* does suggest that Nabokov's own attitude toward its popular ingredients was not sufficiently highlighted by irony or parody. "You're not going to make me believe you'll marry her. When a man wants to marry a respectable girl, he talks to her family about it," Margot's thuggish brother tells Albinus in the *de rigueur* confrontation scene. "Indeed, there was a fine flavor of parody about this talk," interjects Nabokov, telegraphing his opinion like a Victorian novelist (p. 105). That flavor turned out to be faint enough; the broad ordonnances of the plot recommended it to three other film producers, and *King, Queen, Knave*, another upended love triangle, is now headed for the screen (directed by Jerzy Skolimowski, with Gina Lollobrigida as Martha, David Niven as Dreyer).

Nabokov's low opinion of the novel in all its versions tacitly acknowledges his failure to control or realize fully its "cinematic pattern." "She tottered and pretended to faint. It was an indifferent performance, but it worked," he writes of Margot (p. 99), and that judgment may apply to Nabokov's projection of his "general [film] idea." He had set no easy goal for himself, of course, and figurative effects are asked to carry a heavy load: "In her distress [Margot] went to a dance-hall as abandoned damsels do in films" (p. 38); Albinus jumps out of a taxi and "paid as men do in films—blindly thrusting out a coin" (p. 80); Margot's eyes gradually dim "as if they were being slowly extinguished like the lights in a theatre" (p. 92). Seated between Rex and Albinus, "she felt as though she were the chief actress in a mysterious and passionate film-drama" (p. 147), a fair claim, and the last page of *Laughter in the Dark* (but not *Camera Obscura*) is explicitly staged, a setup awaiting a camera crew. When Albinus was informed of his daughter's birth early in the novel, there appeared before his eyes "a fine dark rain like the flickering of some very old film (1910, a brisk jerky funeral procession with legs moving too fast)" (p. 18). The parenthetical footage, sustained by the participle, prefigures her death and illuminates Nabokov's struggle to transcend the prepositional limitations of simile, as though the author of "The Beast in the Jungle" (1901), with its concluding figurative leap, were straining to write *The Metamorphosis* (1912), a visualization of the beast itself. Minor revisions in *Laughter in the Dark* point to Nabokov's frustrations.

Although Nabokov says he "wasn't thinking of the form of a screenplay," the American edition interpolates many parenthetical remarks that at first glance seem to imitate the stage directions of a scenario ("they were finishing supper," p. 11). Other parentheses contain wry authorial asides ("mirrors were having plenty of work that day," p. 61) or old-fashioned omniscient revelations (Margot's thoughts on p. 227). The inconsistency of these effects flaws the design of the novel as well as its cinematic surface. Curious too is *Laughter in the Dark*'s omission of significant passages concerning Horn's major contribution to world cinema. *Camera Obscura* opens with four pages that should be quoted in their entirety since the novel is virtually unobtainable:

Round about the year 1925 an amusing little animal enjoyed world-wide popularity. It is now almost forgotten, but for a period of some three to four years it was to be seen everywhere: from Alaska to Patagonia, from Manchuria to New Zealand, from Lapland to the Cape of Good Hope—in a word, in every region accessible to picture post cards. This little creature rejoiced in the seductive name of "Cheepy," and it was a guinea-pig.

The origin of its rise to fame is said to have been connected with the question of vivisection. Robert Horn, the caricaturist, was once lunching in New York with a chance acquaintance, a young physiologist. They were talking about experiments on living animals, and the physiologist, a very sensitive man, maintained that in the dissecting room scientists permitted dumb animals to be tortured more than was really necessary.

"I tell you what," he said to Horn. "You do charming sketches for the newspapers. Take up the cause of one of these long-suffering creatures—for instance, the guinea-pig, and create a vogue for it. Make drawings of it with some droll heading, and refer incidentally to the tragic connection between the guinea-pig and the laboratory. In this way you might not only create a very original and amusing type, but also draw the attention of the public to the sad fate of this most lovable little animal."

"I don't know," replied Horn. "Guinea-pigs always remind me of rats. I can't stand them. Let them squeal under the dissecting knife for all I care."

But a month after this conversation, when Horn was trying to think of a subject for a series of drawings which an illustrated paper had commissioned from him, he recalled the advice of the tender-hearted physiologist—and, on that same evening, the first paper guinea-pig was swiftly and painlessly born. The public was immediately charmed with the sketch. The sly expression of the round, twinkling eyes, the plump little figure of the guinea-pig, with its stout hind-quarters, the sleek head, the skin with its patches of black, brown and yellow, and, above all, the creature's delicious and comical sprightliness won it extraordinary popularity. For Horn had succeeded in hitting off the characteristic outline of the animal, emphasizing its drollness and yet at the same time investing it with something curiously human. One of his guinea-pigs, for instance, was holding in its small paws the skull of a rodent and exclaiming: "Alas! poor Yorick!" Another was shown lying on its back on the bench of a laboratory and trying to do fashionable gymnastic exercises—feet to head (and you can imagine how far it could reach with its short hind legs); a third was calmly trimming its claws with a suspiciously fine pair of scissors, surrounded by cotton wool, a lancet, needles and all sorts of other instruments . . .

Very soon, however, the allusions to vivisection were dropped, and the guinea-pig appeared in quite unexpected positions—dancing the Charleston, burning itself quite black in the sun, and so on. These guinea-pigs were reproduced on picture post cards and in film cartoons, as well as in solid form, for soon there grew a demand for guinea-pigs in plush, cloth, wood and clay; and Horn made a great deal of money by them. The physiologist often used to tell people how he had given Horn the idea of drawing guinea-pigs, but no one believed him, and so he gave up talking about it.

In Berlin, at the beginning of 1928, Bruno Kretschmar, the art connoisseur, a learned, but by no means brilliant individual, was invited to give his expert opinion regarding a ridiculous—yes really, a quite absurd matter. Kok [from *kokett;* German, "coquettish"], a fashionable artist, had painted a portrait of Dorianna Karenina, the film actress. A firm which manufactured face-cream had acquired from the actress the right to reproduce this picture as an advertisement for its lipstick. In this portrait, Dorianna was clasping a hugh plush guinea-pig to her bare shoulder. Horn, from New York, immediately brought an action against the firm.

All the parties concerned had really only one end in view: to get themselves talked about as much as possible. Articles were written about the picture and about the actress; the lipstick was sold; and the guinea-pig—which was in need of a little boost, since it was getting out-of-date—appeared in a new drawing by Horn, with eyes modestly lowered, a flower in its paw, and the laconic title: *Noli me tangere.*

"This fellow Horn seems quite in love with his guinea-pig," remarked Kretschmar one day to his brother-in-law, Max, a stout, good-natured man, with rolls of fat bulging over his collar.

"Do you know him?" asked Max.

"No; how should I? He lives in America. But he will win his case if he succeeds in proving that the public attention is captivated by the guinea-pig more than by the film star."

The animals in cartoons of the nineteen-twenties were highly stylized, Disney's included, and Cheepy's "curiously human" attributes anticipate the subsequent procedures of Disney, whose Mickey Mouse (né Mortimer Mouse, 1928) was not yet an international star or a wellspring of merchandise. Although the wordplay on Cheepy may be too obvious, the passage is excellent because it presages the global village established by popular culture; Cheepy's reappearances throughout *Camera Obscura* underscore the powers wielded so cynically by the Rex-Horns of the "media." Why did Nabokov drop all of this appropriate material? "Accidental dove droppings," he answers.

Nothing in Nabokov is an accident. The stream of handwritten revisions that wend their way across the typeface and down the margins of almost every page of Nabokov's own copy of *Camera Obscura* testify to the care with which he revised it. Cheepy's disappearance adheres to a pattern. In *Camera Obscura*, "An American, a famous tennis-player, with a horse-like face and sunburnt hands, offered to give [Margot] lessons" at their Riviera hotel (p. 199). The player is Bill Tilden, who will one day instruct Lolita (pp. 164 and 234),[11] but the passage in *Laughter in the Dark* is reduced to the bland "youths who played tennis with

her" (p. 207). Horn affects American clothes, Rex does not, and Hollywood is mentioned far more frequently in *Camera Obscura* than *Laughter in the Dark*, Nabokov's first American publication. It is quite possible that the Paris-based *émigré*, already anticipating another move, did not wish to alienate or offend his new audience. By 1937 Cheepy had become a Disneyesque reality, a dear figure too close to hearth and home. *Lolita* would be considerably less circumspect. Yet many "Germanisms" are also omitted from *Laughter in the Dark*, suggesting that these revisions, like the new opening paragraph, were meant to distance the narrative from any specific landscape and allow the reader to color the transparent spaces in the story of "a man called Albinus."

Measured against Nabokov's announced intentions, it seems that the revisions both help and hinder *Laughter in the Dark*, making it difficult if not pointless to say which is the "better" version. Moreover, the most affecting aspect of *Laughter in the Dark*, an adjunct to the cinema theme, is articulated in both versions. "I have realized that the only happiness in this world is to observe, to spy, to watch, to scrutinize oneself and others, to be nothing but a big, slightly vitreous, somewhat bloodshot, unblinking eye," states the narrator at the end of *The Eye* (1930).[12] Consciousness is an optical instrument to Nabokov, and the renaming of Kretschmar is a considerable improvement. Albinus, as his name suggests, suffers from a veritable congenital deficiency; his eyes fail him in every way. His art collection includes fakes, and he believes cuckolder Rex to be homosexual. "Love is blind," remarks a postman, and his "thoughtful" attitude implies that Albinus's inability to see the truth does not distinguish him from every reader (p. 185). "I couldn't believe my eyes, as the blind man said," jokes Axel Rex (p. 135), who has earlier suggested that they animate Brueghel's *Proverbs* (p. 11). The blind lead the blind toward a ditch on Brueghel's horizon line, and Albinus's proverbial delusions, his tumble into that ditch, are pictured no less forcefully. Rex, as clear-eyed as he is clever, has adumbrated the grotesque isolation of Albinus, who appears to be the only person seated in the well-named Argus Theatre, a "velvety dark" cranial chamber. "Standing at the exit next to a horribly purple curtain which she had just drawn to one side" (p. 21), Margot guards the enchanted cave of myth and legend.

Alone in his own camera obscura, Albinus appropriates Margot's shadowy image—"the swift walk in the darkness, the pretty movement of her black-sleeved arm" (p. 22)—investing it with the glamor of a hundred unrealized daydreams. After the car acci-

Odilon Redon: *The Eye, Like a Strange Balloon Mounts Towards Infinity,* Plate I from *To Edgar Allan Poe.* 1882, lithograph.

dent blinds him permanently, "all that was left of her was a voice, a rustle, and a perfume; it was as though she had returned to the darkness of the little cinema from which he had once withdrawn her" (p. 257). But Albinus has been in the dark all along, despite his name, and the "vista of mirrors" (p. 58) in his camera obscura has failed to correct his distorted perceptions. Only when his aperture is closed for ever does he recognize, in horror, "how little he had used his eyes" (p. 257). "The impenetrable black shroud in which Albinus now lived infused an element of austerity and even of nobility into his thoughts and feelings" (p. 256), and he finally realizes his etymology, as it were (*albus*), and the optical fact that white reflects to the eye all the rays of the spectrum combined. "The picture gallery of his mind" comes alive (p. 256), deploying a rainbow of colors, most vividly at the moment of his death.

Rescued from Rex and Margot by his brother-in-law, the blind man is reunited with his wife and installed in his dead daughter's nursery. "The sacred slumber of that little room" (p. 282), Professor Grimm's domain, is not disturbed by its silent lodger, who plots Margot's death, all the while clutching the key to the chest in which he has locked his gun. The key "seemed to him a kind of Sesame that would . . . one day unlock the door of his blindness" (p. 283), a metaphor reinforced at the end of the novel. Finally left alone on his fourth day home, Albinus sneaks

away, takes a cab to Margot's apartment, and corners her. They struggle for the weapon, in a straightforward version of the Humbert-Quilty tumble, "and, together with a faint detonation that seemed miles away, in another world, there came a stab in his side which filled his eyes with a dazzling glory. 'So that's all,' he thought softly, as if he were lying in bed. 'I must keep quiet for a little space and then walk slowly along that bright sand of pain, toward that blue, blue wave. What bliss there is in blueness. I never knew how blue blueness could be. What a mess life has been. Now I know everything. Coming, coming, coming to drown me . . .'" (pp. 291-92). The earlier color values have been infused with a new intensity. "The cradle rocks above an abyss, and common sense tells us that our existence is but a brief crack of light between two eternities of darkness," Nabokov would write in the opening sentence of *Speak, Memory*. Albinus's short happy life is over, and *Laughter in the Dark*'s conclusion improves upon *Camera Obscura*'s, as this pairing indicates:

[*Camera Obscura*] He sat on the floor, with bowed head, bent slowly forward and fell obliquely to one side.

Silence. The door to the hall was wide open. The table was thrust to one side. The chair lay by the dead body in the light purple suit. The revolver was nowhere to be seen. It was lying beneath him.

On the little table, on which once, when Annalisa was still living here, the porcelain ballet-dancer had stood (it had later been transferred to another room), lay a crumpled woman's glove.

By the striped sofa stood an elegant little trunk, with a coloured label pasted on it: "Solfi, Hotel Adriatique."

The door leading from the hall to the landing was also wide open.

[*Laughter in the Dark*] He sat on the floor with bowed head, then bent slowly forward and fell, like a big, soft doll, to one side.

Stage-directions for last silent scene: door—wide open. Table—thrust away from it. Carpet—bulging up at table-foot in a frozen wave. Chair—lying close by dead body of man in a purplish brown suit and felt slippers. Automatic pistol not visible. It is under him. Cabinet where the miniatures had been—empty. On the other (small) table, on which ages ago a porcelain ballet-dancer stood (later transferred to another room) lies a woman's glove, black outside, white inside. By the striped sofa stands a smart suitcase, with a colored label still adhering to it: "Rouginard, Hôtel Britannia."

The door leading from the hall to the landing is wide open, too.

The revised passage emphasizes that "the end" is a regression as well as a fatal progression. Stumbling toward Margot, Albinus had thought of "blind man's buff, blind man's buff . . . in a country-house on a winter night, long, long ago" (p. 290), the arena of creative play that would be explored in Nabokov's next novel, *Invitation to a Beheading*. Mortally wounded, Albinus thinks he is in bed. Sinking into death, he becomes a soft doll, the companion of the bewitched purple toy in the nursery he has recently occupied. The purple exit curtain manipulated by Margot has closed upon him, and the prosaic color scheme is reasserted by the scenarist. The brilliant blue light of death gives way to the basic black and white of the glove, and Kretschmar's "light purple suit" has been neutralized by a brown gouache or filter. Reduced by a cinematic plot of his own design, Albinus is a nameless object in a *mise-en-scène*. He has entered another dimension, as has the novel, moving beyond narrative—and simile and metaphor. The two open doors, ironic signs or symbols of escape and new vistas of vision, are an old movie convention (MacMurray struggling toward the door in *Double Indemnity*), but the verbs of the "stage directions" which arrange the glove, suitcase, and second door—"lies," "stands," "is"—are also a startling and deceptively simple rendering of movie time. On the screen verbs are always in the present tense, and the closing lines of *Laughter in the Dark* (1938) point toward "The Assistant Producer" (1943), a brave approximation of the film form itself and a story whose ambitious use of movie time anticipates the novels that Robbe-Grillet and Butor have "filmed," as it were, in the present tense.

The title *Camera Obscura* evokes a specific condition where *Laughter in the Dark* speaks to the experience of an entire generation of Russian wanderers.

Vladimir Nabokov, age thirty-four, a pastel by Magda Nachman-Archarya, 1933.

The sorrows of exile were infinite: isolation, poverty, despair, disease, early death, suicide. A statistical enumeration of the sudden deaths in Nabokov's fiction alone would produce an awesome, disheartening figure, and a fair representation of *émigré* life and letters. If the writer survived, languageless in some distant land, his options were painfully simple: the obscurity of writing in Russian for a minuscule audience; a second life in a new tongue; or silence, and the nightmare of nostalgia—an *émigré* reality in any instance. "What is the use of time and rhyme? / We live in peril, paupers all," declared Vladislav Khodasevich in "Poem" (1927).[13] "I haf nofing," cries Nabokov's Pnin thirty years later, a material truth rather than an indulgence of self-pity (p. 61). Although *Camera Obscura* assiduously avoids Russian characters, its dark mood reflects those *émigré* realities. "Death often is the point of life's joke," says Axel Rex (p. 182), thoroughly enjoying his role as the invisible cosmic puppeteer who toys with blind Albinus much as history has buffeted the Russian *émigrés*, that "mythical tribe whose bird-signs and moon-signs I now retrieve from the desert dust," writes Nabokov in his 1963 Foreword to *The Gift*.

Berlin is indeed a desolate place in Nabokov's poem "Evening on a Vacant Lot" (1932), published the same year as *Camera Obscura* and written to commemorate the tenth anniversary of his father's murder. "Never did I want so much to cry," he writes, contemplating the trash-filled lot and a "weedy little stalk with teardrop, / skull of happiness, long, slender, / like the skull of a borzoi." His mind returns to early efforts at rhyme-making, to Russia, and the light of a kerosene lamp "penetrating dense woods." The poem concludes:

> Blinking, a fiery eye looks,
> through the fingerlike black stacks
> of a factory, at weedy flowers
> and a deformed tin can.
> Across the vacant lot in darkening dust
> I glimpse a slender hound with snow-white coat.
> Lost, I presume. But in the distance sounds
> insistently and tenderly a whistling,
> And in the twilight toward me a man
> comes, calls. I recognize
> your energetic stride. You haven't
> changed much since you died.[14]

Albinus is surely no autobiographical portrait, but his phantasms and optical delusions are not the product of a tranquil authorial mind, and Nabokov's agent, Udo Conrad, talks to Albinus, thereby narrowing the distance between character and creator. "The door leading from the hall to the landing is wide open, too," along with its open-ended implications, a symbolic resonance that includes the reality of *émigré* escape and travel. Wakened in the morning in his temporary lodging—the foreground plane in an infinite regress of rented rooms in many towns and cities and countries—the *émigré* might wonder for a moment where (if not who) he was, and might well say that his life, if not history itself, had become a fiction, an unbelievable celluloid melodrama; *The Horizon Book of the Arts of Russia* (1970) does not even mention the Russian emigration. "Meaning? Well, because sometimes life is merely that—an Assistant Producer. Tonight we shall go to the movies. Back to the Thirties, and down the Twenties, and round the corner to the old Europe Picture Palace," writes Nabokov at the outset of his most cinematic creation, which ends by offering the movie-goer the "exit-bound stream" of his choice.

The producer is a mere assistant because Russian history has begotten a stream of B-pictures that are in their way as distorted as the monstrous jokes perpetrated by Soviet revisionists. "The Assistant Producer" also renders personal history as fiction by redeveloping one of Nabokov's most arresting phantasmagoric images of *émigré* life in Berlin, the spectacle of Russian film extras playing themselves, as it were, in German films. In *Mashenka*, Nabokov's first novel (1926, translated as *Mary*),

Nothing was beneath [*émigré* Ganin's] dignity; more than once he had even sold his shadow, as many of us have. In other words he went out to the [Berlin] suburbs to work as a movie extra on a set, in a fairground barn, where light seethed with a mystical hiss from the huge facets of lamps that were aimed, like cannon, at a crowd of extras, lit to a deathly brightness. They would fire a barrage of murderous brilliance, illuminating the painted wax of motionless faces, then expiring with a click—but for a long time yet there would glow, in those elaborate crystals, dying red sunsets—our human shame. The deal was clinched, and our anonymous shadows sent out all over the world.[15]

The figurative violence of that dark but well-lit scene is striking, and Nabokov's dying sunset is the right directorial and historical touch, defining the emigration's pervasive twilight mood. On a subsequent evening, Ganin takes his silly girlfriend to the cinema: "On the screen moved luminous, bluish-gray shapes. A prima donna, who had once in her life committed an involuntary murder, suddenly remembered it while playing the role of a murderess in opera. Rolling her improbably large eyes, she collapsed supine onto the stage. The auditorium swam slowly into view, the public applauded, the boxes and stalls rose in an ecstasy of approval. Suddenly Ganin sensed that he was watching something vaguely yet horribly familiar" (pp. 20-21); it is the film in which he had appeared as an extra, "acting in total ignorance of what the film was about. He remembered young men in threadbare but marvelously tailored clothes, women's faces smeared with mauve and yellow make-up, and those innocent exiles, old men and plain girls who

were banished far to the rear simply to fill in the background. On the screen that cold barn was now transformed into a comfortable auditorium, sacking became velvet, and a mob of paupers a theatre audience" (p. 21). The reader will soon realize (as Ganin does not) that the young man's horror is compounded subliminally by the fact that the bogus musicale in the "cold barn" is a travesty of "a charity concert staged in a barn on the border of his parents' estate" in pre-Revolutionary Russia (p. 44), where, "amid the hot yellow glare" and the sounds of an opera bass from St. Petersburg supported by the village school choir, Ganin had first glimpsed lovely Mary, his emblem of the past (pp. 45-46). Seated unhappily in a Berlin cinema, "straining his eyes, with a deep shudder of shame he recognized himself among all those people clapping to order" on the screen (p. 21).

Ganin's doppelgänger also stood and clapped, over there, alongside the very striking-looking man with the black beard and the ribbon across his chest. Because of that beard and his starched shirt he had always landed in the front row; in the intervals he munched a sandwich and then, after the take, would put on a wretched old coat over his evening dress and return home to a distant part of Berlin, where he worked as a compositor in a printing plant.

And at the present moment Ganin felt not only shame but also a sense of the fleeting evanescence of human life. There on the screen his haggard image, his sharp uplifted face and clapping hands merged into the gray kaleidoscope of other figures; a moment later, swinging like a ship, the auditorium vanished and now the scene showed an aging, world-famous actress giving a very skillful representation of a dead young woman (pp. 21-22).

Only when Mary is "buried" will Ganin come to life. Later that night, "when he went to bed and listened to the trains passing through that cheerless house in which lived seven Russian lost shades, the whole of life seemed like a piece of film-making where heedless extras knew nothing of the picture in which they were taking part" (p. 22). At the end of *Mary*, he stands by the deathbed of Podtyagin, the *émigré* poet who has lost his passport and all remaining hope: "Ganin, gripping the edge of the bed with a strong white hand, looked in the old man's face, and once again he remembered these flickering, shadowy doppelgängers, the casual Russian film extras, sold for ten marks apiece and still flitting, God knows where, across the white gleam of a screen" (p. 110), the animate and inanimate rendered in death's monochrome.

The terrible fate and shame of the *émigré* poet Marina Tsvetaeva were in their way "cinematic" too. *I Am a Fugitive from a Chain Gang* (1932, with Paul Muni) was her favorite film because it mirrored her life, she said—and her husband, who on the eve of World War II turned out to be a double-agent, also worked as a movie extra, underscoring the meta-

"Because of that beard and his starched shirt he had always landed in the front row": Emil Jannings as an extra in *The Last Command;* the other men are authentic Russian *émigré* extras.

I Am a Fugitive from a Chain Gang, Marina Tsvetaeva's sense of the alternative open to the lonely *émigré:* Soviet bondage.

phoric possibilities of that precarious and surreal occupation. (Tsvetaeva followed him back to the Soviet Union and committed suicide in 1941.) Nabokov's first spy thriller, *Chelovek iz SSSR* ("The Man from the USSR"), an untranslated five-act play which was produced in Berlin in 1926, again evokes the shadowy trade in extras: an elderly, studio-bound ex-Baron, now a waiter, is the Soviet agent's "contact" in Act One's basement night club scene, and still wears his movie eye make-up in order to save time between jobs and thus gain tips. Marianna, the play's young *émigré* heroine, is a full-time film actress; role-playing and survival coincide. "You certainly are an unbelievable character," she says to the bold undercover agent who has designs on her person. Marianna is "terribly tired" from that day's filming; the star, Pia Mora, has acted and behaved badly, requiring eighteen takes for a single scene. "My role is the most crucial one in the whole movie, the role of a Communist. A hellishly difficult part," Marianna complains, unaware that she is about to become involved with a real Communist, and that her fiction will now be activated and unreeled.[16]

Seventeen years later, in "The Assistant Producer," Nabokov once more records how "German film companies, which kept sprouting like poisonous mushrooms in those days (just before the child of light learned to talk), found cheap labor in hiring those among the Russian *émigrés* whose only hope and profession was their past—that is, a set of totally unreal people—to represent 'real' audiences in pictures." Nabokov's "mushroom" image is not fanciful; in 1925 German film companies produced 228 features, as opposed to France's 77 and Britain's 44. "The dovetailing of one phantasm into another produced upon a sensitive person the impression of living in a Hall of Mirrors, or rather a prison of mirrors, and not even knowing which was the glass and which was yourself" (p. 83), he concludes, compressing *Mary*'s dominant metaphor. "Yes," said Nabokov in 1971, "I have been a tuxedoed extra as Ganin had been (and a threadbare extra officer, too), and that passage in *Mashenka* is a rather raw bit of 'real life.' No, I don't remember the names of those films," and one can imagine a demented biographer, his eye on a definitive volume, squinting at grainy old German movies for a fleeting glimpse of Nabokov.

The cinema has at least twice developed that "Hall of Mirrors" image of *émigré* existence. *Surrender* (1927) represents the only American appearance of the famous Russian actor Ivan Mosjoukine (né Mozzhukin, 1889-1939), whose romantic swashbuckler roles were much admired by adolescent Nabokov (1912-16). Mosjoukine made his own miraged appearance in the first stage of young Nabokov's life as exile. After the Revolution his family moved to the Crimea, where Nabokov senior became Minister of Justice in the hopeful Regional Government. One

morning in the summer of 1918, with real battles raging in the north (the Civil War), Nabokov suddenly met on a mountain trail

a strange cavalier, clad in a Circassian costume, with a tense, perspiring face painted a fantastic yellow. He kept furiously tugging at his horse, which, without heeding him, proceeded down the steep path at a curiously purposeful walk, like that of an offended person leaving a party. I had seen runaway horses, but I had never seen a walkaway one before, and my astonishment was given a still more pleasurable edge when I recognized the unfortunate rider as Mozzhuhin, whom Tamara [his first love, the model for Mary—A. A.] and I had so often admired on the screen. The film *Haji Murad* (after Tolstoy's tale of that gallant, rough-riding mountain chief) was being rehearsed on the mountain pastures of the range. "Stop that brute [*Derzhite proklyatoe zhivotnoe*]," he said through his teeth as he saw me, but at the same moment, with a mighty sound of crunching and crashing stones, two authentic Tatars came running down to the rescue, and I trudged on, with my butterfly net, toward the upper crags where the Euxine race of the Hippolyte Grayling was expecting me (*Speak, Memory*, p. 247).

All rehearsals concluded, the party over, both actor and carefree lepidopterist would soon become permanent *émigrés*; *Surrender* starred Mosjoukine as a White Army officer who loses everything in the Civil War that had provided a backdrop for the actor's unreal meeting with Nabokov. A publicity photograph poses Mosjoukine with Edward Sloman, *Surrender*'s

Personal history as fiction: *Surrender* (Mosjoukine and director Sloman at the center), and its *émigré* extras. "I wore such a uniform in one film," said Nabokov when shown this still, and he pointed to the officer on the far right. "Am I here? No."

director, and some of those dazed Russian *émigré* extras "whose only hope and profession was their past." The theme is memorably orchestrated in Josef von Sternberg's *The Last Command* (1928), in which Emil Jannings plays an ex-tsarist general who, now a poor old man in Hollywood, applies for work as an extra and is cast to replay his glorious former self in the film-within-the-film. The cruel, dizzying commission and that film's Communist director (William Powell) combine to drive Jannings insane. (Sternberg's scenario was inspired by a "true story" rather than, say, Pirandello's play *Henry IV*, 1922.) Still photos often fail to communicate the essence of a tragic performance or, even worse, freeze what seems to be an overblown expression (always a possibility in the context of the more stylized "theatrical" acting of the silent cinema). The haunting quality of *The Last Command*, however, is preserved in several stills: Jannings about to don his "costume" in the extras' common dressing room; Jannings being inspected like a young recruit by the assistant director and prop man, ready with a box of authentic medals; or the spectacle of Grand Duke Jannings, imprisoned by mirrors and carried away by his re-creation of the past as he bravely confronts a mob of revolutionaries or arrogantly reviews the troops of his last command, many of them played by actual Russian *émigrés*. "I had fortified my image of the Russian Revolution by including in my cast of extra players an assortment of

Russian ex-admirals and generals, a dozen Cossacks, and two former members of the Duma, all victims of the Bolsheviks, and, in particular, an expert on borscht by the name of Koblianski. These men, especially one Cossack general who insisted on keeping my car spotless, viewed Jannings' effort to be Russian with such disdain that I had to order them to conceal it," writes Field Marshal von Sternberg in his autobiography, *Fun in a Chinese Laundry* (1965).[17]

The most literally terrible version of Nabokov's prison trope was achieved by the Nazis, sustaining a chilling link of associations. One of the Russian monarchist assassins who had murdered V. D. Nabokov in 1922 was later released from his Berlin jail by the Nazis and put in charge of the Gestapo's efficient *émigré* section. Countless Russian Jews thus passed through Theresienstadt (Terezin), the "showplace" concentration camp maintained for inspectors from the International Red Cross. Also interned there was German filmmaker Kurt Gerron (né Gerson), who was forced to direct the sanguine anti-Semitic propaganda film *The Führer Gives the Jews a City* (1944), which cast Jews of many nationalities as "Jews." "We are all happy here in Theresienstadt," they said, smiling over the sumptuous meals which, off-camera, they were not permitted to eat. When the filming was completed, Gerron, his technical crew, and his actors were shipped to Auschwitz and killed. *Transport from Paradise* (1961), a Czech film, re-creates that

Jannings is "inspected" in *The Last Command*.

Right, top:
A prison of mirrors: Jannings faces the extras in *The Last Command*'s film-within-the-film, Reds played by extra Whites.

Personal history as fiction (continued): "Welcome to Theresienstadt!" A "guest" arrives (above) in *Transport to Paradise*'s film-within-the-film, "before death with its clapstick closes the scene" (*Ada*, p. 254). Left: The transport from paradise departs for Auschwitz.

cinematic infamy and commemorates the privileged inmates of Terezin as no gravestones ever can.

Shame, rather than terror, and a vertiginous sense of illusion were experienced by many of Hollywood's more successful *émigré* directors, musicians, and performers, and it must have hurt less if one possessed a mordant sense of humor. Unable to obtain work as a director, Otto Preminger had to play monocled Nazi generals—a fate preferable to Gerron's, however. Many other Austrian and German refugees (most of them Jewish) were cast as Nazi officers, spies, or leaders: Conrad Veidt and Hans von Twardowski (two of *Dr. Caligari's* alumni), Peter Lorre, Fritz Kortner, and resolute Martin Kosleck (né Nikolai Yoshkin in 1907), a veteran of both the Russian and German stage who impersonated Josef Goebbels in five films, including *The Hitler Gang* (1944), with its cast of German, Russian, Dutch, and Polish exiles playing the men who had oppressed them. Kosleck also played the evil doctor who mortally drains the blood of blond Russian children in *The North Star* (1943), one of several contemporary tributes to beleaguered, bucolic Mother Russia that ignored or distorted history in behalf of freedom, and in so doing contributed to Nabokov's cinematic vision in "The Assistant Producer." The publicity still from *The North Star* on p. 282 is by the famous photographer Margaret Bourke-White, who had covered the Russian front in 1941-42 and was flown back from the North African campaign (courtesy of Samuel Goldwyn) to document Hollywood's front. The bathetic results of her mission enlarge the faults implicit in her initial, typically sentimental picture-book, *Eyes on Russia* (1931).

Red Army victories also warmed and softened at least one *émigré* heart and mind; thus director Gregory Ratoff's (1897-1961) saccharine *Song of Russia* (1944), a musical tribute to Russia's fighting spirit. The story, as reviewer Bosley Crowther capsuled it, is about "a young American caught in Russia by love and war."[18] Before the war Robert Taylor, a symphonic conductor, meets and marries a musical Russian girl. The war separates them. Reunited at the end of the film, they are dispatched to America by plane "to state the spirit of Russia through their art" (Crowther). The film's musical score is adapted from Tchaikovsky; an additional number, "Russia is Her Name," was provided by Jerome Kern and E. Y. Harburg, and performed by a chorus of villagers. *Song of Russia* is an embarrassing companion to the pro-Stalin, fellow-traveling *Mission to Moscow* (1943), whose portrait of kindly Uncle Joe and his justifiable purge trials, his reasonable pact with Germany, and his fair-minded invasion of Finland—recent history as instant fiction—would surely have moved moviegoer Pnin to tears. *Mission to Moscow* couldn't have made *émigré* participants such as Vladimir Sokoloff (1889-1962) too happy, either. An actor and director in Moscow, Sokoloff had emigrated to Berlin in 1923, where he played a Red revolutionary in *The Love of Jeanne Ney* (1927). He emigrated to France in 1932, and to Hollywood in 1937, where he returned to "Moscow" in 1943 and presided benevolently as M. I. Kalinin, the president of the USSR. His movie desk features a set of *Mining and Metallurgical Engineering* volumes, conspicuous evidence of constructive Five Year Plans rather than lethal Siberian labor camps. A Soviet propaganda exhibit is maintained today at the Nabokovs' former summer estate at Vyra, near Leningrad. It asserts, among other fictions, that Vladimir Nabokov returned there in 1943 as a Nazi SS officer (played by Conrad Veidt or Martin Kosleck?).

Because of their heavy accents, gifted Russians were usually cast, humiliatingly, as stereotyped Comic Russians (Decadent ex-Count or Countess, Compulsive Gambler, Gabby Bartender, Aristocratic Cabdriver—the *émigré* equivalents of the black actor's Uncle Tom roles) or, when not being asked to parody their past, were limited to character parts. Witness the long Hollywood career of versatile Akim Tamiroff (1899-1972), whose range of caricature and mimicry —Arab trader, American Indian, Italian gangster, Chinese warlord, Corsican killer, Spanish guerrilla, Mexican *bandido* or bodyguard—begs an unhappy question. Tamiroff's performance in *Touch of Evil* as a grotesque, avuncular Tiajuana racketeer is wonderfully bizarre and typically skillful, but the patent-leather toupee, pencil-line moustache, and dusky make-up cannot mask the intelligent eyes that belong to an actor who more than once must have pondered (if not lamented) the straight dramatic roles that many aging American "heavies" were allowed to play (e.g., Edward G. Robinson). "Think of all your countrymen who have made it big in the movies," says Groucho Marx to Sasha the Comic Russian Waiter in *Room Service* (1938), trying to cadge a free meal with a bogus offer of stardom. "*Who?*" asks the innocent Sasha (Russian waiters and barmen are invariably Sashas). "Gregory Ratoff!" "Nazimova!" "Ginger Rogerovich!!" answer Chico and Groucho in rapid-fire succession; their concluding riposte alludes to Ginger's role in *Roberta* (1935), a "White Russian" musical.[19] Alla Nazimova (1879-1945), an early expatriate, played the Stoic Peasant in several World War II films; Olga Baclanova (1899-   ), a well-known singer and actress in Russia, became a hen-woman in *Freaks* (1932); Mischa Auer (né Unkovsky, 1905-67), having played small Hollywood roles for years, successfully impersonated a gorilla in *My Man Godfrey* (1936), thereby convincing producers he could play idiotic, popeyed ex-noblemen or gloomy ballet masters (*You Can't Take It With You*, 1938); and Maria Ouspenskaya (1876-1949), an exile from the Moscow Art Theatre, appeared as Mother Gin Sling's aged, silent Chinese amah in Sternberg's *Shanghai Gesture* (1941) and as the gypsy fortuneteller in *The Wolf*

Man (1941) and *Frankenstein Meets the Wolf Man* (1943). Her role as the queen of the hidden valley of women under the Apeman's protection in *Tarzan and the Amazons* (1945) was a far (jungle) cry from *The Three Sisters*. "Tha-a-nk you ver-r-y much ladies and gentleman, I would like jost to say one thing, dot Helen Hayes is a fink. I am the real Anastasia," croaks Lenny Bruce in the "Maria Ouspenskaya Interview," his shortest routine (ten seconds).[20] The reference to Hayes's stage role as Anastasia, the self-proclaimed "heir" to the illusory throne and fortune of the Romanovs, dramatizes once more the idea of history as fiction, the bizarre production of an assistant producer.

One generation's trash (and individual pain) is another's comedy and camp, as college presentations of Ouspenskaya movies amply prove. "The Assistant Producer" succeeds so well because Nabokov's fundamental seriousness is never compromised or trivialized by the base content he transmogrifies so amusingly and succinctly. The story is fortified by first-hand knowledge and firm attitudes toward history as well as popular culture. Its illusory world reflects Nabokov's experiences as a film extra at the same time that it evokes the plight of the professional *émigré* actor. "M. Auer's real name was Unkovsky—not 'Ounskowsky,'" Nabokov corrected me after an earlier version of the above paragraph had appeared as part of an

Conrad Veidt fled in 1932 to England, where he appeared in many films, including *The Wandering Jew* (1933). He moved to Hollywood in 1940 and was immediately drafted to play a Nazi officer in *Escape* (above, with Norma Shearer).

Hitler (Robert Watson) and Goebbels (Martin Kosleck) in *The Hitler Gang*, a veritable Madame Tussaud's Wax Works of Nazi leaders impersonated by refugee and *émigré* actors. The Reichstag burns behind them.

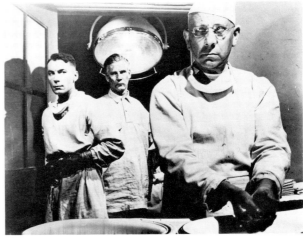

Walter Huston, a Russian peasant in *The North Star*, flanked by Nazi doctors Martin Kosleck (left) and Austrian-born Erich von Stroheim, who played Field Marshal Rommel in the same year's *Five Graves to Cairo*.

Mothers Russia, memorialized by Bourke-White: Ann Harding, Anne Baxter, and Ann Carter, Russian peasants awaiting the German army in *The North Star*. Their humble wall is graced by a portrait of Pushkin, curtained by a clean towel.

Poshlost' forms a united front: the farewell scene at the airport in *Song of Russia*, whose spirit has been invested in the hands of conductor Robert Taylor.

The chorus of villagers in *Song of Russia*. The *émigrés* in the cast of "Soviets" included Vladimir Sokoloff, Feodor Chaliapin, and Michael Chekhov, the founder of actors' schools in London and New York, who had his Hollywood debut in *North Star*.

Celluloid Stalinism: Left to right, U.S. Ambassador Joseph E. Davies (Walter Huston), Stalin (Manart Kippen), and Kalinin (Vladimir Sokoloff).

Emigré Leonid Kinsky played a Soviet revolutionary in *Trouble in Paradise* (1932), sang "I'm an Old Cowpoke" in *Rhythm on the Range* (1936), and was Sasha the *émigré* bartender in *Casablanca* (1943).

Tamiroff about to be killed by Orson Welles in *Touch of Evil*.

Olga Baclanova in *Freaks*.

Igor Stravinsky (center) visits Hollywood, 1937. Movie executive Boris Morros, an *émigré* and a U.S. agent (see his *Ten Years a Counterspy*, 1957), is on the left, next to Claire Trevor. Just behind Stravinsky on the right is Akim Tamiroff.

Emigré gorilla Mischa Auer enthralls Eugene Pallette, Carole Lombard, and Alice Brady in *My Man Godfrey.*

Mischa Auer (far right) in *You Can't Take It With You.* "Confidentially, eet steenks!" he says of everything in the film, from the Bolshevik Revolution to the dancing of pupil Ann Miller, who aspires to be a Pavlova.

Lon Chaney, Jr., Bela Lugosi (*not* Karloff), and *émigrée* Maria Ouspenskaya in *Frankenstein Meets the Wolf Man.*

"Think of all your countrymen who have made it big in the movies": Johnny Weismuller, Shirley O'Hara (prone), and inscrutable Ouspenskaya in *Tarzan and the Amazons.*

insufficiently learned article in an otherwise respectable journal.[21]

Role-playing is more than a metaphor in "The Assistant Producer." One of its co-stars, General Golubkov, is a triple-agent, and his wife is more literally a performer:

She was a celebrated singer. Not opera, not even *Cavalleria Rusticana*, not anything like that. "La Slavska"—that is what the French called her. Style: one-tenth *tzigane* [= "gypsy"], one-seventh Russian peasant girl (she had been that herself originally), and five-ninths popular—and by popular I mean a hodgepodge of artificial folklore, military melodrama, and official patriotism. The fraction left unfilled seems sufficient to represent the physical splendor of her prodigious voice (*Nabokov's Dozen*, p. 75).

"She was an Elvis Presley in period dress," says Nabokov. "Her real name was Plevitskaya, and we met many times in Berlin and Paris. She would sing at the drop of a glass. Her songs had a certain emotional impact—Russia buried in the snow, that sort of thing —and the lost souls in the audience would weep into their vodka." "The Assistant Producer" presents her actual story as though it were a fiction, a movie as contrived as her performances: "And now, ladies and gentlemen, we have the great pleasure and honor— There she would stand against a dreadful background of palms and national flags, and moisten her rich painted lips with her pale tongue, and leisurely clasp her kid-gloved hands on her corseted stomach. . . . Her artistic taste was nowhere . . . but the kind of people for whom music and sentiment are one, or who like songs to be mediums for the spirits of circumstances under which they had been first apprehended in an individual past, gratefully found in the tremendous sonorities of her voice both a nostalgic solace and a patriotic kick" (pp. 84-85).

"A venerable but worldly priest, with his cross gently heaving on his ample chest, sits in the front row [at one of Slavska's performances] and looks straight ahead," writes Nabokov (p. 83), who quietly places the reader/viewer in an adjacent seat as he animates that "hodgepodge of artificial folklore [and] military melodrama"; its bit players are as accomplished as Akim Tamiroff and Mischa Auer, and the customary "self-conscious samovar reflect[s] [their] distorted faces" during one of La Slavska's histrionic numbers (p. 78). Viewing Golubkov's White Army camp, "we get a gloomy glimpse of ravens, or crows, or whatever birds proved available, wheeling in the dusk and slowly descending upon a plain littered with bodies somewhere in Ventura County," a geographic detail that locates the production company in California (p. 77). "Ghostly multitudes of ghostly Cossacks on ghost-horseback are seen charging through the fading name of the assistant producer," writes Nabokov. "Then dapper General Golubkov

"Bodies somewhere in Ventura County": Jane Withers and Farley Granger, who seems to be deciding whether to laugh or cry in this scene from *The North Star*.

[from *Golub Mira*, "Dove of Peace"] is disclosed idly scanning the battlefield through a pair of opera glasses. When movies and we were young, we used to be shown what the sights divulged neatly framed in two connected circles. Not now" (pp. 76-77). If the ensuing panoramic action is familiar it is because that tireless brigade and its brave leader, who "loom[s] sky-high for an instant on his rearing horse" (p. 77), have charged through countless Hollywood *ruskie* Westerns, ranging from *The Cossacks* (1928) to *The North Star* (1943), by which time the ghostly horsemen have donned Red outfits. "The Assistant Producer," characterized within the story as a "vile script" (p. 77), was also created in 1943, and it builds upon a tradition of cinematic nonsense.

There was a great vogue for "Russian" subjects in German as well as American films of the late twenties and early thirties, and there are two reasons why their historical inaccuracies are even worse than what one would expect: producers and scenarists were infatuated with the tragic glamor embodied by a fallen aristocracy, or, as Nabokov says of American intellectuals, they were "bewitched by Communist propaganda, [and] saw us [the *émigrés*] merely as villainous generals, oil magnates, and gaunt ladies with lorgnettes" (Foreword to *The Gift*).[22] American films such as *The Guardsman* (1931), *Rasputin and the Empress* (1932, with the three Barrymores), *Scarlet Dawn* (1932, with Douglas Fairbanks, Jr., as an exiled aristocrat), and *Mata Hari* (1932, with Ramon Novarro as Garbo's doomed White lover) are typical of the first category,[23] while Garbo's earlier performance as a White Russian spy in *The Mysterious Lady* (1928), with Gustav von Seyffentitz as the "villainous general," exemplifies a more deadly kind of caricature, quite consistent with Hollywood's ongoing travesty of Russian history.

"We should define, should we not, what we mean by 'history,'" says Nabokov. Like most artists, he adheres to no systematic "philosophy," but his attitude toward historiography clearly aligns him with the idealists rather than the Aristotelian realists: "If 'history' means 'a written account of events' . . . then let us inquire *who* actually—what scribes, what secretaries—took it down and how qualified they were for the job. I am inclined to guess that a big part of 'history' (the unnatural history of man—not the naive testimony of rocks) has been modified by mediocre writers and prejudiced observers. We know that police states (e.g., the Soviets) have actually snipped out and destroyed such past events in old books as did not conform to the falsehoods of the present. But even the most talented and conscientious historian may err. . . . If I try to select a keeper of records, I think it safer (for my comfort, at least) to choose my own self."[24] The keeper of records in "The Assistant Producer" is a first-person narrator, nameless at first. Subsequent hints and remarks indicate that he is the

Lynn Fontanne and Alfred Lunt in *The Guardsman*.

The Mysterious Lady: Tania the Russia spy (Garbo) and General Alexandroff (Gustav von Seyffertitz). He subsequently served as head of the Austrian Secret Service in *Dishonored* (1931), in which he enlists streetwalker Marlene Dietrich as spy "X-27"— who, alas, falls in love with her quarry, Russian agent "H-14" (Victor McLaglen). Dietrich brings glamor to the Russian Revolution in *Knight Without Armor* (1937).

"worldly priest" seated in the front row (p. 83), who seems to have lost his congregation if not his calling in the process of emigrating to America (p. 89). Who exactly is this narrator? "It's me, of course, disguised as a priest," says Nabokov. Why a priest? "He tells the truth," answers Nabokov. Although Nabokov states that "several of the facts in the story are true to nature," his priest is actually a poor servant to circumstantial truth, insofar as it is discernible in "The Assistant Producer." All truths are suspect in the "old Europe Picture Palace" (p. 75), and the "information" dispensed to the Soviets and the Nazis by the White Russian double- and triple-agents in the story is as irrelevant or confused as their own sense of the "historical" moment.[25]

"The Assistant Producer" is based on a Parisian incident of 1938 that involved competing factions of a White Army alumni organization. "They weren't really political," says Nabokov. "They were interested only in the welfare of army survivors, and entertained pathetic dreams of re-invading Russia, a threat that did not trouble the Soviets greatly. Its membership probably included more double-agents and informers than 'true believers.' I was quite familiar with all this because General E. K. Miller [= Fedchenko in the story] lived near us in Paris. La Slavska's husband, Skoblin [= Golubkov], kidnapped old Miller, and the entire affair was well documented by journalists." "The Assistant Producer" transforms these activities and straightforward events into a mysterious fiction, a mystery story in fact. The amply chested narrator, Father Fedor by name (p. 88), evokes G. K. Chesterton's portly Father Brown, once a favorite character of Nabokov's. "My boyhood passion for the Sherlock Holmes and Father Brown stories may yield some twisted clue," said Nabokov when asked why he has so often transmuted the mechanisms of the detective genre.[26] "The Assistant Producer" looks back to that early passion.

Father Fedor the impresario and scenarist also represents the historian as detective. "I myself have known at least two reliable witnesses of the event; and the sentries of history have let it pass unchallenged" he says early in the story (p. 77). The priest tries to reconstruct that recent event. "I still think . . . that if Father Fedor insists on paying for all those lodgings out of his own funds, the least we can do is to supply the fuel," says General Fedchenko (p. 88), demonstrating that Fedor our narrator is one of those witnesses and is well acquainted with his characters and the kind of empirical data (leases and bills for those lodgings) that is requisite to reliable history. As Fedchenko walks past a long wall near a dark church (the narrator's, no doubt), a little green door opens and "three pairs of hands with incredible speed and skill whisked the old man out of sight"— for ever (p. 88). "I frequently passed that green door.

It led into an abandoned villa," says Nabokov with certitude; but Father Fedor has considerable trouble with such concrete matter. The abduction takes place on a lane "named by some well-read city father Rue Pierre Labime," supposedly after a philosopher; the obvious play on "father" and the awkward run-on ("father Rue") contribute to the story's *trompe-l'œil* surface, its spoor of clues (p. 87). When the historian-detective returns to the scene of the crime he discovers that "it was but an optical trick. There is no green door, but only a gray one, which no human strength can burst open. I have vainly searched through admirable encyclopedias: there is no philosopher called Pierre Labime," admits the "worldly priest" (p. 88), who has missed the rueful pun in "Labime." Suspicious Fedchenko, fearing the worst, has left behind an incriminating letter, but General Golubkov, an unconcerned husband, disappears quickly; the Slavska is arrested, tried, and convicted. "By an amusing coincidence both a German press agency and a Soviet one laconically stated that a pair of White Russian generals in Paris had absconded with the White Army funds," a false report evidently based on the solid information provided by a trustworthy triple-agent (p. 92). Father Fedor, a realist who thinks he can definitively reconstruct a given event, is no longer so confident: "it is useless to retell all those lame rumors" (p. 93). He employs various qualifying phrases in his remaining reel, though he is far too creative an historian to overlook scenes to which he was not privy:

> We get a few last glimpses of the Slavska in prison. Meekly knitting in a corner. Writing to Mrs. Fedchenko tear-stained letters in which she said that they were sisters now, because both their husbands had been captured by the Bolsheviks. Begging to be allowed the use of a lipstick. Sobbing and praying in the arms of a pale young Russian nun who had come to tell her of a vision she had had which disclosed the innocence of General Golubkov. Clamoring for the New Testament which the police were keeping—keeping mainly from the experts who had so nicely begun deciphering certain notes scribbled in the margin of St. John's Gospel. Some time after the outbreak of World War II, she developed an obscure internal trouble and when, one summer morning, three German officers arrived at the prison hospital and desired to see her, at once, they were told she was dead—which possibly was the truth (p. 93).

La Slavska died in prison shortly after World War II, though in 1943 her circumstances were quite unknown. Why St. John? We can't locate Slavska's Bible, but we can get up from our seats, as Fedor has been forced to do, and parallel his quest for the truth, a quest parodied in the Index to *Pale Fire* (see "Crown Jewels" and "Word Golf"). "And the Word was made flesh, and dwelt among us" reads the text (John 1:14); "The Assistant Producer" realizes the message in secular fashion, if the reader-detective identifies Golubkov and Labime as the Word(s) in question. The wayward general is produced in the flesh at the last possible moment, as befits a mystery story.

The readily available version of "The Assistant Producer" ends with that quoted passage, alas. "Where did [Golubkov] go, poor *perdu?*" wonders Father Fedor on a concluding page which appears in *Nine Stories* (1947) but was inadvertently omitted from *Nabokov's Dozen*—"a terrible error," agrees Nabokov. "Perhaps he found a haven in Germany and was given there some small administrative job in the Baedecker Training School for Young Spies," says the narrator. "Perhaps he returned to the land where he had taken towns singlehanded. Perhaps he did not." The final sentence on this "lost" page answers these questions and suppositions. Earlier in the story Golubkov has been described as "dapper" (p. 76), "lean and frail" (p. 81), a heavy smoker whose "English prune-flavored 'Kapstens,' as he pronounced it, [were] snugly arranged in an old roomy cigarette case of black leather that had accompanied him through the presumable smoke of numberless battles" (p. 83).[27] He "produced his battle-scarred cigarette case" at the scene of Fedchenko's abduction (p. 88); these details are clues in the classic manner of Poe, Conan Doyle, and Agatha Christie. As the story ends, the narrator heads for the exit to welcome "reality": "This tangible cigarette will be very refreshing after all that trashy excitement. See, the thin dapper man walking in front of us lights up too after tapping a 'Lookee' against his old leathern cigarette case." Father Fedor is obviously no Father Brown. Despite his intimate knowledge of the case, he fails to recognize General Golubkov, who has been seated there all along, in the darkness. The parodistic show turns out to be a Chesterton-like anti-thriller, its full thrust concealed by an awful editorial error. The story has opened directly: "Meaning?" Perhaps the priest is not a very good historian. Perhaps he has poor eyesight. Perhaps "history" is impossible. General Fedchenko was spirited away through a door, and "The Assistant Producer" stops at the threshold of another meaningful door.

The story approximates "movie time" by frequently employing the present tense[28] or gerunds which suspend linear development and freeze the moment, suggesting the characters' entrapment in the past tense, the "prison of mirrors" of their hopeless nostalgia. La Slavska sings for them, buttressing their mirrors, and the narrator speaks for Nabokov when he scorns her sentimental vulgar shamming (p. 85), a musical version of her husband's "vision of presiding over an organization that was but a sunset behind a cemetery" (p. 80). Comedy releases the narrator from that prison, distances him from the "old Europe Picture Palace" of history, and deposits him in the lobby, at the threshold of an exit of his choice: "Perhaps he was summoned by whoever his arch-boss was and told with that slight foreign accent and special brand of blandness that we all know: 'I am afraid, my friend, you are nott nee-ded any more'—and as X turns to go Dr. Puppenmeister's delicate index presses a button at the edge of his impassive writing desk and a trap yawns under X, who plunges to his death (he who knows 'too much'), or breaks his funny bone by crashing right through into the living room of the elderly couple below," he writes on the "lost" page, burlesquing a melodramatic scene that extends from *The Mysterious Lady* (1928) and Lang's *Spies* (1928) to *All Through the Night* (1942) and the *Falcon* series which Nabokov endured with Dmitri in 1943. Father Fedor tells the truth after all, and his comic course of survival parallels that of Nabokov, Dr. Puppenmeister himself, the ventriloquist and anthropomorphic deity. "This is the disciple [John] which testifieth of these things, and wrote these things: and we know that his testimony is true" (John 21:24). The other featured disciple is of course Peter, or Pierre, if you will. "Rue Pierre Labime" is a punning authorial tribute to the priest, Nabokov's disciple in matters pertaining to survival, and it is immaterial that Fedor fails to remember that the title character in Nabokov's "Lik" (1938), written at the time of "Fedchenko's" disappearance, had performed in a French play called *L'Abîme* ("The Abyss"). The gray door on Rue La-

"You are nott nee-ded any more," the iconography of the Master Spy: Above, Seyffertitz in *The Mysterious Lady*. Right, Conrad Veidt as the Nazi spy in *All Through the Night*. Veidt died the following year (1943), aged fifty.

bime won't open because, like his *émigré* creator and the resurrected Golubkov, Fedor's "human strength" has withstood the pull of the abyss. They are not lone miraculous figures in the fictional world of an author who often has been accused of manipulating his characters with a uniform cold contempt.

The figure of the exile embodies the human condition in our time, and it has become a commonplace to point out how many writers have either chosen this role or been cast literally in it: Joyce, Mann, Broch, Toller, Brecht, Beckett, Ionesco, Cabrera Infante, and Russians too numerous to list, for they seem to have had all of modern history with which to contend. Nabokov's Pnin, who weeps in the dark, is a representative figure, and he testifies to the humanism of his creator. "I haf nofing left, nofing, nofing!" wails Pnin, who doesn't see himself with complete detachment (p. 61). The oldest assistant professor in the world, fired from his job, addlepated Pnin nevertheless possesses something precious enough—a spirited resiliency. Readers tend to focus on and retain abject or sorrowful images of homeless Pnin while overlooking his zestful game of croquet, the passion with which he discusses Tolstoy, the fact that the dropped nutcracker misses his cherished glass bowl at the bottom of the soapy crowded sink. When Pnin glides into the water at The Pines, a resort owned by *émigré* Al Cook (né Kukolniko), "his dignified breast stroke [sent] off ripples on either side. Around the natural basin, Pnin

swam in state" (p. 129), and the Miltonic syntax complements that dignity. At the end of the novel Nabokov treats his unemployed *émigré* to a suitably hopeful send-off: "Hardly had I taken a couple of steps when a great truck carrying beer rumbled up the street, immediately followed by a small pale blue sedan with the white head of a dog looking out, after which came another great truck, exactly similar to the first. The humble sedan was crammed with bundles and suitcases; its driver was Pnin," hemmed in by the trucks which had tormented refugee Humbert. The "next moment the light turned green . . . and everything surged forward—truck one, Pnin, truck two. From where I stood I watched them recede in the frame of the roadway, between the Moorish house and the Lombardy poplar. Then the little sedan boldly swung past the front truck and, free at last, spurted up the shining road, which one could make out narrowing to a thread of gold in the soft mist where hill after hill made beauty of distance, and where there was simply no saying what miracle might happen." The miracle is not a self-congratulatory reflection of Nabokov's American success. *Lolita* was not yet a best-seller, and miracles may not even be necessary; Pnin is a figure of pathos rather than a pathetic figure. He didn't laugh at Chaplin's comedy (p. 80) because his own life is too Chaplinesque, in the happiest sense, however. Although Pnin is accompanied by a yapping dog rather than a grateful orphan girl,

"The shining road": Chaplin and Paulette Goddard at the end of
Modern Times, in a happier place than Robert Frank's American road (p. 219).

his unsentimental departure echoes the Little Tramp's smiling exit from *Modern Times* (1936), a farewell performance. Unlike Charlie, whose Tramp would never return (the distant hills are symbolic), Pnin reappears in *Pale Fire* (1962), firmly on his feet, on high ground indeed: a Departmental Chairman, a "martinet" in a Hawaiian shirt!

Pnin's academic triumph (such as it is) underscores the optimistic rhythm which pulsates through much of Nabokov's *émigré* fiction. Although Nabokov's spectral *émigré* world is circumscribed by loss and grief, there is almost always a redeeming sense of gaiety at its center; like Luzhin, Albinus plunges into the abyss, but *émigré* mountain-climber Martin had joyfully negotiated it in *Glory* (1932), Nabokov's previous novel (pp. 169-70). Cincinnatus, a dream projection, does even better, while *Despair* (1936) and *The Gift* (1937-1938) variously employ a signal narrative dateline—April 1—and not because it is Gogol's birthday. Even the most minor characters in *Transparent Things* (1972) are in mourning and dress in black. Death is everywhere because the compact novel—*The Eye*'s (1930) brightened, lifted shade—is deftly structured as a ghost story, and its omniscient overseer, in conversation, concurs with this reading: "Ghosts see our world as transparent, everything sinks so fast. Yes, it is a kind of thriller." Only authorial comedy can transfigure and transcend all the dread in Nabokov's gay "pocket requiem," to borrow Stravin-

Vladimir Nabokov (right), Soliès-Pont (Var), France, summer, 1923: "Naked to the waist, his back already the hue of terra cotta, Martin, to humor the young maize, loosened and heaped up the soil, grubbed out with the sharp corner of his hoe the wily and stubborn speargrass, or for hours on end stood bend-

Keaton in *Sherlock, Jr.,* his reel running even faster than his fantasies.

ing over the shoots of infant trees, apple and pear, clicking his pruning shears. He especially enjoyed conducting the water from the reservoir in the yard to the nurseries, where the mattocked furrows joined with one another and with the hollows dug around the stems. As the water spread all over the young plantation, it picked its way like a live thing; here it would stop, there run on, extending bright tentacles. . . . He felt happy he knew how to satisfy a plant's thirst, happy that chance had helped him to find work that could serve to try out his shrewdness and his endurance. Together with the other laborers he lodged in a shed, drank, as they did, one and a half liters of wine a day, and found satisfaction in looking like them"—*Glory* (pp. 163-64).

sky's characterization of his own *Requiem Canticles* (1966). *Émigré* Nabokov's present apotheosis in world literature is singular, but his spirit is not unique. The sustaining efficacy of art celebrated by Vladimir Markov in his excellent "Mozart" (1956) is sounded by other *émigrés* too: the sardonic idiom of Tsvetaeva's Mayakovsky poems (1930) and the incandescent prose of Boris Poplavsky's *Homeward from Heaven* (c. 1934); the exhilarating rhythms of Alexei Remizov and the music of Khodasevich's "Orpheus" (1927), rising out of his customary gloom.[29] Stravinsky's ebullient *Symphony in C* (1940) is bracing as well as dramatic, for it was begun at a time of deep grief, amidst the confusion and turmoil created by modern history. "But my reel is going too fast," says the narrator of "The Assistant Producer" at one point (p. 79), busily recording and projecting history as "trashy entertainment"; "I want all your attention now, for it would be a pity to miss the subtleties of the situation" (p. 80).

While *Ada* (1969) offers Nabokov's most ambitious, literally global translation of the theme, *Pale Fire* represents his most subtle and labyrinthine and personal "historical" situation; through Kinbote, Nabokov *has* cut the pages of *Solus Rex* by submitting its *donnée* and surviving sheets (1939) to comedy's hall of mirrors, thereby retrieving and reviving several shadows of the *émigré* work-in-progress literally sacrificed to history. "I do not believe that 'history' exists

History as fiction: Marlene Dietrich as Catherine the Great in Sternberg's *The Scarlet Empress* ("Based on a diary of Catherine II"—only one point of view, tsarina as unreliable narrator or prejudiced witness). Sternberg's Russian music, art, costume, and decor are a carefully stylized, anachronistic historical mishmash—High Church Tchaikovsky and Wagner, eighteenth-century Art Deco, Byzantine Expressionism, Romanesque Art Nouveau, *Belle Epoque-Wizard of Oz* couture—which is one reason the film has become a camp classic, though the cultists (along with the Marxist critics of the thirties) miss the point of its parody of "authentic" historiography, as do the purists who would dismiss it as *poshlost'*, or a product of the Germanic vision of barbaric, "oriental" Russia. Note the "cross" growing out of Dietrich's head; if it is anything save an askew tuberculosis Christmas seal emblem, it is surely upside down. If the ship is secular, it doesn't belong in an icon; nor would icons be arranged in this order, or incorporate a keyhole ornament—or decorate in so ostentatious a manner the royal nuptial chamber of a palace. The aureoled figure to the left of the cross is particularly droll: the iconography suggests that he is the ascetic St. Simeon Stylites, who lived on top of a column. What is a saint doing with a bow and arrow? Unlike the naive, kitschy anachronisms in many costume melodramas or the foolishness of *The Guardsman* or *The Mysterious Lady*, these "mistakes" are intentional and thematically correct. The world of the film was of course "not a replica," says Sternberg in his autobiography, *Fun in a Chinese Laundry*. Like the clockwork toy in *Pale Fire*, Grand Duke Peter's beautifully made toy soldiers are emblematic; the creator's playfulness is serious indeed. The intuitive insights of these artists are confirmed by current historical revisionism. Hitler, as it turns out, was not down and out in Vienna; the author of *Mein Kampf* had been accepted as a reliable narrator, the rarest of birds in modern fiction.

Sam Jaffe in *The Scarlet Empress*.

apart from the historian," says Nabokov, and in *Pale Fire* the illusory modes of memoir and historiography blend in King Charles II's Zemblan realm, Clio serving Nabokov as a zany assistant producer. "Opéra bouffe!" exclaimed at least one dismayed reader, lost in Zembla's palace intrigue and extremist politics. Similar complaints, also predicated on an otiose belief in history, were made of Sternberg's treatment of history as farce in *The Scarlet Empress* (1934), a film that surely learned something from the Marx Brothers' *Duck Soup* (1933). An intentionally ill-chosen wig and a bit of eye-rolling turn Grand Duke Peter (Sam Jaffe) into a veritable Harpo Marx, and Tsarina Dietrich looks considerably Greater than Russia's Catherine II. The reviewers who unfavorably compared *The Scarlet Empress* with the straightforward *Catherine the Great* (1934) had accepted fiction as fact; Sternberg's farce undercuts such assumptions. "Don't be silly! Don't be old-fashioned! This is the eighteenth century," exclaims Empress Elizabeth (Louise Dresser), exercising the same kind of extraordinary historical self-consciousness that Humbert will mock: " 'We,' I quip-quoted, 'medieval mariners, have placed in this bottle—' " (p. 167). "Get out! I have a war on my hands!" commands Dresser, and Grand Duke Peter plays with an army of toy soldiers. At his wedding, Peter chews up the sacramental wafer, an unchronicled augury of a less than happy union. "I'm sure history was far from her mind at the time," says a palace retainer, discussing Catherine's begetting of an illegitimate son, another broadly "Nabokovian" reminder that the entire show is illusion, *this* history is fiction. The metaphor is more elaborate in *Pale Fire*.

"We must wonder or remember," says Nabokov, contemplating history, "who exactly is telling the story," and Zembla's not altogether disinterested scholar has a penchant for young lads which affects and infects his pages. The Zemblan entries in *Pale Fire's* Index form a brilliant parody of chronicles (and their unreliable narrators), of neatly packaged "definitive" histories and their trusting readers: "*Uran* [from *uranist*, or "homosexual," a *nineteenth*-century usage!] *the Last*, Emperor of Zembla, reigned 1798-1799; an incredibly brilliant, luxurious, and cruel monarch whose whistling whip made Zembla spin like a rainbow top; dispatched one night by a group of his sister's united favorites" (a heterosexual conspiracy?). Loaded adjectives continually fix the "truth," not without feline humor (Baron A. is succinctly immortalized as a "puny traitor"), and history's heterosexual figures are somehow less heroic than Uran the Last: the "bald spot" of stylish, womanizing Count Otar highlights his entry. Question marks are too frequently affixed to the names of mock-historical figures, and a search for the buried "Crown Jewels" (*q.v.*) through the Index's cross-referenced entries reveals nothing, a dead end in a metagame. The monarchial name Alfin the Vague summarizes

Nabokov's attitude, and the Index self-consciously underscores its own fictiveness, as well as history's: O'Donnell, Sylvia, "was in the act of divorcing Lionel Lavender . . . when last seen in this Index." Charles the Beloved's kingdom proper is staged as a technicolored costume extravaganza, as though any one of the many movie versions of *The Scarlet Pimpernel* (1917, 1929, 1935, 1938, 1941, 1950)—as various as history itself—or *The Prisoner of Zenda* (1927, 1937, 1952), the most famous of the Ruritanian romances of impersonation and escape, had been crossed with Laurel and Hardy's *Fra Diavolo* (1933) or *Duck Soup*, the Marx Brothers's Ruritanian burlesque. *Pale Fire's* kingdom of Zembla recalls the fun-house palace of *Duck Soup,* with its ludicrous functionaries, uniformed guards, and mirror walls, as well as the sequence in *A Night at the Opera* (1935) in which Chico, Harpo, and Allan Jones (managed by Groucho) disguise themselves as the three identically bearded Russian aviators, Chicoski, Harpotski, and Baronoff. Witness Kinbote in *Pale Fire,* as King Charles (p. 76), modestly "lectur[ing] under an assumed name and in a heavy make-up, with wig and false whiskers" (his real, immense, American-grown beard will earn him his obscene sobriquet, the Great Beaver), or making his escape from Zembla, aided by a hundred loyalist "clowns" who, in a brilliant diversionary ploy, don red caps and sweaters identical to the king's, in their apprehension packing the local

In *Duck Soup,* left to right: Mrs. Teasdale (Margaret Dumont); Pinkie (Harpo Marx) Ambassador Trentino (Louis Calhern); and Chicolini (Chico Marx).

prison, which is "much too small for more kings"— shades of *A Night at the Opera*'s crowded cabin (p. 144). King Charles's escape is directed and abetted by Odon, Zembla's most famous actor, a master of disguise, and when, in *Pale Fire*'s closing paragraph, the masked author suspends the fiction and renders his plot and players transparent, he envisions his return in "other disguises, other forms"; "I may join forces with [exile] Odon in a new motion picture: *Escape from Zembla* (ball in the palace, bomb in the palace square)." It is an old celluloid melodrama, of course, which we have already seen, most recently in *Pale Fire*. (Earlier in the novel [p. 149], Odon himself had "direct[ed] the making of a cinema film in Paris!"— resembling, no doubt, the Zemblan portion of *Pale Fire*.) "Oh, I may do many things! History permitting, I may sail back to my recovered kingdom, and with a great sob greet the gray coastline and the gleam of a roof in the rain," a sensuous visual detail localizing the sense of loss, the pain. History will not oblige *émigré* Nabokov. *Laughter in the Dark*'s stage door is open, but beyond reach. Distanced by space, internalized, as is everyone's past, the exile's resplendent Russian land and language grow more fabulous with time as the "future" is devoured by each rapidly passing day. "Anyhow the show is over," as Nabokov writes at the end of "The Assistant Producer," on the concluding, omitted page. Let us complete our rescue of the wayward end, that ghostly *émigré* page, and

"*Escape from Zembla* (ball in the palace, bomb in the palace square)": Harold Lloyd (*Why Worry,* 1923), assuming the Prospero-like stance of Nabokov in *Pale Fire,* surveys the triumph of art. "A bigger, more respectable, more competent Gradus" will one day arrive, states Nabokov in his final phrase, but for now Death has been contained by the authorial magic of comedy.

circle back to our opening departure from the Play-house Theatre:

. . . You help your girl into her coat and join the slow exit-bound stream of your likes. Safety doors open into unexpected side portions of night, diverting proximal trickles. If, like me, you prefer for reasons of orientation to go out the way you came in, you will pass again by those posters that seemed so attractive a couple of hours ago. The Russian cavalryman in his half-Polish uniform bends from his polo-pony to scoop up red-booted romance, her black hair tumbling from under her astrakhan cap. The Arc de Triomphe rubs shoulders with a dim-domed Kremlin. The monocled agent of a Foreign Power is handed a bundle of secret papers by General Golubkov. . . . Quick, children, let us get out of here into the sober night, into the shuffling peace of familiar sidewalks, into the solid world of good freckled boys and the spirit of comradeship. Welcome, reality! . . .

THE END

Notes

1. Frederick's of Hollywood

1. James Joyce, *Finnegans Wake* (New York, 1963), p. 164.
2. *Ibid.*, p. 166.
3. James Joyce, *Ulysses* (New York, 1961), p. 368.
4. James Huneker, "The Seven Arts," *Puck*, 80 (July 29, 1916), 12, 21.
5. Larry Swindell, *Spencer Tracy* (Cleveland and New York, 1969), p. 139.
6. Aaron Latham, *Crazy Sundays: F. Scott Fitzgerald in Hollywood* (New York, 1971), p. 178.
7. Vladimir Nabokov, *Lolita* (New York, 1958), p. 299. All subsequent parenthetical page references are to this edition and my own edition, *The Annotated Lolita* (New York, 1970), which have the same pagination.
8. The authors are, respectively, S. J. Perelman; Ring Lardner; Fitzgerald; Fitzgerald; Gavin Lambert; Christopher Isherwood; Irwin Shaw; and West, of course. Unlike Fitzgerald's Pat Hobby stories (1939-40) or Isherwood's *Prater Violet* (1945), a long-suffering writer is not at the center of *The Day of the Locust*. Its excellence may in part be due to this fact. West's (possible) surrogate in the novel is a painter-set designer, rather than a novelist-screenwriter, a strategy that distances the author from his own experiences and grievances. The focus is on the demimonde of Hollywood, and screenwriter Claude Estes, an unsympathetic character, figures but briefly. The screenwriter is literally a whore in Billy Wilder's *Sunset Boulevard* (1950), where failed scenarist William Holden is hired as a gigolo by faded screen star Gloria Swanson.
9. See Dorothy Gardiner and Katherine S. Walker, eds., *Raymond Chandler Speaking* (Boston, 1962).
10. William Faulkner's career as novelist and screenwriter proved that eight or ten weeks in Hollywood per year (over a ten-year period) is no worse for a writer than ten months spent reading Freshman English themes and the manuscripts of "creative writers." Of course boorish, ignorant producers abused and misused American writers, but that's only part of the story. The Martyrdom Myth has too long obscured the positive contributions made by American writers to American films. Important correctives are offered by *Film Comment*'s special issue, "The Hollywood Screenwriter" (V, 4 [Winter 1970-71]), issued under that title as a paperback in 1972 (Richard Corliss, ed.); Pauline Kael's general remarks about the verbal style of nineteen-thirties screen comedy (but not her praise of screenwriter Herman J. Mankiewicz at Orson Welles's expense) in "Raising Kane" in *The Citizen Kane Book* (Boston, 1971); William Froug's interview-book, *The Screenwriter Looks at the Screenwriter* (New York, 1972); and The

Viking Press's series, The M-G-M Library of Film Scripts, which, unlike other such ventures, gives top billing to the screenwriter, rather than the director. *Talking Pictures: Screenwriters in the American Cinema* (New York, 1974), by Richard Corliss, is indispensable.

11. Andrew Sarris, "An Aesthete at the Movies," *Commentary*, 51, 2 (February 1971), 81-82.

12. The poem is included in Hollander's collection *Movie-Going and Other Poems* (New York, 1962) and in *The Cosmos Reader*, Edgar Z. Friedenberg *et al.*, eds. (New York, 1971), pp. 447-50.

13. Lionel Trilling, "Bergman Unseen," *The Mid-Century*, No. 20 (December 1960), 2-10. Trilling's elegant rationale for his "alienation" from cinema is archetypal.

14. Anatole Broyard, "No, But I Read the Review" [Pauline Kael's *Deeper Into Movies*], *The New York Times*, February 22, 1973, p. 37.

15. Jay Martin, *Nathanael West: The Art of His Life* (Boston, 1970), p. 211.

16. See Saul Bellow, "Culture Now: Some Animadversions, Some Laughs," *Modern Occasions*, II (Winter, 1971), the loudest *cri de guerre* of the new cultural conservatism.

17. "The Strong Opinions of Vladimir Nabokov—As Imparted to Nicholas Garnham," *The Listener* (10 October 1968), p. 463. All the interviews quoted herein are collected in Nabokov's *Strong Opinions* (New York, 1973), whose texts sometimes differ from the original, published versions of the interviews.

18. Vladimir Nabokov, *Pale Fire* (New York, 1962), p. 69. Textual references are to this edition (hardcover first editions are always the rule).

2. Negative Images

1. Vladimir Nabokov, *Ada* (New York, 1969), p. 399. Subsequent parenthetical page references are to this edition.

2. Vladimir Nabokov, *Transparent Things* (New York, 1972), p. 14. Textual references are to this edition.

3. Unless otherwise noted, such quotations are drawn from informal conversations with the Nabokovs in Montreux, Switzerland (September 1966; January 1968; August 1970; September 1971; and November 1972). One of Nabokov's own cartoons is reproduced in *The Annotated Lolita*, p. 419. He dashed it off when neither author nor annotator could remember the name of a "repulsive strip" mentioned by Humbert (p. 256). This challenge to future scholarship can now be met; the strip is *Kerry Drake*. Nabokov is an accomplished draftsman, and has exercised his ability in lepidopterological drawings. The last chapter of this book includes a capricious product of his color-pencil set.

4. Vladimir Nabokov, "Spring in Fialta," in *Nabokov's Dozen* (New York, 1958), p. 18.

5. Vladimir Nabokov, *Laughter in the Dark* (New York, 1938), p. 26. Textual references are to this edition.

6. Vladimir Nabokov, *King, Queen, Knave* (New York, 1968), p. 50. Textual references are to this edition. See also pp. 52, 61, 87, 115, and 117-18.

7. Vladimir Nabokov, *Despair* (New York, 1966), p. 87. Textual references are to this edition. See also pp. 54, 83, and 218.

8. Vladimir Nabokov, *The Eye* (New York, 1965), p. 39. Textual references are to this edition.

9. Vladimir Nabokov, *The Defense* (New York, 1964), p. 86. Textual references are to this edition.

10. Vladimir Nabokov, *Glory* (New York, 1971), p. 35. Textual references are to this edition.

11. Vladimir Nabokov, *Pnin* (New York, 1957), p. 80. Textual references are to this edition.

12. Vladimir Nabokov, "Lik," in *Nabokov's Quartet* (New York, 1966), p. 49.

13. Vladimir Nabokov, *The Real Life of Sebastian Knight* (New York, 1941), p. 147. Textual references are to this edition.

14. An eidetic memory serves Nabokov in life as well as art. These conversational remarks (September 1971) repeat, almost verbatim, a passage in the Foreword to the *Lolita*

screenplay, written in October 1970 and revised three years later. See *Lolita: A Screenplay* (New York, 1974), p. xii. Textual references are to this edition.

15. Vladimir Nabokov, *Nikolai Gogol* (Greenwich, Conn., 1944), p. 70. Also see pp. 63-69. Textual references are to this edition. Nabokov keeps his definition of *poshlost'* up-to-date; see any of several interviews, especially *Paris Review*, No. 41 (Summer-Fall 1967), 103-4, where *poshlost'* ranges from airline stewardesses to Mann's *Death in Venice*.

16. Vladimir Nabokov, *The Gift* (New York, 1963), p. 102. Textual references are to this edition.

17. Vladimir Nabokov, *Bend Sinister* (New York, 1947), p. 222. Textual references are to this edition.

18. See Joyce, *Ulysses*, p. 609, and compare with Nabokov's description: "The murdered child had a crimson and gold turban around its head; its face was skilfully painted and powdered: a mauve blanket, exquisitely smooth, came up to its chin" (*Bend Sinister*, p. 224).

19. Alfred Appel, Jr., "Conversations With Nabokov," *Novel: A Forum on Fiction*, IV, 3 (Spring 1971), 213.

20. *Ibid.*, 212. The 1963 film was directed by Tony Richardson, adapted by Edward Bond, and starred Nicol Williamson and Mlle Karina, the setting disastrously moved from old Berlin to Richardson's own mod London. Because of the liberties of the adaptation and the fact that Nabokov had nothing to do with the scenario or production, Richardson's version will not be discussed here. For Nabokov's comments on it, see pp. 134-35.

21. Vladimir Nabokov, *Speak, Memory* (New York, 1966), p. 191. Textual references are to this edition. In Nabokov's story, "An Affair of Honor" (1927), set in Germany, an unhappy, disoriented expatriate, Anton Petrovich, thinks about his imminent duel, and imagines how he would turn up his jacket collar against the chill of the early morning: "That's how they did it in that film I saw." Although he also alludes to diluted Pushkin ("What does Onegin do in the opera?"), his initial vision defines the absurd and

pitiable incongruity manifest in his attempt to assert old codes in the strange new world of the emigration (*Nabokov's Quartet*, pp. 31-32). This idea, the pity and pathos qualified considerably, is central to the story "The Assistant Producer" (1943).

22. Vladimir Nabokov, "The Assistant Producer," in *Nabokov's Dozen*, p. 77.

23. Raymond Chandler, *The Little Sister* (New York, 1971), p. 203.

24. "Conversations With Nabokov," 214-15.

25. Jorge Luis Borges, "Citizen Kane," *Sur* 83 (1945), reprinted in *Focus on Citizen Kane*, Ronald Gottesman, ed. (Englewood Cliffs, N.J., 1971), pp. 127-28.

26. "More recently, on French TV I saw a Laurel and Hardy short in which the 'dubbers' had the atrocious taste to have the two men speak fluent French with an English accent," notes Nabokov ("Conversations With Nabokov," 213-14); that idle moment may well have inspired the parodies of dubbing in *Ada*: the cast's "macedoine of accents—English, French, Italian" in *Four Sisters* (pp. 427-28), and a "madhouse" of bilingual babble that is rendered in scenario form (pp. 516-18).

27. "The Strong Opinions of Vladimir Nabokov," p. 463.

3. *Tristram in Movielove*

1. I extend this line of argument in *The Annotated Lolita*; see the third section of the Introduction, "The Artifice of *Lolita*," and Note 253/15 (p. 418), which summarizes the verbal contrivances.

2. The stories discussed in the following pages are collected in *Nabokov's Dozen*, and the textual references are to this edition.

3. Vladimir Nabokov, "The Refrigerator Awakes," in *Poems and Problems* (New York, 1970), pp. 153-54.

4. Despite the complaints of the narrator in "Time and Ebb," Nabokov does not dismiss photography per se. The walls of the art teacher's studio in *Pnin* are adorned by only

"two identically framed pictures: a copy of Gertrude Käsebier's photographic masterpiece 'Mother and Child' (1897), with the wistful, angelic infant looking up and away (at what?); and a similarly toned reproduction of the head of Christ from Rembrandt's 'The Pilgrims of Emmaus,' with the same, though slightly less celestial, expression of eyes and mouth" (p. 95). Käsebier, an excellent American photographer (1852-1934), is not in today's pantheon, and the literary anatomist becomes a curator of sorts. Rembrandt's title and iconography clarify his "meaning," but Käsebier's masterful photo begs a parenthetical question. Nabokov's juxtapositioning of "high" and "low" forms is nonetheless instructive. "The mechanical process can exist in a ludicrous daub, and inspiration can be found in a photographer's choice of landscape and in his manner of seeing it," he told me in 1970, doubtless having in mind the distinguished work of photographers such as Paul Strand, Edward Weston, Ansel Adams, Minor White, and Douglas Cole.

5. See Joyce's *Ulysses,* pp. 68-69. The author of the story, Mr. Philip Beaufoy, appears in Nighttown to denounce Bloom. "No born gentleman, no one with the most rudimentary promptings of a gentleman would stoop to such particularly loathsome conduct," he says (pp. 458-59).

6. Nathanael West, "Some Notes on Miss L.," *Contempo,* III (May 15, 1933), 1-2.

7. Nathanael West, *Miss Lonelyhearts and The Day of the Locust* (New York, 1969), p. 8. Textual references are to this edition.

8. Vladimir Nabokov, "Perfection," *The New Yorker,* May 19, 1973, p. 38.

9. Richard Brautigan, *Trout Fishing in America* (San Francisco, 1967), pp. 89-91.

10. Eudora Welty, "Why I Live at the P.O.," *Selected Stories of Eudora Welty* (New York, 1954), pp. 99-100.

11. In retrospect, *Freaks* would seem to have been shocking not so much for its subject matter but for the way it attacked the corrupt (and abnormal) "big people's" manipulation and humiliation of the deformed members of the circus sideshow, particularly its women. "Go ahead and laugh! Women are funny, ain't they?" says a hermaphrodite named Venus to a clown who is grinning at her.

12. Contemporary comic strips, after all, also featured children: *Wash Tubs; Dickie Dare; Tim Tyler's Luck; Little Orphan Annie;* Junior in *Dick Tracy;* and Terry, only ten when *Terry and the Pirates* began. But these comics, variants of earlier child strips, were basically adventure stories, and, except for the right-wing proselytizing of Annie's Daddy Warbucks, they do not belie their genre. And in the late thirties, when an adolescent Terry has a series of "crushes"—on a very experienced older woman, Burma, or his contemporary, April Kane—they are rendered most innocently, as opposed to the adult sexuality of his sidekick Pat Ryan and the Dragon Lady. Comic books, a development of the late thirties, are another matter entirely. Unlike the newspaper strips and the movies in question, they were created exclusively for children.

13. Thomas Pynchon, *Gravity's Rainbow* (New York, 1973), pp. 419-22.

14. *Ibid.,* pp. 465-68.

15. Albert J. Guerard, "Was Lia de Putti Dead at 22?," *Tri-Quarterly* 20 (Winter 1971), 255-83.

16. James Thurber, "The Remarkable Case of Mr. Bruhl," *The Thurber Carnival* (New York, 1945), p. 147.

17. Lolita is "Dolores on the dotted line" (p. 11), but an evolving diminutive to others: Dolly, Lola, Lolita, Lo. By describing her on the novel's first page as "Lola in slacks" (p. 11), Humbert would seem to be aptly connecting mother and daughter through an allusion to Marlene's "scandalous" wearing of slacks and her famous role as Lola Lola (a double name, too), the young cabaret entertainer who ruinously enchants an aging professor in Sternberg's classic German film *The Blue Angel* (1930). But Nabokov says that this is "probably a happy coincidence. I doubt I had the association in mind," especially since he has never seen that film. "The first-run cinema palaces in Berlin were

quite expensive, you know," he says, recalling that period of *émigré* life. "In Europe we usually went to the neighborhood cinema," though they did see Dietrich in *Shanghai Express*. Yet Nabokov *has* seen still photos of *The Blue Angel*, so. . .

18. The most readily available illustration of the painting is in William S. Rubin, *Dada and Surrealist Art* (New York, n.d.), p. 65.

19. Johan Huizinga, *Homo Ludens: A Study of the Play Element in Culture* (Boston, 1955), p. 10.

20. See Alfred Appel, Jr., "*Lolita*: The Springboard of Parody," *Wisconsin Studies in Contemporary Literature*, VIII (Spring 1967), reprinted in L. S. Dembo, ed., *Nabokov: The Man and his Work* (Madison, 1967), or the Introduction to *The Annotated Lolita*, pp. lxiii-lxviii. For Nabokov's remarks on the Double, see my "Interview with Vladimir Nabokov" in the previously cited issue of *Wisconsin Studies* (also reprinted in Dembo), 145.

21. Vladimir Nabokov, "Rowe's Symbols" [a review of Rowe's *Nabokov's Deceptive World*], *New York Review*, October 7, 1971, p. 8. Nabokov includes it in his *Strong Opinions*.

22. *Ulysses*, p. 368.

23. *Ibid.*, pp. 367-68.

24. Julian Symons, *The Players and the Game* (New York, 1972), p. 19.

25. François Truffaut, *Hitchcock* (New York, 1967), p. 186.

26. André Bazin, *What Is Cinema?*, Vol. II, Hugh Gray, ed. and trans. (Berkeley and Los Angeles, 1971), p. 167.

27. Symons, pp. 3-4.

28. Nabokov, *Strong Opinions*, p. 137.

29. See "*Lolita*: The Springboard of Parody" and, for a more succinct discussion, the Introduction to *The Annotated Lolita*.

30. James M. Cain, *Double Indemnity*, in *Cain X 3* (New York, 1969), p. 408.

31. Everything in *Lolita* is constantly in the process of metamorphosis, including the novel and the reader; see Note 18/6, *The Annotated Lolita* (pp. 340-41).

32. For more on the "fairy tale" in Nabokov, see Note 33/3 in *The Annotated Lolita* (pp. 346-47) and the discussion of *Laughter in the Dark* in my concluding chapter here.

33. "An Interview with Vladimir Nabokov," 142.

34. Some of Nabokov's fun recalls films which he has never seen: *Baby Face Harrington* (1935), Raoul Walsh's wonderful satire on the gangster genre, and the black-garbed hoodlums' dance number in Vincente Minnelli's *The Band Wagon* (1953). The entire chapter, in tone and conception, shares many qualities with the John Huston-Truman Capote collaboration, *Beat the Devil* (1954), the shaggy-dog thriller that casts Bogart, Peter Lorre, Jennifer Jones, Gina Lollobrigida, et al., in comic inversions of their standard roles. Lorre as a German named O'Hara is particularly delightful, an Ur-Quilty. As an undergraduate at Cornell, I sat behind Nabokov at a downtown showing of the film in the spring of 1954 (an Ur-Kinbote?), and vividly remember his loud laughter, especially at the moment when Lorre pauses before a character who is having his portrait painted, and says, in his inimitable nasal whine, "That doesn't look like him! It has only one ear!" The film didn't influence Nabokov, however; *Lolita* had just been completed, and the killing of Quilty had been written several years before, out-of-sequence, as Nabokov often works. It might be claimed, however, that Lorre's performance, here and elsewhere, influenced Peter Sellers's Quilty in the film version of *Lolita*.

4. Positive Images

1. "Conversations With Nabokov," 213.

2. For a paraphrase of these untranslated works, see Andrew Field, *Nabokov: His Life in Art* (Boston, 1967), pp. 75-78.

3. "Conversations With Nabokov," 214.

4. Vladimir Nabokov, *Invitation to a Beheading* (New York, 1959), p. 97. Textual references are to this edition.

5. "Conversations With Nabokov," 214.

6. Vladimir Nabokov, "Terra Incognita," in *A Russian Beauty and Other Stories* (New York, 1973), p. 127.

7. *Nabokov's Dozen*, p. 141.

8. "Conversations With Nabokov," 213.

9. These devices are done to death, figuratively speaking, in the most violent *Tom and Jerry* cartoons. They demonstrate how imaginative and sophisticated devices can be vulgarized or exhausted all too quickly, in "high" as well as "low" forms of art.

10. I have not seen this cartoon, and am drawing upon Barbara Deming's recollection of it in *Running Away from Myself* (New York, 1969), p. 190.

11. The anti-hero of Nathanael West's parodistic *A Cool Million* (1934, subtitled "The Dismantling of Lemuel Pitkin") suffers in similar fashion. Over the course of the novel he loses several working parts, and, as the stooge in a vaudeville finale, is divested of his remaining good eye, toupee, and wooden leg, which is knocked into the audience—a scene that Nabokov's Cornell student, Thomas Pynchon, seems to have drawn upon in V. (1963) for the interlude in which the gang of Maltese urchins unhinges the prefabricated and helpless transvestite priest.

12. *Ulysses*, p. 523. Prior to his three class-weeks on Joyce, Nabokov would lecture on "three tales of transformation": Gogol's *The Overcoat*, Stevenson's *Dr. Jekyll and Mr. Hyde*, and Kafka's *The Metamorphosis*, "a supreme, perfect masterpiece." He might also have included Gogol's *The Nose*, a lengthy and bona fide sight gag which Nabokov loves.

13. Vladimir Nabokov, "An Evening of Russian Poetry," *Poems and Problems* (New York, 1970), pp. 159-60. The kingly images in the poem clearly point to *Solus Rex*, a loss now partially recouped; translated versions of "Ultima Thule" and the excerpt titled "Solus Rex" now appear in *A Russian Beauty and Other Stories*.

14. See "An Interview with Vladimir Nabokov," 152.

5. Dark Cinema

1. For cinematic tropes typical of Nabokov, see *Despair*, p. 83; *The Gift*, p. 17; *Bend Sinister*, p. 172; "Scenes from the Life of a Double Monster," in *Nabokov's Dozen*, p. 174; and *Lolita*, pp. 213-14.

2. This point is also stressed by Raymond Durgnat in "Paint it Black" (*Cinema*, 6 & 7 [August 1970]) and Paul Schrader in "Notes on Film Noir" (*Film Comment*, VIII, 1 [Spring 1972]).

3. See Lotte H. Eisner's amply illustrated discussion of *Stimmung* in *The Haunted Screen* (Berkeley, 1969), pp. 199-206.

4. Lang, tape-recorded in 1965; from Peter Bogdanovich's interview-book, *Fritz Lang in America* (New York, 1969), p. 15.

5. *Cain X* 3, p. 347.

6. *Ibid.*, p. 315.

7. Carlos Baker, *Ernest Hemingway: A Life Story* (New York, 1969), p. 457.

8. *Gravity's Rainbow*, p. 264.

9. See Durgnat's article (*op. cit.*). His survey of some 300 films encompasses several genres and posits no less than eleven taxonomic subdivisions. Since his *noir* criteria are so loose—violence, psychological quirks, political commitment, low-life tableaux, and so forth—most anything save a musical may turn out to be a *film noir* (e.g., *High Noon*).

10. Gene Phillips, "Kubrick," *Film Comment*, VII, 4 (Winter 1971-72), 32.

11. Pauline Kael, "Lolita," *I Lost it At the Movies* (New York, 1966), p. 187.

12. *A Russian Beauty and Other Stories*, p. 220.

13. See Nabokov's *Strong Opinions*, p. 21. This interview, one of Nabokov's best, first appeared in *Playboy*, XI (January 1964) and is also included in *The Twelfth Anniversary Playboy Reader* (Chicago, 1965).

14. Pauline Kael, "Stanley Strangelove," *Deeper Into Movies*

(Boston, 1973), pp. 373-78. Walter Benjamin, whom I read only after completing this study, was also astute on the subject of violence. Writing in the thirties in advance of rampant screen violence, he lamented Marinetti's celebration of the beauty of war, and concluded that mankind's "self-alienation has reached such a degree that it can experience its own destruction as an aesthetic pleasure of the first order. This is the situation of politics which Fascism is rendering aesthetic" (Benjamin, "The Work of Art in the Age of Mechanical Reproduction," in *Illuminations*, Hannah Arendt, ed., New York, 1969, pp. 241-42).

15. Nabokov's self-conscious (or involuted) strategies are schematized in my article, "Nabokov's Puppet Show," included in *The Single Voice*, Jerome Charyn, ed. (New York, 1969). A somewhat different version appears in the first part of the Introduction to *The Annotated Lolita*.

16. Jorge Luis Borges, "Partial Magic in the Quixote," *Labyrinths* (New York, 1964), p. 196.

17. Everything should cohere elegantly, in life, art and criticism. Melville appears in the satirical role of a novelist named Parvulesco (from the French *parvenir* ["to attain, to reach, to succeed"] and *parvis* [poetical; "hall, temple"]), who is interviewed by Patricia (Jean Seberg). "I had seen Nabokov in a televised interview," says Melville, "and being like him, subtle, pretentious, pedantic, a bit cynical, naive, etc., I based the character on him" (from Rui Nogueira's interview-book, *Melville on Melville* [New York, 1971], p. 76).

18. Quoted by Homer Dickens in *The Films of Marlene Dietrich* (New York, 1968), p. 179.

19. *Ulysses*, p. 769.

6. Form and Metaphor: Exit Smiling

1. "Graham Greene: On the Screen," an interview by Gene D. Phillips, included in *Graham Greene: A Collection of Critical Essays*, Samuel Lynn Hynes, ed. (Englewood Cliffs, N.J., 1973), p. 169. Greene's critics are understandably anxious to demonstrate the influence of the cinema on his work. Too often they stop short at novelistic equivalents of a "closeup," "pan," or "long shot," ignoring a more fundamental source of inspiration: film content. In a 1935 review of *The Case of the Lucky Legs*, a Perry Mason film, Greene unfavorably compares William Powell with Warren William's Mason. "Mr. Powell is a little too immaculate, his wit is too well turned just as his clothes are too well made, he drinks hard but only at the best bars. . . . I find the cadaverous, not very well-dressed Perry Mason more real in his seedy straw hat with his straggly moustache; one does not find him only in the best bars . . ." (*Graham Greene On Film*, p. 49). "Cheap" and "squalor" are terms of praise in his criticism, and the squalid and mean content of his novels and "entertainments" owe not a little to B-picture subject matter.

2. J. D. Salinger, *Franny and Zooey* (New York, 1964), p. 47.

3. In his article "On Inspiration" (1972), Nabokov singles out six exemplary stories from some thirty anthologies, and Schwartz's "In Dreams Begin Responsibility" is one of them: "there are several . . . divine vibrations in this story that so miraculously blends an old cinema film with a personal past" (*Strong Opinions*, p. 313).

4. *A Russian Beauty*, p. 251.

5. *Ibid.*, p. 133. Nabokov is uncertain of the story's date of composition and publication (in an *émigré* journal).

6. Nabokov, *Laughter in the Dark* (New York, 1938), p. 58.

7. The original name afforded hermetic revenge, years after the fact. Schoolboy lepidopterist Nabokov thought he had discovered a new moth, and sent its description and picture to the editor of *The Entomologist* (in England), who informed him that it had been discovered long before by Kretschmar (see *Speak, Memory*, p. 134).

8. Suspense techniques are frequently sent up, as when Margot playfully locks Albinus in a room and disappears as his brother-in-law Paul returns unexpectedly. Albinus pretends that a burglar had locked him up and the two men search

the apartment. "A pang of horror" shoots through Albinus when he sees "the edge of a bright red frock" showing from behind a revolving bookstand. Paul overlooks it, the suspense builds. After Paul departs, Albinus feverishly opens the library door: "Margot, you mad little thing." A scarlet silk cushion awaits him (pp. 64-67).

9. Val Lewton realized the *tableau vivant* idea in a feature film. His *Bedlam* (1946) is based on Hogarth's famous painting, and individual scenes in the film follow the "set-ups" in the seventh and eighth sequences of *The Rake's Progress* print cycle.

10. The situation has certain obvious similarities with *Lolita*. Rex is clearly a forerunner of Quilty. In *Camera Obscura,* for example, he has prepared sketches "which a pornographic publishing firm in Berlin had commissioned" (*CO,* London, 1936, p. 244). This is deleted from *Laughter in the Dark* but realized in Quilty's Duk Duk movies. Margot's dreams of stardom parallel Lolita's, but the connections between the respective amours of A. A. and H. H. have been exaggerated ("Nabokov Returns to Young Girl, Old Man Theme," declared a typical review, after *Laughter in the Dark* had been reissued in 1960). Margot, a sixteen-year-old who looks eighteen, is no nymphet, and Albinus's passion is not pathological. His downfall has also been compared with Emil Jannings's in *The Blue Angel,* but that is a misreading of the film, whose focus is not on Lola's deceit but on the bachelor professor's puritanical rigidity and the ossified class consciousness which isolates him after he has married "beneath" him. *The Blue Angel* is also a portrait of a failed marriage: Lola strays only after having endured several years of an unsatisfactory union.

11. Tilden appears in *Lolita* as "Ned Litam," the simple anagrammatic pseudonym ("Ma Tilden") under which the tennis star chose to write articles and fiction, a verbal disguise enabling him to preserve his "amateur status" and darkly allude to his inverted sexual games. The literary anatomist's memory for quirky facts provides Nabokov with a double life analogous to Humbert's.

12. Also see Nabokov's poem "Oculus" (1939), in *Poems and Problems,* p. 101.

13. Vladislav Khodasevich, "Poem," Vladimir Nabokov, trans., *TriQuarterly* 27, "Russian Literature and Culture in the West: 1922-1972" (Spring 1973), 69.

14. *Poems and Problems,* pp. 69-73.

15. Vladimir Nabokov, *Mary* (New York, 1970), p. 9. Textual references are to this edition.

16. Act One is the only part of the play ever to appear in print, in *Rul'* ("The Rudder") January 1, 1927. Pia Mora's exotic assumed name is the kind of satirical touch which will be extended in *Laughter in the Dark, Lolita,* and *Ada.* Pia = Pola (Negri); Mora = "love" and "death" by way of Theda Bara (né Theodosia Goodman), *her* assumed name an anagram of "Arab death," as everyone in the twenties knew.

17. Josef von Sternberg, *Fun in a Chinese Laundry* (New York, 1965), p. 132.

18. Bosley Crowther, *Song of Russia, The New York Times,* February 11, 1944, p. 17.

19. Ginger appears in *Roberta* as Lizzie Gatz, a girl from Indiana who finds success in the supposedly glamorous Russian *émigré* community of Paris. Because "you have to have a title to croon over here," Lizzie assumes the name of the "Countess Scharwenka" and lands a singing job at the Café Russe, the kind of artificial environment Nabokov mocks in "The Assistant Producer."

20. *The Best of Lenny Bruce,* Fantasy LP 7012.

21. Vladimir Nabokov, letter to the author, June 15, 1973.

22. *Émigré* writers were victimized by this western liberal demonology. At the height of Stalin's blood purges in the mid nineteen-thirties, a "liberal" magazine in London refused to publish Nabokov because he was a "White Russian" (i.e., a reactionary). In 1943, when the Book-of-the Month Club deigned to offer a translation of *émigré* Mark Aldanov's novel *The Fifth Seal,* a letter of protest was signed and published by a host of well-known American "intellectuals," none of whom, as Simon Karlinsky points

out, had read the book. McCarthyism is not a right-wing phenomenon.

23. "A young girl is cruising on her father's yacht in the South Seas. She is engaged to marry a Russian count, who is tall, thin and old, but with beautiful manners," writes West in *The Day of the Locust* (1939), describing the scenario of one of Faye Greener's dreams and summarizing the cheap appeal of "White" subjects (pp. 105-6).

24. *Strong Opinions*, p. 138.

25. Allen Dulles, late director of the C.I.A., deemed "The Assistant Producer" authentic enough to include an abridged version in his anthology *Great Spy Stories from Fiction* (New York, 1969). He omitted its most problematical and comical passages, however, perhaps because they might have appeared to parody some of his other selections (by Conan Doyle, Eric Ambler, E. Phillips Oppenheim, Len Deighton, John Le Carré, Ian Fleming, etc.).

26. "Conversations With Nabokov," 221.

27. The boxes of the old Capstan cigarettes, a man of action's brand, pictured a sailor peering at the horizon, as Golubkov does at the outset of "The Assistant Producer" (p. 76).

28. Schwartz's "In Dreams Begin Responsibilities" (1939) brilliantly uses the present tense. When did Nabokov first read his story? "I see the connection between 'The Assistant Producer' and the Delmore Schwartz story but it is not a creative radical link," replied Nabokov. "I read it only four or five years ago in Klein and Pack's anthology *Short Stories, 1967*" (letter to the author, February 5, 1973). Schwartz and Nabokov clearly anticipate Robbe-Grillet, whose use of movie time is perhaps the most arresting of such experiments. The narrator's jealousy, in the novel of that name (1957), is a unified field, and his fearfulness is sustained by the film tense.

29. These writings are collected in the first volume of the *TriQuarterly émigré* compendium, which I co-edited with Simon Karlinsky (*op. cit.*). One evening, during a visit to Montreux, I showed its table of contents to Nabokov. The next morning he handed me a note card. "The product of my insomnia," he said. "You may use it as an epigraph for your Tsvetaeva section, or however you wish." The card reads:

> Amidst the dust of bookshops, wide dispersed
> And never purchased there by anyone,
> Yet similar to precious wines, my verse
> Can wait: its turn shall come.
>
> Marina Tsvetaeva
> Translated by Vladimir Nabokov
> Nov. 12, 1972

Index

Numerals in boldface refer to pictures and their captions.